Hot Stuff

Hot Stuff

Disco and the Remaking of American Culture

Alice Echols

W. W. NORTON & COMPANY

NEW YORK · LONDON

For information about permission to reproduce
selections from this book, write to Permissions,
W. W. Norton & Company, Inc.,
500 Fifth Avenue, New York, NY 10110

For information about special discounts for bulk
purchases, please contact W. W. Norton Special Sales at
specialsales@wwnorton.com or 800-233-4830

Manufacturing by RR Donnelley, Harrisonburg, VA.
Book design by Chris Welch
Production manager: Andrew Marasia

Library of Congress Cataloging-in-Publication Data

Echols, Alice.
Hot stuff : disco and the remaking of American
culture / Alice Echols. — 1st ed.
p. cm.
Includes bibliographical references and index.
ISBN 978-0-393-06675-3 (hardcover)
1. Disco music—United States—History and criticism.
2. Popular culture—United States—History—20th century.
3. Music—Social aspects. I. Title.
ML3526.E34 2010
781.64--dc22

2009040997

W. W. Norton & Company, Inc.
500 Fifth Avenue, New York, N.Y. 10110
www.wwnorton.com

W. W. Norton & Company Ltd.
Castle House, 75/76 Wells Street, London W1T 3QT

1 2 3 4 5 6 7 8 9 0

To Kate

CONTENTS

CONTENTS

ACKNOWLEDGMENTS

Researching *Hot Stuff* involved poring over old issues of *Rolling Stone*, the *Village Voice*, *Sounds*, *Melody Maker*, and *New Musical Express*, as well as the pop music sections of the *New York Times* and the *Los Angeles Times*. I don't blame other scholars at Oxford's Bodleian Library for covetously eyeing my reading material while I took notes on, say, a John Peel column in *Sounds*. While I have learned a great deal from other academics about popular music, I've learned just as much from the music critics and journalists whose work I have followed over the years. The writer and cultural critic whose work has most influenced me never, to the best of my knowledge, wrote about disco. Indeed, if memory serves, the one time Ellen Willis came to Ann Arbor and a group of us took her to the Rubaiyat she was seriously underwhelmed. Nonetheless, Ellen's writing and her approach to cultural criticism influenced me profoundly. Among the most brilliant thinkers of her generation, Ellen was intellectually curious, but absolutely impervious to the sort of trendiness that sometimes characterizes academia. Although she identified herself as a leftist and a feminist, she never pulled any punches, even when it meant alienating allies. Ellen probed deeply into American culture in essays that were lucid, supple, and often wickedly funny. Had she lived we would doubtless have had a conversation or two about the disco years, and I would have been the wiser for it.

Nevertheless, I did have many useful conversations while at work on *Hot Stuff*. I presented parts of this book to the following groups: the International Association for the Study of Popular Music's 2009 conference, "Don't Fence Me In: Borders, Frontiers, Diasporas"; the American Studies and History Departments at Rutgers University, fall 2008; the Roundtable on Gender and Popular Culture at the 2008 Berkshire Conference of Women Historians; "How Do We Keep Knowing?," a 2008 symposium at Texas A & M University's Melbern G. Glasscock Center for Humanities Research; Cornell University's 2007 Feminist, Gender, and Sexuality Studies lecture series; the 2007 Sexuality series of the English Department at Rutgers University; Northeastern University's 2007 lecture series on Gender Studies; Columbia University's 2006 seminar on Women and Society; the roundtable discussion "Intimate but Indirect: Examining the relationship between Music and Politics," at the American Studies Association's 2006 annual meeting; the History Department at Arizona State University, 2004; and the English Department at the University of Southern California, 2003. At these events, I benefited from the comments of many scholars, including Daphne Brooks, my interlocutor at Columbia University; Maureen Mahon at the IASPM conference; Jim Rosenheim, Melanie Hawthorne, and Kathleen Woodward at the Glasscock Center symposium; Rhonda Hammer and Jim Schultz at UCLA; Charles Kronengold and Judith Peraino at Cornell; Joe Boone, Judith Jackson Fossett, and Bruce Smith at USC; Marianne DeKoven, Ann Fabian, Billy Galperin, Vincent Lankewish, Carter Mathes, and Carolyn Williams at Rutgers; Barry Shank at the ASA; and Ruth Feldstein, Gayle Wald, and Jane Gerhard at the Berks.

I am indebted to the following people who agreed to be interviewed: the wondrous Nona Hendryx of Labelle; veteran Detroit deejays Mike

Conboy, Jerry Jackson, and Marty Ross; journalism professor and writer Abe Peck; and documentary filmmaker Mark Page. I am also grateful to Tim Lawrence, Jeanne Cordova, and Martin Meeker, who answered questions via email. My longtime Santa Fe friend bassist Dave Moir, and the musicologist Charles Kronengold spoke with me at length about the sonics of disco. Any errors, however, are mine alone.

Over the years I have talked at length about the Rubaiyat, and disco more broadly, with three Thursday night regulars: Bette Skandalis, André Wilson, and my partner during the disco years, Connie Samaras. These conversations have been enormously helpful in helping me to think freshly about that time. My debt to Connie, who supported my deejay ambitions in all kinds of ways and was a keen observer of the scene, is enormous. Connie is my closest friend in Los Angeles and our conversations about politics and culture, many of them had while walking around the Silverlake reservoir, are always fun and enlightening.

Angelenas Lois Banner, Ellen DuBois, Maria Lepowsky, Vivian Rothstein, Marla Stone, Devra Weber, and Alice Wexler—the "girl gang"—and more recent friends and colleagues from USC—Joe Boone, Bill Handley, Sharon Hays, Heather James, and Beth Meyerowitz—have been terrifically supportive throughout the process of researching and writing *Hot Stuff*. I am grateful to the following people who generously gave of their time and read parts of the manuscript: Casey Blake, Joe Boone, Bob Currie, John Di Stefano, Karen Dubinsky, Daniel Goode, Rhonda Hammer, Bill Handley, Janis Butler Holm, Doug Kellner, Eric Lott, Beth Meyerowitz, Charlotte Nekola, Paula Rabinowitz, Connie Samaras, Jim Schultz, Jeff Solomon, and Devra Weber. Wini Breines, Daphne Brooks, Carla Kaplan, Maureen Mahon, Moshe Sluhovsky, Chris Stansell, and Scott Tucker gave me particularly thorough comments on the material that they read. Greg Bills burned me seven CDs of post-disco disco, with an accompanying commentary that proved immensely helpful. Barbara Mello chased down people for photo permissions and Mariko Dawson converted footnotes into endnotes. I would not have come close to meeting my deadline without their very able assistance.

Throughout the writing of this book, Dave Moir, Torrey Reade, Leon Simis, Lydia Szamraj, and Lisa Udelson have been encouraging. So has my sister, MJ Echols. Joy and Ray Flint have provided a welcoming home away from home. Several students deserve mention as well. Shannon Carlock, Jovita Carpenter, Bill Hutson, Sheryl Smith, and Jonathan Snipes (Captain Ahab) from UCLA, as well as Renée Martin and almost all of my spring 2009 T.O. students from USC were standouts. Adrienne Lennix very usefully (and tactfully) suggested I take another look at *Boys in the Band.* Not to be forgotten are our cats. Writing can be a vexing process, but Emmett, Lola, LucyFur, and DandeLion provided plenty of diversionary pleasures . . . or at least distractions.

I began working on this book in earnest in 2005 shortly after joining the faculty at the University of Southern California. USC provided generous funding, many wonderful colleagues, and some exceptional students. I want to thank in particular Joe Boone for his role in bringing me to USC as part of the College's Senior Hiring Initiative. In addition to those colleagues whom I have already mentioned, I want to thank Elinor Accampo, Leo Braudy, Alice Gambrell, Larry Gross, Lon Kurashige, Rebecca Lemon, Philippa Levine, Teresa McKenna, Susan McCabe, Richard Meyer, David Rollo, David Roman, Meg Russett, Bruce Smith, and David St. John. Nellie Ayala Reyes, Kaye Watson, Flora Ruiz, and Rebecca Woods—the administrative staff of the English Department—and Jeanne Weiss and Raquel Gutierrez of Gender Studies were always efficient and friendly. In the spring of 2007, I taught at Rutgers University as a visiting professor in the English Department. This was a move made for personal reasons. My partner had agreed to serve as the interim chair of the English Department, and we knew we would see very little of each other unless I temporarily relocated. I was skeptical at first: New Jersey? But the community of scholars there proved exceptionally supportive of my work, so much so that I have accepted a position in American Studies and History at Rutgers. I want to thank all those who have welcomed me, particularly Louise Barnett, Emily Bartels, Marianne DeKoven, Ann Fabian, Leslie Fishbein, Nicole Fleetwood, Angus Gillespie, Douglas Greenberg, Helene Grynberg, Nancy Hewitt, Allan Isaac, Alison Isenberg, Temma Kaplan, Seth Koven, John Kucich, Rick Lee, Quionne Matchett, Meredith McGill, Michael McKeon, Richard Miller, Cheryl Robinson, Michael Rockland, Ben Sifuentes-Jáuregui, Cheryl Wall, Carolyn Williams, Ginny Yans, and the supernal Barry Qualls.

Hot Stuff builds on (and occasionally contests) the critical writing about disco that stretches back to the seventies, including the incisive work of Vince Aletti, Richard Dyer, Walter Hughes, Andrew Kopkind, Frank Rose, and Tom Smucker. Two recent books proved indispensable to me as I worked on *Hot Stuff*: Tim Lawrence's *Love Saves the Day* and Peter Shapiro's *Turn the Beat Around*. Although I take issue with some of the arguments put forward in these books, they are crucial foundational texts and great reads.

My literary agent, Geri Thoma, has been unfailingly supportive, reading drafts on short notice and offering sound advice at every step of the way. Everyone at Norton has been splendid, but Amy Cherry has been a dream editor. Her criticisms and suggestions have been absolutely spot-on, and throughout she has remained blissfully calm. Allegra Huston's meticulous and smart copyediting saved me from making a number of really embarrassing mistakes. Many thanks as well to Chris Welch who came up with such a terrific design for *Hot Stuff.* Throughout, Erica Stern has been cheerfully on top of all the pesky details.

My biggest debt is to my partner, Kate Flint. Anyone who's ever had a substantial conversation with Kate knows that she is brilliant and possessed of a scarily encyclopedic knowledge about everything from literature to livestock. But Kate is also disarmingly unpretentious, a woman who at the end of the day loves to kick back, margarita in hand, at our favorite Santa Fe restaurant, Harry's Roadhouse, and talk about the latest star gossip in the *Daily Mail* or, I don't know, collegiate

ACKNOWLEDGMENTS

sports. As for her contributions to *Hot Stuff*, Kate read many, many drafts, emailed me relevant links, suggested what turned out to be crucial research paths, and listened to disco when her own musical taste runs to alt-country and northern New Mexico fiddle music. That would have been more than enough, but Kate also opened her heart to me. I have no idea how I got so lucky.

Introduction

Plastic Fantastic

THE DISCO YEARS

N othing seems to conjure up the 1970s quite so effectively as disco. Even at the time, critics remarked upon disco's neat encapsulation of that decade's zeitgeist. "It must be clear by now to everyone with an ear or an eye that this era," wrote journalist Andrew Kopkind in 1979, "is already the Disco Years, whether it will be called by that name or not." A former sixties' radical, Kopkind was by turns fascinated, bemused, and appalled by the disco epoch, and he likely imagined that in years to come fellow cultural critics would share his interest. But the seventies have not loomed large in our national imagination, except perhaps as comic relief. For many Americans, these were the forgettable years.

That forgettability owes a lot to the 1960s, the outsize decade that dwarfs all others in recent memory. The sixties will always be remembered for their audacity, whether found in the courage of civil rights protestors who put their bodies on the line or in those doomed but beautiful rock stars who tried breaking through to the other side. By contrast, the seventies seem the decade when nothing, or nothing good, happened—an era memorable for the country's hapless presidents, declining prestige, bad fashions, ludicrous music, and such over-the-top narcissism that Tom Wolfe dubbed it the "Me Decade." Before the decade was out, this narrative of decline had become routine. "After the poetry of the Beatles comes the monotonous bass-pedal bombardment of Donna Summer," huffed one *New York Times* writer in 1979. It is a measure of the era's persistent bad press that a recent book challenging this view carries the pleading title *Something Happened.* As for the sixties, it doesn't matter how much silliness went down, we still invest those times with seismic significance. Take Joe Cocker's performance at Woodstock. His spasmodic thrashing about and his vocals, slurred to the point of incomprehensibility, are something of a joke today. Cringe-making though it may be, however, Cocker's performance is never made to stand in for the whole of the sixties. The sixties remain enveloped in the gauzy sentimentalism of what might have been. Yet the iconic image of John Travolta as dance-floor king Tony Manero in white polyester suit, arm thrust to the disco heavens, has come to symbolize the narcissistic imbecility and inconsequentiality of the disco years.

Were it not for the Rubaiyat, I, too, might well regard the seventies as a lamentable and regrettable period in American history. The Rubaiyat was, yes, a disco. It was located in the heart of sixtiesland: Ann Arbor, Michigan, the home of the University of Michigan and legendary incubator of radical activism. At the height of the seventies, the town's annual Hash Bash—a smoke-in to reform marijuana laws—was still going strong and so were its two food co-ops—one reform, the other orthodox when it came to selling white foods (that is, rice, sugar, and flour of the white variety). Ann Arbor also had bookstores galore, including the original, wonderful Borders Bookstore, and any number of hippie-ish restaurants and bars such as the Fleetwood Diner, the Del Rio, and the Blind Pig. Musically, it prided itself on its vintage music (it hosted one of the earliest blues festivals), but at heart it was a rock town besotted with Iggy Pop and the Stooges and Sonic's Rendezvous, a band fronted by Patti Smith's future husband, Fred Smith. Its leading music store, Schoolkids' Records, stocked disco, but never played it. All of this is to say that disco-averse Ann Arbor came close to providing something like a safe haven from glitterball culture.

That disco had any presence in Ann Arbor owes a lot to the Rubaiyat, which was about a fifteen-minute walk from the university, where I was a graduate student. More town than gown, it nonetheless attracted some students, although not many graduate students, whose musical ecumenism did not usually extend to disco. The Rubaiyat's crowd included flight attendants and librarians—a good number of them gay men—and lesbian-feminist bus drivers, some of whom moonlighted as prostitutes at a nearby massage parlor. You could say it was a gay bar, but that's far too generic a description. The Rubaiyat was a fly-trap for the fringe—snagging performance artists, con artists, and even Madonna Ciccone, who is said to have danced there before dropping out of U of M and heading off to New York.

Rubaiyat cocktail napkin, ca. 1980

However, the club's customers had no monopoly on weirdness. The Rubaiyat's owner, a middle-aged Greek immigrant who drove a late-model, cherry-red Cadillac convertible, spent most of his time on the floor below at the Italian restaurant he owned. He was a splashy character with an alarming array of facial tics and hair in the strawberry blond range. Although he was flamboyant, he was emphatically not gay. On those occasions when he ventured upstairs, he would search the club hopefully for stray heterosexuals or for any sign that the club was tilting straight. The woman he chose to manage the place, a gravelly-voiced Korean American, was someone best given a very wide berth. Rumor had it that one night when a thief demanded the club's cover money, she thwarted the robbery by ferociously grabbing his knife by the blade. Neither she nor the owner knew anything about disco, so when it came to music they gladly deferred to the club's waiters and bartenders—small-town gays, almost all of them blond and with names like Jimmy, Johnny, or Joey.

The Rubaiyat was no red-velvet-rope disco where fashionista doormen determined who was sufficiently fabulous to gain entry. This would never have worked in a town where down jackets and army surplus were hardly an unusual sight. The club did have some pretensions to classiness, but the mismatched, sagging booths and bordello red carpets defeated occasional efforts at upmarket sophistication. What the Rubaiyat did have were better-than-average speakers, a heterogeneous clientele, and a weekend cover of three dollars. As a consequence, during disco's peak years the Rubaiyat was often bursting at the seams, with upward of four hundred people jammed up against one another. At the Rubaiyat you were spared loudmouth deejays, line dances, floor-clearing solo dancing, and all but a sprinkling of polyester. In other words, if you came looking for something on the order of 2001 Odyssey, the disco in *Saturday Night Fever*, you were in the wrong club.

What the Rubaiyat offered instead was the experience of being blasted inside of one's body. This effect was achieved through megadecibel levels and the sound system's determined emphasis on the music's resonant lows—so throbbing that it felt as if the beat had taken up residence inside of you. Disco's penetrative thump was a different sensation from anything I had experienced at a rock concert, where sound reverberated inside your ears. Dancing at the Rubaiyat entailed a shared surrender to the beat—quite unlike the 1960s, when dancing often seemed an interior experience where people moved to the rhythm of their own freaky orbit. Something about this collective yielding to the rhythmic was thrilling to me.

I grew to love dancing, but my addiction to pop music long predated it. Records had always taken a chunk of my income, and during the early disco years, when Stevie Wonder, Labelle, Rufus, AWB, the Ohio Players, and Earth Wind and Fire were at their peak, my record-buying accelerated. Largely because I had more records than anyone else, I began deejaying informally at parties and benefits. Spinning records at the Rubaiyat never seemed remotely possible to me. It wasn't just that club deejaying, like playing lead guitar, was strictly guysville territory in those days; it was also that I had no idea how to achieve the smooth segues characteristic of disco.

Then, toward the end of 1979, the Rubaiyat suffered what looked like twin calamities—the death of disco and the loss of its chief deejay, who had moved to New York City. It was likely one of the waiters who came up with the idea of hiring a deejay whose specialty was danceable new wave. In practice, this meant fifteen minutes of Gary Numan's "Cars" followed by about ten of Blondie's "Heart of Glass" and another fifteen of the B-52's track "Rock Lobster." A few months into the new regime, a friend suggested that I approach the manager about getting a tryout. We were feeling heady from a recent political mobilization in which we had stopped the university from scaling back its fledgling women's studies program. (This followed on the heels of other political campaigns including "Free the VA Nurses" and "Decriminalize Prostitution.") We gave little thought to what we might do if the Rubaiyat refused, but I think we talked vaguely of a boycott.

It was no accident that management decided to give me a try just at the moment when it seemed to many that the bottom was falling out of the disco business. I was hired on a strictly trial basis for Thursdays, one of the club's slow nights. "A girl deejay?" was the wait staff's skeptical response. As for me, I might have said it was a lark, but I was determined to make a go of it, especially now that I was meant to begin working in earnest on my dissertation. Anxious that my mixes not sound embarrassingly primitive, I spent days hunched over my Pioneer turntables and newly acquired Numark mixer. When I wasn't teaching myself how to mix, I was scouring record bins for the latest 12-inch releases. As a part-timer I was not eligible for the record pool that provided club deejays with free releases. I often shopped at a small Detroit record store that catered to working-class African Americans and was owned by a brother of Eddie Kendricks, the ex-Temptation with the fabulous falsetto. My record-buying was made less hit-or-miss because of musician Ronń Matlock, today an "underground legend" among British fans of R&B and disco, who worked at the shop and played me the hottest new tracks. Disco deejaying proved a highly effective form of procrastination, and much more fun than other strategies of dissertation-avoidance I had encountered.

It wasn't long before Thursdays were nearly as popular as weekend nights. By summer, Fridays were part of my schedule, too. Technically, I was no great shakes, nailing some segues, but with others producing a terrible cacophony as beats slammed up against each other rather than melding together smoothly. My popularity stemmed largely from the fact that no one else in Ann Arbor was playing as full a range of disco, including the funkier tip of disco, the sort of music programmed by Detroit's maverick radio deejay Electrifyin' Mojo. Also critical was the feminist community, which came out to support a woman deejay, even if some of my musical choices, particularly Parliament–Funkadelic, Prince, and Rick James, seemed dismayingly "male-identified."

The nights I played attracted more African Americans, lesbians, bisexuals, and heterosexuals than usually turned up at the Rubaiyat. The club's mainstay, white gay men, showed up, too, but in diminished numbers. Nothing in my life—certainly not working on my dissertation—was more gratifying than bringing this polymorphic crowd together in its shared love of an unexpected mix or a knockout song such as Kurtis Blow's "The Breaks," an early rap song that was among 1980's summer hits. In those moments social distinctions seemed to fall away. More than that, identities that had felt solid and immutable sometimes turned blurry with a touch or a glance. These dance-floor epiphanies could last a few hours or, well, a lifetime.

However, as the Rubaiyat dance floor grew more heterogeneous, the tensions became palpable. Although a feel-good vibe gripped the dance floor when a song like Sister Sledge's "We Are Family" played, relations were not always warm and fuzzy between gay men and lesbians or between straights and gays. These were further complicated by racial tensions, although they did not always play out in predictable ways. The one time I cleared the dance floor, with a deliberately spiky choice—Jimi Hendrix's "Foxy Lady"—an exasperated black gay man was overheard complaining about my "white trash music."

It turned out that discontent among the club's staff had been brewing for some time. They preferred hi-NRG diva-driven disco, which I included but did not feature. Matters came to a head when a handful of Jheri-curled, heterosexual black men started showing up on the nights that I deejayed. The club's waiters and bartenders had tolerated the funkier disco and the growing numbers of women, but they put their collective foot down over these guys. "It's not that they're black," they insisted, "it's that they harass us." They had a solution. "Switch the music!" they urged. "Play whiter-sounding stuff." It's true that this group of black men was noticeably more street than other black men who danced at the Rubaiyat. But from what I could see they seemed, like their white counterparts, much less interested in harassing gay men than in pursuing women, who, curiously, never lodged a complaint. My refusal to buckle under annoyed the management, which began to withhold the bonuses I was owed for high-capacity crowds. Then I was relieved of Friday nights, despite the fact that I was still drawing plenty of customers. Was the staff racist, or at the very least parochial? Or was I putting the Rubaiyat, the only queer disco of its kind in a many-mile radius, at risk? I was fired before I could find out.

I begin with my Rubaiyat adventure because it departs from the usual disco narrative. For one, my story takes place at that moment when disco is generally believed to have died. Moreover, it takes place in a club that bears little resemblance to America's two best known discos—the hardscrabble, thwarted world of 2001 Odyssey and the high-end, glitterati scene of Studio 54. Instead it explores the texture of disco culture a full six hundred miles away from its epicenter in New York. My story also features women, who, despite their centrality to disco as artists and consumers, are usually consigned to its sidelines. Moreover, my Rubaiyat narrative gives the lie to the idea that among African Americans disco was an affected taste to which only middle-class strivers succumbed. It illustrates a point made by Ralph Ellison some forty years ago, that efforts to make a "rigid correlation" between color, class, and musical taste always fail to take into account the complexities of lived experience. It highlights the fact that there was no single disco experience, even among those who shared the same wood parquet dance floor. Finally, my story calls into question the wisdom of pitting the socially conscious sixties against the solipsistic, hedonistic seventies, as though the history of this period pivots on the supplanting of high-minded we-ness by shameful me-ness.

Mine is not the first book to contest the usual depiction of the 1970s. Revisionist histories have begun to pry apart the thirty-year lock that Me Decade clichés have had on our thinking about the period. But these days seventies' revisionism is up against sixties' revisionism, which increasingly argues for the "long sixties," so long that it is now considered by some the longest decade of the twentieth century. This extended-play version of the 1960s lasts at least until the oil embargo of 1973, possibly through the Watergate crisis of the following year, and might even include the ignominious fall of Saigon in 1975. Certainly there is a case to be made for the incredibly expanding sixties. Skepticism about government, a sense of loss, and a grudging recognition of limits did not arrive at the dawning of the new decade. But if the sixties swallow up half of the following decade, if the seventies become a mere sliver, we risk making those years little more than a prelude to Reaganism rather than the contentious, contradictory years they were. After all, the seventies were the decade when some of the most significant movements of the sixties—feminism, gay rights, and the struggles of racial and ethnic minorities—had their greatest impact. This is when the culture wars heated up as abortion rights, affirmative action, school busing, multicultural education, gay rights, and the battle over the Equal Rights Amendment roiled America.

The 1970s are often remembered for block-long gas lines, shuttered factories, high unemployment and stagflation, all of which combined to give the period a feeling of inertia giving way to slow-moving collapse. Yet these years were characterized by considerable flux as well. Small but growing numbers of African Americans entered the ranks of the middle class, women moved into the workplace *and* into nightlife, and gays vacated the shadowy margins of American life. Disco's one-nation-under-a-thump impulse sometimes gave way to tribal reversion, but it nonetheless succeeded in integrating American nightlife to an extent unthinkable just a decade earlier. Pornography began moving out of seedy red-light districts and into respectable businesses—corner newsstands, drugstores, and convenience stores—and into American homes, as a result of video technology. The near ubiquity of pornography, the resurgence of feminism, the ready availability of the birth-control pill, the legalization of abortion, and the discofying of nightlife remade America's sexual landscape in ways that created unprecedented (and sometimes risky) possibilities of sexual pleasure for women. Meanwhile, the feminist assault on masculine privilege, defeat in Vietnam, deindustrialization, and affirmative action posed challenges for American men. These were combustible times.

Of course, the seventies *were* also a time of hot tubs, polyester, platform shoes, and disco. Certainly disco entailed nothing short of an assault on the rules of rock music. Rock's embrace of the serious or the "heavy," its privileging of artistic integrity and emotional sincerity over the imperatives of show business, were almost utterly disregarded by disco. The ethos of naturalness that so defined sixties' rock (be it Dylan's untuneful voice or Janis Joplin's raspy near-screech) did not much interest disco, which favored the slick and the synthetic, and, indeed, some would say the plastic. Where the Jefferson Airplane assailed the seductiveness of technology in 1967's "Plastic Fantastic Lover," disco producers like Giorgio Moroder were fascinated by the possibilities of technology. It was a culture that, in contrast to rock, didn't trade on "realness," preferring instead to revel in the pleasures of the artificial, what theorist Walter Benjamin called "the sex appeal of the inorganic." Indifferent to the battles over authenticity that raged in other quarters, disco embraced even arrivistes like Rod Stewart and Cher. Had Ethel Merman cut a *good* disco record, she, too, might have found a place on the dance floor. Like the great pop of the sixties that Phil Spector, Jeff Barry, and Motown churned out, disco was producers' music, not something that emerged more or less organically from garages, basements, street corners, and bedrooms. Shamelessly commercial, disco gleefully ransacked other genres, discofying everything from Eddie Floyd's R&B masterpiece "Knock on Wood" to Beethoven's Fifth Symphony, impervious to the damage done. Disco was on the make and on the take, just like the Hustle, the dance craze it inspired. Years later, purists declared certain tracks "real" disco and others commercial dreck, but authenticity was not relevant to its seventies' fans. This was not a world where the charge of selling out enjoyed much currency, where performers had to fret about damaging their credibility if they scored a big hit. Promiscuous and omnivorous, disco absorbed sounds and styles from all over, and in the process accelerated the transnational flow of musical ideas and idioms.

Disco's influence extended beyond the realm of popular music. The 1970s are associated with identity politics, but they were also a time when numbers of gay men, African Americans, and women ditched predictable social scripts. Disco played a central role in this process, which broadened the contours of blackness, femininity, and male homosexuality. Black musicians and producers experimented with lavish, sophisticated arrangements that didn't always sound recognizably "black," and which became the foundation of disco. Concomitant with the disco turn, black masculinity moved away from the "sex machine" model advanced by James Brown towards the "love man" style of Barry White. As for gay men, as they became newly visible, largely through the dissemination of disco culture, their self-presentation shifted as effeminacy gave way to a macho style recognizable to anyone who has ever glimpsed the Village People. Feminism's critique of three-minute sex found its voice in disco, and black female performers broke with representational strategies rooted in respectability—those white gloves and gowns that were worn with greatest effect by the Supremes.

All of these changes provoked controversy. Was disco a repudiation of pernicious racial profiling or was it turning R&B "beige," transmogrifying it into a "mush of vacuous Muzak," as one critic alleged? And what about the new gay masculinism? Was it best understood as a parody or as a mimicking of conventional heterosexual masculinity? Was it liberating in its rejection of the age-old association of homosexuality with effeminacy, or was it regressive in its stigmatizing of sissiness? Disco filled the air with what one singer called "women's love rights." Disco's move into X-rated territory and its attention to women's sexual pleasure both reflected and abetted a shift in African American women's sexual presentation. The move toward greater sexual expressiveness caused uneasiness among some performers, most notably Donna Summer, and it unnerved Jesse Jackson's civil rights organization Operation PUSH, which threatened to boycott "X-rated disco sex-rock."

Hot Stuff: Disco and the Remaking of American Culture is an interpretive rather than a comprehensive history, one that focuses on these very shifts in identity and representation and the debates they triggered. It takes its title from two identically named (yet completely different) genre-defying songs, which bookend the period of disco's greatest popularity: the Rolling Stones' 1976 track and Donna Summer's 1979 cut. Throughout, I take aim at the stereotypical view of disco, but I also query the depiction of disco that has emerged in recent studies. Too often disco revisionists, in an effort to debunk the pervasive view of disco as crassly commercial, exclusionary, and politically regressive, have emphasized instead its subcultural purity, democratic beginnings, and transgressive practices. Although their recasting of disco has much to recommend it, it follows too faithfully the declension narrative so typical of pop music writing whereby an inventive underground is eclipsed by its debased commercial version. This two-tier schema of "good" versus "bad" disco creates its own distortions, including the by-now routine disparagement of *Saturday Night Fever* as politically reactionary. In the pages that follow I offer a history that appreciates both disco's steamy, illicit roots and its mainstream expression—including, even, the Bee Gees. My definition of disco is expansive, encompassing whatever worked on American dance floors, rather than being limited to what is now codified as "disco." In contrast to rock, which is assumed to be protean, disco is habitually reduced to its narrowest expression, with the result that anything that deviates even slightly from classic disco is always something else. This book does not shortchange the music, but neither does it chronicle in exhaustive detail every important artist, producer, deejay, and club. Rather, throughout *Hot Stuff* I place disco within a discussion of feminism, deindustrialization, globalism, and the ongoing struggles for racial justice and greater sexual expressiveness. The reader comes to understand the centrality of disco to the changing American landscape, and to see why these really were the Disco Years.

Hot Stuff

I Hear a Symphony

BLACK MASCULINITY AND THE DISCO TURN

> You should see this whole Roxy Music thing. It's so elegant and
> cool and fashionable.
>
> —*Nile Rodgers to Bernard Edwards, cofounders of Chic*

isco snuck up on America like a covert operation. This wasn't
how it had been in the sixties, when shifts in popular music—
the arrival of the mop-headed British Invasion bands, Bob
Dylan's galvanizing electric turn, the emergence of psychedelic rock—
were unmissable cultural events immediately accorded the status of
milestones. The rock "revolution" of the sixties, like the Vietnam War
and the protests it provoked, was the object of intense media coverage.
Newsweek, *Life*, *Time*, and all the rest pounced on the story with prairie-
fire speed. In a blink, whole new publications, including that soon-to-
be arbiter of countercultural taste, *Rolling Stone*, emerged to chronicle
the music, personalities, and culture of rock. The major labels may
have been bewildered by the scruffiness, long hair, and druggy vibe of
groups such as Big Brother and the Holding Company and the Grateful Dead, but they barely paused before racing to sign them up, even
when they were little known outside of San Francisco's hippie enclave,
Haight-Ashbury.

Six years later, when another musical revolution was taking shape,
record companies opened neither their arms nor their coffers, with

the result that disco developed slowly and at first largely off the official map. By the time Vince Aletti wrote about what he called "party music" and "discotheque rock," in a fall 1973 issue of *Rolling Stone*, gay men had been dancing in discos for three years. It would take another year before *Billboard* magazine began keeping track of "hot dance club" cuts, and two more before the major labels began to take the music seriously. One reason that disco lingered below the radar was that the clubs in which it incubated were predominantly gay and, with the exception of the glitziest, initially relatively unknown to the larger population. Discos were not nearly so invisible to music business insiders, who began hearing about crowded clubs where danceable R&B or soul records played continuously rather than in between musicians' sets. When Motown's Frank Wilson learned that Eddie Kendricks's "Girl You Need a Change of Mind," a 1973 track he produced, was popular in New York's discos, he was "shocked. That was not what we were going for," he recalls. "We were after radio." Disco's multiracial, largely gay

Chic, album cover for *Real People*. L–R: Bernard Edwards, Alfa Anderson, Nile Rodgers, Luci Martin, Tony Thompson. "In lots of different areas we broke through the color line," recalls Anderson

clientele was not one that the music industry seemed eager to court. To industry executives, the dance crowd represented a mere sliver of the demographic they craved, and, one imagines, a rather unwelcome one at that, given the prejudices of the time.

While the invisibility of the scene kept disco culture underground, the music operated in a more complicated fashion. Indeed, another reason disco registered so feebly during its formative years was that much of the music that club deejays played was anything but underground. Early discos weren't like Bill Graham's Fillmore, which at first featured groups playing freak rock that had yet to find a home on the radio. Although disco deejays sought out and sometimes made clubland hits of less well-known records such as "Soul Makossa" by the Cameroonian-born saxophonist Manu Dibango or "Woman" by the Spanish group Barrabás, many of the tracks they played were staples of R&B radio. Millions of Americans were listening to the same records by the O'Jays, Temptations, and ex-Tempts that were heating up disco dance floors. In a curious twist, disco's reliance on popular soul hits provided the emerging scene with a kind of camouflage. After all, to most consumers, George McRae's "Rock Your Baby" was soul, not disco—a word barely even in circulation outside of industry circles. The fact that disco playlists leaned so heavily on R&B, including that emerging subset of percussive, polyrhythmic, danceable R&B called funk, also meant that record company executives could think that they were supplying discos with plenty of product. At the same time, the lesser status of R&B in the world of popular music exacerbated disco's marginality. By 1971, a third of what was played on Top 40 radio had migrated there from soul radio. Yet even with increased Top 40 radio play and a growing chunk of record sales, R&B lacked the prestige and the capital—cultural and actual—of rock music.

In fact, the first disco track to become a number one pop hit, 1973's "Love's Theme" by Barry White's Love Unlimited Orchestra, would have landed in the dustbin had it not been for the intervention of two enterprising New York club deejays. Spying the record with other "dead albums" about to be chucked at White's label, 20th Century Records, the deejays prevailed upon a promotional staffer to give them copies. Their success in breaking the song persuaded 20th Century to distribute free copies of the record to the city's other leading club deejays. Steady disco play created so much demand for the track that, by the beginning of 1974, "Love's Theme" was swept into the pop Top 20 without radio support—something that rarely happened, and that suggested the potential power of club deejays.

White's single was remarkable for the way it upended the conventional wisdom about the marketing of music, and, like his recent R&B hits, it also underscored a trend in soul music away from the gritty and the raw. White's "Love's Theme" wasn't so much a Wall of Sound as it was a wall of strings that cloyingly swooped and swelled while the beat chugged on . . . and on. To Britain's leading rock critic John Peel, it was a "stunningly dull tune" that sounded like a cross between two movie soundtracks—the Percy Faith Orchestra's 1960 hit "The Theme from *A Summer Place*" and Isaac Hayes's recent smash "Theme from *Shaft*." About the only sonic element that made "Love's Theme" legibly R&B was its wah-wah chank, what Peel called its "obligatory Shaft noises."

Millions loved White's music, including daytime TV host Dinah Shore, who devoted an entire show to White and his music. However, if you were what rock critic Robert Christgau called a "white soul conservative," this was precisely the sort of schmaltz that likely had driven you into the arms of Atlantic and Stax Records in the first place. And then there was White's ingratiating self-presentation, so squishy soft it seemed light years away from the insistent "got-ta, got-ta" masculinity of iconic sixties' soul men. In contrast to James Brown, whose funk tracks featured lots of call-and-response guy talk, White made a point of addressing himself to the ladies. While Brown rapped, "If you hear any noise, it's just me and the boys," White moaned, "Whatever, whatever, girl, I'll do." Gone as well was the sweaty athleticism that powered the performances of so many other soul greats. In concert,

White's languid pillow-talk raps and his baritone crooning did the trick for hundreds of women, who tore off their panties and threw them his way. White's pitch consisted of the very "baby, baby, baby songs" that Stevie Wonder had recently declared African Americans "as a people are not interested in . . . anymore." James Brown may have been all over the map politically (eventually embracing the Republican Party), but at least he championed black pride and power, whereas White operated in a register devoid of racial politics. After attending one of White's concerts, rock critic Lester Bangs declared that he had never seen "anything quite so immaculately vacant."

For Bangs and other fans of old-school soul music, 1974 brought little hope that there would be a turnaround. Among music critics, there was a growing sense that the sound of R&B was shifting. Writing about ex-Temptation Eddie Kendricks's single "Keep On Trucking," John Peel wrote, "We have a crying need for a new word to adequately describe that sort of popping, chucking sound that forms the basis of much of the music wending its way to us from Black America." His suggested term, "snatting," did not take, but it captures the hissing hi-hats so prominent in this new music. Vince Aletti described the new music as "Afro-Latin in sound or instrumentation, heavy on the drums, with minimal lyrics, sometimes in a foreign language, and a repetitive, chant-like chorus." Writing in the summer of 1974 about "the new genre of black rhythm and blues music," New York journalist Mark Jacobson offered the most compelling description of the changing soundscape. "The new songs are like big barroom fans that sweep the air around you as you dance."

Certainly that was true of Gloria Gaynor's cover version of the Jackson 5's 1971 hit "Never Can Say Goodbye," yet another disco record that the music business chose to snub, even after Elton John talked it up. Like "Love's Theme," Gaynor's 1974 record highlights disco's growing distinctiveness from traditional soul music. "Never Can Say Goodbye" is an intoxicating dance-floor romp, but the song's galloping arrangement and Gaynor's strutting vocal go a long way toward stripping the song of its anguish. Another record that demonstrated the growing sonic divide between old-school and new-style R&B was *Love Is the Message* by a band with the anonymous-sounding name of MFSB. Philadelphia International Records, an independent label formed by veteran R&B producers Kenneth Gamble and Leon Huff, released *Love*. By 1974 PIR was already on its way to becoming the Motown of the seventies, in part because of its house band MFSB. *Love Is the Message* contained the propulsive "TSOP (The Sound of Philadelphia)," which became the theme song for the popular TV show *Soul Train*, and won the Grammy for Best R&B Instrumental Performance. While Barry White's "Love's Theme" was still perched in the pop Top 10, *Love Is the Message* stormed the charts, and quickly became the bestselling album on the R&B music chart. "TSOP" catapulted *Love Is the Message* to the head of the class, and it was enormously popular at discos, but the album's sleeper cut, "Love Is the Message," proved much more influential in shaping what became understood as the disco sound. What many disco deejays and dancers found most irresistible about "Love"—its "lush fluidity"—was what set it apart from so much sixties' soul.

There are other records from 1974 that illuminate the difference between old-style soul music and disco, including Jamaican-born Carl Douglass's reggae-tinged "Kung Fu Fighting," which made its way to the number one position on both the pop and R&B charts. Another tropically inflected song, George McCrae's "Rock Your Baby," suggested that sweetness was trumping not just soul-man swagger but even the slinky sexiness of Al Green. The dreamy-sounding "Rock Your Baby" was McCrae's only disco hit, but it emerged from TK Records, a Florida company whose "Miami sound" became an important strand of disco. Singer and keyboardist Harry Wayne (KC) Casey and bassist Richard Finch, who wrote, arranged, and produced "Rock Your Baby," were already recording for TK as members of KC and the Sunshine Band, an interracial outfit known for their "tropical funk." Within a few months they would simplify their sound and begin churning out "bubblegum funk" that topped the pop, disco, and R&B charts. In no time, David Bowie, Elton John, and the Average White Band joined KC on the R&B and pop charts, and they all appeared on *Soul Train.*

The success of white musicians on the R&B chart pointed to a potentially troubling shift. What if disco, which was taking shape as a genre equally hospitable to black and white artists, squeezed black artists off the R&B charts and off black radio? This was not an unreasonable concern. By the midseventies, WBLS, New York's largest black-owned radio station, stopped claiming that it offered "the total black experience" and began boasting that it offered "the world's best-looking sound." WBLS's increasingly colorblind music—its shift from soul to suave—was pioneered by celebrity deejay and programmer Frankie Crocker, who increasingly took his cues from New York's leading disco deejays, particularly Larry Levan. According to one *Village Voice* writer, Crocker's racial ambiguity over the airwaves had some listeners wondering, "He sounds black, but is he?" This trend toward colorblindness was happening elsewhere, including Detroit, where radio deejay Electrifyin' Mojo played Queen and the Stones as well as the two Georges—funk impresario Clinton and smooth jazz guitarist Benson.

It was the apprehension that soul music was surrendering to pop imperatives, content to stake out a place for itself in the commercially fertile but artistically barren and soulless territory of schmaltz, that most upset music critics. Of the Hues Corporation's 1974 disco hit "Rock the Boat," British music critic Mike Flood wrote, "your mother will probably love . . . its hoopity-boopity soulless soul." His colleague Rob Mackie wrote wistfully of a time when soul was "still exciting." To some, disco seemed a crazy reversal of all that the black freedom movement had fought for. After all, it had seemed to many, as Elton John put it in 1973, that "black people are just beginning to do their own thing and it's no longer just five men in a row in satin suits." It was as if the movement's insistence on black pride and self-determination was being thrown over in an effort to take up that most embarrassing of white cultural forms, schlock. "What happened to the days when black music was black and not this . . . pretentious drivel?" lamented a reviewer in Britain's *New Musical Express.*

Through 1973 the people most responsible for the new symphonic soul were veterans of the R&B scene. Like Motown producer Frank Wilson, they saw themselves making music for the radio, not for clubs. But beginning in 1974, the dictates of the dance floor started to shape the sound of this new-style R&B. This wasn't any old dance floor where people were content to stand around during those awkward seconds between the end of one jukebox song and the beginning of the next. This was the newly liberated gay dance floor, which, as Chapter Two explains, boasted a continuous mix of deejay-spun music. "People would kill a DJ who stopped between songs," recalls gay clubber Mel Cheren. Yet mixing this new disco music so the segues between tracks were not jarring was daunting, especially given the primitive resources with which deejays at first had to make do—three-and-a-half-minute 45 rpm singles, turntables that lacked a variable speed mechanism, and often no mixers whatsoever. In Detroit, deejay Marty Ross connected a foot pedal to his amp so he could easily switch from one turntable to the other, but it did not allow him to do beat-on-beat mixing. As a consequence, deejays played whatever danceable music they could get their hands on—James Brown, the Doobie Brothers, even the Doors— none of which was produced with them in mind. This is in large measure why early disco was so heterogeneous.

However, beginning in 1974, as a few record labels began to wake up to the disco market, club deejays began to exert their influence, and in ways that widened the distance between old-style and new-style soul. The first deejay to produce a remix for a record company was Tom Moulton, a model known to New York's fashionable gay crowd as one of the Marlboro Lights men. He soon became even more famous for his impeccably mixed disco tapes, which played at Fire Island's Sandpiper disco. Moulton was among the first deejays to mix in such a way that dancers did not at first know that one song had ended and the next begun. But Moulton's influence would extend far beyond the

Sandpiper, first as the author of *Billboard*'s new column on disco, and then as a much-sought-after remixer. Frustrated by the limitations of available disco records, particularly their brevity and timid bass levels, he began a one-man campaign to get record companies to adjust their product for the dance floor. It is no accident that Mel Cheren, who also worked as a production executive at Scepter Records, was the first to hire Moulton to remix a record. As a habitué of some of the city's hottest gay discos, Cheren understood that these records could be enhanced for maximum danceability.

Moulton's remixes of records such as the B.T. Express's "Do It ('Til You're Satisfied)" created the model for the 12-inch, extended-play disco single—the pounding bass, the stark percussive disco break, and extended instrumental passages, which doubled the length of a record. For those who had never heard tracks of music mixed together, Moulton's remix of Gloria Gaynor's 1975 LP set the standard. Moulton remixed it so that the whole first side moved almost seamlessly from "Honey Bee" to "Never Can Say Goodbye" to another Motown cover, "Reach Out I'll Be There." In an era of primitive mixing technology, this was a treat for dancers and deejays alike, who for eighteen minutes were spared any embarrassingly bumpy transitions.

Moulton did more than just segue the cuts; he transformed each track into a "suite" with distinct movements. After studying a record, Moulton asked the recording studio to eliminate certain tracks so he could hear the recording's "hidden" material. Working in a truly deconstructive fashion, Moulton altered the record's instrumentation by building upon this hidden or repressed material. By looping back, he was able to bulk up a record's instrumental passages. Dancers and deejays loved the embellishment and elongation that Moulton created, and that came to characterize disco. However, as deejays tinkered with the music, the priorities of the dance floor and its deejays began to prevail over everything else. Gradually songs with a steady 4/4 thump that clocked in around 120 beats per minute and featured extended instrumental passages—in other words, songs that were easy to mix in and out of—began to dominate deejays' playlists. And as the dance floor took precedence, singers found that their vocals were no longer the defining feature of a song but rather just one element. "I don't sing much" was Gaynor's wounded response upon hearing Moulton's final mix of her LP. Dismayed, Gaynor asked, "What am I supposed to do when we perform the song?" To which Moulton replied, "You learn to *dance*."

Gaynor was among the first vocalists to come up against the brutal exigencies of disco, which mandated that the dance floor, and therefore the rhythm section, take precedence. Veteran R&B singer Loleatta Holloway had an even ruder awakening several years later when she discovered that deejay Walter Gibbons had excised the first two minutes of her vocal and *all* of her verses from "Hit and Run." The B.T. Express scored a hit in 1974 with Moulton's remix of "Do It," but they disliked the way their music was being chopped up and reassembled for the dance floor. When the group heard Moulton's stark remix, which foregrounded the drummer's hi-hats and cymbal crashes and de-emphasized their vocals, they "hated" it. Moulton remembers the group complaining that "it wasn't the way they recorded it, and that it was unnatural."

Mindless, repetitive, formulaic, and banal were more typical epithets directed at disco. Nonetheless, from very early on the idea of unnaturalness hovered over the discourse about disco. Disco did favor the synthetic over the organic, the cut-up over the whole, the producer over the artist, and the record over live performance. And if you believed that authentic soul music was raw and unpolished, then disco's preference for silky sophistication was further evidence of its inauthenticity. The fact that many of its most committed fans, deejays, and remixers were gay men encouraged this view that disco was not the real thing. Chuck D of Public Enemy called disco "the most artificial shit I ever heard," music that was "sophisticated, anti-black, anti-feel," not to mention gay, and upwardly mobile.

The demands of the dance floor left their mark on disco. That said, black producers and musicians were the leading architects of the disco sound. The idea that disco involved a renunciation or, worse, a perversion of black music does not do justice to the complexity of R&B. Yes, disco staked out new sonic territory, but it drew on a long-standing tradition within both R&B and jazz of sweet vocal and instrumental styles. Without the sweet soul music produced by Motown there simply would have been no disco. And long before Giorgio Moroder began producing Donna Summer's hits, Isaac Hayes's cinematic soul broadened the sonic palette of R&B. Even though disco was not a man's man's man's world, James Brown's musical innovations proved to be critical to its development. The point is that disco did not arrive on American shores courtesy of Giorgio Moroder, the Bee Gees, and Abba. It developed through ongoing transnational exchanges, whose point of origin, while not exclusively American, was nonetheless more American than not.

So how did we get from James Brown to Barry White? This shift is, of course, about music, but it is also about larger cultural shifts that are inextricable from disco. Usually disco functions as an easy trope for the era's narcissism and hedonism. However, I want to examine less familiar cultural concerns, ones that animated black communities but registered only faintly, if at all, in the glitzy, celebrity-studded world of Studio 54, the most common model for disco nightlife. Disco, and the music that anticipated it, provides a partial map of black America's shifting relationship to masculinity, upward mobility, and politics in the post-civil rights era. Although disco had its message music, it put forward its critiques slyly, favoring so much indirection and disguise that one could argue it operated according to what one anthropologist calls a "hidden transcript."

What follows is not a seamless narrative that unfolds gracefully, like those smooth mixes that galvanized dancers of the era. Mapping both the aural and the larger cultural shifts entails some rough transitions and bumpy segues. Even without my stereographic approach—with one eye on the music and the other on the culture—this chronicle would prove daunting, because disco was not monolithic or reducible to one sound, a handful of performers and producers, or one demographic.

Complicating any effort to map a genealogy of disco is the murkiness of its history, which curiously remains more hidden than that of the more ostensibly "underground" punk. Critics may disagree about which continent gave rise to punk or whether certain musicians, such as Patti Smith, were really punk, but these are definitional problems. Because punk, on both sides of the Atlantic, assumed an explicitly rejectionist stance towards established rock, and was confident of its own significance, it took on the quality of a movement. Like most movements, it has left a vast archive and an impressive critical literature. Disco's history, by contrast, can be difficult to trace. Pop music is nothing if not a neverending series of borrowings, but the men and women who made disco—both in recording studios and in the deejay booths— were particularly promiscuous in their musical appropriations, refusing national boundaries as well as the snobbish purism that disdains the popular. As one peels back the layers of sound that make up disco, one discovers some unlikely sources and curious syncretisms.

"I HEAR A SYMPHONY" is the title of a Supremes record, and it was Berry Gordy's dream. At Motown Records, Gordy assembled a group of artists, musicians, songwriters, and producers who made music that often sounded like those "thousand violins in the air" that the Supremes invoked in their 1965 hit. Motown's violins, propulsive bass, and pounding beat created a sound both sweet and urgent, and it provided the aural template for disco. Perhaps the best indicator of the Motown–disco connection is how effortlessly so many of the label's hits were discofied in the late seventies. Like the music that would supersede it, Motown's was producer-driven and followed the logic of the assembly line. Indeed, when an interviewer asked founder Berry Gordy to respond to the criticism that his label was producing a sound rather than songs, Berry was unfazed. "You probably haven't any voice," he told the journalist. "But there are probably three notes you can sing. I can take those three notes and give them an arrangement and some lyrics. That makes a song. And your song will sell." Ten years later disco producers would say much the same thing about their music.

Crucial to the Motown sound was its beat—so insistent and whomping that Beatle John Lennon once asked a member of the Four Tops if their drummer "beat on a bloody *tree*" to get such a loud backbeat. Actually, Lennon was not far off. In order to achieve the heavily accented backbeat on the Supremes' hit "Baby Love," the musicians rigged up two-by-fours hooked together with springs, which someone stomped on. To some, Motown's rhythmic assault was unsubtle, even un-black. Isaac Hayes, who worked at rival Stax Records, regarded Motown's pounding beat somewhat cynically, as part of the company's calculated crossover approach. "Now it was the standard joke with blacks, that whites could *not*, cannot clap on a backbeat," recalled Hayes. "What Motown did was very smart. They beat the kids over the head with it." Hayes claimed that this wasn't considered "soulful" at Stax, but, as he emphasized to journalist Gerri Hirshey, "baby, it *sold*." And not just to rhythm-impaired whites; Motown was massively popular among African Americans, too.

Disco's indebtedness to Motown was more than simply aural, and included Gordy's audacious crossover ambitions. Gordy was committed to creating what he called the "Sound of Young America." Rather than making music that would circulate largely within the charts, radio, and venues of black America, he set out to make music that would take its seat at the front of the bus. In the process, Gordy upended the usual racial dynamics of popular music. Critics have often argued that Gordy's mainstream ambitions resulted in watered-down soul rather than the industrial-strength variety advanced by James Brown, Otis Redding, or Sam and Dave. In his elegiac *Sweet Soul Music*, Peter Guralnick excluded Motown on the grounds that its music was "so much more popular, so much more socially acceptable, so much more arranged and predictable, so much more white." Gordy's strategy did involve compromises. He initially opposed Stevie Wonder's plan to cover Bob Dylan's "Blowing in the Wind," which he considered too controversial. And he went so far as to establish the separate Soul label for records like Junior Walker and the All Stars' "Shotgun" that he (wrongly) judged too raw for Motown.

But if Gordy was sometimes a prisoner of the very racial categories his company was tearing down, that doesn't nullify what was truly radical about Motown: that is, the claims it made on the musical mainstream and American culture more broadly. His artists would no longer be in the background covering pop standards for a much smaller black audience. Nor would they find their own songs covered much more profitably by white artists, as repeatedly happened to early R&B stars such as Ruth Brown and Little Richard. Motown's artists would own pop music. And they pretty much did. Of the 537 singles the company released between 1960 and 1970, a remarkable two-thirds were hit records. Certain records, such as Martha and the Vandellas' "Dancing in the Street," not only seized the airwaves but also seemed to expand the realm of the possible, particularly for African American listeners. Martha Reeves and the Vandellas weren't singing about dancing at a sock hop, but in the streets at a time when streets were sites of protest, and when urban riots were extending the literal meaning of the song. Reeves denied the political import of the song, but, as cultural critic Gerald Early points out, most black people at the time regarded it "a metaphorical theme song for black unity and black revolution."

Philadelphia became the epicenter of disco music, but Motown was hardly out of the picture in the early seventies. With its illustrious songwriting and production trio Holland–Dozier–Holland having abandoned ship to set up their own label in 1967, Motown began drawing upon other talented writers and producers who started experimenting with new sonic textures. Frank Wilson produced Eddie Kendricks's startling 1972 track "Girl You Need a Change of Mind." Although "Girl" didn't burn up the charts, it was enormously influential within the emerging disco scene. Two qualities distinguished the cut from the label's usual sound: Wilson's inversion of Motown's four-on-the-top beat and his deployment of the gospel break, which emptied the track of most instrumentation and then gradually built it back up. This technique became so standard in seventies' dance music that it came to be called the "disco break." Just as important as Wilson's track with Kendricks was the work of Norman Whitfield. A young, ambitious songwriter-producer, Whitfield was further modifying the Motown sound, particularly in his work with the Temptations, who had been made over to seem more relevant to a younger generation. Whitfield's atmospheric funk on tracks like 1972's "Papa Was a Rollin' Stone," which was a hit for the Temptations on the pop and R&B charts and in discos, was widely copied, especially by the musicians at the recently formed Philadelphia International Records. Whitfield devised a dense, polyrhythmic texture made up of subtle conga fills, skittering hi-hats, and hand claps. He would use much the same rhythmic architecture in 1973's "Law of the Land," only this time it was undergirded by an unwavering, bass-driven 4/4 beat—the disco thump that the musicians at rival Philadelphia International Records were starting to employ. Whitfield's influence at the company is undeniable, and within a year another Motown record—the Jackson 5's "Dancing Machine"—was enjoying great success with clubgoers.

Motown artists sometimes scaled the disco charts, but the label's greatest significance to disco was foundational. Motown's unprecedented success ratcheted up the expectations of black artists, including disco's future hit-makers, who felt that the mainstream was now theirs for the taking. Many of the black musicians and producers who were in the forefront of disco, particularly Leon Huff and Kenneth Gamble of Philadelphia International Records, were looking to extend Motown's success and its sound. They set about challenging Detroit with what amounted to an updating of the Motown sound. "The Philly sound was a take-off of Motown, only more sophisticated," says Vince Montana, vibraphonist of MFSB, the house band of PIR. The Philadelphia sound worked the highest end, the sweetest registers of soul music. With its sumptuous, swelling strings, Latin-tinged percussion, and horns (often a French horn and flugelhorn or something even more obscure rather than R&B's familiar sax and trumpet) that were "brassy and up" rather than down and dirty, Philly soul achieved a sound considerably more lush than Detroit-style soul.

Thom Bell was a key architect of Philly soul, both on his own and in collaboration with Gamble and Huff. The Jamaican-born pianist was an important producer, arranger, and songwriter, who racked up an armful of hits including the Delfonics' "La La Means I Love You," the Stylistics' "You Are Everything" and "You Make Me Feel Brand New," and the Spinners' trio of hits, "I'll Be Around," "Could It Be I'm Falling in Love," and "One of a Kind (Love Affair)." Bell's signal achievement was to bring together what one critic calls the "sophisticated compositions and orchestration" of Burt Bacharach with the "smooth vocalizing" of old-style R&B groups like the Platters. The Stylistics' lead singer, Russell Thompkins Jr., even sounded like a more high-pitched version of Bacharach's favorite vocalist, Dionne Warwick. Bell was hardly the only black record producer and arranger listening to Bacharach.

Thom Bell pioneered the lush instrumentation of disco, but it was up to others to show how all that swollen orchestration might really heat up a dance floor. Although it is tricky to pinpoint the one group of musicians who created disco's distinctive rhythms, MFSB is often credited with "turning the beat around" and creating what became known as the disco beat. Besides vibraphonist Vince Montana, MFSB featured Norman Harris on guitar, Ronnie Baker on bass, and Earl Young on drums. These were the musicians playing on Harold Melvin and the Blue Notes' 1973 hit record "The Love I Lost," a track that disco historians often credit with establishing what became known as the disco sound. To writer Peter Shapiro, the cut's "hissing hi-hats, the thumping bass sound, the surging momentum, the uplifting horns, the strings taking flight" and vocalist Teddy Pendergrass's "gospel passion" are the quintessence of disco. Key to the foundational sound of "The Love I Lost" was the drumming of Earl Young, who claims to have come up with the idea of inverting Motown's usual rhythm. "Motown used four-four on the snare—khh, khh, khh, khh—and the heartbeat on the bass—dmm-dmm, dmm-dmm, dmm-dmm, dmm-dmm—and they also used four-four on the tambourines," recalled Young. "I would use cymbals more than the average drummer, and I realized that if I played the four-four on the bass I could work different patterns on the cymbals." That pattern would become the signature rhythmic pattern of much disco, from MFSB's own "TSOP" to Harold Melvin and the Blue Notes' "Bad Luck" and the Trammps' "Disco Inferno."

The Motown–PIR connection was pivotal to disco, but there was another important current that shaped its sound, and its creator was James Brown. Beginning with his epochal "Papa's Got a Brand New Bag," Brown hijacked soul music and took it deep into the territory of the rhythmic. As critic Dave Marsh has argued, just at that moment when the Motown juggernaut made "comparatively ornate records seem the wave of the future," Brown "invented the rhythmic future." With his 1965 chartbuster "Brand New Bag," Brown, who heretofore had found himself mostly confined to black radio where he was the "scream at the end of the dial," achieved an unlikely crossover to the pop world. Even Brown seemed a little awed by what he had accomplished, explaining to one interviewer that the track was "a little beyond me right now . . . It's—it's—it's just *out there*." But with James Brown, "Everything came out of his mind brand new."

Brown's hit record demoted melody and chord changes to such an extent that, in the words of music journalist Robert Palmer, the "rhythmic elements *became* the song." Every voice, every instrument was deployed for its percussive effect. With Brown, the percussive emphasis was on the first downbeat at the start of each bar, or what he called the "One." Dissecting Brown's sound, Palmer notes "the horns played single-note bursts that were often sprung against downbeats. The bass lines were broken into choppy two- and three-note patterns," which, as Palmer notes, was hardly a novelty in Latin music, but was less typical of sixties' R&B. In another innovation, his rhythm guitarist "choked his guitar strings against the instrument's neck so hard," writes Palmer, "that his playing began to sound like a jagged tin can being scraped with a pocketknife."

Repetition was the other critical quality in Brown's sound. From his early days as the lead singer of the Flames, Brown had acquired a name for himself by "crawling the floor and crying out the one essential word of their hit song, 'Please, Please, Please,' over and over again." Once Brown made the rhythmic turn, his vocal contributions sometimes consisted of little more than "uhn"s, "huh"s, and falsetto "eeeaaayowww"s. Brown's voice was never ancillary, but it was very much in service to the overall rhythmic assault, with the result that his vocals sometimes resembled percussive punctuation. Critics (and Brown himself) have often contrasted Brown's supposedly naturalistic funk to the soulessness of mechanistic disco, and yet the Father of

House-wrecking James Brown and the Famous Flames do some damage at the Apollo Theater, 1964. L–R: Johnny Terry, Bobby Byrd, Bobby Bennett, James Brown

JAMES BROWN'S "GET UP OFFA THAT THING"

DETERMINED TO BREAK the disco juggernaut he believed was killing his career, Brown declared war on the mellow dance music sweeping the nation with his 1976 release "Get Up Offa That Thing." Brown
has said that the song came to him in the middle of a dispiriting gig at a
Florida nightspot where the audience seemed determined to sit through
his set. They were "trying to do a sophisticated thing, listening to funk."
Frustrated, he began yelling, "Get up offa that thang and dance till you
feel better." The resulting record, which opened with Brown's declaring,
"I'm back," found the singer throwing down the groove and the gaunt-
let. Mr. Dynamite was on a mission to take back America's airwaves
and dance floors from disco, or what fellow funk artist George Clinton
dubbed "the blahs." For Brown, the song was about "releasing the pressure" by unleashing the hardcore funk that he believed disco was pushing to the margins of popular music.

In the LP's liner notes, Brown made it clear that he understood that
disco had democratized the music scene, pushing aside stars in the
process. "It once was me, now it's the people," he wrote. Brown insisted
that he knew "this game," he had conquered dance floors some ten
years earlier, and he was out to liberate the hearts, minds, and asses
of America once again. The track was bouncier than Brown's fractured
funk, but its only concession to the disco sound was the way the hi-hat
articulates the off-beats. There was nothing smooth, cool, or synthetic
about his latest track, just Brown's boasting, and an especially lively
example of the jive talk that usually passed between Brown and his
backup band the J.B.'s, including jabs at the Ohio Players and Barry
White, whom one band member derisively called "Barry White Boy." It is
a hard-edged jam so funky that Brown predicted it would jolt the disco

crowd to its feet and to its senses. "I can see the disco now, jumping, stomping, shuffling, screaming, roaring, hollering, getting overheated and shacking. Ha!"

"Get Up Offa That Thing" climbed no higher than number four on the R&B charts and barely cracked the disco Top 20. It demonstrated that as badly as Brown wanted to turn the clock back to those days when his music dominated the charts, by 1976 the ground underneath him, the ground he had so skillfully negotiated, had shifted. For the next three years Brown was lucky to get any chart action. Then in 1979, at the very tail end of disco's reign, his record company made a last-ditch effort to market him as the progenitor of disco. The cover of *The Original Disco Man* shows Brown in a white Bee Gees–like jumpsuit in the middle of a cavernous, empty disco, a glitterball above his head and a smile on his face. The album's execrable title track, "The Original Disco Man," a song with all the intensity of a sitcom theme song, transformed Brown into the scream at the back of the disco. Critic Robert Christgau nailed it when he wrote that the LP found Brown "exploring the alien world he founded."

Funk was not techno-averse. As music historian Brian Ward points out, before releasing "Brand New Bag," Brown remastered and sped up the original recording to give it more kick. The resulting record was, Ward maintains, the product of "inspiration, contemplation, and technological manipulation." Finally, Brown stretched out songs into jam-band length. Brown's funk upended the conventions of pop music in ways that disco musicians and producers would exploit.

Brown laid much of the groundwork for disco, but he did not prosper during the years of its hegemony. Most histories position Brown as too raw and too "black" for disco audiences. It is true that Brown's house-wrecking stage style, so explosive it left audiences "completely fucked up," was at odds with the smooth style of much seventies' disco. And the music Brown was best known for—his tense, staccato funk, with its unpredictable breaks and bridges—has a ruptural quality different from the plush, tightly seamed, 4/4 steamroller of disco. But Brown's biggest problem with disco wasn't its polish and sophistication. After all, the Godfather of Soul recorded any number of highly orchestrated ballads, including his monster hit "It's a Man's Man's Man's World." Brown's problem was that he never melded the funky and sophisticated within one track, but rather kept them sequestered. Melding these qualities inside a cut was the genius of disco, which Brown's arranger and trombonist Fred Wesley recognized. "Disco music," Wesley wryly observed, "is funk with a bow tie."

Other funk artists, which is to say those who followed the trail the Godfather blazed, worked the contiguous territory of funk and disco better than Brown. Sly and the Family Stone, who owed their success to their ability to "bridge the gap" between psychedelic Jimi and the tuxedoed Temptations, had largely fallen apart by the time disco hit big. Nonetheless, the group's musical hybridity and its initial optimism in songs like "Everyday People" and "Everybody Is a Star" prefigured disco's universalism. The composition of the band itself, a multiracial outfit in which women played instruments rather than only singing backup, underscored the band's commitment to breaking through established conventions and hierarchies. The group's 1968 hit "Dance to the Music," with its lines "Beat is getting stronger / Music's getting longer too," proved uncannily prescient, and modeled a sound that powered future disco hit-makers KC and the Sunshine Band. 1971's "Family Affair," which topped the pop and R&B charts, anticipated the mellower sound of disco. "Family Affair" featured a primitive drum machine that played a bouncy, featherweight rhythm that was echoed in two early disco hits, George McCrae's "Rock Your Baby" and the Hues Corporation's "Rock the Boat." In 1978, with Sly's best days behind him, his record company tried unsuccessfully to capitalize on the disco craze by rereleasing some of his biggest hits with a standard disco beat instead of the original rhythm tracks.

The success of James Brown and Sly and the Family Stone in the late sixties and early seventies resulted in a funk surge within R&B. Earth Wind and Fire, the Ohio Players, B.T. Express, Rufus, War, Kool and the Gang, and the Isley Brothers were among those galvanizing dance floors and racking up hit after hit on the pop and R&B charts. Records such as "Love Rollercoaster," "Once You Get Started," "Hollywood Swinging," and "City, Country, City" smoothed the edges of Brown's angular funk, which probably accounts for their popularity. Another case in point is "Express," a chugging, largely instrumental single by the New York group B.T. Express that became one of 1974's biggest R&B and disco hits. "Express" moved James Brown's funk into such monotonous territory that Brown's own band (with trombonist Fred Wesley at the helm) recorded a satirical cover, "(It's Not the Express) It's the JB's Monaurail," which mocked the track's easy-listening funk. Brown was exasperated by his imitators' commercial success, and when he wasn't trying to score a dance-floor hit he often criticized disco for capturing only the "repetitious part" of his funk.

However, the line between authentic funk and so-called fake funk— or, as others might construe it, between funk and disco—was not always discernible. George Clinton, who presided over a funk conglomerate that included the bands Parliament and Funkadelic, described the latter's disco-ish single "One Nation Under a Groove" disparagingly as "P-Funk for passives." Funkadelic recorded it, he said, because they needed a hit and bet that with disco's popularity the track might do well on the dance floor. Yet "One Nation" proved so prodigiously popular in black communities that it topped the R&B chart for six weeks in 1978. *Jet* magazine even named it the song of the year, which suggests that, whatever Clinton's intentions, for plenty of African Americans the record successfully worked the overlapping territory of funk and disco.

Writing funk into the history of disco entails calling into question some of the shibboleths about black-authored popular music.

Specifically, it means challenging the view that disco was bourgeois and funk was street, that disco represented an attenuated version of "black" music and that funk was its authentic expression. Writers continue to make these claims, but they never rise above the level of sheer assertion. Pitting disco and funk as antagonists denies the way they rubbed up against each other on the dance floor, on the radio, and in the recording studio. For example, Houston Baker has written dismissively of Johnnie Taylor's 1975 hit "Disco Lady," which he argues was one of the first R&B singles to be marketed to a white audience. Yet the record got heavy disco play and topped the pop and the R&B charts, perhaps because its sinewy sound owed a lot to the musicians playing on it—members of Funkadelic. Like so many disco records, these tracks were massively popular, and not just among rhythm-challenged whites and the upper stratum of black America.

This is not to say that disco and funk were indistinguishable. Disco was fonder of the 4/4 beat than funk, whose growing preference for a thwacking beat (as always "on the one") is audible in the Commodores' "Brick House" or Zapp's "More Bounce to the Ounce." Musicologist Charles Kronengold draws our attention to another difference: in a funk song a single detail might animate the whole as "the heartbeat," whereas the details in a disco record are not nearly so anchored to its sonic architecture, but rather come and go. Finally, disco was more attentive to female desire than funk, which tended toward the guy-centric.

The shift away from James Brown's male-centered sexual politics ("the way I like it is the way it is") to something more reciprocal owes a lot to another key figure in disco's prehistory, Isaac Hayes. A songwriter and musician at Stax Records, Hayes helped to define and popularize hard-edged Southern soul with songs such as "Soul Man" by Sam and Dave. However, Hayes's 1969 solo effort *Hot Buttered Soul* was utterly out of genre—a cross between lounge music, movie soundtracks, and R&B. Hayes favored lush instrumentation, but in contrast to the architects of Philly soul he had a penchant for the truly offbeat.

Years before the arrival of extended disco mixes, Hayes broke out of the two-and-three-quarter-minute straitjacket of R&B radio. His cover of country artist Glen Campbell's recent Top 20 song "By the Time I Get to Phoenix" clocks in at a bloated eighteen-plus minutes.

Critic Ken Tucker observed that Hayes wanted "to make soul music as a jazz artist might, lengthening and improvising on a single idea." The owner of Argent Studio, where Hayes recorded the album, says that the songs were so long that he would have to "walk out onto the studio floor while the band was playing and make a motion with my hand so that Isaac knew to either figure out how to end the song or let us start another reel." Hayes explored the possibilities of repetition, which he considered the key to getting "real deep into a listener's head." For Hayes the point was "to keep at it until even if the head was stubborn, the body couldn't resist." Hayes also experimented with minimalism in his stark cover of Dionne Warwick's "Walk On By" (one of three Bacharach tunes Hayes would cover) as instruments crescendo and then drop out. Indeed, Denise Chapman of the disco label Salsoul Records claimed that Hayes's "By the Time I Get to Phoenix" was the inspiration for deejay Walter Gibbons's stripped-down mix of Loleatta Holloway's "Hit and Run." Hayes's orchestration moved between the lush and the spare—a style that disco producers would pounce upon. And his eagerness to transform others' music—no matter if it was the sophisticated pop of Burt Bacharach or the country of Glen Campbell—suggested that anything was fair game for discofying.

In its repetitiousness, suavity, outsized tracks, orchestration, and audacious covers of unlikely songs, Hot Buttered Soul anticipated disco, but it doesn't sound much like it. However, Hayes's 1971 megahit for Gordon Parks's blaxploitation movie Shaft was a different story. The rhythmic architecture of "Theme from Shaft"—those tireless 4/4 hi-hats—was the prototype for disco's 4/4 thump. A perfect mix of the funky and the cool, the earthy and the synthetic, with Hayes's understated rap floating on top of it all, "Theme from Shaft" was wildly popular. The single sold a million copies, and from 1971 through 1972 it was a staple of Top 40, black, and jazz radio. And it was popular in the earliest discos. "Theme from *Shaft*" went platinum, won a Grammy, and the soundtrack from which it was drawn earned Hayes an Oscar, making him the first black composer to win that award. Decked out in flowing African robes, Spandex tights, and elaborate gold chains across his chest, Hayes toured with a twenty-piece tuxedo-clad orchestra in front of audiences that could not get enough of him.

Hayes enjoyed outsized commercial success, but music critics routinely savaged his music. One *Rolling Stone* reviewer called his follow-up LP *Black Moses* "dull, enervated and . . . pretentious." Another attacked Hayes for substituting gimmicks for "the *native* sensuality of black music" (italics mine). And Vince Aletti indicted him for churning out "black Muzak" that transformed good material into "a drowned and bloated body washed ashore after weeks at sea: pathetic, grossly misshapen, dead." Hayes was by no means the only artist to find himself bashed by critics for ditching his roots in authentically "black" music. Critics also dismissed as too sweet and insufficiently funky the symphonic soul of Thom Bell, Leon Huff, and Kenneth Gamble. The conventional wisdom among critics was that musicians like Hayes had fallen victim to the seductions of the white, bourgeois mainstream.

In pushing past the accepted borders of soul music, it is possible that Bell, Hayes, Gamble and Huff, and all the others *were* moved at least in part by their own upward mobility. It could also be that their fascination with sophisticated symphonic soul reflected what longtime R&B record producer Ahmet Ertegun characterized as African Americans' musical orientation towards the future—"what's next." For these musicians, "what's next" may have meant exploring the freedom to move beyond stultifying racial categorizations that consigned them to a particular kind of R&B—raw, straightforward, and unadorned. Stevie Wonder certainly made music that spoke to the dreams and disappointments of African Americans, and yet he categorically rejected the label "black musician." "That's putting me in a particular box," he insisted, "and saying . . . stay . . . right . . . where . . . you . . . are!" Over

the years, Philly producers Kenneth Gamble and Leon Huff have positioned themselves differently when questioned about the "blackness"
of their music. In early 1973, Gamble argued that black artists no longer had to go through a "whitening process" because the black market
was now large enough to sustain them. (Certainly PIR produced any
number of socially relevant songs geared to black listeners.) He also
said that he and his partner "never thought along the lines of a black
music thing," and on yet other occasions that they thought "green."
But the critical disparagement of PIR's sweet soul (mostly at the hands
of white critics of rock music) infuriated the two producers. Huff went
so far as to complain that these critics "cannot really hear black music"
and find it difficult "respecting black cats without patronizing us."

The critical commentary on the new soul music was often patronizing and, frankly, obtuse. Critics often could not grasp that to black
audiences Hayes, for one, was breaking new ground in all kinds of ways,
not the least in his self-presentation. For starters, he made sure that
the cover of Hot Buttered Soul was designed for maximum provocation,
unlike the covers of most R&B albums, whose sole design require-
ment seemed to be maximum innocuousness. Instead of a conventional photograph of Hayes either performing or posed smiling at the
camera, the from-above shot on the cover of Hot Buttered Soul captured
little beyond the top of Hayes's shiny, clean-shaven head, his shades,
and the hefty gold chains around his neck. Although Hayes recalls the
photo starting as a "joke," he says that he and the others involved in
the shoot quickly came to appreciate how "different and out front" it
was. By 1969 when the Afro was just beginning to become as much a
matter of style as a signifier of militance, Hayes's gleaming Afro-free
head suggested a shift in the sixties' hair wars. Maybe, as Hayes put it,
"bald was as black as you could get."

Likewise, Hayes's bare-chested-gold-chains look, which became de
rigueur in hip-hop circles some twenty years later, was another signifier of blackness. Hayes's chains and the African robes he often wore
tagged him a militant to some whites, including TV station managers

who were known to eye him nervously when he arrived to perform. To many African Americans, Hayes was the quintessence of black pride and black power. The image of Isaac Hayes at 1972's Wattstax Festival, an event often dubbed the black Woodstock, shaking off his cape to reveal his buff black chest and gold-chain vest is, as one historian has argued, perhaps the most powerful representation of "the impact of Black Power in America." Like the "black private dick" John Shaft about whom he sang, Hayes represented black people winning. This was the crucial element that most critics missed about both blaxploitation and the nascent disco sound: they represented black people getting over.

However, the critical establishment at rock-oriented publications such as *Rolling Stone* favored more overtly political music, of which there was much in early seventies' R&B. Indeed, the critical drubbing of Hayes and the other architects of disco reflected in large part an apprehension that this new soul music marked an abrupt move away from political engagement toward embourgoisement and political apathy. It's true that many of the soul records topping the R&B and pop charts

The nervy cover of Isaac Hayes's 1969 album *Hot Buttered Soul*

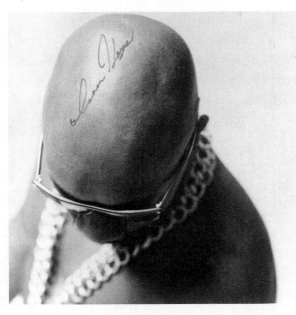

from the summer of 1970 until 1974 were what critic Greil Marcus called music of "worry," in which disenchantment and disillusionment loomed large. The Temptations' "Ball of Confusion" and "Papa Was a Rollin' Stone," Stevie Wonder's "Living for the City," Edwin Starr's anti-war anthem "War," Marvin Gaye's trilogy "What's Going On," "Inner City Blues," and "Mercy Mercy Me," the Undisputed Truth's "Smiling Faces," Sly Stone's *There's a Riot Goin' On*, Curtis Mayfield's *Superfly* soundtrack, the O'Jays' "Backstabbers" and "For the Love of Money," and War's "Slippin' into Darkness"—all were staples of Top 40 and R&B radio in this period. And this trouble music heaved its last gasp in 1975 with the Isley Brothers' uncompromising "Fight the Power," which after several weeks topping the charts gave way to KC and the Sunshine Band's disco number "Get Down Tonight."

To critics and observers it seemed obvious: the dance floor and the bedroom were trumping politics. Most attributed the turn away from politics to black America's resignation or capitulation. Critic Greil Marcus thought the new soul reflected the black community's "drift into accommodation," which he blamed on persistent racism, internal fragmentation, and the unraveling of the black freedom movement, largely through government repression. Most histories have echoed Marcus's downbeat assessment. In his book on Philadelphia International Records, John Jackson likewise stressed the negative, particularly the growing racial divide in the country. African American studies scholar Mark Anthony Neal also viewed the seventies as a time of "deterioration," when blackness was reduced to a commodity, and black middle-class flight from the inner city intensified the decline of black public life. And Brian Ward argued that with the rise of disco and funk, black Americans "were dancing to keep from crying."

Without question, there's much truth in these assessments, but they either disregard or diminish the important cultural transformations that were the legacy of civil rights. Affirmative action, growing black electoral muscle, greater and occasionally less caricatured representation in TV, film, and music, and the elimination of restrictive covenants created more opportunities (and some new conundrums) for African Americans. These changes were complicated by the depletion of the black freedom movement, stagflation (a combination of economic stagnation and inflation), growing class fissures, and continued police brutality in black communities. Equally important was the growing unemployment fed by the rust-belting of the Northeast and Midwest, which wiped out large numbers of unionized factory jobs of the sort that had been the traditional path out of poverty for poorer Americans. These were unsettled and unsettling times, but they were not characterized by unmitigated gloom. It was a period when the imperative was to "rock steady" because the ground was "shaky."

The focus on defeat and accommodation as *the* defining experiences of African Americans in the seventies has blinded critics and historians to the heightened sense of possibility that also characterized those years. Funk historian Rickey Vincent's belief that "black folks could go anywhere (almost) in America by 1970" is too optimistic, but he is right to emphasize the mobility—psychic as well as physical—that came with desegregation. The focus on black accommodation and capitulation misses the exhilaration of hearing Isaac Hayes have his way with pop standards just as John Shaft did with white cops. It fails to take into account the glee of watching the Oscars ceremony where Hayes, ("my weird black self") dressed in a fur-trimmed tuxedo, rose, Black Moses–like, on a pneumatic platform to perform "Theme from *Shaft*." It overlooks the sense of pride and power engendered by the success of Funkadelic's "One Nation Under a Groove," a song that championed a united, unstoppable people. And it ignores the triumph that black musicians and producers felt about breaching the racial boundaries of American music.

For black musicians, claiming the mantle of sophistication was a thrilling proposition, even if the end result sounded like schmaltz and looked like a sellout to some. Even James Brown felt the lure of sophistication. J.B. bandleader and trombonist Fred Wesley recalled how in the seventies he and Brown went "harp crazy, trying to put harp on

anything and everything." No one went about appropriating sophistication in a more determined way than the disco group Chic. Committed
to "reversing the traffic," they fashioned a tony style drawn from the
look and posture that Bryan Ferry and David Bowie put forward during
their "decadent" period. Chic cofounder Nile Rodgers recalls thinking,
"If we take this sophistication, high-fashion, aristocratic, interesting,
cerebral stuff, put a beat to it, make it black and our own thing, we
could really be happening, too." More recently, Rodgers has said that
with Chic he and his partner Edwards were trying to create funk music
distinct from that of the South, Midwest, or the West Coast. They
decided that "New York funk is slick, it's sophisticated, it's chic, it's . . .
French." With the women dressed in Norma Kamali and the men in
Armani and Cerruti, Chic advanced an elegant, classy look. Once they
became established, they traveled with three violinists as well. No one
rammed this music down the throats of black listeners, who, as Stevie
Wonder noted, "were looking for this change in their music."

Still, the movement away from overtly political R&B wasn't just
about the transgressive pleasure of seizing what traditionally had
been white turf—sophistication, class, those thousand violins in the
air. There was likely another reason that these musicians backed away
from songs like the O'Jays' "Backstabbers," which chronicled white
America's "broken promises" and black America's "faded hopes." In
part the answer lies in the evanescence of popular music. The detail-
ing of duplicity and disappointment that produced goose bumps of
recognition in 1970 had grown formulaic by 1974. Song after song had
taken to recycling what discographer Peter Shapiro calls the "smiling
face trope," the image of the backstabbing (white) politician or (black)
brother. Perhaps more to the point, by this juncture the realization
that the sixties' dream of peace, justice, and love had fallen short was
old hat. What was the point of belaboring it in song after song? To
radical cultural critic Michele Wallace, it was simply a foregone conclusion by the midseventies that the Black Power movement had passed,
largely as a result of the FBI's campaign against it. "Everybody knew, I

thought, that the possibility of radical politics was over." Her response was not more handwringing, but rather to conclude "at least you could be famous and then tell them all to fuck themselves."

For disco's architects, fame may have been its own revenge. They weren't interested in cataloguing disappointments, but rather in breaking expected racial stereotypes and "taking it to the bank," which is not quite the same thing as accommodation. Chic's Nile Rodgers was a sixties' person (he says he wrote Sister Sledge's big disco hit "We Are Family" at 1969's Woodstock Festival), but he was committed to making music that "uplifted the race," albeit cagily. What Rodgers and his bandmates "would do was hide it in our songs," sometimes so successfully that the political message was discernible to only the most maximally competent listeners. A case in point is the backstory to Chic's "Le Freak," which became Atlantic Records' bestselling single of all time. The story of "Le Freak" begins on New Year's Eve 1977, when the doorman at Studio 54 refused to admit the group's cofounders, Nile Rodgers and Bernard Edwards, who were guests of the singer Grace Jones. Infuriated at the snub, they retreated to Rodgers's apartment where they got wasted and jammed. As they played, they shouted, "fuck Studio 54 . . . fuck em," and "Aaaaaaaah, fuck off." The final version, which substituted "freak out" for "fuck off," seemed a paean to the newly opened but already famous New York disco. However, anyone familiar with the club's legendary snobbishness might have smiled at Chic's seemingly guileless suggestion, "Just come on down to 54 / And find a spot out on the floor." This was the way that Chic worked—through indirection.

And so it was with "Good Times," their 1979 track that many took as a clueless, head-in-the-sand celebration of the good life at the height of hard times. "People asked how we could write a song called 'Good Times' in the middle of the greatest recession since the 1930s," says Rodgers. A former Black Panther, Rodgers maintains the song was always meant ironically. "Listen to the lyrics, we are comparing it to the Great Depression!" But most listeners didn't pick up on Rodgers's rip-off of a line from an Al Jolson song or anything else. "If Dylan was standing in front of a tank singing 'happy days are here again' people would say 'oh, check Bob,'" Rodgers observed. "It would be loved and would make all the sense in the world." But something that arch coming from a black disco group, Rodgers pointed out, "sounds totally different."

There were some disco songs that grappled with political issues in a straightforward manner. The best known include Machine's "There But for the Grace of God Go I," Gladys Knight's "Bourgie Bourgie," and two PIR songs, McFadden and Whitehead's "Ain't No Stoppin' Us Now," and the O'Jays' "Message in the Music." But for the most part, disco was politically oblique rather than explicit. From the beginning disco favored manifestos of love, songs such as "Love Train," "I Love Music," "Love's Theme," and "Love Is the Message." As disco congealed, the noirish music that had been a strand of early disco (songs such as "Papa Was a Rollin' Stone") gave way to upbeat, broadly humanist tracks such as the Temptations' "Happy People," and most famously "We Are Family," the song that Edwards and Rodgers wrote and produced for Sister Sledge. Given half a chance disco would almost always dodge the politically controversial.

However this hardly means that disco was emptied of political meaning. Just as the shift toward sophistication was in a broad sense political, so was the shift in the representation of black masculinity that occurred in these years. At the beginning of the 1970s James Brown was the undisputed Godfather of Soul and his style of masculinity, which journalist Nelson George considered one of "unbridled machismo," still held sway among many. Brown advanced a cocky masculinity rooted in the streets that, as one fan recalls, "hooked most black men (including me) to the James Brown culture." Activist Al Sharpton Jr. has said of Brown, "We look at James Brown, and we say, 'Hey, *that's* how I'm gonna be a man.'" With his hard-edged funk and his political audacity (recording his anthem of black pride, "Say It Loud—I'm Black and I'm Proud"), Brown configured black masculinity in the sixties as surely as the Black Panthers did in their black berets and leather jackets. Much of Brown's appeal lay in his swaggering, boastful sexuality. In songs like "Get Up (I Feel Like Being a) Sex Machine" and "I'm a Greedy Man," Brown advertised his outsized libido. Even in his late forties, Brown appeared onstage "in a red jumpsuit with the word SEX stitched across the front." George Clinton is likely not the only man whose love of Brown's funk has something to do with the way "it makes your dick hard."

On the surface, Hayes also seemed like a "black stud," as rock critic Ken Tucker put it. After all, he described John Shaft as a "sex machine," and likely Hayes enjoyed the inevitable slippage between himself and the "black private dick" he sang about. But while "Theme from *Shaft*" suggested that black power is phallic power—that it emerges from the shaft of . . . you name it—Hayes's self-representation leaned toward the ironic. Reviewing his 1973 London concert, *Melody Maker* noted that Hayes "didn't take himself seriously, thank God, but came on with a maximum of showbiz camp." Hayes has said that his tough-guy pose gave him the necessary cover to express emotions usually considered unseemly in men. In his view, much of his popularity stemmed from the way he expanded the emotional parameters of masculinity in a way that both men and women found appealing. Even a cursory listening to Hayes's music reveals that underneath all the Spandex and chains, he was as much a love man as a sex machine, as apt to sing about getting hurt as about getting laid, and able to move seamlessly from baritone croon to falsetto wail. In the lugubrious "By the Time I Get to Phoenix" the narrator only leaves his wife after the *eighth* time he's found her in their bed with another man.

Hayes was a race man and a love man—a combination that no other R&B singer of his generation, even Marvin Gaye, was able to pull off quite as effectively. As critic Carol Cooper has persuasively argued, Hayes was simultaneously sexy and warriorlike. Hayes pioneered a different kind of black masculinity in which toughness, rather than being an end in itself, could be harnessed for the purpose of tenderness. He was a transitional figure whose soul-baring R&B and tough but vulnerable masculinity bridged the sixties and the seventies and prepared America's airwaves and dance floors for disco. With Marvin "Let's Get It On" Gaye, Hayes also pushed the boundaries of respectability with his X-rated bedroom music. It was Hayes's 1973 album *Joy* that, with Sylvia Robinson's "Pillow Talk," pioneered the orgasmic gasps and moans that would later turn up in Marvin Gaye's "Since I Had You," Major Harris's "Love Won't Let Me Wait," Leon Ware's "Body Heat," and most famously of all in Donna Summer's 1975 record "Love to Love You Baby," her first hit.

Given Hayes's love-man credentials, he should have been positioned to take advantage of the disco turn. But by late 1973 he was playing catch-up with Barry White, who as a solo artist racked up five Top 10 hits (and even more on the R&B and disco charts) between 1973 and 1979. By comparison, Hayes managed three disco hits, "Disco Connection," "Don't Let Go," and "I Ain't Never," but they were far from his most memorable or bestselling tracks. Writing about this turn of events in the mideighties, critic Dave Marsh said it was hard to believe that Hayes, whom he called the master of the "personalized epic," had actually been "laying the groundwork for Barry White." Indeed, White so copped Hayes's baritone croon, raconteur vocalizing, and pillow-talk soul that he was widely recognized as an Isaac Hayes imitator. Hayes edged R&B closer to disco, but, like Brown, he found it difficult to adjust to disco's diminution of the performer. His mini-epics about the betrayals and loss that come with loving were too Ike-centric for the disco years, when dancers expected a singer to commit himself to *their* pleasure and not, as Hayes often did, to the exploration of his already much-examined psyche. Moreover, Hayes's love songs remained focused on his needs at the very moment when women's liberation was making an issue of women's desires.

Barry White did take an armful of pages out of Hayes's musical playbook—the buttery baritone, the plush orchestration, the languorous come-ons. White's breakthrough single, 1973's "I'm Gonna Love You

Just a Little More Baby," easily could have been the latest Hayes record . . . except for the fact that with its intense strings-versus-rhythm structure the song was tighter and tenser than anything Hayes was putting out. Jon Landau was one of the few rock critics to appreciate White, and in 1975 he wrote that at his best he was one of rock's great bandleaders, someone who could "perform any song at what feels like the beat of the universe." White had more than his music going for him. In contrast to "Black Moses," White "erased the difference between black and white," contended music promoter Howard Stein. With his "easy emotion, no challenges," and a twenty-piece orchestra, half of them middle-aged white men, he was, in Stein's view, "accessible to everyone."

White's success also owed a lot to his enthusiastic proclamations on behalf of the ladies. When it came to lovemaking, his aim always was to "please her and please her / any time or any place." Before most male musicians, White was onto the country's shifting sexual terrain, one in which women's sexual desire actually mattered. White presented himself as a heterosexual woman's fantasy of fidelity, devotion, and desire. At concerts he asked how many men in the audience really "know how to love their women." Longtime nightclub owner Trude Heller marveled at what she called his "women's liberation rap."

White was the vital ingredient in his woman's pleasure, but it was *her* pleasure that he claimed to be after. Always, she was "his first, his last, his everything." White advanced a more idealized vision of romantic love and a more selfless masculinity than just about anyone else on the scene. Certainly there were plenty of R&B and funk artists whose music reflected the usual masculine prerogatives. Even Stevie Wonder, who produced plenty of songs of adoration like "Golden Lady," turned regressive in "Superwoman," reprimanding an ambitious woman for "trying to boss the bull around." Marvin Gaye's falsetto was so seductive that it was easy to miss that *his* sexual healing took precedence. Falsetto Eddie Kendricks's "Girl You Need a Change of Mind," in which he sang, "Why march in picket lines? Burn bras and carry signs?" is

A one-time gang-banger, Barry White said that had
his mother not been a loving presence in his life he
might well have developed into "another kind of
human being"

explicitly anti-feminist. And funk musicians of the time—Rick James,
P-Funk, Cameo, the Ohio Players, the Commodores, among others—
celebrated "freaky girls" known for "letting it all hang out."

However, White had plenty of company when it came to this
women-first music. In 1975 the Miracles had a hit tweaking James
Brown's sex machine mantra by declaring, "I'm just a love machine /
and I don't work for nobody but you." Teddy Pendergrass's popularity
soared with steamy songs such as "Close the Door" and "Turn Off the
Lights," in which he implored his girlfriend to "tell me what you wanna
do." Even the onetime funk outfit Kool and the Gang abandoned their

"Jungle Boogie" for "Ladies Night," a number one disco hit. Although more romantic than sexual, falsetto-fueled groups often put forward a woman-identified vision of romantic love. The Dells scored a hit with "Give Your Baby a Standing Ovation," as did the Intruders with "I'll Always Love My Mama," a song that African American scholar Cornel West recently sang on Tavis Smiley's radio episode for Mother's Day. Under the direction of Thom Bell and often in collaboration with lyricist Linda Creed, also from Philadelphia, the Stylistics churned out woman-friendly songs of romance like "Betcha By Golly, Wow." So did the Spinners with records such as "Mighty Love," "I'll Be Around," and "Could It Be I'm Falling in Love."

One can't know the extent to which White's gospel of love prevailed in the discos, bars, and bedrooms of the seventies where his music played. After all, the relationship between the textual and the social is tricky. We do know that as the seventies came to a close his woman-centered love songs, and disco more generally, provoked a backlash among the young black men who began to turn toward the harsher sounds of hip-hop. Public Enemy had no truck with the cruder sort of misogyny peddled by the likes of 2 Live Crew; nonetheless, they went out of their way to make guys' music. Chuck D has said that the group "intentionally made records girls [would] hate and once they hated it, we knew we had some shit." Even though they knew their records were danceable, they preferred to think of them instead as "driving" or even "fighting" records. Coming of age in the days before bitches and hos, Michael Jackson, Prince, and Luther Vandross were among those who struggled in the post-disco landscape where masculine hardness and performative streetness mattered. Indeed, from *Thriller* onward, Jackson sometimes cast himself in his videos as an alien—too soft and androgynous to fit in with the ghetto-tough black men around him.

Performers like Jackson and Vandross, who consciously defied the mandate against "softening up," could situate themselves in a seventies' tradition of male sensitivity that included Isaac Hayes and Barry White. These love men could be schlocky, but they helped to make the seventies a time when vulnerability and tenderness weren't the sole preserve of women, when men's "rhymes could still sigh," as critic Thulani Davis so beautifully put it. But if these male architects of disco were refusing black macho, the men most gripped by dance fever were opting for butchness.

More, More, More

ONE AND ONENESS IN GAY DISCO

There is a force that connects us. And if I connect with that force, which I think is love . . . and I'm playing from that center, we're all gonna get it, we're all gonna get off on it.

—*Nicky Siano, deejay at the Gallery*

This is one massive cake of solid body, thousands, Hot Men, radiating enough heat to defrost Arctic wastes and I am being pulled into it and I am dancing and dancing, oh we are so many bodies, plowing my way through bodies, bashing and twisting and poppers passed like party favors and seven men now hold me and we swing and sway and sweat becoming One!

Larry Kramer, Faggots

In the summer of 1970 the first-person protagonist of Edmund White's autobiographical novel *The Farewell Symphony* returns to New York City after a six-month stay in Rome. What he sees upon his return astonishes him. "Where before there had been a few gay boys hanging out on a stoop along Christopher Street, now there were armies of men marching in every direction off Sheridan Square." Greenwich Village felt like a liberated zone. "Even the previously timid white boys of lower Manhattan were now out in sawed-off shorts and guinea T-shirts, shouting and waving and surging into the traffic." "Is this a holiday or what?" was his protagonist's ecstatic, bewildered response.

What had happened? How had timorousness been supplanted by

this surge of brash gay energy? Perhaps it was the June 1969 uprising at one of the Village's better-known gay bars, the Stonewall Inn. After all, many historians argue that the pitched battles between the police raiding the bar and its gay patrons helped to launch the modern gay liberation movement. But, curiously, White's account of those times did not mention Stonewall or contemplate its political reverberations. Rather, he seemed to link gay men's newfound visibility and boldness to all the gay discos that had "sprung up like magic mushrooms" in the six months he had been gone. It was that same summer, a year after Stonewall, that the "sound and light and people" first came together on Fire Island, too. This was 1970, three years before music critic Vince Aletti dubbed the new dance music "discotheque rock" in the pages of *Rolling Stone*, and two years before ex-Temptation Eddie Kendricks recorded one of the earliest disco-ish hits, "Girl You Need a Change of Mind." Disco had not yet developed a distinct sound or even a name, nor had deejays developed the mixing techniques that allowed them to seam together a night's tracks. Yet disco was already changing the city and transforming the lives of gay men in ways both superficial and profound.

Today the connection between disco and gay men is so well established that it is hard to imagine a time when disco was understood as anything but queer. Gay men were among the genre's first and most legendary deejays, its earliest audience, and at the height of the glitter-ball mania practically ran the industry. At one point gay men held the top three positions in the field of disco record promotion. Each worked at a different label, but the three shared an apartment where they convened after work and smoked grass, snorted coke, and strategized about their upcoming releases. "You're going to have to wait with your Instant Funk," one might say, "because I'm putting out the Donna Summer this week . . ." Mel Cheren, who cofounded the disco label West End, says, "It was like musical monopoly, and gay people ran the bank."

Of course, before disco there was the Broadway musical, whose architects and most ardent fans were often gay men. Indeed, many gay

American men growing up in the post-Second World War years came to understand their difference from other boys as they sang along to the soundtracks of *Gypsy*, *Oklahoma*, and other Broadway hits. Literary critic D. A. Miller has argued that for gay men musicals advanced the "solitude, shame, and secretiveness by which the impossibility of social integration was first internalized." More often than not the Broadway musical presumed "a depressive status quo" best tackled through steely persistence and a cheery denial of suffering. In the way it veered between "some version of hellish and some version of swellish," the musical seemed to replicate gay life in these years. And while disco served up plenty of songs of romantic sorrow, it fashioned itself as the new swellish status quo in which injury and solitude were banished and the principle of sybaritic moreness ruled. One hears this shift in Linda Clifford's disco version of "If My Friends Could See Me Now" with its line, "I rejoice with all my friends," which so completely upends the meaning of the original. One sees it in William Friedkin's controversial 1980 movie about the gay leather scene, *Cruising*. "No sad, solitary longing here," writes Miller, "instead, a superabundant spectacle, as crowded with bodies as a Bosch painting, of acts and pleasures."

The contrast between the shadowy, almost quarantined quality of homosexual culture in the years before disco and its in-your-face visibility at the height of mirror-ball mania has sometimes encouraged the view that gay liberation and disco moved—or better still, danced—hand in hand. While the relationship between "going out and coming out" (and between consumer capitalism and gay liberation) was deep and reciprocal, it was not untroubled.

THE SIXTIES ARE so mythologized as a time of revolutionary rupture that the humiliations and constraints of gay life during the Age of Aquarius seem almost inconceivable. Even if heterosexuals weren't quite doing it in the road, as the Beatles put it in 1968, they were finding far fewer impediments to sexual expressiveness. Yet as the sexual revolution swept across straight America, gays still could be arrested for simply holding hands. Homophobia and harassment were the norm even in big cities, and as a result, "you were always taking a chance when you went to a gay place." In 1969 alone the Los Angeles Police Department made a staggering 3,858 arrests under the category of crime that it used to prosecute gays. Police entrapment in this period made hooking up with another man a high-risk affair, as gay historian and activist Martin Duberman recalls. The police "would choose the hunkiest young cops and dress them in the standard gay uniform of the day—chino pants, penny loafers and T-shirt—and send them out to entrap gay men. The guy would come up and say, 'Hey, what're you doing tonight?' And because they were generally gorgeous, you said, 'Nothing. What are you doing?' And then, snap! On went the handcuffs. Just like that."

Even the counterculture, which dismissed monogamy as a bourgeois hang-up, could be narrow-minded about homosexuality. In 1966, when a group of San Francisco hippie entrepreneurs transformed a gay porno theater into a hip rock ballroom, they named it the Straight Theater in large part so that gay men would stay away. On the other coast in Greenwich Village, the liberal *Village Voice* refused to carry ads that used the word homosexual or homophile. Even on Fire Island, which had a reputation as a "carefree" gay resort, homosexual men who visited the cruising areas risked being rounded up by police who treated them like vermin. Chained together to a telephone pole that sat in the middle of the Fire Island Pines dock, the men waited until the police had made thirty or forty arrests. Then they were loaded onto a police launch and taken to the Long Island town of Sayville, where they were led into the back of a drugstore that functioned as a kind of kangaroo court. Worried about losing their jobs or being exposed, they paid the steep fine and accepted the thirty-day suspended sentence.

This climate of repression extended to gay bars nationally, which were often operated by crime syndicates that seemed as committed to dispensing humiliation as alcohol. According to one study, gay bars in Chicago prohibited virtually everything but getting drunk. Touching, dancing, even eating, were strictly off-limits. Often contemptuous of their clientele, bar managers vigorously enforced the prohibitions against same-sex dancing that existed throughout much of America. Gay activist Craig Rodwell worked at a popular Fire Island bar, the Botel, from 1966 through 1967. Employees there "had to take turns sitting on top of a ladder, ten rungs high, and be ready to shine a flashlight as rudely as possible into the eyes of anyone engaging in 'illegal' behavior." At the Botel, according to Rodwell, this included just facing another man while dancing. "All male eyes on the dance floor were supposed to be aimed exclusively at the occasional female—somebody's lesbian friend or one of the straight women from the yachts—who had been persuaded to participate."

The dance floor had long been contested territory in nightlife establishments that served sexual minorities. In New York City during the first third of the twentieth century, social purity organizations committed to fighting vice were a bigger thorn in the side of such businesses than the police. When these groups or the state did intervene in their operations, they usually did so against the wishes of managers who saw little harm and considerable profit in tolerating gays. During the Roaring Twenties, gay men became such a feature of New York's nightlife that some thought the city had succumbed to a "pansy craze." Anxious that the fairies (and the much smaller number of butch lesbians) not attract the attention of the authorities, most managers established limits on permissible gay sociability. Very often dancing was a flashpoint.

New York police could and sometimes did use laws against "degenerate disorderly conduct" to arrest gays engaging in "non-normative" behavior in public spaces. However, the policing of the gay nightworld did not become systematic until the 1930s, when authorities began to crack down on sexual minorities who had grown increasingly eager to test the limits of "decency." Historian George Chauncey reports that their restiveness, manifested in large part in the growth of same-sex dancing, combined with the growing attentiveness of the police, led the organizers of the last big drag balls of the 1930–31 season to cancel them rather than risk being raided.

With the repeal of Prohibition in 1933, New York nightlife, which had been largely underground and unpoliced, became highly regulated. New state regulations promulgated by the State Liquor Authority defined as "disorderly" any establishment in which gays and lesbians were even a presence. Within a few years, the SLA, which systematically targeted queer establishments, achieved its goal of shoving New York's gay world into the closet. Remarkably, many of these very same laws and regulations continued to tyrannize gays until the end of the sixties. It was this vulnerability to harassment and license revocation that allowed the Mafia and corrupt police officers to muscle in on gay bars. It bears mention that there is some speculation that the Mafia's involvement with gay bars also stems from a "lavender streak" running through the Mob's lower levels. It raises the intriguing possibility that Vito Spatafore, *The Sopranos*' gay mobster, who was based on a real-life gay member of the Gambino family, may not have been completely anomalous.

In this period gay bars across America offered their patrons a distinctly equivocal experience: the pleasures of sociability on one hand, and on the other the likelihood of crummy treatment and police raids. By the late sixties, San Francisco and Washington D.C. finally permitted dancing, but gay bars in Baltimore, Chicago, and Los Angeles risked being raided if their patrons danced. As for New York, police there ignored the January 1968 ruling by state judge Kenneth Keating establishing the legality of close dancing between homosexuals. Despite this, when the Stonewall Inn opened in the spring of 1967, management and customers alike behaved as if the dance floor had been won. The unlicensed bar was a firetrap that doled out watered-down drinks in dirty glasses, but it quickly developed a loyal clientele because it was the only gay bar in New York City that as a matter of course permitted dancing between men. In contrast to another gay bar, the Tenth of Always, where "you knew that when the chandelier would flick on, you'd have to sit down," at the Stonewall "you were never told not to dance." Indeed, the only time the dancing came to a halt was when the police arrived. "I had such a thrill in my stomach," recalls a patron of his first visit to the Stonewall. Walking into its back room and seeing several male couples dancing together was "like an electric shock . . . it was so fucking exciting." Within a year of opening, it was the Village's most popular gay bar and a "money machine" for its Mafia owners. Despite the fact that its owners made regular payoffs to the police, the bar was raided on June 27, 1969. This was hardly the first time that the police hit the Stonewall, but it was the first time that they had not given advance notice to the management. And it was the first time that gays, angry about being treated like scum, fought back. Soon the police found themselves under siege, cowering inside the bar in order to escape the fury of the queens whom they had always bullied. The officer in charge during the first night of rioting concedes that for the police "things were completely changed" afterward, because gays "were not submissive anymore." When Beat poet Allen Ginsberg surveyed the partially cleaned-up bar later that weekend, he declared its patrons "beautiful—they've lost that wounded look fags all had 10 years ago."

By the time of the Stonewall uprising, the homophile movement, as it was then known, had been active for almost two decades. Moreover, Stonewall did not mark the first time that gays took to the streets. Independent scholar Susan Stryker has uncovered the story of the long-forgotten Compton's Cafeteria disturbance of 1966, in which gays and transgender people fought the San Francisco police. Nonetheless, many scholars contend that the June riots at the Stonewall Inn brought about a much fuller mobilization and politicization of gays and lesbians. David Carter, author of *Stonewall: The Riots That Sparked the Gay Revolution*, points out that within nine months of the uprising three gay newspapers—*Gay Power, Come Out!* and *Gay*—began publishing in New York City and two militant gay liberation organizations had formed. In his book about the riots, historian Martin Duberman argues that Stonewall engendered a "kind of seismic shift" in the consciousness of gays and lesbians. Even Stryker, who has argued for the importance of the Compton's Cafeteria riot in queer history, concedes that Stonewall had a catalytic effect in the Bay Area, where new militant organizations formed almost immediately.

Indeed, the idea of "Gay Power" exerted such a pull that established homosexual rights groups, which believed that bland conventionality would win gays and lesbians admittance to American society, came to seem quaint and wrongheaded. One week after the riots, at a homophile demonstration at Philadelphia's Independence Hall, two lesbian activists had the temerity to walk the picket line hand in hand. This was radical stuff in the homophile movement, where public displays of affection were regarded negatively as being a provocation to straight America's sense of propriety. As soon as he spotted them, the veteran activist Frank Kameny rushed over to the couple, indignantly yelling, "None of that! None of that!" Although he broke up their handholding, neither Kameny nor the larger homophile movement he was a part of could quash the spirit of Stonewall. Suddenly gay liberation groups such as the Gay Liberation Front and the Gay Activist Alliance that were committed to transforming rather than joining American society formed, and flaunting it became the way forward.

But if the Stonewall riot brought about a sea change in gay and lesbian life, it was also building on shifts already under way. Several historians have argued that if homosexual men and lesbians were receptive to gay liberation, it followed from the fact that in participating in bar culture they were already engaged in everyday resistance. However, those historians have yet to connect the riots to the changing dynamics inside the Stonewall itself. Perhaps because the Stonewall seemed such an outpost of wounded, pre-liberation consciousness, historians have been slow to consider that the bar might have been a site of transformation. What if the bar's two dance floors helped to undermine the sort of sexual indirection and repression that characterized most other gay bars? One of the many young street queens who frequented the Stonewall contends that the unrestrained dancing there fostered the "articulation" of gay sexual desire. At other gay bars, he says, "you could look across the room and see sexy Vinnie over there and you could get into the longing, but you couldn't go over and ask him to dance." Another regular credits the Stonewall with making him confront his own sexual inhibitions and internalized homophobia. On his first visit there, when someone asked him if he was going to dance, he blurted out, "I don't dance with men. I don't do that." And yet, as he hung out at the Stonewall, he came to see that dancing was a prelude to sex, and that no matter how "embarrassed and nervous" he might at first feel about dancing with another man, if he wanted to do more than daydream he would have to give the dance floor a try. Even if the Stonewall was in many ways part of the "old gay" world, its dance floor encouraged greater sexual expressiveness, which in turn forged a closer connection between going out and coming out.

The idea that the Stonewall Inn was changing consciousness was hardly the view of either button-down homophile activists or the long-haired "freaks" of gay liberation, both of whom viewed the bar queasily. Three years earlier, New York's Mattachine Society, the city's best-known homophile group, had organized a successful "sip-in" to eliminate the New York State Liquor Authority's policy that made it illegal for a restaurant or bar to serve liquor to a group of three or more homosexuals. However, its leaders were hardly keen on the Stonewall Inn or the other seedy bars that were making money off gays. Activist Craig Rodwell believed in the historical significance of the Stonewall riot, but in a broadside he called on gays to boycott Mob-owned gay bars. Certainly some within Mattachine considered the Stonewall's core clientele of working-class drag queens a pretty disreputable lot—alcoholics, drug users, hustlers—and symptomatic of what was wrong with gay life. Mattachine's Randy Wicker was mortified by the flamboyant queens in the forefront of the rioting at the Stonewall. The "tacky and cheap" queens "went against everything that I wanted people to think about homosexuals."

Most hippie-styled radical gay liberationists were ecstatic about the rioters' energy and anger. However, many would have agreed with activist Jim Fouratt, who thought the Stonewall was a "real dive, an awful sleazy place set up by the Mob." Moreover, younger activists often took a dim view of drag, which seemed a throwback to the days when gay men were considered (and often thought themselves) gender "inverts," internally female if externally male. Lesbian feminists of gay liberation developed a different critique of drag for fetishizing the very things that were oppressing women—girdles, corsets, stockings, high heels, and makeup. Although drag's tarted-up femininity caused unease among both respectable homophile activists and hippie-ish gay liberationists, the alternatives advanced by these groups were substantially different. While many inside Mattachine thought gays should aspire to conventional masculinity, gay liberationists generally saw themselves as working toward a radically androgynous future in which gender ceased to matter.

The liberationists' skittishness about the Stonewall (and gay bars more generally) also stemmed from their hostility to capitalism, and more specifically to commercial forms of leisure. Many were already active in other sixties' social change movements and had come to regard capitalism as an incubator of inequality and consumption as an activity that propped up "the system." By the end of the sixties some movement activists were calling for the creation of organizations and institutions that would allow people to pull their support from capitalist businesses and to nurture revolutionary consciousness. Within a few years many large cities boasted a range of alternative organizations and businesses—food co-ops, women's centers, feminist bookstores, people's legal services, free universities, and gay and lesbian community centers. In the heady days after Stonewall, gay liberationists hoped that "a genuine eroticism of everyday life" would take hold of their communities and banish to the dustbin of history all the tawdry bathhouses, massage parlors, and dives, which they considered relics of the bad old days when secrecy was demanded and gay shame and self-hate were not uncommon.

In an effort to provide alternatives to bar culture, many gay liberation groups forming across the country began to organize dances. New
York's Gay Liberation Front, which was established in the aftermath of
Stonewall, sponsored weekend ones that featured psychedelic rock at
the lefty Alternative University. Charging only a $1.50 entrance fee and
a mere twenty-five cents for beer and soda, the dances quickly became
popular—and contentious. GLF dances were meant to engender love
and acceptance and to create community, which they tried to achieve
through hippie-like circle dances. However, GLF dances also featured a
disco ball, go-go boys, and to some radical lesbians a lot of "groping and
dryfucking" among men as well. "These were by far the wildest parties
I had ever been to," recalls GLF member Karla Jay. To many lesbians
newly sensitized to male sexual objectification, it didn't much matter
that men, not women, were being objectified. To them, the dimly lit,
sexualized, overcrowded GLF dances "simulated a gay men's bar." In
fact, these dances were far less restrained than your average gay bar, as
men tore off their T-shirts and waved them above their heads as they
danced bare-chested.

The next gay group to organize alternative dances dispensed entirely
with the warm-and-fuzzy circle dances and acid rock. By the time the
Gay Activist Alliance, a more moderate group, began sponsoring Saturday night dances in May 1971, gay disco was already taking shape in
Manhattan. GAA held its dances in an abandoned SoHo firehouse that
the group had leased to house its gay and lesbian center. Their deejayed
disco dances became wildly popular, drawing on average 1,500 people.
"These were great jubilant shindigs," recalls one participant, and they
brought together "hippies and macho men, outrageous glitter queens
and intense politicos." Ray Caviano, who would become the most powerful promotional man in disco (the "head Homo Promo"), said the
Firehouse was the first club he ever attended. Two of New York's most
popular gay deejays, Barry Lederer and Richie Rivera, got their start
spinning records there. Mel Cheren, who worked in record promotions
and later formed the disco label West End, and his boyfriend at the

time, Michael Brody, who subsequently owned the Paradise Garage disco, loved dancing there. The Firehouse dances continued to go strong until 1973, but a year later the building was destroyed in an arson attack that to this day remains unsolved.

The GAA dances suggest the intimate and synergistic connection between gay liberation and gay disco. Here we have some of the first gay activists throwing dances that attracted men who would become pivotal players in the disco scene. Sometimes the dance floor became the launching pad for political action, as it did one Saturday night in June 1971. Frustrated by the opposition of New York City councilman Saul Sharison to a proposed gay rights bill, GAA decided to mobilize the dance floor for an action, or "zap." At 1:30 a.m. they pulled the plug on the music and told the crowd that they were going to "stroll" over to Sharison's luxury apartment building in "a show of gay/lesbian pride." A thousand dancers-turned-protestors poured out of the Firehouse and into the streets. Once at the councilman's residence, they created

Shirtless at the Firehouse. The scene at a 1971 Saturday night dance sponsored by New York City's Gay Activist Alliance

such a ruckus that his neighbors subsequently organized a petition drive to have him evicted as an undesirable tenant. "Now," wrote GAA member Arthur Evans, "he, too, knew what it was like to lack housing protection."

But what of all those gay men—and there were scads of them—who never set foot in a movement-sponsored dance, much less a meeting? Jorge La Torre was among New York's first disco dancers, but he never went to a gay liberation dance. A party hound, he frequented the Sanctuary, originally a straight disco with a gay following. Stonewall meant little to him; it certainly didn't get him out on the dance floor. Were other early adopters of disco similarly unaffected? What about the armies of men that Edmund White observed a year after Stonewall? Was their boldness attributable to a few months of club life rather than to the "seismic shifts" caused by Stonewall?

It's been argued that the eight-month lapse between Stonewall and the opening of the first for-profit gay disco proves that disco was on its own track, developing independently of the riots of '69. And, yet, social change rarely proceeds neatly or in an easily mappable fashion. Shifts in consciousness are devilishly difficult to map, not the least in this case where change was more a matter of conjunction than straightforward cause-and-effect. Is it even possible to disaggregate dancing from protesting when dancing itself constituted a kind of protest and entailed its own alterations of identity and subjectivity? The Stonewall riot was the result of all kinds of cultural and social reverberations— from the turbulence of the sixties to the shifts in gay sociability and gay desire that followed from the Stonewall's dance floors. Likewise the sense of empowerment that came from gays' "days of rage" at the Stonewall remade New York's gay nightlife. Mel Cheren recalls that the "aftermath of Stonewall almost took your breath away." Gay life in the city just "seemed to explode." His friend, the future gay activist Bill Scott, doubts that "those of us on Fire Island and in the clubs in the city could have danced the way we did without our newfound sense of freedom." Pioneering deejay Francis Grasso connected the opening of New York's first gay disco to Stonewall. Even those gays who took little notice of Stonewall could not help but be affected by its reverberations. After all, it was GAA that successfully fought a whole battery of laws regulating New York City nightlife, including the prohibition against same-sex dancing. This, as much as anything, facilitated the explosive growth of commercial gay discos—many of the clubs where La Torre and thousands of other gays partied in the years to come.

Once homosexual sociability was effectively decriminalized, gays became a desirable demographic, and the crime syndicates gradually lost their stranglehold on gay bars. Gay men forged a new relationship to public space, bold instead of furtive. If their new boldness grew out of gay liberation protests at City Hall, it also grew out of new post-Stonewall bars and discos. These were not the gay bars of old, which Edmund White once described as "temples to despair, where self-mocking queens . . . 'rubbed pussies' with one another before they got the courage to go out in search of the real thing, a bit of rough trade to rob and beat them."

Take the Picadilly [sic] Pub, which opened in 1971 on the Upper West Side. Here the jukebox leaned heavily toward soul music, with Judy Garland at first relegated to the far right corner of the menu, and then replaced entirely by Barbra Streisand. Its bartenders favored a look that anticipated "clone" style—"flannel shirts, veeeery tight Levi 501's and boots or work shoes." And even though the bar featured no dancing, the volume was set so high, according to the wonderful chronicler of gay life who runs the webpage nycnotkansas, that patrons had to dispense with the usual formalities and chitchat. " 'The music's so fucking loud I can't hear you,' said with a grin and a shake of your head, invited moving yourselves shoulder to shoulder and bringing your heads together—a business that could have taken half an hour to all evening in former bar environments." Full-fledged discos would intensify this shift toward greater sexual straightforwardness, which, in tandem with gay liberation, would help to put an end to gay men behaving like "arch and bitchy caricatures of middle-class women of the past," as Edmund White once put it.

That said, by 1971 the beneficiary of gay liberation's cry, "out of the closets and into the streets," was not so much the movement as the discotheques and bathhouses that catered to gays yearning to be out and proud. The Stonewall riot and the fallout from it had the effect of legitimizing gay space. Bathhouses and discos, rather than meeting halls or community centers, became what journalist Andrew Kopkind called the "sensational glue" holding these communities together. Gay liberationists praised movement-organized, noncommercial dances where gays and lesbians could know "people as people, not anonymous bodies," but these would gradually recede like the movements they grew out of. It was on the disco dance floor surging with the energy of "so many bodies becoming One" that gay men discovered their own "true" selves. Gay liberationists could decry gay institutions for fostering a "boring and pacified ghetto" and advocate instead a gay culture made up of such activities as "music, poetry . . . kissing, loving, painting . . . and sewing," but gay America wasn't sewing. It was dancing.

Indeed it took gay liberationists a decade to acknowledge the obvious—that gay men were about as likely as the working class to renounce the pleasures of consumption and sign onto a socialist revolution. Dennis Altman was hardly the only gay activist to find it both ironic and more than a little disappointing that as gays became freer in their sexuality they also became more dependent upon businesses. But there was no denying the fact that gay neighborhoods were bursting at the seams with bathhouses, discos, gyms, sex clubs, clothing shops, restaurants, and bookstores. By 1980, gay bathhouses and sex clubs in North America represented a hundred-million-dollar industry. Moreover, their influence was not simply economic. It was not unusual for gay entrepreneurs, who often gave money to movement groups, to become leaders within the gay community. Scott Forbes, the owner of the West Hollywood disco behemoth Studio One, served on the boards of the gay community's most important organizations, including the influential Municipal Elections Committee of Los Angeles.

For sixties' radicals, the seventies made Americans' investment in consumer capitalism depressingly clear. But for gay liberationists this reckoning was made somewhat more complicated by the fact that seventies' cultural critics, from the conservative Midge Decter to the liberal Christopher Lasch, were targeting consumer capitalism in ways that seemed to implicate homosexuality. Even when these critics weren't attacking homosexuals per se, their description of the modern personality as narcissistic, hedonistic, malleable, and marketable matched rather well the traits often associated with gay men. British sociologist Jeremy Seabrook was among the first to explicitly link capitalism and gay identity, claiming that the homosexual was a "pioneer of the new kind of human being that has come into existence under the protective shelter of plenty."

Gay liberationist Dennis Altman did not disagree with Seabrook, but he thought him shortsighted for not comprehending capitalism's liberatory potential. Although he would have preferred that the movement played a greater role in gay life, he accepted, albeit somewhat wistfully, that discos and bathhouses had become the real engine of change, bringing people into the gay community and fostering pride and acceptance. Indeed, Altman went so far as to claim that "no other minority had depended so heavily on commercial enterprises to define itself." British cultural critic Richard Dyer went further, becoming perhaps the first gay academic to suggest that capitalist cultural production might have "subversive potential." Rather than defend gays against the charge that they were overly invested in materialism, Dyer, using the example of gay disco, argued, "the anarchy of capitalism throws up commodities that an oppressed group can take up and use to cobble together its own culture." As we shall see in the pages ahead, gay men did a lot of cobbling in these years with jeans, leather, tees, s/m paraphernalia, poppers, gay-themed books, the latest 12-inch disco records, and, when within reach, memberships at gyms, bathhouses, sex clubs, and discos—all of which proved the power of gay money, or what in Britain soon came to be known as the "pink pound."

NEW YORK CITY'S first important discotheque was Le Club, which opened on New Year's Eve of 1962. Owned by a Frenchman, the snobbish Le Club became a magnet for the monied, jet-setting crowd. "To put it bluntly," wrote journalist Albert Goldman, "Le Club was a French playboy's dream of the ultimate seduction pad." By 1965 the city boasted fifteen discotheques, including Arthur, which was much more inclusive and for a year or two one of the city's happening nightspots. However, just as the discotheque was coming into its own in the States, a new kind of nightlife emerged. By 1968, hippie rock ballrooms such as Chet Helms's Avalon Ballroom and Bill Graham's Fillmore in San Francisco (and later in New York, too) were the new hip destinations. Some discos were able to hold on for a while, but most seemed hopelessly square and plastic by comparison to the electric ballrooms where bands like the Jefferson Airplane and the Grateful Dead played. There, young people dispensed with the Boogaloo and the Jerk and danced, not always very gracefully, to their own inner drummer.

Although the counterculture preached free love, it leaned decisively in the direction of heterosexuality. As a result, most gays, even youthful ones, patronized gay bars, which typically relied for music on jukeboxes rather than live rock bands. It wasn't just that most rock bands were reluctant to play gay bars; it was also that the bar owners were notoriously tight and wouldn't shell out the money for live entertainment. Dependent on jukeboxes, gay men began fiddling with them, adjusting them so that the gap between records grew briefer and briefer.

While gay bars struggled along with jukeboxes, music lover David Mancuso, who had been on the fringes of New York's counterculture, developed what became the prototype of the gay disco. Mancuso has traced the roots of his ur-disco, the Loft, to Harlem rent parties, but in its origins the Loft also bears some resemblance to the very first San

Francisco hippie dances. Like his hippie predecessors, Mancuso was cash-strapped and looking to ignite a scene when he decided to organize his first party. arlem'He held it on Valentine's Day and named it "Love Saves the Day," whose acronym signaled his own drug of choice. Mancuso's parties were by invitation only, but because he counted among his friends African Americans, Puerto Ricans, and women, not just white gay men, his dances were mixed in just about every way. Mancuso served no liquor, but with his acid-spiked punch no one much complained. Despite the LSD, Mancuso's hippie rhetoric of love, and participants' countercultural style of non-partnered dancing, critic Vince Aletti insists that the Loft "didn't feel like any hippie outpost to anybody who was there." Mancuso's weekly parties, which ran from midnight until six in the morning, became wildly popular, and before long there was a substantial waiting list of people eager to attend them. "By the end of 1970 you couldn't squeeze anyone else in, and it stayed like that for four and a half years," Mancuso recalls.

The Loft was a professional house party, the very opposite of the "dressy, Saturday night out feeling" usually identified with disco. But as Mancuso's parties were beginning to take off, glitzier commercial discos that grew out of sixties' discotheque culture began to take hold. Perhaps the most important was the Sanctuary, a club whose scandalousness earned it an appearance in the psychological thriller *Klute*. Occupying what had been an old German Baptist church in Hell's Kitchen, the Sanctuary featured an enormous pornographic mural of a gleamy-eyed devil surrounded by cherubs engaged in a variety of "depraved" sexual activities. The club quickly became a magnet for men and women in fashion, acting, and design. The Sanctuary was a gay-friendly space that underscored the point by hiring gay men to handle the door. With its huge dance floor, it became the first club where gay men could safely come together in a large crowd. Eight months after the Stonewall riot, the club changed hands, and its new gay owners made it more decisively gay. They ditched the jukebox for a deejay, making it, claims club deejay Francis Grasso, the first gay bar without a jukebox.

The Sanctuary was the home of the Bump, but, as journalist Albert Gold-man observes, on its dance floor the Bump was not "the cute little hip-hugger tushie-touching step that it became in the straight world," but rather what he indignantly called "a frank pantomime of buggery."

Although the Sanctuary's sexual explicitness contributed to its rep-utation, equally important was its trailblazing deejay Francis Grasso, one of the many Italian Americans manning the turntables at New York discos. Rather than make the crowd "catch the beat again" at the end of every record, Grasso kept the beat going by slip-cueing, a method that allows the deejay to introduce the first beat of a new track on the beat of the song that's ending. Unlike other deejays who didn't yet "know how to bring the crowd to a height, and then level them back down, and bring them back up again," Grasso introduced sexual know-how to the dance floor. Deejays soon developed a variety of mixing strategies that spared dancers the embarrassment of standing around awkwardly on the dance floor between cuts.

For gay men accustomed to being surveilled and harassed on the dance floor and arrested during bar raids, the tightly seamed disco mix was especially meaningful. Denied the opportunity of uninterrupted dancing with other men, gay men took to disco like a drug. Nonstop music was central to the "throbbing lights, the engulfing sound, the heightened energy, and the hyperbolic heat," which together created what gay journalist Andrew Kopkind described as the feeling that "the world is enclosed in this hall, that there is only *now*, in this place and time." From the beginning, discos fostered the feeling of being in a "timeless, mindless state." At the Loft you felt "cut off from the out-side world" as soon as you walked inside. "There was actually a clock in the back room but it only had one hand," recalls David Mancuso. "It was made out of wood and after a short while it stopped working."

Of course, drugs played no small role in pushing people into a state of suspended "nowness." "Without drugs," writes art critic Douglas Crimp, "disco can be fun, but only just fun." According to Crimp, one needed "the incredible level of energy [that drugs] give the illusion of supplying . . . and their disinhibiting quality to allow the music's beat to take over your body and inhabit it . . ." Disco-goers used a variety of drugs: poppers, LSD, Quaaludes, cocaine, speed, MDA, and PCP. Amyl nitrate, the active ingredient in poppers, was intended for people with angina, and was available as an over-the-counter drug for much of the sixties. However, amyl nitrate's vasodilatory effects, which relax the body's smooth muscles, made it popular among people looking for a high, too. Poppers produce a euphoric head rush and relax the sphincter muscles in the anus and the vagina. Amyl nitrate's effects are short-lived—a mere minute or two—but as the author of nycnotkansas.com notes, "having received this kind of boost the ensuing sex was likely to be rather terrific." Poppers were so widely used in the back rooms and dance floors of discos that their fumes were sometimes overpowering. Amyl nitrate was also used in conjunction with heavier drugs. Flamingo's deejay, Howard Merritt, remembers basing his playlist upon that week's drug of choice. "I would call drug dealers up and ask, 'What's been your big seller this week?'" Depending on the answer, his playlist would lean toward the upbeat or the heavy.

By altering the sonics of the music they played, deejays contributed to the feeling of timeless nowness. "I would turn everything off except the tweeter arrays and have them dancing tss, tss, tss, tss, tss, tss, tss, tss for a while," explained Gallery deejay Nicky Siano. "Then I would turn on the bass, and then I'd turn on the main speakers. When I did that the room would just explode."

Deejay Bob Casey experienced a few such "dance orgasms" at Siano's club.

> Every once in a while, everybody would be so together with it . . . and they'd be singing along—and Nicky would bring it up and all of a sudden BOOM! Out would drop the center and everybody would be stunned—"Awwwww!"—and then BLAMM!! in would come this incredible bass. And by that time—and there's essence of amyl nitrate all over the place—it was flawless.

As the technology of discos improved it became possible to engineer sound so that the bass felt as if it were penetrating one's body. At the Paradise Garage disco, the bass was so thunderously earthquaking that to deejay Casey it felt like it "put your balls up your ass."

Many accounts of gay disco stress the intensely sexual and tribal quality of the dance floor. When the protagonist of Larry Kramer's bestselling novel *Faggots* dances among thousands of other half-naked men on Fire Island at Cherry Grove's Ice Palace, he allows himself to succumb to the disco heat produced by the commingling of music, men, and the feeling of brotherhood. With fists "pounding to the beat of one of their own disco anthems," the dance floor becomes a site of "Release." For many gay New Yorkers no disco had quite the libidinal charge of the notorious Flamingo, a private club that opened in December 1974. The height of gay trendiness, Flamingo was known for its model-beautiful men and its color-coded theme parties. Andrew Kopkind wrote about 1979's Black Party, which featured leathermen performing s/m in a cage. "Some of the goings-on were semimentionable: people (actors?) were in chains, under the whip, groveling and groping, disheveled," he wrote. "Other attractions were unmentionable, and getting more so as the evening wore on." In his gay travelogue *States of Desire*, Edmund White wrote about his night at Flamingo, where the "drugs and the music and the exhilaration" banished his physical inhibitions. "We were packed in so tightly," he wrote, "we were forced to slither across each other's wet bodies and arms." The feeling proved irresistible, and White "surrendered to the idea that I was just like everyone else. A body among bodies."

If the feeling of tribal oneness was especially intense at Flamingo, it was in large measure because it was exclusively gay. Yet the very first discos that gay men typically patronized were not exclusively homosexual. For example, in Detroit, Disco Mondays at the Roostertail, apparently the first disco to attract gay men, was geared to men and women who worked in and patronized particular boutiques and hair salons. In New York, the Sanctuary was initially mixed, and the Loft counted a fair number of women among the dancers. And Galaxy 21, a black and Latino club near the Chelsea Hotel, was, like most clubs where gays of color partied, mixed. Some say that it was not until the upscale Continental Baths got into the disco business in 1970 that New York's gay men actually had a space in the city that was unequivocally theirs. Best known as the bathhouse where Bette Midler first sang and told her off-kilter, off-color jokes, the Baths was "opulent with steam rooms, swimming pool, private apartments, restaurant and disco," but it was also "dark, sexually charged, and clandestine." Deejay Nicky Siano recalls, "It was like, 'We were so chi-chi in our towels, cruising each other and slapping each others' dicks' . . . It was like a kind of orgy." At the Baths dancing and having sex melded in a way that became a part of the gay disco experience.

With men, nude except for the towels that hung from their waists, moving freely between their cubicles in the downstairs bathhouse and the dance floor upstairs, disco's get-down-tonight ethos was fully realized at the Baths. However, this state of affairs didn't last long once the Baths became a celebrity destination publicized in the press. Jorge La Torre recalls the moment in early 1972 when a magazine article about the Continental Baths made it "terribly chic to go to the Baths—to this *steam box*." Once the owner opened the Baths on Saturday nights to "regular-clothed outsiders," women started encroaching on the backrooms, and gay men, not wanting to share their space, went elsewhere.

Through disco, celebrities and trendsetting (and trend-following) heterosexuals, at least on the island of Manhattan, pursued the frisson of the illicit that still clung to homosexuality. Even during the repressive midcentury years, gay (and bisexual) men had been curiously influential as artists, writers, filmmakers, and composers. Tennessee Williams, Stephen Sondheim, Truman Capote, Andy Warhol, Robert Rauschenberg, Samuel Barber, Leonard Bernstein, Allen Ginsberg, James Baldwin, Edward Albee, and Gore Vidal are just a few that come to mind. However, straight America had not been this curious about gay nightlife since the Roaring Twenties. Its interest was fed in large part by articles in mainstream magazines about the new "gay chic." Straight curiosity about gay men was not limited to New York. Writing about a popular Chicago club called Dugan's Bistro, one journalist noted that it was both "unabashedly gay" and "the essence of hipness." Eager that her readers get her drift, she added, "in case you haven't noticed, the two have become synonymous to a certain degree." Understandably, there were some heterosexuals who wanted to get in on the new hipness.

Gay men may have swooned over the glitterati in their midst—musicians such as Mick Jagger and David Bowie who between 1973 and 1974 spent time in what Bowie later called Manhattan's "great little disco scene." However, they were not enamored of the less glamorous tourists, for whom homosexuals were simply the latest trend. As the narrator of the novel *Dancer from the Dance* explains, as "the public began to dance, we had to abandon places when they became too professional, too knowing, too slick." In the worst-case scenario, discos where the gay crowd once thronged would end up catering to "a mob of teen-agers and couples from Queens whose place it was now."

This process whereby below-the-radar gay clubs were "discovered" by celebrities, set upon by those judged unhip, and then abandoned by the original gay partygoers occurred time and again. It happened in 1973 at trendy Le Jardin, whose owner initially advertised it as offering "a total gay experience." However, with writer Truman Capote on *The Tonight Show* raving about the club, which he described as "churning like a . . . buttermilk machine," and its glitterati clientele—from the Warhol crowd to Diana Ross—garnering it press attention, Le Jardin became yet another spectacle, and inevitably more mixed. So it went at Infinity, whose only street signage was the six-foot neon pink penis that stood at its entrance. Infinity was meant to be a gay club, too, but its owner, knowing gay men's preference for late-night partying, hoped to maximize his profits by attracting heterosexual revelers to the early shift. On the club's opening night, the straight people whom the owner had bargained on leaving at ten o'clock were still partying, to the dismay of arriving gays. Infinity was enormously profitable, but

"MORE, MORE, MORE"

BEGINNING WITH THE Hues Corporation, which struck gold in 1974 with "Rock the Boat," disco advertised its facelessness. There were bands and orchestras, of course, but there were also machines, committees, corporations, sources, families, crews, commissions, conventions, and connections . . . so many connections. The Andrea True Connection was unlike all the other entities, though. It was fronted by a star, which couldn't have been said of the Rotary Connection or the T-Connection. Admittedly, she wasn't a Hollywood star and most of America had never heard of her, but to viewers of adult films the woman who sometimes went by the name of Andrea True was instantly recognizable. She had been in sixty porno films by the time she got into the disco business.

Given disco's fondness for the X-rated, it's not surprising that someone in the sex industry should have thought to exploit the link. However, True's route into the field was unusual. She had worked as a singer in supper clubs in the early seventies, but no one was beating down her door to record her. In 1975 she filmed a TV commercial in Jamaica, but as the island succumbed to political turmoil, she was blocked from leaving the country with her earnings. Stuck in Jamaica, she somehow convinced a friend, musician Gregg Diamond, to travel to the island to record a disco track with her. The idea was that she would spend her money locally on the recording and leave the island with the tape of the session.

Diamond was hardly a heavy hitter in the New York music scene. A percussionist who had played on the road with Joey Dee and the gay non-sensation Jobriath, his biggest claim to fame was that his brother had worked as a sound engineer on David Bowie's *Young Americans* LP. He would go on to produce singer Luther Vandross, whom he knew from his role as a backup singer on that same recording session, but he was still on the margins of the music business. Perhaps that's why Diamond thought it worth his while to travel to embattled Jamaica to record a porn star whom he had never before heard sing. In disco the way it usually worked was that the producer hired the singer, but in this instance it was the other way around. Diamond arrived on the island with a tape of a disco track he had cut in New York with his brother and several other musicians. Soon after arriving he had the good fortune to run into the entourage of calypso star Mighty Sparrow, and he quickly made arrangements to hire his horn section for overdubs. Like the films True performed in, the track was low-budget, with studio costs under $1,500.

After leaving Jamaica, True (and her Connection) signed with Buddah Records and Tom Moulton was hired to remix the track. Eager to flog her new record, True stopped by the New York offices of *Rolling Stone* with an acetate of it in hand. After listening to a bit of it and dismissing True, staff writer Chet Flippo reported that he and his colleague shook their heads over the delusions of the untalented, and agreed it was the last they would see of her. A few days later a coworker showed them the latest trade magazines whose charts revealed that "More, More, More" was "dripping bullets." Indeed, it climbed to number one on the *Record World* pop charts and number four on the *Billboard* charts.

Like so much early disco music, the track, with its clave-type rhythm pattern and its Mighty Sparrow horn section, had a tropical quality. The horns, which were both energetic and languidly funky, kept the song from sounding like generic disco. True's vocals were passable, in the tradition of the coy disco coo. Moulton's mix emphasized what musicologist Charles Kronengold calls the "arbitrariness" of disco's instrumentation, the way that certain details seem detached from other elements as they come and go. The song reveals its constructedness, its seams, as it moves between vocals, horns, and percussion. Just as the cut wears its studio imprint on its sleeve, True made no effort to sound authentically soulful or even sincere. When she proclaims the realness of her love she is as believably passionate as *Klute*'s call girl Bree Walker, looking distractedly at her watch while faking an orgasm with a client. And with the reference to cameras and action, the song is more redolent of a porn shoot than a spontaneous bedroom encounter.

No one could accuse "More, More, More" of lyrical depth. Diamond wrote its few words on the spot, which is just the way the song sounds. Critics, time and again, have written about the lyrical shallowness of disco music—its preference for sensation over meaning, style over substance. Walter Hughes attributes this to disco's emphatic commitment to the beat. Language is so subordinated to the beat, he argues, that in some cases it becomes a "mere verbal echo of the beat itself." There was a rhythmic hegemony at work in disco, but that does not fully explain disco's penchant for the superficial. Literary theorist D. A. Miller's work suggests the appeal of the shallow, if not the reason for its musical manufacture. Perhaps for gays, he argues, the realm of the superficial operates as a refusal of "substance," which is culturally inscribed in heteronormative terms. Lives of substance involve solemn vows, and, of course, children. Gay lives oriented around disco participate in a giddy consumption of moreness, which, like the denim and flannel, began to penetrate straight America, where monogamous marriage became for some an option rather than one's fate.

according to one longtime disco scenester, "gays never took the place seriously," which left a vacuum that the despised bridge-and-tunnel crowd eventually filled. The same process happened in Los Angeles and other cities. One night three straight couples who had been turned away from the leading gay disco Studio One returned later in a Rolls Royce, which one of the men drove through the club's front door. If police harassment and archaic laws had been the main obstacle to gay nightlife before disco took off, it was now the chic appeal of gay disco among fashionable and fashion-hungry heterosexuals that was thwarting the brotherly reverie of dance-floor oneness that gay men were chasing. Even though straight men had to become accustomed to being called "baby" rather than "sir," some still wanted in. Over time, gay discos increasingly became exclusively gay, and women, who had once partied as friends or as dance-floor "beards," sometimes found their entry to top-end gay discos blocked.

The scarcity of exclusively gay space was in part what motivated a group of gay men to open the Tenth Floor disco. The starkly minimal Tenth Floor was responsible for the "industrial, hi-tech, chic look" that other New York discos were soon scrambling to copy. The men behind the Tenth Floor wanted to fashion it after David Mancuso's club, with one important difference. They did not want their clubbers to find themselves dancing next to a "three-hundred-pound black lady" as they might at the Loft. According to Mancuso, whose advice they sought, they "wanted to open a Loft-style party that would be strictly gay and white." Like the Loft, the Tenth Floor operated on an invitation-only system, and much of its exclusive membership consisted of the moneyed men (some of them gay celebrities) who regularly vacationed on Fire Island. To those not part of this gay elite, the atmosphere at the Tenth Floor was one where attitude (and sex) trumped partying. Its members indulged in so much attitudinizing that Richard Brezner, whose best friend was an owner of the club, felt that "it turned into *the* pretentious party of all time." To gays of color, it could feel even more alienating. Tenth Floor devotees practically created the clone look of dressing up (or down) in the masculine drag of Levi's 501 button-fly jeans, aviator jackets, tees, work boots, etc. Perfecting the desired look took more time and money than many gays of color had. African American Nathan Bush was comfortable mixing with whites, but he recalls that at the Tenth Floor "if you tried to dance or socialize, people gave you a look like, 'Jesus, what are you doing here?'" Although there were a few men of color at the club, they were usually there as boyfriends and one-night stands, not as full-fledged members. Even the normally magnanimous Mancuso concluded that the Tenth Floor was "a white male gay thing."

The Tenth Floor was not the only club where the vibe was "if you're white you're right, if you're black stay back." So it was at the aforementioned Flamingo, which catered to the glamorous A-list gay crowd. Yearly membership cost $75, with hefty fees for each visit. Nonetheless, within its first month of operation the club proved so popular that its owner, Michael Fesco, had to close its membership rolls. This had the effect of ratcheting up the disco's cachet, and soon Flamingo memberships were selling for $500 on the black market. Although those who ran the club claim not to have actively excluded blacks, others say they made a point of admitting few blacks lest their white members decide to go elsewhere. As the president of Yves Saint Laurent, Alan Harris was precisely the sort of man whose membership the disco sought, but he, too, found it very "cliquish." Flamingo was "going after a very affluent crowd and you really needed to know a whole group of people," recalls Harris, "if you were going to get in." For that matter, even a hole-in-the-wall like the s/m club the Anvil could discriminate. The narrator of Brad Gooch's novel *The Golden Age of Promiscuity* considers "The door of the Anvil worse than [Studio 54's] because all the ploys of caste, like the signed cards from attorney Roy Cohn that could get you into Studio anytime, no matter how crowded, were negligible at the Anvil. Dispossession ruled."

Private clubs were not the only discos that practiced dispossession. And if money counted for little at the Anvil, it mattered at most discos, which sometimes charged prohibitively expensive entrance fees.

At a time when America was suffering from stagflation, and lots of gay people, especially racial and ethnic minorities, were financially hurting, the cost of glitterball culture kept some gays out. When pricey door fees and pricier drinks failed to keep out or reduce those deemed undesirable, upscale discos across America sometimes employed a variety of strategies—stringent carding (requiring multiple forms of picture ID), providing slow or nonexistent drink service, and playing nonstop Eurodisco—to keep the dance floor predominantly white. In a 1973 article on "homosexual lives," a writer for the *Washington Post* noted the double standard for admission to one popular downtown gay bar. Several of D.C.'s new "super discos" reportedly used carding policies to exclude African Americans as well as women and female impersonators. And L.A.'s Studio One admitted so few men who did not meet the "Hollywood Golden Boy standard" that for years it was picketed by gay activists.

Disco exclusionism could also provoke greater inclusiveness, as it did in New York when Alan Harris and his lover decided to open a disco designed to serve a wider swath of the gay community. 12 West, which opened in March 1975, was meant to be "a completely safe and nonelitist environment." Harris retained a membership system, but it was one in which members could bring with them one guest. In less than six months, 12 West had 1,250 members, and the *New York Post* reported that its owners were planning to "add a restaurant, to present cabaret, sponsor charter flights, [and] market teeshirts." And that wasn't the end of it, according to the *Post*, which revealed that Bloomingdale's would soon open a disco shop that would sell bathrobes and toothbrushes displaying 12 West's logo.

12 West was more racially mixed than many gay New York discos, and it was wildly successful for a few years. Doubtless some men welcomed clubs that broke down the color line. However, not all gay discos, even those whose owners wanted to create a multiracial environment, were able to overcome the clannish tribalism of gay New York. At the Paradise Garage, where the legendary Larry Levan deejayed, owner

Michael Brody discovered that the A-list white gays he had hoped to lure away from Flamingo simply would not go to his disco on Saturday nights. It was not just that the club had a disastrous opening night or that its island motif—corrugated steel and painted banana leaves—was at odds with the prevailing industrial aesthetic of white gay discos. The Flamingo crowd was turned off by Levan's R&B-inflected disco and by not finding more of their own kind on the club's expansive dance floor. To Mark Riley, who worked security at the Garage, Brody was in no way racist, "but he knew that the white gay crowd was not comfortable being around a lot of black people." White deejay Robbie Leslie agrees that for the white affluent gays Brody was trying to bring into the mix, the Garage "was NOCD: not our club, dearie." To attract that crowd, Brody resolved to make Friday nights for blacks and Saturday nights for whites—a decision that infuriated many of his black, and some of his white, customers. "Suddenly," recalls longtime deejay Steve D'Acquisto, "the Garage was like one of those restricted clubs where they won't let Jews in." David Mancuso blamed the Garage's policy of racial segregation on money. "It wasn't as if they weren't making money, but they wanted more of it." In the end, despite Brody's best efforts, the Garage remained NOCD to many of the A-list white gays whose business he sought.

Racial exclusion has not generated much discussion among dis-cologists, perhaps because they have been at such pains to disabuse readers of the widely held view that discos were agents of pernicious velvet-rope elitism. Most revisionist accounts emphasize the demo-cratic and underground quality of disco's first years. Anxious to prove disco's underground bona fides, revisionists often linger on the racial egalitarianism of the Loft and novelist Andrew Holleran's evocation of gay disco in *Dancer from the Dance.* The novel's narrator describes the book's fictional disco, the Twelfth Floor, as a "strictly classless" world in which the anarchy of "erotic love" dissolved the usual class and racial barriers. In a much-quoted passage, he describes a scene in which "[t]he boy passed out on the sofa from an overdose of Tuinols [*sic*] was a Puerto Rican who washed dishes in the employees' cafeteria at CBS, but the doctor bending over him had treated presidents." However, Holleran hardly depicts the white patrons of the Twelfth Floor as oblivious to race and class. The book's reigning queen, Andrew Sutherland, is forever referring to blacks as "dinge" or "Shvartzers," and mouthing utterly predictable clichés about Latinos as dangerously, even lethally romantic and blacks as more stylish and more agile on the dance floor. The Twelfth Floor may have operated according to a democracy that privileged good looks, but Holleran makes it clear that it also delivered the "thrill of exclusivity."

I linger on race not to berate middle-class white gay men, most of whom had more meaningful encounters across color and class lines than their heterosexual counterparts, but rather to complicate the usual declension narrative in which a democratic underground—be it punk, rave, or disco—is undone by the forces of commodification. Too much writing about music ignores what theorist Sarah Thornton calls the subcultural capital—the "right" look, lingo, moves, attitude, and all-important taste—that underwrites an underground, and dismisses mainstream audiences as homogenous, conformist, and politically quiescent, even conservative. Certainly within gay disco the inclusive always vied with the exclusive, the democratic with the elitist, in a process that was aided but not determined by the commercial exploitation of glitterball culture. The Loft, for example, may have been racially inclusive, but its underground cachet made the club both a destination disco for celebrities and "the favored domain of disco snobs," as Mel Cheren once put it.

Operating as private clubs, as many gay discos did, allowed them not only to weed out the "wrong" kind of men but also to exclude women legally. Women had partied at the earliest discos, but at many of the chicest gay clubs they soon discovered they were viewed as a nuisance—a relic of the bad old days. When the Sanctuary turned gay in the wake of Stonewall, the owners sacked many of their female employees because they no longer wanted women there. Indeed during the filming of *Klute*, actress Jane Fonda got into an argument with the club's owners because they would not allow lesbians inside. Over the course of the decade the proscription against women only grew more intense. At Manhattan's Saint, which opened in 1980, "women were as rare as dinosaurs." Even less exclusive gay discos developed strategies, including dress codes that prohibited, say, open-toed shoes, which were designed to exclude women (and queens). L.A.'s Studio One, for example, established an ever-changing dress code so that only a woman with an inside connection could avoid being turned away at the door.

Two films that bookend the decade—1970's *Boys in the Band* and 1978's *Thank God It's Friday*—capture some of these transformations in gay sociability. In *Boys*, dancing together is intoxicating fun, but profoundly stigmatizing. When a straight man walks into a party of campy "boys" line-dancing to Motown music, his presence stops them dead in their tracks. All but the most incorrigibly queer of them quickly assume a conventionally masculine comportment, but the damage is done. He knows that "boys" who dance together, unaccompanied by women, are fairies. Fast-forward to 1978 and the cheesy *Thank God It's Friday*. A box-office clunker, this movie about a glitzy L.A. disco presents same-sex dancing as though it's unremarkable. In one scene, a minor character played by Debra Winger dances with a hunky guy when another handsome man asks to cut in. She registers only slight surprise when it turns out it's her dancing partner who has taken his fancy. The gender-free future that gay liberationists had dreamed of just a few years earlier was a distant blur in this new disco brotherhood where women, gay men's onetime dance-floor beards, were now largely obsolescent.

Gay men may not have wanted women on their dance floors, yet when it came to singers, they favored the divas of disco—Donna Summer, Labelle, Gloria Gaynor, Chaka Khan, and Grace Jones, among others. Indeed, as disco grew in popularity, female performers discovered that disco music was becoming the domain of "the ladies."

Ladies' Night

WOMEN AND DISCO

... they used to tell her, everybody, the gym teacher, the Episcopalian minister, Mother, even one awful embarrassing time, not to make your body a plaything when that's just what it was ...
—*John Updike,* Rabbit Redux

I really came in Philadelphia.
—*Sarah Dash of Labelle to a* Rolling Stone *reporter*

Few aspects of disco are as confounding as its relationship to women. Was it a cultural arm of feminism or a part of the backlash against it? During her 2006 "Confessions" tour, Madonna came down on the side of disco as Woman Power. Each show began with a ton-and-a-half, crystal-covered disco ball that was slowly lowered onstage, where it opened to reveal the Material Girl. Later in the show, she unveiled "Music Inferno," built around a sample from the famous track "Disco Inferno." This number found Madonna outstrutting and outdancing that other Italian American, John Travolta, whose solo dance in *Saturday Night Fever* she reprised. Throughout, she treated her acrobatic, roller-skating male dancers like boy toys and her female dancers (dressed, like her, in white, three-piece Travolta suits) as comrades-in-arms. In Madonna's reworking of *Fever*, the girls run the show, doing the Bump with each other and hanging up on, rather than waiting around on, guys who can't be bothered to express themselves. Madonna turned the disco seventies into a culture where girls ruled, yet others have come to no consensus on the question of disco's empowerment of women.

Whether one sees disco's sexual politics as regressive or progressive, one thing is certain: as disco moved out of the underground and into the pop mainstream it became marked, even tainted, not just as "soulless soul" but as girls' music. Although disco's prioritizing of the rhythmic over the melodic, its circular structure, and the sheer length of its songs actually put it at odds with pop music conventions, most rock 'n' rollers nonetheless viewed disco as the worst sort of pop fluff. The denigration of pop as sappy and nice (and feminine) and the elevation of rock as hard-hitting and risk-taking (and masculine) date back to the beginnings of rock. But this gendered formulation was bolstered in the midsixties when Dylan, the Beatles (and other British Invasion groups), and the American bands they inspired transformed rock into "art"—serious, and resonant with meaning. Rock marketed itself on the basis of its distinctiveness from pop, which increasingly became understood as the domain of teenyboppers, who were simply assumed to be girls.

Many rockers thought the battle had been won until disco came along and threatened a return to the old regime that had privileged the commercial over the artistic, the formulaic over the experimental, and the producer over the artist. In contrast to the world-changing, or at least mind-blowing quality of rock, disco seemed to be about nothing more meaningful than getting down—the preoccupation, it would seem, of girls (and gays). Instead of rock's mystical musings, enigmatic rhymes, or insolent nose-thumb, disco offered overblown orchestration, lame lyrics, and that super-sized thump. Disco was all beat and no message. Indeed, it seemed emptied of meaning. As critic Tom Smucker cannily noted, the disco turn was encapsulated in the reinvention of the 45 single. Record companies still produced 45s, but most consumers of rock favored albums. Disco not only reclaimed the single, it had the audacity to "inflate it back up to 12-inch proportions."

To rock aficionados, the new dance music threatened to catapult society back to the bad old days of bubblegum, when the bedroom yearnings of teenaged girls dictated what ruled the charts, when "It has a good beat, I give it a ten"—the *American Bandstand* measure of musical worthiness—reigned. For those convinced of disco's calamitous effect on popular music, the fact that the king of sixties' bubblegum, Neil Bogart, presided over the leading disco label, Casablanca Records, seemed all the proof needed that American music was succumbing to the forces of regression.

The fact that disco music was unabashedly about dancing consolidated rockers' conviction that it was chick music. Rockers' antagonism toward disco's "boogie down, baby" imperative may have represented Western culture's uneasiness about the body and its elevation of the rational over the physical. However, rockers' discomfort with disco's physicality also reflected their own bodily diffidence. Writing in 2003, Nick Hornby, the author of *High Fidelity*, observed that for white males, especially for fortysomethings like himself, the "dance floor is like the social equivalent of the North Sea during English seaside holidays—something to be treated with the utmost fear and caution . . . something that leaves lots of important parts of you feeling shriveled." It was no different on this side of the Atlantic, where many men lived by the same principle as rock journalist and heavy-metal enthusiast Chuck Klosterman: "If I am sober enough to drive, I am too sober to dance."

Certainly, by the midseventies, with hippie free-style dancing in eclipse and arena rock in ascendance, audience physicality was often reduced to so much fist-pumping and flick-your-Bic waving. True, punk featured pogoing, but it was a kind of anti-dancing, deliberately devoid of rhythm or skill. By contrast, disco required graceful rhythmic motion that had never much characterized the free-form dance styles of the largely white sixties' counterculture. If you were a less than agile dancer, disco could evoke the dance-floor humiliations so typical of high-school sock hops. Shirley and Company's 1975 hit "Shame

Shame Shame," which warned, "you can't stop the groove / 'coz you just won't move," located male resistance to disco in dance-floor phobia. Clearly not all men, even white rockers, were held hostage by bad dance-floor memories, but women usually were much more keen than men to pull out their dancing shoes and head for the discotheque. This is the premise of the disco episode of *That Seventies Show*, where the guys reluctantly accompany the girls to a disco. Once there, it's Fez, the brown-skinned foreign exchange student, who heats up the dance floor and impresses the girls. Scorned as mindless pop, denigrated for its lowly (and scary) aspirations of boogieing, disco, at least within rock circles, was experienced, if not always clearly understood, as the territory of the Other. *Rolling Stone* writer Peter Herbst admitted that much of the paper's discophobia stemmed from the staff's perception that disco belonged to those "outside of the rock & roll population that we belonged to personally . . . blacks and gays and women."

This is not to say that women (or blacks or gays) embraced disco en masse. After all, Herbst notwithstanding, women read *Rolling Stone*, bought albums by Bob Seger, Fleetwood Mac, and the Ramones. Young women eager to be part of the rock scene sometimes developed an allergic reaction to disco, especially if they had once loved it. Poet Lavinia Greenlaw has written of the humiliation she felt as a teenage girl for having once been part of a "disco gang." She swore off dancing and ditched her disco and soul records. If someone discovered those records in her room, "they would discover something *terrible* about me."

Disco may have been perceived as a woman's genre, but critics and scholars have drawn starkly different conclusions about disco's relationship to women's liberation. Some contend that disco "reduced women to sexual playthings." *Rolling Stone*'s Stephen Holden characterized Donna Summer as "an inflatable sex machine as insatiable as she is helpless." To *Rolling Stone* critic Ken Emerson, disco represented the triumph of "multiorgasmic kewpie dolls" such as Donna Summer over the "tough-talkin' mamas" of seventies' soul—singers such as Jean

Knight and Denise LaSalle. Analyzing the Hustle, one scholar argued that it elevated the male as the initiator, who sets the pace, physically holds up the female, and throughout remains the center of attention. To this observer, disco "actually heralded the return of Western society's traditional assumptions of gender."

However, a radically different view of disco as feminist and anti-masculinist emerges in the revisionist work of some cultural studies scholars. In their view, women, particularly black women, ruled the mirror-ball world. It is not just that the "classic disco singer was a black diva," but that the very sound of disco was, in contrast to most European-derived music, sonically open-ended (or "anti-teleological") and therefore anti-phallic. Writing at the height of the disco craze, critic and gay liberationist Richard Dyer claimed that disco "releases you in an open-ended succession of repetitions" that operated in contrast to rock whose "repeated phrases trap you in their relentless push." To Dyer, disco's rhythmic complexity and play—its "delaying, jumping, countering of rhythm"—encouraged "whole-body eroticism" as opposed to the "thrusting and grinding" he identified with rock music. Literary critic Walter Hughes pushed this analysis further, arguing that in allowing the insistent, penetrative disco beat to become part of them, gay men "disturbed the very foundations of conventional constructions of masculine selfhood." For Hughes, disco, with its "seemingly endless cycles and plateaus," evoked the open-endedness and fluidity of the female orgasm. Disco was the music of "jouissance"—blissful pleasure.

Disco did represent a break from pop music conventions in its fragmenting of narrative musical structure. That's why Diana Ross initially balked at recording "Love Hangover," which she felt "wasn't exactly a song," and required "a lot of improvising." However, as anyone who has ever danced the night away at a discotheque knows, disco records were not usually climax-less exercises in the open-ended. Yes, Donna Summer's records sometimes did "ease off before reaching a climax." But in most disco records the climax occurs during the instrumental

"break," which critic Vince Aletti described as the "pivot and the anticipated peak of the song." Aletti's view is corroborated by a well-known
East Coast deejay, Danae, who said of a disco climax that "the mix starts
at a certain place, builds, teases, builds again, and then picks up on
the other side. The break is the high point. It's like asking a question,
repeating and repeating it, waiting for an answer—and then giving the
answer. That is the great, satisfying moment."

Disco was no more a stranger to the great satisfying moment than
most women are, and one can hear it in what many consider the very

Diana Ross gets down like she never did as a
Supreme at a New York disco, August 1979

first disco record, Eddie Kendricks's "Girl You Need a Change of Mind." About midway through the track, just as it gains heat and Kendricks's soaring falsetto is fading out, the sound turns stark. Motown producer Frank Wilson, drawing on his background in gospel, instructed the musicians to "break it down to nothing, then gradually come in one by one and rebuild to the original fervor of the song." It's at that moment, as the song regains its momentum, that the music climaxes along with the dancers, who shout, wave their shirts in the air, sniff poppers, and in the words of disco's premier remixer, Tom Moulton, "get off." Dee-jays also built climaxes into their sets so that over the course of the night they would get a dance floor hot, tease it, bring it to climax, then ease it down and slowly rebuild the energy.

If the claims that disco music resisted narrative closure are exaggerated, so is the view that disco space was necessarily congenial to women. The gay male discos of New York, for example, were sites of intense sexual energy. They were nothing short of liberated zones for men who as recently as 1969 had been unable to dance legally with one another. To *Village Voice* writer and gay activist Richard Goldstein, the disco years constituted a "psychic Intifada: a sloughing off of centuries of shame and a venting of pent-up desire." Women, who had for years operated as dance-floor beards (that is, as heterosexualizing covers) for gay men, were suddenly expendable, and often unwelcome in the new clubs. Maybe the throbbing disco beat unsettled conventional masculinity at some clubs, but at those like the trendy Flamingo where gay macho ruled, gay men hewed to what writer Fran Lebowitz calls the "absolutely narrowest notion of masculinity." Even at gay clubs where relations between gay men and women were friendlier, heterosexual women sometimes came to the discouraging conclusion that discos were not always organized around their pleasure. Or, as Betty Wright sang in "Loving Is Really My Game," "I can't get no man hanging out at a discotheque."

As for female artists' relationship to the music industry, over time black divas came to dominate disco. However, their prominence did not usually translate into real power. Disco did offer female singers significantly more opportunities than rock. Nonetheless, disco was a producers' genre where performers rarely achieved the sort of control that even lesser-known rock musicians took for granted. And as disco became a commercial juggernaut and grew more feminized, female vocalists found their musical options narrowing. Record labels pushed them toward it, while funk increasingly defined itself in opposition to disco. Funk became the genuine article, "real" black music played by real black men.

However, if claims of disco's liberatory qualities are overdrawn, so are claims that disco diminished and degraded women. The contention that disco dancing subordinated women seems largely based upon the dance-floor dynamics in *Saturday Night Fever*. Yet most actual discos featured free-form, improvised dancing. In many clubs the Hustle was performed as a line dance rather than in a coupled fashion.

But what about the claim that disco turned women into sexual play-things? Well, it tried its best, and in this regard disco was hardly alone. The seventies were the decade of the Big O, the female orgasm. Millions of women whose relationship to their sexuality had been more vigilant than relaxed began, like Janice in *Rabbit Redux*, to experience their bodies as playthings. Feminism was crucial to this shift, as it exposed the yawning gap between women's sexual desires and standard three-minute, missionary-position sex. In the process, women's sexuality, long treated as inscrutable and negligible, became a force to be reckoned with. Suddenly, there was no escaping the female orgasm. In addition to countless magazine articles devoted to "What Women Want!" bestselling books such as Shere Hite's *The Hite Report*, Nancy Friday's *My Secret Garden*, the self-help manual *Our Bodies, Ourselves*, and Erica Jong's *Fear of Flying* explored female desire.

For those women's liberationists who believed that feminism entailed sexual liberation, women's embrace of their orgasmic potential—selfishly multiple and for itself—was radical. With the popularization of feminist ideas about women's sexuality the focus upon pleasuring oneself sometimes dropped out of the equation as "coming"—multiply and spectacularly—became yet another measure of one's femininity, and a sure-fire way to please one's man. In plenty of disco songs women's sexuality was oriented towards pleasing others. "How do you like it?" cooed ex-porn star Andrea True in her hit "More, More, More." And disco *was* often unabashedly sleazy. As the 1997 movie *Boogie Nights* rightfully suggests, there was an undeniably X-rated aura that clung to disco. One hears it in disco's irrepressibly (t)humping beat, Donna Summer's soft-core moaning in "Love to Love You Baby," the breathy female vocals of the Salsoul Orchestra's "You're Just the Right Size," and Musique's aggressively explicit "In the Bush."

Nonetheless, disco foregrounded female desire to a far greater extent than rock music. There were exceptions, of course, most notably Bonnie Raitt, whose reworking of songs such as Sippie Wallace's "You Got to Know How" introduced audiences to the wit and lust of twenties' blues queens, and Patti Smith, whose snarling "Gloria" made female desire sound thrillingly dangerous. But until the eighties it was disco that most reliably gave voice to women's lust. Take the lyrics of Summer's "Love to Love You Baby," which were focused on her pleasure ("do it to me again and again / you put me in such an awful spin, a spin"), a point italicized by her orgasmic gasps and cries. Even "Right Size," which makes a dubious correlation between size and performance, nevertheless vocalizes female desire. Disco's concern with "the ladies" goes a long way to explaining why feminists reserved their ire for rockers such as the Rolling Stones, whose ad campaign for their 1976 album *Black and Blue* suggested that for women the experience of getting beat up is one big turn-on. How likely was it that feminists would have campaigned against women singing campy lyrics like "Voulez-vous couchez avec moi?" and "You can ring my bell," especially when for many women the biggest problem with discos was not sexual harassment but gay men's sexual indifference? Indeed, disco was irresistible to all kinds of women.

But was it irresistible to those African American women who comprised the majority of disco's divas? It was to Chic singer Alfa Anderson, who argued that the group's penchant for elegant designer clothes was nothing short of radical. "Being asked to wear something that elevated me to the level of a woman, not a toy. How political is that?" But if Anderson felt that disco's upmarket sophistication enabled her to broaden her representational repertoire, others offer more mixed assessments. Some felt as if disco deposited them on the front lines of the sexual revolution. Moreover, divas sometimes found themselves in the curious position of playing up their sexuality when, historically, black women's sexuality (or white fantasies of their hypersexuality) was the very thing that had been used against them.

The question of whether sexual freedom advances or retards women's liberation became especially fraught in the 1970s, as pornography grew ever more available and explicit. Scholars have discussed that era's "sex wars," in which feminists clashed over the meaning of sexuality and its representations in the media, especially in pornography. But the further loosening of sexual conventions *and* growing feminist consciousness (which was often articulated in racially and ethnically distinct groups) reverberated beyond the pages of *Ms.* magazine. Music critic Stephen Holden, reviewing a Donna Summer album, asked two questions on the minds of many women in this period. "Isn't sex more erotic when spiced with a sense of danger? But how much danger?" And just how explicit can women, particularly black women, safely be? Certainly these questions were alive for a number of disco's biggest divas, including the women who dominate this chapter, Donna Summer, Chaka Khan, and the women of Labelle. As disco enthusiasts know, these women are not fully representative of disco, a genre that included legions of anonymous female vocalists oohing and cooing away in the background. Khan and the vocal trio Labelle were never in the background, nor was Summer after a short stay there. Indeed, they are among the few artists with a history in disco who could be said to be genuine personalities.

EVEN THOSE WHO disagree on the question of whether disco promoted female empowerment would likely agree that America's sexual rules were substantially rewritten in the seventies. Although the sexual revolution took off in the 1960s, its impact was most keenly felt in the 1970s. Hippie electric ballrooms, for example, fostered a freewheeling sexuality, but most young people had little or no contact with countercultural spaces like San Francisco's Fillmore auditorium. By contrast, once disco became popular, it was everywhere, including in established businesses like the local Holiday Inn that drew a wider swath of the population. It was during the seventies that the sexual revolution burrowed deeply into American culture, with disco operating as both cause and effect.

R&B, the incubator of disco, was no stranger to the risqué. Nevertheless, R&B registered the shock waves of change that followed from the sexual revolution. Most sixties' soul had revolved around love— love lost, love won, love betrayed, love thwarted, love obsessed—and no one, least of all female singers, escaped singing what Stevie Wonder called these " 'baby, baby, baby' songs." There were, of course, notable exceptions such as Aretha Franklin's anthem of reciprocity "Respect," Betty Everett's exasperated "You're No Good," and the duet "Tramp," in which Carla Thomas mocked Otis Redding's overalls, unkempt hair, and chronic lack of cash. However, more typical were songs such as the Supremes' "You Keep Me Hanging On," Fontella Bass's "Rescue Me," Martha and the Vandellas' "Nowhere to Run," and the Crystals' "He's Sure the Boy I Love." Most successful R&B women singers focused their attention on the micropolitical, or what feminists were calling personal politics. While the soul men of the early seventies decried the smiling faces of white politicians and brothers on the make, soul music's divas, like their counterparts in country music, were more apt to look closer to home, at scheming boyfriends, cheating husbands, and worthless lotharios.

Perhaps this calling out of men was related to Black Power's masculinism—its tendency to equate black people's advancement with the attainment of patriarchal privilege, which historically had been denied to black men. Whatever its cause, by 1971, a good eight years before the publication of Michele Wallace's groundbreaking bestseller *Black Macho and the Myth of the Superwoman*, the floodgates of female anger and disappointment had opened. Among the first songs to tap these emotions was "Want Ads" by the briefly successful group Honey Cone. Produced by former Motown producers Holland–Dozier–Holland, "Want Ads" tells the story of a woman who dumps a philandering boyfriend and begins searching the personals for a "young, single, and free man." He doesn't have to be an experienced lover, but he has to be willing to apprentice himself as a "young trainee." Honey Cone's tune held down the number one R&B spot in early June 1971, until it was knocked down a notch by "Mr. Big Stuff," in which Jean Knight mocks a jive-talking, boastful man for thinking his money is enough to win him a woman's love. Knight's single, the biggest of her career, took the R&B charts by storm, and by mid-June 1971 the top three R&B singles were "Mr. Big Stuff," "Want Ads," and Wilson Pickett's "Don't Knock My Love," which could be read as a rebuttal to both these tunes.

The R&B charts featured plenty of other songs, particularly those by Roberta Flack and Donny Hathaway, in which romantic coupling suggested racial solidarity. However, like the songs of discontent and disappointment that male artists were recording in this same period, songs of female discontent kept coming. In October, Denise LaSalle's "Trapped in a Thing Called Love" topped the R&B charts. The Staple Singers' "Respect Yourself" hit the Top 10 in November 1971. Although it was about achieving racial advancement through self-respect, its fiercest line, sung by Mavis Staples, targeted men who were "dumb enough" to think that cursing in the company of women somehow made you "a big ol' man." Within three months, Laura Lee's daring album *Women's Love Rights* had tied down the number one position on the R&B charts. Lee's hit single of the same title assailed the sexual double standard, noting that women should "love who they wanna /

'coz the man's surely gonna." For Lee, women's love rights included a set of car keys, a meal out at least once a week, and having a claim on your lover's earnings while maintaining your own untouchable bank account. As Vince Aletti pointed out, in this and other songs such as "Wedlock Is a Padlock," Lee sang to women. While not all of these songs were critical of black men—Betty Wright's "Clean Up Woman" suggested that men wouldn't stray if their women would simply satisfy them sexually—many pointed the finger squarely at them.

A number of these songs were written by men, who may have been as dismayed by the apparent appeal of black macho, and as eager to critique it, as the women doing the singing. They may have used female singers to express their own discontent with the new black masculinity. This might well be the case with "Make Me Believe in You," which was penned and produced by Curtis Mayfield for sixteen-year-old singer Patti Jo. This 1973 record was not a big radio hit, but it was a club favorite in the earliest days of disco. When Patti Jo demands that her lover "move out of [his] hard-rapping world" so she can believe in him, it's hard not to think of Mayfield's recent *Superfly* soundtrack, which made explicit his disapproval of the hustling, drug-peddling style the movie celebrated. If R&B's men were not enthusiastically behind the new black macho, it might explain why songs like "Mr. Big Stuff" and "Women's Love Rights" elicited so little in the way of grumbling from male singers. In contrast to ex-Temptation Eddie Kendricks, who on the proto-disco "Girl You Need a Change of Mind" chided a women's libber for being anti-male and boasted that a night with him would turn her around, many male R&B singers were working overtime in an effort to celebrate women—girlfriends, wives, mothers, all of them. Al Green's "I'm Still in Love with You," the Dells' "Give Your Baby a Standing Ovation," Stevie Wonder's "You Are the Sunshine of My Life," the Intruders' "I'll Always Love My Mama," the Spinners' "I'll Be Around," and all of Barry White's oeuvre represent a mere sampling of this voluminous genre of female veneration.

R&B was a site in which African American men and women entered into a dialogue about sexual politics, one in which sex talk was becoming much more sexually graphic. Of course there were R&B artists who for some time had challenged notions of feminine propriety, most famously Dinah Washington, Tina Turner, and Etta James. However, throughout the sixties female soul singers tended toward sexual circumspection lest they reinforce any lingering assumptions about black women's sexual looseness. Their understandable discretion, which stands in such contrast to late forties' and early fifties' R&B—in which Dinah Washington sang of getting drilled by her dentist and Etta James thrilled to rolling with Henry—was particularly true at Motown, whose female singers were groomed to walk the tightrope of being sexually desirable yet respectable. The Supremes radiated hipness, but white stars like the Beatles who assumed that they were "party girls" quickly learned otherwise.

However, within just a few short years concerns about black female respectability among pop-minded soul singers receded considerably. In part, white women's abdication of good-girl femininity meant that the purportedly high standard against which black women were judged no longer resonated. With Janis Joplin, in her sometimes awkward emulation of twenties' blues queen Bessie Smith's sassy sexuality, advertising her sexual availability and proclaiming that performance was for her literally orgasmic, the Supremes could ditch their gloves and gowns for jeans and black leather and sing about extramarital sex, as they did in 1968. There was another, perhaps more powerful reason for black female performers (and their record companies) to become more explicit in their sexual presentation. Black pride and Black Power celebrated the black body, and this inevitably encouraged its commodification. Male artists were the first to take advantage of the changed circumstances. Whether it was Isaac Hayes, James Brown, or Al Green baring his chest on the cover of an LP, the move was sexy, race-conscious, and profitable. By contrast, the earliest overtly sexual images of black women to appear on American record album covers featured models, not singers, to sell albums by male artists. Among the first of these appeared on the album covers of the Ohio Players. Purveyors of an especially slinky funk, the Ohio Players put out album art that routinely pictured beautiful black women, nude or semi-nude, in provocative poses often suggestive of sadomasochistic sex.

Black women performers were more tentative and conflicted than their male counterparts when it came to baring their flesh. It is telling that the first female R&B artist of the seventies to unambiguously embrace greater sexual explicitness owned her own record label and recording studio, and was mostly moonlighting as a singer. Sylvia Robinson is best known for her role in breaking out rap music. The owner of Sugarhill Records, she was the first producer to comprehend rap's commercial potential, and for several years hers was the most prominent rap label in the business. However, Robinson had her first big success in 1956 when she and her singing partner Mickey Baker scored a million-selling hit with the quirky tune "Love Is Strange." Although she had no hits in the sixties, Robinson wrote, produced, and played guitar for a variety of R&B acts, including Ike and Tina Turner. In the midsixties she and her husband Joe Robinson formed All Platinum Records and All Platinum Studios in Englewood, New Jersey—not far from Manhattan—where they reached the charts with the smooth Philly-style soul of the Moments. The trio's plaintive falsetto ballad "Love on a Two-Way Street," which Robinson cowrote and produced, was the group's biggest hit.

A shrewd businesswoman, Robinson clearly saw that there was room for a woman's voice in the slinky, sexy music that was coming to dominate the charts. Her 1973 album *Pillow Talk* succeeded in seizing the bedroom from the likes of Isaac Hayes. Released on her own label, Vibration Records, *Pillow Talk* is a low-rent effort with abrupt fade-outs, cheesy cover art, and synthesized strings, but it broke new ground in its presentation of black woman's desire. Indeed, radio programmers initially resisted playing the record. Even after selling 750,000 copies, the album's eponymous single was being played by only one-third of America's major pop stations. Eventually the record took hold, and "Pillow Talk" was a number one R&B hit for two weeks in early spring. In it, Robinson takes the traditional male role, sweet-talking her boyfriend into putting down his "stop sign," ignoring his gossipy friends, and letting her light his fire. Sex is a place to "meet and compete," and if one missed the sex-role reversal, she makes it explicit with a line about borrowing his pants. More curious is another album track, "Had Any Lately," an explicitly antiwar song ("have you had any peace lately?" she asks) that declares, as would Grandmaster Flash and the Furious Five some nine years later, that life's a jungle. Throughout, Robinson sexes it up with orgasmic oohs, ahs, and "oh my God!"s all performed in a breathless, chirpy Diana Ross–like voice that floats atop a bed of lush strings. Nor did she hold back on the cover art, which pictured the thirty-seven-year-old Robinson decked out in cleav-age-revealing lingerie, huge hoop earrings, and a wedding ring. Equally suggestive was the back cover, which showed her in a thigh-revealing slit robe, a champagne glass in one hand, a phone in the other.

While "Pillow Talk" held down the number one position on the R&B singles chart, "I'm Gonna Love You Just a Little More Baby" by newcomer Barry White was climbing the charts. Robinson noticed that deejays were playing the two records back-to-back, as if "they're trying to marry us off." Even more serious competition turned up by 1975, when glamorous, sexy Donna Summer began recording music that owed more than a little to Robinson's music. Robinson continued to cut tracks in the seventies, including even racier tunes, most nota-bly a cover of Marvin Gaye's "You Sure Love to Ball." She would chart twice more herself in the seventies, once with a Eurodisco cut that fea-tured a robotic male voice vowing to be Robinson's "automatic lover." However, Robinson's biggest success before hitting on rap was "Shame Shame Shame," which she wrote and produced. Sung by Shirley Good-man (of Shirley and Lee "Let the Good Times Roll" fame) this early disco hit, which put men on notice that if they continued shunning the dance floor women might just shun them, landed at the top of the R&B charts in the spring of 1975.

Sylvia Robinson reintroduced women's sexual assertiveness to the R&B Top 10, and many followed her cue. Millie Jackson's raunchy raps far outstripped anything Robinson recorded. Soon even that "matriarch of the black protest movement," Aretha Franklin, who had been known for wearing colorful but unrevealing African-inspired clothing, had taken to appearing on record covers in what appeared to be little more than fur coats. That same year the gospel-rooted Staples, with Mavis singing lead, recorded that great ode to getting down, "Let's Do It Again." But if Robinson helped to move R&B singers toward greater sexual expressiveness, she never became a personality or the model of a new black womanhood in the way that James Brown or Isaac Hayes represented new styles of black masculinity. Roberta Flack offered up a compelling mix, conveying both black pride and sensuality in songs such as "Killing Me Softly with His Song" and "Feel Like Makin' Love." Powerful though she was, Flack remained restrained, never "out there" the way that Brown and Hayes so often were. The first woman to bring together black power and sexuality as persuasively as they did was Chaka Khan.

From the moment she hit the scene, Chaka Khan was unmissably different. Decades before Michelle Johnson renamed herself Meshell Ndegeocello, Yvette Marie Stevens had taken the African name Chaka, which she chose because of its association with "fire, war, heat—the color red." By the time Khan began making records in 1973, there were, of course, other black women singers sporting Afros, a hairstyle whose "naturalness" made it seem authentically black and politically right-on. Even the cautious Supremes turned themselves out in Afros (or Afro wigs) at one point. Doubtless this was a sincere move for many performers, perhaps none more so than Aretha Franklin, who went natural, donned African robes, and even offered to post bail for imprisoned radical Angela Davis.

But Khan, who was called "Little Aretha" as a teenage performer, took after no other R&B singer, including Franklin. For one, Khan may have sung in the choir, but she wasn't a traditional church girl, belonging instead to the "Church of Khan." She grew up on Chicago's South Side, where her father was a freelance photographer and her mother worked as a research supervisor at the University of Chicago. The relative who most fascinated her as she was growing up was her great-grandmother Naomi Bagby, a "Kansas City bootlegger and quasi-madam-turned-spiritualist in Chicago." Likely Khan owed some of her freewheeling ways to Bagby, who was married seven times. Although she has said that she was raised in a competitive environment, she nevertheless dropped out of high school, and from then on made the public library her school. Feeling it was "half-past time for us to be bold," she joined the Chicago chapter of the Black Panther Party, which was led by the charismatic Fred Hampton. She attended Panther meetings at the Loop City College campus, hawked Panther newspapers on street corners, and volunteered with their free breakfast-for-kids program.

Khan's musical interests set her apart from the Queen of Soul and many other R&B musicians, too. Aretha Franklin's taste in material was wonderfully catholic, but her covers of rock songs seemed obligatory. Khan, by contrast, always sounded at home with rock. Their differences were at least in part generational. Franklin was born in 1942 and Khan eleven years later, by which point Top 40 radio had grown more integrated. By the time Khan started singing in clubs, Berry Gordy's success in making Motown the "Sound of Young America," coupled with white rock musicians' indifference to pop music's racial barriers, had opened a space for the sort of musical cross-fertilization practiced by the groundbreaking band Sly and the Family Stone. It was this space between rock and R&B that funk artists such as Khan and her band Rufus struggled to expand. Khan's voice was big, and initially it lacked the restraint of Franklin and other R&B singers. Indeed, she wailed in a way that recalled Janis Joplin whose "Half Moon" she covered on 1974's *Rufusized*.

Chaka Khan was interested in crossing racial borders, and she had more than a little of the hippie about her—the torn jeans, wild mane, guilt-free love, and "everyone-has-an-aura" rap. Part of what attracted her to Rufus was that the band was racially mixed. She has said that she had never before seen a "white band fronted by a black chick." Khan developed a close friendship with the group's lead singer, Paulette McWilliams, and when McWilliams left, Rufus Khan replaced her. In her music, stance, and self-presentation Khan seems strikingly similar to the black rockers studied by anthropologist Maureen Mahon in *Right to Rock*. When one of Mahon's subjects describes himself as a "black hippie," and as coming out of "that kind of progressive, political, sort of countercultural, black kind of environment," it seems very much the territory that Khan occupied for a time. Khan has said that life before Rufus included nights spent "dropping acid or in a reefer cloud listening to Jimi Hendrix and Stevie Wonder . . . like so many other make-love-not-war types." She never formally married Hassan Khan, the Afro-Indian bass player whose last name she took. Instead they "went through some Indian rituals." But, as she told *Rolling Stone*, "marriage is a state of mind anyway."

Khan later regretted putting herself forward as a "sex symbol"—a move that her record label wholeheartedly encouraged—but at the time she was fearless. With Khan it seemed as if there were no vestiges of the old sexual order, none of the sexual propriety demanded of black women, especially in the integrationist fifties and sixties. Rufus's first hit record, 1974's "Tell Me Something Good," which Stevie Wonder penned for the group, showcased Khan's slinkiness and sassiness as she boasted, "what I got will knock all your pride aside." And then there were her "fiendishly sexy outfits," many of which she put together.

No other black female hit-maker—not Roberta Flack, Mavis Staples, Gladys Knight, or Aretha Franklin—was as unapologetically sexy as Khan. The photograph on the cover of *Rufusized* pictured her with a supersized Afro, midriff-baring tight tee, and even tighter bell-bottom jeans. With Khan laughing and holding onto band mates as they grasp her, the photo reinforced her sexy image. The centerfold photo shows her on an unmade bed, barefoot in those same street clothes, while mugging for the camera. Diana Ross may have paved the way for this with her 1970 debut solo album, where she posed unglamorously in funky cut-off jeans and a tee, but it was easy enough to write it off as a calculated updating of her look, part of Motown's effort to stay relevant. With Khan it seemed like self-invention and it was all of a piece—the hippie look, get-it-on songs, and her African name. When Khan's fur bikini top burst a strap during a concert at Madison Square Garden, it honestly was a "wardrobe malfunction." When she sang of

Chaka Khan, shown here performing with Rufus on *Soul Train,* designed outfits to reflect her Native American heritage

her desire, she breached the old walls of sexual silence and respectability that had necessarily defined the lives of many black women. Khan was the New Woman and she was irresistible. "We were all Chaka clones at that time," recalls R&B singer Anita Baker.

Intelligent and adventurous—both sexually and musically—Khan inspired a small army of wannabes. Her musical tastes strayed far from R&B and included Joni Mitchell's *Hejira* and *Don Juan's Restless Daughter*, on which she sang. Khan was more than a vocalist; she worked on arrangements, wrote songs, and was not afraid to tackle offbeat material. In 1979's haunting "What Am I Missing?" which she cowrote with her brother, she sings of feeling emotionally "jack-knifed," and of being worn down by "white lies." Among her most melancholy songs, "Missing" finds Khan singing, "You could say I've been everywhere / But you can't say what I've seen."

Earlier, on *Rufusized*, she tackled the meaning of black womanhood. Written by Lalomie Washburn, one of the band's backup singers, "I'm a Woman (I'm a Backbone)" was one of Khan's favorite concert numbers, and she sometimes played drums while singing it. Washburn's song lacks the humor that fires Laura Lee's "Women's Love Rights" and Jean Knight's "Mr. Big Stuff," but then it wasn't intended as a critique of philandering, no-good men. Rather, Washburn's song is a meditation on what it means to be the proverbial backbone—the resilient, sturdy black woman. Like some other writing by black women in this period, "I'm a Woman" finds satisfaction in being capable and steadfast. Khan's defense of black women's strength stands as a rebuttal of sorts to white feminism, which to many black women seemed a litany of velvet woes. Strength in adversity was a way of declaring one's superiority to white women, whose time on the pedestal too often made them seem "childlike" rather than "competent," as Toni Morrison once put it. But it also seems a response to black power, which sometimes treated black women's strength as evidence of what Black Panther Eldridge Cleaver once called their "subfemininity." With lines like "Smile and then I need to cry / Never knowin if I lie (or die)," Washburn's "I'm a

Woman" is not an upbeat song. Yet Khan transformed it into a celebration of the healing power of black women's steely resoluteness and an expression of black feminism.

Khan went solo in 1978 and her hit disco single "I'm Every Woman" had none of the snarl or ambivalence of the earlier "I'm a Woman." Penned by the husband-and-wife singer-songwriter team Nicholas Ashford and Valerie Simpson, the track has the same exuberant energy of the couple's incandescent "Ain't No Mountain High Enough." Khan has described the track as "right on time" because when she recorded it disco so dominated the charts. "I'm Every Woman" is about a "natural" woman with Superwoman, even supernatural, qualities—someone who can read her lover's mind, "cast a spell of secrets," and dispense "plenty of good old-fashioned love." Although the woman of this song appears omnipotent, her power is deployed on behalf of her man. Yet because "I'm Every Woman" is powered by Khan's irresistible, soaring vocal, the record registered to many as an anthem of seventies' feminism. A *Rolling Stone* writer thought it revealed her as "more of a feminist." And Khan seemed to agree—up to a point. "This is not your basic Helen Reddy song," she told a New York audience. But if it wasn't "I Am Woman" with its call to action ("I am woman, hear me roar / In numbers too big to ignore") Khan admitted that the song nonetheless "*does* celebrate womanhood." And she told an interviewer that as the lone woman in a group of men, she had to "overwork a lot to prove I could carry my bucket of water." Khan has said that as a result of being in the Panthers, she "put empowerment" in her music, and nowhere is this better showcased than in "I'm Every Woman." The Panthers were hardly Khan's only influence. In her autobiography she emphasizes that "woman-power was definitely in the air," a change she ties to the emergence of the "slick, snappy" *Essence* magazine, which she praises for not only profiling the accomplishments of professional black women but for showing "ourselves being mod."

To disco's detractors, the sort of female empowerment that "I'm Every Woman" advanced seemed hopelessly baggy, loose enough to accommodate even the most politically conservative woman. Certainly the song blurs differences, and in a way that some could criticize as post-racial. Yet one could also argue that by positioning Khan as America's Everywoman the track was every bit as audacious in its crossover ambitions as Berry Gordy's aim to make Detroit soul America's leading pop music. Disco staked out a position of sly inclusiveness, one that worked to "blur the lines, to bring everybody together," not into some homogenous nightlife—white-bread and heterosexual—but into one that was multiracial and sexually varied. As music critic Carol Cooper argues, disco's audience was in fact "a vast, multiethnic subculture."

Moreover, what sounded like toothless feelgood music to some could register differently among the marginalized groups that constituted disco's core audience. British punk rocker Tom Robinson, whose "Glad to Be Gay" made him one of the very few aboveground gay artists to treat their sexuality in an explicitly political manner, understood that even disco's many "do-it-to-me-one-more-time" tracks could feel empowering. Despite being a punk during the seventies, Robinson found himself drawn to disco, particularly the work of Dan Hartman, who was gay but not out. Hartman wrote, produced, and sang a number of disco hits, including "Instant Replay." When Robinson first heard the track, during the era of "disco sucks," he was blown away by what a "life-affirming and upbeat song" it was. "Instant Replay" isn't a gay record per se, although the song's opening line "You set my lips on fire" does seem a bit of a wink and a nudge to a gay crowd. Like "I'm Every Woman" and Sister Sledge's blockbuster "We Are Family," the record performed political work as surely as Dylan's "finger-pointing" songs or the more obviously political R&B songs of the late sixties and early seventies. Who is to say that the people dancing and singing along to Khan's "I'm Every Woman" at a jammed disco were any less political than the audience at a late sixties' James Brown concert chanting "I'm black and I'm proud"?

Black feminist critics and writers such as Michele Wallace, Ntozake Shange, Alice Walker, Toni Cade Bambara, and Toni Morrison usually get credited with the emergence of black feminism. But perhaps it is time to acknowledge that black women musicians played a role as well. Historian Ruth Feldstein has shown the importance of Nina Simone in generating black feminism in the sixties. But Simone, powerful and brilliant though she was, never attained the popularity of Chaka Khan or Labelle, whose music and self-presentation brought Black Power, feminism, and sexiness all together. Alice Walker has written that for her "Zora Neale Hurston, Billie Holiday, and Bessie Smith form a sort of unholy trinity." Young black feminists coming of age in the seventies similarly might find it hard to disaggregate Chaka Khan and Labelle from Alice Walker or Toni Morrison. Indeed, Khan was the first choice to play Shug Avery, the charismatic blues singer, in the film version of Alice Walker's *The Color Purple*. Although she turned down that role, many years later, in 2007, she played Sophia in the Broadway production of Walker's piece. Sophia, she said, was a "forefronter of women's liberation," like herself.

Chaka Khan is a piece of the story of black feminism, and she is also part of the history of funk. When Chaka and Rufus hit their stride in 1974, they were part of the new wave of funk artists eager to experiment with rock. They emphasized that the band wasn't R&B but was pioneering a different sound, one that they (curiously) dubbed "Krudde." However, even before Khan went solo in 1978, she and Rufus, having been relegated to the bottom half of the pop Top 10, began to shift gears in the direction of disco-inflected pop and jazz fusion. Khan claimed that her musical moves didn't portend a recalibration of her image, assuring one interviewer that she had no plans to begin "appearing in long evening gowns!" Yet her plans changed. With the musical shift came the evening gowns and Las Vegas shows. Rock critic Robert Christgau mocked Khan's makeover for the way it strained to be "classy" and "sophisticated." *Rolling Stone*'s Laura Fissinger lamented Khan's transformation from a musician full of promise and "bad-girl cheekiness" to an "overly facile stylist." Doubtless her record company saw bigger sales in this area than in funk, but Khan herself yearned to record jazz and she had grown uneasy about her sexpot image. Dance-floor success came again in 1984 with her cover of Prince's "I Feel for You," which featured rapper Melle Mel and became her biggest hit. It wasn't until 1998 that she returned to her funky roots with the Prince-produced record *Come 2 My House*.

BEFORE THERE WAS LABELLE, there was Patti LaBelle and the Bluebelles, a second-tier girl group whose members included Nona Hendryx, Sarah Dash, Cindy Birdsong, and, of course, the lead singer. The Bluebelles were stitched together from two earlier groups that hailed from Philadelphia and nearby Trenton, New Jersey, the Del Capris and the Ordettes. The group's biggest hit, 1962's "I Sold My Heart to the Junkman," climbed to number fifteen on the pop charts. The group's subsequent records, which included the chestnut "Danny Boy," generated only modest chart action, but their dynamic live shows made them perennial favorites with the legendarily hard-to-please crowds at Harlem's Apollo Theater, where they were known as the Sweethearts of the Apollo. The group languished in the late sixties, a period that brought hard times to the most successful girl groups, even that once impregnable hit-making machine the Supremes, on whom lead singer Diana Ross bailed in 1969. The styles of the midsixties' "rock revolution" and the reigniting of feminism made girl groups, with their bouffant 'dos, matching outfits, white gloves, and boy-obsessed lyrics, seem like relics of a blander, more uptight era. If girl-group music exploited the tension between escaping from yet capitulating to a male-dominated society, it was clear by 1969 that its days were numbered.

While American rockers treated girl groups as though they were the most debased expression of commercial rock 'n' roll, British rockers often responded differently. The Beatles covered lots of girl-group music (the Marvelettes' "Please Mr. Postman," the Cookies' "Chains," and two by the Shirelles, "Baby It's You" and "Boys"). Bad-boy rockers the Rolling Stones didn't cover their tunes, but they did tour with the Ronettes. Even fussy Mods, who looked down their noses at the Beatles as a "girls' band," were apparently less rejecting of girl groups. Another Brit who adored them (and American soul music more generally) was folkie-turned-pop-star Dusty Springfield. Springfield had fallen so in love with this music when she first toured the U.S. that in 1965 she hosted *The Sounds of Motown*, the TV special that introduced Berry Gordy's stable of hit-makers to Britain. Springfield wasn't just an avid promoter; she was also a diligent student. Like the Beatles and the Stones and other British Invasion bands that were finding success in the U.S. by recycling American blues and R&B, Springfield was engaged in some transatlantic cultural ransacking of her own. She personified Swinging London, but her vocal style, bouffant hairdo, and exaggerated eye makeup owed quite a lot to the American girl groups she idolized.

It was Springfield who brought Patti LaBelle and the Bluebelles, and many other R&B performers, to the attention of producer Vicki Wickham and the rest of the staff of *Ready, Steady, Go*, Britain's hippest music show. "Nobody in England had ever seen these people," recalls Wickham, who produced the TV show. "Only people like Dusty or the Beatles or the Rolling Stones, who were going to America and buying their records." From the time Patti LaBelle and the Bluebelles appeared on her show in 1964, Wickham was among their biggest fans, and by the close of the decade, she was managing the group (minus Birdsong, who left in 1967 to replace Florence Ballard in the Supremes). Wickham worried that the trio needed someone who knew the American music business better than she did, but her ignorance proved to be her strong suit, enabling her to reconceive the group in ways that most American managers likely would not have imagined. "I had no concept of the problems a black act had in America," she later acknowledged. But she thinks her naiveté worked in Labelle's favor. "When the girls would say, 'We can't do that,' I'd say, 'I don't see why not.'"

Wickham believed that the traditional girl group was a thing of the past. She didn't think the Bluebelles should disband, but she did advise the group to ditch its name, which she streamlined to the hipper-sounding Labelle. However, Wickham and the women of Labelle had more in mind than a simple name change. They wanted to revolutionize the representation of black women performers, to overturn the predictable ideas that music industry insiders and fans alike shared about black women's place in the music world. "When we were Patti LaBelle and the Bluebelles," recalled Sarah Dash, "we all wore the same wigs, the same dresses, and the same heels." Fed up with the idea that "black women all have to look alike because they're singing together," they resolved "to break the mold." Labelle was an experiment, their effort to see whether or not "black girls," in the words of Wickham, could "just be a group in the way that the Animals or the Who" were. Labelle was about nothing less than claiming the same privileged turf— the creative freedom, individuality, sexual forthrightness, and right of reinvention—so effortlessly occupied by male rockers. It felt like "the other side of the moon" from the Bluebelles, said Nona Hendryx. "You could be something that had never been before."

Breaking the mold proved no easy task. As soon as they set about working with Wickham, they found that they didn't always agree on the terms of the makeover. Patti LaBelle resisted the abbreviated name, the new material, and the greater sexual openness that Wickham advocated. "I fought the whole time in London with Vicki, and after," she recalled. "Me and her—just Joe Frazier and Muhammad Ali." LaBelle clearly saw herself, like Frazier, as old school, and so did Wickham, who years later attributed the lead singer's resistance to her "prudishness." Wickham's reaction suggests that she may not have comprehended that stressing the trio's sexual audacity, particularly in a crossover context, might be dicey given that racist assumptions about black women's sexuality still lingered. In a 1975 interview, Patti LaBelle suggested that her biggest fear actually was that the group might lose its loyal black following. "I didn't want to sing about screwing in the morning. I didn't want to change our name or style of clothing because I was afraid of losing our black following." However, she came to see that people were ready for a change.

Labelle's look and sound didn't come together immediately. It wasn't until the group teamed up with singer-songwriter Laura Nyro on *Gonna Take a Miracle*, her 1971 album of R&B and pop classics, that the group began to cross over to rock and pop audiences. Produced by Kenneth Gamble and Leon Huff, who became important architects of disco, *Miracle* turned out to be an inspired pairing in which Labelle worked as Nyro's collaborators rather than her backup singers. Indeed, Hendryx has said that Nyro was "almost like another member of Labelle." Music critic Dave Marsh believed the record was actually "pushed into shape by Labelle." The album's back cover showcased them with a stark photo. Shot from the chest up, Hendryx, LaBelle, and Dash stare at the camera—cool, unsmiling, somewhat forbidding. Although they're dressed in identical black turtleneck sweaters, theirs is not a girl-group get-up. Rather it's a transatlantic steal, a look and a pose that inevitably evokes the famous photo of the Fab Four in black turtlenecks that graced the cover of *Meet the Beatles*.

Less than two years after *Miracle*, Labelle released *Pressure Cookin'*. It was on this LP, their third as Labelle, that everything began to come together. *Pressure Cookin'* featured the group's explosive cover of Gil Scott-Heron's caustic "The Revolution Will Not Be Televised," Nina Simone's hard-hitting "Four Women," and Nona Hendryx's poignant "(Can I Speak to You Before You Go to) Hollywood?" Hendryx would become the group's writer, and she penned songs unique in their scrutiny of power relations. Labelle's preference for making politically meaningful music and their focus upon albums rather than singles caused them problems with TV producers, but it helped make them "darlings of the pop avant-garde." The group's underground cachet was further enhanced when up-and-coming singer Bette Midler recommended Labelle as her replacement at the Continental Baths, the popular gay Manhattan bathhouse. About this time an enthusiastic fan and clothes designer, Larry LeGaspi, came up with the idea of making them over into glam rockers. With their silver lamé outfits, feather headdresses, wacky helmets, and eye-grabbing breastplates (anticipating Jean Paul

Futuristic funksters Labelle onstage in 1976. L–R:
Nona Hendryx, Sarah Dash, Patti LaBelle

Gaultier's for Madonna by nearly two decades), Labelle rivaled Bowie
and T.Rex. By 1974, even *Rolling Stone*, which was indifferent to most
contemporary black performers, raved that Labelle had a "decidedly
right now and musically expanded consciousness."

When "Lady Marmalade" hit the airwaves later that year Labelle
became a phenomenon and among the earliest stars of disco. "The
right song, sung by the right group, produced and played by the right
musicians and released at the right time," enthused Jon Landau. The
Rolling Stone critic, who went on to manage Bruce Springsteen, pre-
sciently argued that the record's impact was so great that it would be
remembered twenty years later. Even more, it proved, he argued, "that
something good can come out of disco-music." Labelle first heard

"Lady Marmalade" when they were partying with music producer Bob Crewe, best known for his work with the sixties' hit-makers the Four Seasons. Crewe cowrote the song with Kenny Nolan, and he had produced its first recorded version, which appeared on a disco album by the Eleventh Hour. But Labelle's version, which began with the arresting chant, "Hey sister, go sister, soul sister, go sister!" was an intensely sensuous slab of funk. Recorded in New Orleans with R&B veteran Allen Toussaint producing and the funky Meters backing them up, Labelle had never rocked harder.

"Lady Marmalade" is about a regular "grey-flannel" guy who is haunted by his sexual encounter with a Creole streetwalker. Its refrain, "Voulez-vous couchez avec moi?" was racy enough to mobilize a segment of the right wing. Ostensibly the song is about male pleasure, but from the beginning it's Marmalade, not the john, who has the upper hand. She's blasé whereas he's overcome with desire, driven to crying, "more, more, more." Labelle didn't coo the lyrics either, as some disco vocalists might, but rather turned the song into a taunt, thereby underscoring the song's reversal of predictable power relations.

"Lady Marmalade" scaled the heights of the pop charts, and soon Labelle found itself on the cover of *Rolling Stone*. Always a hot concert act, they became the first black pop group to play New York's Metropolitan Opera House. Yet Labelle continued to make music for their core audience—people who were "sophisticated, streetwise, and ready for a change." Labelle sang about revolutions—on the streets *and* in the bedroom—and their concerts offered hints of what that revolution might look (and feel) like. And they were candid with the press. "This whole image men have about women wearing white gloves," said Sarah Dash before Patti LaBelle interrupted her. "*Lady* is a man-made word. It's 'woman' or leave it out," she declared. In *Rolling Stone*'s lavish cover article, the women of Labelle made no bones about the orgasmic quality of their performances. Dash revealed that they had told their backup band, "Now we like to reach orgasms onstage." Looking dreamy, Dash told the startled reporter, "I really came in Philadelphia."

In Atlanta, Hendryx appeared onstage with a pair of handcuffs and a riding crop, and acknowledged later to that same interviewer that she had always had a "handcuff fetish." In marked contrast to some other disco divas, who were more comfortable with gay money than gay people, Labelle embraced difference and outsiderness. From the early sixties the group had a "healthy homosexual following," because they weren't homophobic and they played the *gay* chitlin circuit.

Most chronicles of disco cite Sylvester and Grace Jones as exemplars of disco gender-bending. But Labelle did some serious bending, too. And in contrast to Jones and Sylvester, who remained largely underground figures, Labelle, propelled by the success of their hit record, took their act to America's heartland. Dressed like sisters from another planet, and sometimes singing about some other planet, Labelle helped to shape culture here on Earth. A Labelle concert was, as one fan says, "a place where you could go to be gay." He recalls one concert in Milwaukee where fans of headliner Chuck Berry turned hostile as gays took to the aisles dancing when Labelle hit the stage singing "What Can I Do for You." Labelle avoided trouble by quickly turning to "Lady Marmalade," which got the oldies fans out of their seats, dancing and singing alongside the very people they had wanted to pummel just minutes earlier. When they performed in Los Angeles at the Santa Monica Civic Auditorium, one newscaster covering their concert emphasized in his broadcast the queerness of the group's following. "There's six different sexes round the soda fountain, and they're mixing and matching really great." In Atlanta a member of that city's Feminist Lesbian Alliance told a reporter, "Lesbians love Labelle," in part because of the group's "heavy feminist message." Right down to their lyrical alteration of Gil Scott-Heron's "The Revolution Will Not Be Televised" (deleting the demeaning reference to "hairy-armed women liberationists"), Labelle gave voice to the varieties of feminism alive at the time. "We saw ourselves representing *all* women," says Hendryx.

Hendryx was particularly daring, telling *Rolling Stone* in 1975, "I don't know what a heterosexual or a bisexual or a homosexual or

Jamaican-born model and singer Grace Jones,
whose brother is a preacher in South Los Angeles,
singing at the Savoy Club in 1981

a monosexual is. I don't understand the differences." Onstage, the
women of Labelle enacted such an erotically charged display of sisterhood that it demolished those differences. In their commitment to
going "as far as we felt like going," they demonstrated to their fans
another way of being in the world. Music critic Vince Aletti nailed it
when he wrote that the group's fans were drawn to them "as if to a
cause, a movement, or, perhaps, a mirror." Lesbianism has never carried

the same cachet as male homosexuality in either the music business or in disco studies. Disco's only self-declared and unambiguously lesbian performer, Alicia Bridges, came out twenty years after she scaled the charts with her 1978 hit "I Love the Nightlife." And yet lesbian and bisexual women were part of disco culture—both in their own bars and in gay male and mixed clubs.

Labelle's story suggests the role that bisexual and gay women played in disco. It also illuminates the gendered and racial contours of popular music in the seventies. When groups like Labelle and Rufus first began their musical experimentation, the music industry was more open to genre-busting artists, in large measure because artists such as Sly and the Family Stone and Stevie Wonder proved that there was a market for their syncretic sounds. They were joined by others, including Rufus, the Parliament–Funkadelic constellation, the Isley Brothers, and the Pointer Sisters, all of whom worked interstitially, refusing to abide by the borders separating R&B and rock. The early seventies witnessed rich cross-racial musical collaborations, and there was no reason to think that the space for such out-of-genre work would not expand. In 1974, Hendryx optimistically ventured that the record industry had finally learned that "progressive black music can sell to anybody." But with radio embracing "narrowcasting" and consolidation gripping the record industry, there was less and less space for black artists trying to make funky music that rocked. As journalist Nelson George has argued, black artists who were signed to major labels—and this included Labelle and Rufus with Chaka Khan—were under pressure to cross over, and not with rock-inflected funk, which was enjoying only intermittent success on the pop charts. Stargard, a female funk trio fashioned after Labelle and the Pointer Sisters, is a case in point. They scored a number one R&B hit with "Which Way Is Up?" that failed to even register on the pop Top 10. Crossover had distinct advantages— greater exposure and better distribution—but over time it grew less accommodating of genre-busting artists. Labelle found its music dismissed as too rock for R&B radio and too R&B for rock radio.

As the afterglow from "Lady Marmalade" faded, it became clear that Wickham's vision for the group was not commercially feasible in the long term. After all, a group like the Who did not need a string of hit singles to be successful because their albums (and their older hits) were staples of AOR, album-oriented radio, which featured album tracks of heavy rock by mostly white artists. Labelle managed to score three gold albums in the wake of "Lady Marmalade," but they did not come up with Top 10 pop singles. Sexually explicit songs such as "Going Down Makes Me Shiver," political records such as "Who's Watching the Watcher," not to mention tracks about outer space such as "Phoenix: The Amazing Flight of a Lone Star," were not destined for America's Top 40. "What Can I Do for You," the group's fiery 1975 follow-up to "Lady Marmalade," reached number seven on the disco charts, but barely made a ripple on the pop and R&B charts. But, then, the song was unapologetically political, demanding peace and power at a time when popular music was moving away from overtly political themes. And Labelle, as one critic noted, was interested in "shuffling minds, not feet."

Moreover, by 1977 there was no escaping the fact that disco and funk were diverging, with the former becoming more of a woman's genre and the latter more of a man's. Female African American artists, whom the music industry typically treated as more likely candidates for crossover success than their male counterparts, seem to have been particularly affected by the growing disco–funk divide. Rick James's protégé Teena Marie seemed poised to become a major funk artist with "I'm Just a Sucker for Your Love" and "Behind the Groove" before she moved into jazzy pop. Stargard went on tour with George Clinton's P-Funk, but the hit records quickly dried up and the group soon broke up. Betty Davis, who introduced her husband Miles Davis to Jimi Hendrix (thus sparking, it is argued, the jazz trumpeter's foray into fusion), specialized in raunchy funk, and perhaps because of that was unable to penetrate charts of any sort. Rick James's coquettish Mary Jane Girls and George Clinton's Brides of Funkenstein recorded as solo artists, but they never had much autonomy.

By 1977 the thread uniting the women of Labelle had grown impossibly frayed. Citing artistic differences—particularly Nona Hendryx's preference for rock and Patti LaBelle's for pop—Labelle called it quits. Patti LaBelle would go on to enormous success as a pop-oriented singer who moved easily between ballads and high-energy disco. Hendryx teamed up with the Talking Heads and funk/rock/jazz fusionists Material, and cut many compelling solo albums that expanded the parameters of funk and rock. Her 1983 track "Design for Living" featured an all-female band that included bassist Tina Weymouth of the Heads, Nancy Wilson of Heart, Valerie Simpson of Ashford and Simpson, Gina Schock of the Go-Go's, and Laurie Anderson. Her 1981 single "Bustin' Out," with Material, made it to number two on the dance charts, but sustained commercial success eluded her. Dash hit the disco Top 10 with the track "Sinner Man," and over the years did dazzling session work for everyone from Sylvester to Keith Richards of the Rolling Stones.

In the end, Labelle's disbanding proved that three very talented but uncompromising black women could go only so far in the music industry. Race ruled, if somewhat less so in discos than on the radio. Labelle was very much of a piece with their music, which both advocated material change in the "here and now" and, with their futuristic glam, offered listeners an escape from reality altogether. Conceived transatlantically, sustained by their audacious pursuit of the unattainable, Labelle slammed up against the realities of the American music industry. When they reunited more than thirty years later, they mesmerized audiences all over again with their distinctive blend of funk and rock. The appropriately titled album, released in 2008, *Back to Now*, underlines the thread that runs from their work to the genre-busting music of today's visionaries—artists such as Santogold and Gnarls Barkley.

WE HAVE COME TO THINK of disco as a genre dominated by divas, and certainly it had plenty. However, disco also featured lots of tiny-voiced singers who seemed to take their inspiration from ex-Supreme

Diana Ross's crystalline, petite voice. Not all of them had Ross's affective range. (One reviewer described the women of Silver Convention, who performed "Fly Robin Fly," as singing "in unison with all the style of distracted typists.") And few if any enjoyed Ross's power. Especially in disco groups where the singing amounted to mere vocal punctuation, female vocalists were fungible.

Ross's vocals were shaped by doo-wop rather than the church, and have been unfavorably compared to the earthy singing of the Queen of Soul, Aretha Franklin, not to mention that of Supreme Florence Ballard. Yet Ross's vocal style, which was more in the tradition of Dionne Warwick, influenced Michael and Janet Jackson, Evelyn "Champagne" King, Stephanie Mills, and many disco singers. By the time Diana Ross entered the disco market in 1976, her record label likely figured it was time she got a piece of the action that her own breathy vocals had helped to inspire. Ross's luminous "Love Hangover," the first explicitly disco track by a star of her stature, demonstrates how intoxicating a good disco record could be. Starting slow and sultry, Ross tells her listeners that the hangover, the afterglow of lovemaking is so sweet, so addictive, that she's dispensing with doctors and preachers, the usual enforcers of female sexual respectability, and following her desire. On "Love Hangover" Ross sounds disarmingly uninhibited, like maybe she's spent the afternoon in bed, as she tosses off casual asides, sings in conscious imitation of Billie Holiday, and, midway through the song, cracks up and laughs. Producer Don Davis recalls her "having a ball" recording the track.

By the time "Love Hangover" was burning up the charts, Donna Summer had already begun to make a name for herself in disco. Born LaDonna Adrian Gaines, she grew up in Boston where her father worked as an electrician and her mother as a schoolteacher. Although Summer sang in her church choir, by the time she was a teenager she was going through what she described as the "Janis Joplin part of my life." In 1967, at age nineteen, she made her first professional appearance as the lead singer of a rock band called Crow, apparently because she was the lone black person in the group. The band managed to snag some gigs, including one at Boston's Psychedelic Supermarket, but it gradually dawned on her that Crow was unlikely to go any further. At that point she successfully auditioned for the Munich production of the musical *Hair*. Summer played a hippie, but she later described herself as "a clean-cut, funny American girl," albeit one with an Afro as big as that of radical activist Angela Davis, who was one of her "personal heroes." She began doing what she later described as "top European music," including the Vienna Folk Opera versions of *Porgy and Bess* and *Showboat*, and she married Austrian actor Helmut Sommer. Their marriage ended in divorce, but she kept her married name, which she Anglicized. Low on money, she began working as a backup singer for record producers Giorgio Moroder and Pete Bellotte at Munich's Musicland Studios.

Moroder and Bellotte created the sonic template for Eurodisco, but at the beginning they were trying to make disco music in the style of Philadelphia International Records. Italian-born Moroder and British-born Bellotte scored a couple of hits with Summer on the European charts, but they were hoping to penetrate the U.S. charts with "something sexier" and more discofied than their previous efforts. Moroder had noticed that "Je t'aime . . . moi non plus," the steamy 1969 duet between French singer-songwriter Serge Gainsbourg and his lover, British actress Jane Birkin, was once again on the British charts. Summer suggested that they should record their own "love song." Soon she came up with the lyrics, which consisted of little more than the words "love to love you baby." Moroder has said that he and his crew knew precisely the sound they were aiming for—"a very catchy bass-line, a very emphatic bass drum part and a funky guitar, sort of Philadelphia feel."

Moroder knew what he wanted from Summer, too, whom he asked to moan and groan as though she were having sex. After some cajoling, Summer agreed to record a demo of the song—in a blackened studio, on the floor, without any crew members to embarrass her as she pretended to give herself over to orgasmic ecstasy. Summer saw herself as a theatrical singer, and she later revealed that she had gotten through the experience of recording the song by acting a role: she imagined that she was Marilyn Monroe in the throes of passion. Summer has said that she had no intention of allowing Moroder to release the song under her own name. She thought that the final recording might go to Peggy McLean of the German disco act Silver Convention, but Moroder was so taken with her demo version that he persuaded her to let him release it. "Love to Love You Baby" reached number four on the British charts, although the BBC banned the record for its groans and heavy breathing. Not a chartbuster in the rest of Europe, it was one in America where Casablanca president Neil Bogart saw its potential, both on the dance floor and in the bedroom. Bogart apparently envisioned the song as a sexual enhancement, and instructed Moroder and Bellotte to extend it to twenty minutes so that it would fill the entire side of an album and allow for something other than old-school, three-minute sex. They managed to bulk it up to seventeen minutes with the help of a drum machine that let them extend the song for as long as they wanted.

Released in the U.S. in November 1975, "Love to Love You Baby" climbed to the number two spot on the pop charts by early 1976. It was quite a debut for Summer, who reported that the record upset her mother, who refused to believe that those were her daughter's moans and gasps on the radio. "Love to Love You Baby" was sensational in the larger culture, as well, with *Time* magazine reporting that it contained twenty-two orgasms. (The BBC counted twenty-three.) However, most music critics treated the record as a novelty. *Rolling Stone* ran no review of the album or of the singer's next LP. Disco-tolerant Robert Christgau of the *Village Voice* dismissed the record, but at least he did not turn prissily condemnatory. His review consisted of three questions: "Did you come yet? Huh? Did you come yet?" (Oddly, given his feminism, Christgau did not ask the critical fourth question, "Did you come again?") Some critics later admitted that they discounted Summer's early work as so much "erotic Muzak" and "packaged aural sex."

This was precisely the reaction Summer had feared. From the moment she allowed her vocal to be used on "Love to Love You Baby," she had worried that it might typecast her as an X-rated disco tart whose talents lay in the bedroom rather than in the recording studio. When she embarked on her first U.S. tour, she made a point of telling *Rolling Stone* that she was eager to prove she was capable of a lot more than moaning into a mike. Actually the album showcasing "Love to Love You Baby" was surprisingly varied and included a few twangy cuts that hinted at Summer's fondness for country music, a genre that the Pointer Sisters had managed to crack. While her racial ventriloquism distanced Summer from all those embarrassing moans, groans, and sighs of "Love to Love You Baby," it did nothing to protect her from those who mistook her for the sex-kitten performance she gave on the record, and in her first American concert appearances. If anything, her first live performance seemed designed to cement her reputation as the "Linda Lovelace of pop music." According to Richard Cromelin of *Rolling Stone*, she sang her first songs that evening with "her knees bent and her head thrown back, undulating her crotch in a circular motion at the audience." Worse still, as she performed her hit "Love to Love You Baby," three couples positioned behind her performed various Kama Sutra positions. Perhaps her record company or her managers urged her to ratchet up her sexiness. After all, Casablanca used a suggestive ad campaign promising buyers of Summer's record that they were purchasing seventeen minutes of love with the singer. Bogart went further, urging radio stations to play the track at midnight with the promise of seventeen sexy minutes with Summer.

In the wake of Summer's success, Jesse Jackson's Operation PUSH convened several conferences on disco, which he condemned as "garbage and pollution," although the preacher had shown no qualms about Isaac Hayes's bedroom music. Summer's performance of nubile sexiness and Casablanca's promotional campaign no doubt accounted for some of the overheated reaction. But the response to "Love to Love You Baby" also reveals how much had changed in the year and a half

Donna Summer twirling her leopard print dress as she performs at the Universal Amphitheater in L.A. in April 1979

since Sylvia Robinson released "Pillow Talk." For critics attached to the fading sixties, "Love to Love You Baby" was further evidence that their culture was giving way to a new era that was disconcertingly "stylish, sleek, smooth, contrived, and controlled."

Although disco's in-your-face sexuality would have been unthinkable without the sixties, the mirror-ball world dispensed with the naturalized version advanced by the counterculture. Sex wasn't free;

it was an exchange, brokered in singles bars and discos, with maximum orgiastic pleasure and minimal emotional engagement—what novelist Erica Jong dubbed the "zipless fuck." This wasn't the hippie ethic of free love that aimed to banish the sleaze and the snicker from sexuality, and which believed that pornography might just follow capitalism into the dustbin of history. Disco was a culture of getting down, one where fifties-style guilt lingered, which is why so many of the women on its albums look like tarted-up call girls and why the sex celebrated on its tracks was often of the "skinflick variety," as Stephen Holden put it.

To its critics, disco threatened to hurtle America back to a time when sex was a dirty joke. As glitzy and futuristic as disco was, it also seemed a throwback to the days when plastic ruled. By the time of "Love to Love You Baby," America was awash in fifties' nostalgia, jump-started by the Carpenters, George Lucas's *American Graffiti*, and the TV series *Happy Days*. Of course, the sixties could not be so readily banished. Karen Carpenter's melancholy vocals could not be disconnected from women's discontent any more than Summer's moaning could be heard without reference to *Our Bodies, Ourselves*, Masters and Johnson, or the first mainstream porno flick, 1972's *Deep Throat*. Made for $25,000, which was seen as an absurdly large sum for a porno movie, *Deep Throat* grossed $600 million and became the eleventh biggest-grossing domestic movie of 1973. *Deep Throat* was controversial for all sorts of reasons, not the least for advancing the idea that the protagonist was unable to reach orgasm (to hear any bells ringing) because her clitoris was located deep in her throat. During the film's trial on obscenity charges in New York, one psychiatrist lambasted the movie for popularizing the "Women's Lib thesis" that the clitoral orgasm was better than the vaginal variety.

In fact, the association between disco and pornography was forged even before disco became an identifiable music and culture. Alan Pakula's 1971 movie about a high-end New York call girl, *Klute*, included a scene shot in one of Manhattan's first discos, the Sanctuary. The scene is meant to underscore the tawdriness of the new "liberated" sexuality, a point made in plenty of seventies' fiction and filmmaking, including *Looking for Mr. Goodbar*, the movie version of which leaned heavily on disco tracks. Jazz flutist Herbie Mann, whose "Hijack" topped the dance charts in 1975, summed up the feelings of many when he joked that disco, like a good porno flick, is "great for five minutes."

No record captured this synthetic sexuality quite as well as Donna Summer's next big hit, "I Feel Love." Summer originally dismissed the record as "popcorn tracks" and viewed her vocal on it as "sort of as a joke." But the 1977 record represented a break from American disco, which still sounded like a relative of R&B. Built upon a speeding Moog bass line, a metronomic beat, futuristic sonic swooshes, and Summer's chilly vocal, "I Feel Love" took disco in a different direction, one that laid the foundation for Eurodisco. Even those who found fault with much disco understood the cut's distinctiveness. Critic Ken Tucker called it "thrilling." Musician and producer Brian Eno was won over by its odd pairing of opposites—Summer's "luxurious voice" with that "mechanical, Teutonic beat." "I Feel Love" took the singer even further away from her days as a gospel and Broadway belter. For those who believed disco was bleaching R&B, Summer's frosty vocal was another depressing piece of corroborating evidence. Critic Greg Tate was so sure that disco was demolishing authentically black music that he cleverly dubbed it disCOINTELPRO after COINTELPRO, the FBI's program to undermine oppositional movements in America. To R&B critic Nelson George, the music that Summer made with Moroder represented the "worst tendencies of Eurodisco"—its lack of rhythmic subtlety and its "almost inflectionless vocals and metallic sexuality."

Disco chronicler Peter Shapiro attributed Summer's "Teutonic ice queen" vocals to Moroder and Bellotte, whom he believed wanted to "piss" on the idea that black people are naturally more soulful, and that as a black woman Summer should be a "sensuous soul sista." However, Moroder, who in a 1978 interview called disco today's R&B, actually believed that black singers excelled at disco because "they just feel it more." In fact, it is far from obvious that Summer's sometimes wispy, sometimes icy vocalizing was entirely the creation of her producers. While it is true that Summer spoke of growing tired of the "soft songs" that had made her famous, she also emphasized that she never saw herself as a soul singer. Moroder and Bellotte may have encouraged her to employ this vocal style, but she may have had her own reasons for dispensing with her natural voice. After all, she tended to play against type—as a Monroe-like sexpot or an icy "Teutonic"—on explicitly sexual tracks, suggesting that for her racial ventriloquism created a necessary distance between herself and the super-sexy narrator of these songs. Onstage when she sang "I Feel Love" she moved like a robot and locked her face in what critic Gilmore described as a "dazed mechanical mask."

As for Summer's embrace of the mechanical, it may also have been her way of literalizing the distress she felt about her career. She told *Rolling Stone*'s Mikal Gilmore that her career sometimes felt like "this monstrous, monstrous force, this whole production of people and props that you're responsible for, by audiences and everything that rules you until you take it upon yourself to be a *machine*." She added, "And at some point a machine breaks down." Summer has said that fame diminished her, making her feel like a "commodity." Articles about her in this period demonstrate that she took some pains to distinguish herself from the woman whose moans jump-started many a make-out. She told *Penthouse* that if anything she was "undersexed." She insisted upon removing her eye makeup before meeting another journalist because she didn't want to "look like a hooker." And at a Lake Tahoe nightclub, Gilmore observed the way in which Summer iced out an obnoxious male patron who wrongly assumed that her sexy persona suggested sexual approachability. But if Summer was sexually circumspect offstage, as a performer she seemed almost determined to confirm people's expectations of her. Gilmore could not help but notice that when she performed at this same Tahoe club, she "came

"BAD GIRLS"

SUMMER WROTE "BAD GIRLS" —both the music and the lyrics—in 1977, only to have her record label nix it, apparently on the grounds that it leaned too much toward rock to be commercially successful. Two years later, Summer, Moroder, and Bellotte discovered it in the recording studio among some older tracks, and went about resurrecting the song. Moroder did not cut many demo tracks with Summer, but he did one for "Bad Girls," and for those who know the radio version by heart, the demo is revelatory. Released for the first time in 2003, it is stripped-down funk of the sort one might expect from the Gap Band or the Isley Brothers. Without the horns, four-on-the-floor bass drum, sassy backup singers, disco whistles, or "toot-toot, beep-beep" chanting, the song sounds more like a lament than a party stomper. Summer said she wrote the song after her secretary stepped out of the office one day and was stopped by cops who thought she was a hooker. That's when Summer says she began to get interested in who the real bad girls were. In the demo track Summer asks a series of questions about the selling and buying of sex, culminating in the question that haunts the song—"Is the price ever really right?" Throughout the demo, Summer keeps her distance from the bad/sad

damn close to copulating with her mike stand, writhing up and down its length with palpable shivers."

"When you start out whispering," Summer once observed, "the only way is up." By the time she recorded *Bad Girls* in 1979, Summer was hitting her stride professionally. Yes, she had gone through a crushing depression and a suicide attempt, and she was becoming a born-again Christian—all or much of it brought on, predictably enough, by the emptiness and loneliness of stardom. However, she was also a bona girls, upbraiding them with lines like "Who you trying to fool? / Don't you know everyone mistreats you?"

The final version of "Bad Girls" still refers to bad girls as sad girls, but Summer and Moroder dispensed with the demo's explicit critique of prostitution. Instead of calling into question the psychic price of sex work, this version accepts sex work on its own terms, with girls picking up strangers "if the price is right." But if the final version pulled its punches in many respects, it also positioned Summer not as a judgmental outsider but as one of the girls. Summer isn't celebrating prostitution, even if the track's lusty arrangement suggests otherwise. Rather, she is confronting what she shares with those streetwalkers, which is why she declares that she and the girls "are just the same." If Summer sounds unusually exuberant, especially as she yells out to a john, "Hey, mista, have you got a dime," it may be because Summer knows something about the experience of being made into a commodity, of being reduced to a seductive whisper. Tellingly, in a television interview some years later Summer said that "Bad Girls" marked the moment when she stopped being an object and became a subject. Needless to say, millions of listeners likely missed this because "Bad Girls" comes across as a dancefloor romp rather than an exercise in black female subjectivity.

fide superstar who was not about to be confined to cooing come-on songs. *Bad Girls* was her most solid effort to date, and found her singing with more passion and knowingness than ever before. Yet the way in which Summer cast herself in the role of a "bad girl," both in the album art and on the title track, proved troubling to some.

Stephen Holden, never one of Summer's bigger fans, penned *Rolling Stone*'s lead review of the album. Holden praised her prodigious vocal talent, and he claimed that the double album could have been "a Seventies masterpiece" had it been released on a single disc without the filler. He appreciated how hard Summer rocks on "Hot Stuff," which also featured a searing guitar solo by Jeff Baxter. He found her "hard-boiled, street-cookie directness" a welcome relief from her usual coyness. Holden admired the energy of "Bad Girls," which he thought evoked the "trash-flash vitality of tawdry disco dolls." But he also found the album, which he characterized as "a virtual paean to commercial sex," disconcerting. Holden understood that the hi-NRG cut "Sunset People" revealed the ennui and exhaustion entailed in "doing it right—night after night." He even called "Sunset People" disco culture's "A Day in the Life." In the end, however, Holden concluded that Summer typified the "Fifties child-woman sexual ideal 'liberated' into a Seventies, multiorgasmic *Cosmopolitan* clone." As for the picture of Summer posed as a prostitute with producer Giorgio Moroder as her pimp, Holden believed it "as good a metaphor as any of their musical collaboration."

1979 was the year of Donna Summer, with the success of *Bad Girls*, her two-disk greatest hits collection *On the Radio*, and "Enough Is Enough," her duet with Barbra Streisand, soaring to the top of the charts. "Enough" became her fourth number one pop hit. Disco may have been crashing, but *Bad Girls* alone sold seven million copies worldwide and "Hot Stuff" earned her a Grammy for best female rock vocal performance. But while "Bad Girls" and "Hot Stuff" were burning up the dance floors, Summer was finding Jesus. At the height of her fame she ditched disco and signed with David Geffen's new record company, where she released a rock-oriented LP, *The Wanderer*, which closed with the self-penned "I Believe in Jesus." Writing in *Rolling Stone*, veteran rock critic Dave Marsh argued it was her most mature and satisfying effort in large measure because at heart Summer was a rock 'n' roller. He was perhaps the first to emphasize that Summer, for so long dismissed as a virtual cipher, was an artist in her own right. He pointed to the fact that she had a hand in writing most of her material. Even more, he stressed her "collaborative role" with Moroder, Bellotte, and engineer Harold Faltermeyer, a four-some that he argued "function as a rock band."

Despite positive reviews, *The Wanderer* was a commercial disappointment as Summer, like Khan and Labelle, came up against the difficulty of making music that failed to conform to racially coded musical genres. Subsequent releases found her returning to disco, or what was now called "dance music," but minus her usual team. Moroder was never able to convince her to perform the sort of material that had launched her career. For Moroder, Summer's religious conversion marked the nadir of his career. "Having her biggest hit with a sexy song, she was suddenly saying that she wouldn't sing that type of song anymore, and then she insisted on having a song about Jesus on her album." In fact, it seemed to some that Summer was eager to sever all connections to her disco past when she was quoted (inaccurately, she claimed) as saying that AIDS was God's revenge upon homosexuals. Summer continued to make music, some of it chart-topping dance hits, such as "Love Is in Control (Finger on the Trigger)" and "She Works Hard for the Money," but she has never again experienced, nor did she seem to want, the red-hot popularity she enjoyed in the late seventies. In the 1990s she once again teamed up with Moroder and scored a number of dance-floor hits, although they have not crossed over to the pop charts. Her most recent CD, 2008's *Crayons*, included "I'm a Fire," which was a number one hit on the dance charts.

Summer's experience is not anomalous even in the world of disco, where Gloria Gaynor became a born-again Christian and urged gays to change their ways. If most disco books barely mention their renunciation of the nightlife they helped to script it's because most chroniclers of disco are fascinated with disco as a narrative of gay liberation. Even critic Walter Hughes, who at least acknowledged the power of the disco diva, was most interested in exploring the seventies' dance floor as a site of transracial identification between black vocalists and white gay male dancers.

To disco revisionists such as Hughes, the seventies represented a watershed when "feminine 'jouissance'" was all the rage, and not just among trendy poststructuralists. Although it is unlikely that the term made its way very often from the seminar room to the dance floor, it is true that disco contributed to the discourse of female pleasure. Song after song, from "Love to Love You Baby" to "Love Hangover," positioned female desire front and center. I don't think one can over-estimate the importance of this shift in which female desire—what women wanted—actually mattered culturally. Musically speaking, alt-country rocker Emmylou Harris is miles away from disco, and yet she recalls feeling moved by Summer's "I Feel Love." It's no accident that when female rappers—first Monie Love and then Missy Elliott—strug-gled to make the desires of women integral to hip-hop, the song they referenced was none other than Anita Ward's disco hit "Ring My Bell." Without this music there would have been no Madonna, Janet Jackson, Missy Elliott, or Lil' Kim. There would have been no "Slow Hand" or "Girls Just Want to Have Fun."

However, any consideration of disco's relationship to women must concern itself with the genre's actual women as well as the lyr-ics they sang. Certainly one of the significant stories behind disco is the tension between women's liberation and sexual expressiveness. Donna Summer was not the only seventies' sex symbol to repudiate the sexual revolution she helped to make. About the same time that Summer was proclaiming herself born-again, *Deep Throat*'s Linda Lovelace, declaring that she was now a feminist, claimed that her hus-band had coerced her into making pornography. Theirs are very differ-ent stories, for sure, but they suggest how deeply unsettling the new sexual expressiveness could feel. This was precisely the period when some feminists began to agitate against pornography and the sexual objectification of women. Although feminists, most notably Andrea Dworkin, produced a monocausal theory that granted far too much determinative power to pornography in upholding inequality between the sexes, their ideas resonated with women for whom the threat of sexual danger outweighed the promise of sexual pleasure. After all, this was a decade in which sexuality seemed to be cutting loose as films and music embraced sexual explicitness, pornography became respectable, and casual sex became more commonplace. Meanwhile, social and legal policy that would ensure a more level playing field for women lagged behind. Laws and policies regarding rape and domestic violence were very much in flux and sexual harassment was just beginning to be defined.

Many women, while skeptical of the sexual revolution, nonetheless believed that the risks associated with women's pursuit of sexual freedom did not outweigh the dangers of sexual repression for women. They would have agreed with feminist Ellen Willis, who once quipped that she "felt about the sexual revolution what Gandhi reputedly thought of Western Civilization . . . that it would be a good idea." There was no single disco experience for the women whose vocals powered so many dance-floor hits. Labelle pushed deep into the territory of sexual liberation in ways that seem to have been both personally and artistically satisfying. When they sing of going as far as they felt like going, or of "climbing in perfect timing" on "Going Down Makes Me Shiver," one hears their ecstasy at breaking through long-standing sexual silences. And while Chaka Khan expressed some apprehension about being typecast as a sex goddess, she also admitted what early videos of her performing with Rufus make abundantly clear, that she was a "wild-natured type of person" whose ease at demanding "love me now or I'll go crazy" helped to normalize female sexual assertiveness.

The shock waves set off by America's changing sexual politics were unsettling, generating ambivalence and provoking resistance in the world of popular music, where "disco sucks" became the rallying cry, especially for beleaguered rockers fed up with the hegemonic thump. Meanwhile, within disco, the thump grew more unrelenting and the heterogeneity that had marked early disco diminished. As disco became "disco," it grew more feminized, and despite the feminist advances of the seventies, more devalued. But disco's depreciation is doubtless also related to its association with the mustachioed, muscled gay men who became "shock troops" in the struggle against their continued invisibility and negligibility.

The Homo Superiors

DISCO AND THE RISE OF GAY MACHO

We're the men we've been looking for.
                    —*Edmund White,* The Farewell Symphony

B y the summer of 1974 all the elements of gay glitterball culture were coming together—the music, mix, drugs, lights, sound systems, and an unmistakable uniformity of dress. All of a sudden it seemed as if 501 button-fly Levis, flannel shirts, aviator jackets, work boots, and belt-dangling key chains took the place of ironed chinos, cashmere sweaters, and penny loafers. Sweaty and ecstatic as they spilled out of discos at dawn, these men were conspicuous in other ways as well. They wore their hair strikingly short, unlike most young men who still favored longer hair, and many of them sported curiously similar mustaches. At the time, gay writer and activist Douglas Crimp tried to make sense of what he was seeing on the dance floors of gay New York. It looked to him as though gay men were developing identical bodies fashioned for a specific activity. At first he thought they were designed for particularly athletic sex, but then it dawned on him: "These bodies have been made into dancing machines."

With their short hair, mustaches, and gym-built bodies encased in jeans, tees, flannel shirts, and leather, gay men—or clones, as they were called once the look grew nearly ubiquitous in gay communities

—sometimes transformed themselves into better copies than the "original." Gay men's macho style first took off in the discos of New York and San Francisco, where it was most strenuously cultivated, but it spread even to European cities. At New York's Flamingo disco, the East Coast epicenter of clonedom, it "was like being at a twins convention," observed writer and clubber Fran Lebowitz. Although other gay communities were less slavish in their devotion to clone style, its impact was felt throughout gay America, and beyond. What journalist Blair Sobel dubbed "phys. ed. fashion" had its beginnings in New York's West Village and San Francisco's Castro, but it didn't stay put in these gay ghettos as it drove unisex fashions out of style. "Ever notice how many straight guys stuff red hankies into and hang keys out of their faded Levis?" asked a writer in the gay magazine the *Advocate*. Such was the absorption of gay style by the mainstream that gay writer and activist Dennis Altman dubbed it the "homosexualization of America."

The Village People became the ambassadors of gay macho to the rest of the world. Yet initially, many heterosexuals, accustomed to thinking of homosexuals as limp-wristed, lisping girly men, took the disco group's hyper-masculine presentation at face value. Looking back at thirty-year-old footage of the Village People, one wonders how anyone could have mistaken their fastidiously masculine uniforms, girl-free lyrics, and hip-swiveling swishiness for heterosexual masculinity, but some did. However much this macho drag came to signify queerness within gay communities, the straight world largely registered it as standard-issue masculinity at first. Kenn Friedman, who handled record promotion at Casablanca Records and was himself gay, conducted market research into heterosexual awareness of homosexuality in disco, and concluded that "straights don't see the gay culture, they've only seen what they've made—the styles." Indeed, navy officials were so oblivious that they not only permitted Casablanca Records to film the Village People on one of their warships for the group's video of "In the Navy," they seriously considered using footage of that shoot as part of their own recruitment campaign.

It would be easy enough to treat gay macho as nothing more than a matter of shifting fashions. But embedded in this macho turn were changes in gay men's identity and subjectivity. Gays not only presented themselves differently, they regarded themselves differently, searched out unfamiliar sorts of sexual partners, and expanded their sexual repertoire. Whether gay macho was a parody or a sincere emulation of "normal" masculinity, it provided protective cover for gay men who during the 1970s became a much more visible presence in the urban landscape. While gay macho was facilitated by the recent introduction of Nautilus machines, its causes lay elsewhere—in gay liberation and in disco. Despite its pervasiveness, gay masculinism could be fraught—for the tongue-in-cheek Village People, the uncomprisingly queer Sylvester, militant gay liberationists, and the masses of young gay men whose sense of themselves was remade on the disco dance floor.

The Village People greet the New Year of 1980 with a photo shoot to promote the movie *Can't Stop the Music*. L–R: Randy Jones, Glenn Hughes, Ray Simpson (a new addition and the brother of Valerie Simpson), David Hodo, Alix Briley, Felipe Rose

MASCULINE GAY MEN were not unheard of before the 1970s. At least as far back as the 1910s, some gay men, particularly those of the middle class, had been trying to undo the rigid association of homosexuality with effeminacy. Jeb Alexander, a homosexual and a government clerk who left a detailed diary of his life, often despaired of the fairies who were so much a part of gay life in the early twentieth century. Men such as Alexander, who tended to favor a more conventionally masculine style, would find an ally in Sigmund Freud, whose work helped to recast homosexuality as a matter of sexual object choice rather than gender inversion.

By midcentury, however, effeminacy was still the dominant style both in representations of homosexuality and, it would seem, in homosexual communities. For example, when Truman Capote first hit the literary scene, he put forward a style that literary scholar Jeff Solomon characterizes as "young, effeminate, and strange." Tennessee Williams leaned toward the swishy in his public presentation, and his sexual encounters were often high-risk affairs with masculine men, often trade. Writer Gore Vidal is an important exception, but the story he tells in 1948's *The City and the Pillar* suggests the prevalence of effeminacy in homosexual communities. Vidal's novel, which is sometimes described as the first overtly gay American novel, tells the story of Jim, who is typically masculine in all ways but his sexual preference. Jim yearns for the sort of "natural and complete" brotherly love that he felt for another boy with whom he shared a physical relationship in high school. Yet, his explorations of gay life turn up more "strange womanish creatures" than masculine men like himself. Twenty years later, in *The Boys in the Band*, gay playwright Mart Crowley presented a range of gay men, from the screamingly effeminate to the most ruggedly masculine. In the end, however, he emphasized gay men's narcissistic effeminacy and destructive bitchiness.

Gay men's reminiscences also suggest that homosexual culture was hardly overrun with macho men. The author of the website nycnotkansas.com recalls that at Jacob Riis Park "the few worked-out bodies . . . were like a constellation of beach gods." And he notes that in the early 1960s gay men were apt to "look askance" at the leather-men in their midst. Martin Duberman remembers that at the close of the 1960s the sight of a "perfectly muscled form was still an event, enough to elicit murmurous beach-sighs rather than bored stares . . ."

During the 1950s homosexuality remained closely aligned with "ideas of morbid, narcissistic femininity." But the fifties also marked the moment when this alignment began to weaken. Both newly formed homophile groups and the emergence of gay-oriented muscle magazines challenged the notion of the homosexual as sissy. Homophile groups encouraged a more conventional, button-down masculinity. Male physique publications not only created a "physique ideal," they also urged their readers to "pursue its materialization at home, in gyms, on Muscle Beach." Christopher Nealon has studied these magazines and contends that a generation of gay male bodies was quite literally shaped by these publications. Perhaps these magazines played some role in the emergence in the late fifties and early sixties of gay men—bodybuilders, bikers, and leathermen—who cultivated hyper-masculine styles. Historian Martin Meeker has found evidence of motorcycle bars in the early 1960s in New York, Los Angeles, San Francisco, and Chicago. And *Mattachine Review*, a homophile publication, sometimes featured on its covers drawings of James Dean–like men. One especially memorable cover pictured three men in super-tight jeans and leather jackets, one of them bare-chested. By 1965, it would seem, the "college boy" look of chinos and button-down Oxford shirt was starting to lose ground to jeans and leather.

By the mid-1960s masculine gay men were becoming a discernible presence even beyond the gay community. Gay underground filmmaker Kenneth Anger helped to establish the homosexual biker archetype with his 1964 cult film *Scorpio Rising*. That same year *Life* magazine published an investigative piece on homosexuality that included an eye-grabbing photograph of the Tool Box, a San Francisco leather bar that tossed out anybody "too swishy." Three years later, *Life* ran a story that relied on the usual stereotypes about homosexuals. But then, right on the cusp of the new macho, in late 1969, six months after Stonewall, Tom Burke of *Esquire* magazine spotted the trend—the emergence of what he called "red-blooded, all-American, with-it faggots." Burke declared that the sort of homosexual with which straight America was familiar—"the curio shop proprietor with an uncertain mouth, wet basset eyes, a Coppertone tan and a miniature Yorkshire, who lives in a white and silver Jean Harlow apartment and mourns Judy"—was over, done, dead. In truth, the majority of American gay men at decade's end probably would not have been entirely comfortable at San Francisco's Tool Bar, but gay culture was certainly shifting.

It wasn't until the disco years, however, that "lumberjack masculinity" became the predominant style. It wasn't just that the music's volume and relentlessness encouraged physical intimacy and greater sexual straightforwardness between men. Disco's sonics, with its thunderous bass and its bass drum kick, operated like an "audio orgasmatron," which, as journalist Frank Owen puts it, worked on "erogenous zones you never knew you had." The music and the drugs pretty well obliterated any lingering sexual shyness. Moreover, the sweatbox quality of many gay discos made stripping to the waist all but necessary, which in turn made working out practically obligatory. Flamingo's gay owner, Michael Fesco, was a gym enthusiast and claims to have "engineered" the practice of dancing bare-chested. Flamingo had no air conditioning, and Fesco made sure the windows were shut so the place would heat up. "They *had* to take off their shirts." The evidence suggests that gay men were dancing shirtless several years earlier at those GLF dances. But at Flamingo and the Tenth Floor and other exclusively gay discos ripping off one's shirt was about self-display, and it quickly became enmeshed with working out. "Within a short five years, sculpted pectoral muscles had become one of the main attributes of gay male desirability," writes Douglas Crimp, "and Flamingo institutionalized the fact." Worked-out pecs came to be called "disco tits."

The buff body was about style, but it also was critical to the recon-figuring of gay identity and desire. Before, gay men had often been "hunters after the same prey," recalls Mel Cheren, "rather than allies or prospective partners." Now gay men rather than heterosexual men became the embodiment of masculinity and the fantasized object of desire for each other. "We're brothers," was the feeling. "We're the men we've been looking for," as the protagonist of White's *The Fare-well Symphony* puts it.

In this changed world, trade—those putatively straight, often working-class, masculine hustlers who allowed gay men to sexually ser-vice them for a price—lost their luster. Masculine working-class homo-sexuals and gays of color, who had been symbols of hyper-masculinity in the white gay imagination, may have lost some of their appeal in this new regime of desire, too. Several factors contributed to the growing racial segmentation of gay disco culture, including the process of gentri-fication that was changing the downtowns of many big cities. Although gentrification, parochial clannishness, and racism doubtless figured in the desire of some white gay men for a space of their own, it's also pos-sible that the thrill of discovering one's own kind attractive played a role in the racial compartmentalizing of gay disco.

The changing sexual landscape proved even more daunting to effem-inate gay men, particularly drag queens, who in the post-Stonewall seventies found themselves shoved to the sidelines of gay life. Gay liberationists—men and women alike—were hostile to drag, but their promotion of androgyny hardly proved the undoing of drag queens. Indeed, both liberationists' vision of a gender-blurred future and the drag-queen style that they frowned upon were made obsolete by some-thing that they had never anticipated—younger gay men's preference for masculinity over androgyny. For them, gay liberation became the opportunity to engage with rather than reject one's masculinity. In New York and San Francisco, and to a lesser extent elsewhere, younger gay men began to put together the clone look. To gay San Francisco journalist Randy Shilts, it was the end of the "Judy Garland style."

Gays' camp style—their identification with tragic, doomed women like Garland and obsession with Broadway musicals—no longer had the same resonance now that gayness no longer signaled failed masculinity and disco was reshaping the status quo itself. There were holdouts, of course—gay men who refused to turn themselves into disco-loving macho men. Activist and writer Vito Russo, author of *The Celluloid Closet*, had absolutely no use for disco. "All I could hear," he said, "was this one horrible beat." But Russo was outnumbered and soon disco dancing and Nautilus-powered workouts were becoming the new signifiers of homosexuality.

This shift sidelined whole categories of gay existence, as devotees of Garland and lovers of Broadway musicals came to seem antique. The shift was discernible in big cities across America. By 1975 the *Advocate*, which published a cover story on the changing image of gay men, observed that long-haired gay men had become an endangered species. In Los Angeles, the hyper-effeminate men of John Rechy's novel *City of Night* were "fast disappearing." And so it was in America's first gay resort community, Cherry Grove, where one veteran bartender recalls that drag-loving gays were completely out of fashion in the 1970s. "They used to sit around the bar and complain to me how dejected and rejected they felt. No one wanted their drag and no one wanted them sexually. It was all disco and drugs, and a big problem."

The sexual geography of Fire Island, where the funky and unfashionably campy Cherry Grove was but a fifteen-minute walk from the glamorous, macho-man Pines, made for a palpable tension between the two communities. Cherry Grove may have boasted the Ice Palace, the first discotheque on the island (and some would argue in all of New York), but the Sandpiper in the trendier Pines had supplanted it. So had the Pines' butch style, which to older Grovers seemed both "ridiculous and a sham." As anthropologist Esther Newton discovered, gay Grovers simply took it for granted that a homosexual man "*is* effeminate, whether he likes it or not, because of his 'female' position relative to 'normal' men." However, Grovers' skepticism about the emerging gay

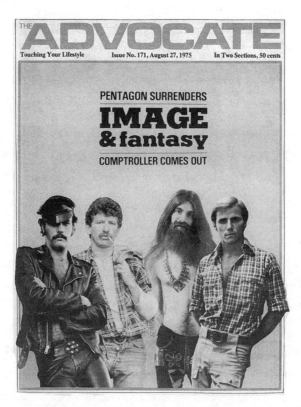

The shape of things to come: gay macho

masculinism did little to dent what Newton calls the "new sense of masculine entitlement" that Pines' gays were relishing.

For Grovers, the situation reached a breaking point in 1976 when the Botel's owner, John B. Whyte, who had been a magazine model, refused to serve one of the Grove's best-known drag queens because he was not "properly attired." Tired of being sneered at by drag-averse butch gays in desert boots and jeans, a small group of Grovers (most of them male) decided to mount an "invasion" of the Pines. But the invaders, decked out in purposefully ludicrous drag, were greeted with bemusement rather than hostility. Startled by this ragtag bunch of Grovers carrying signs saying things like "Pines People are Plastic," the Pines residents' reaction was "What the hell is that?" One Grover remembers that although the catcalls and hoots that greeted them at the disco were friendly, they cleared the dance floor. She suspected Pines people thought, "These people were weird! Where did these people come from?"

In Andrew Holleran's *Dancer from the Dance* the "weird people" have not yet become extinct, but their nights, at least in Manhattan's most exclusive gay discos, are numbered. The novel's only explicit reference to the post-Stonewall macho turn occurs when the relentlessly campy Sutherland, spotting an ex-lover in a crowd of s/m leathermen, remarks, "When I knew her she was all cashmere sweaters and penny loafers." Yet Holleran's novel, which limns gay Manhattan during the years that disco became "an industry," is nothing less than an extended meditation on the nature of gay masculinity. *Dancer* explores gay New York just at the moment when obstinately weird and desperately doomed "old-time queens" like Sutherland are losing ground to a younger generation of men who are "utterly indistinguishable from straight boys . . . and completely calm about being gay." Sutherland might get himself up "like a lumberjack one night, a Gucci queen the next," but he considered himself, like all homosexuals, essentially feminized. For him, homosexuality involves "being looked at," "Being Attractive to others," in short, being consumed. And just like the clones that Martin Levine studied in his monograph *Gay Macho*, most of the men in *Dancer* spend their days "pumping iron, dieting, and dressing 'butch,' all for an approving glance or wink."

The novel's protagonist, Anthony Malone, whose classically handsome face, big dick, and buff body help to make him the heartthrob of gay Manhattan, is a liminal figure poised between the world of the clone and that of the queen. It's Malone's charismatic wholesomeness, his ability to conjure up the "smell of grass when it's cut in August, the heat of a summer day"—his authentic all-American masculinity, if you will—that makes him so irresistible to all the men who yearn for his attention. His boyish hopefulness and nearly indefatigable faith in love stand in stark contrast to Sutherland's jaded weariness. Even when he becomes a high-class call boy administering enemas to one client and pissing on another, he remains somehow uncorrupted. But he is perplexed about the life he's landed. Drawn to piers and bathhouses and discos, Malone pines away for the normal life that might have been his. When he engages in one of his many dreamy reveries about life outside of hothouse gay New York City, and imagines himself dressed in starched white trousers and a starched white shirt, working as an air-traffic controller in the Florida Keys, Sutherland is incredulous. "Is that what you really want?" he asks. "You want to be a man?" Sutherland managed to avoid such questions himself with the help of speed, Valium, Quaaludes, camp ripostes, and the Twelfth Floor. As for Malone, it's a question he cannot answer, except to say that being "free to do anything" is a "horror."

Dancer from the Dance is full of apprehension about the armies of newly minted, well-adjusted homosexuals displacing old-time queens and about the "roller-rink" disco that was displacing the noirish disco that once made the Twelfth Floor so irresistible. "There is no love left in this city," groans Sutherland to Malone, "only discotheques— and they too are going fast, under the relentless pressure of capitalist exploitation."

Dancer is an ambivalent text that longs for assimilation in sleepy small towns, but revels in the homosexually-specific culture of dancing, cruising, and working out. In an interview published shortly after the release of *Dancer*, Holleran suggested that the real horror of post-Stonewall gay life was that freedom had brought a narrowing of choice. The rise of a self-defined gay community had led, he argued, to a "ghettoization" that paradoxically resulted in gays leading more diminished, rather than fuller lives. He cited as proof the ubiquitous "fucking uniform" of the plaid shirt and bomber jacket, which he argued was turning gay men into "Barbie dolls." And yet after fulminating about clone style, he admitted that it had its uses. Holleran's grudging admission followed from his own short-lived resolve to buy a non-clone winter coat, a course of action he abandoned once he realized that it guaranteed he "wouldn't get cruised." That prospect reminded him, he told the interviewer, "the original reason we dressed that way was to identify ourselves to other gay people in a populace that wasn't gay."

Much of what bothered Holleran about the clone was his underlying femininity—he's a Barbie doll preoccupied with his attractiveness to others—but it was the hyper-masculinity of the clone that troubled most observers. Many gay writers, reluctant to view the macho turn as a simple embrace of conventional masculinity, bent over backward to emphasize its parodic qualities. The clone's meticulous masculinity, which so lacked the casualness that marked the self-presentation of straight men, revealed, they argued, that the clone was a masquerade of conventional masculinity, not an effort at emulating the "real" thing.

Martin Levine's *Gay Macho* makes little effort to justify the macho turn or to prove its subversive potential. Gay sociologist Levine thought the emergence of gay macho signaled homosexuals' growing self-worth as they rejected society's view that they were "failed men." Indeed, for Levine, the problem was less macho than effeminacy, which he saw as a potent signifier of gay oppression, of how thoroughly gay men had absorbed society's conviction that they were sad and pathetic creatures. By making themselves over into enviable specimens of masculinity gay men were throwing off decades of homophobic ideology. Likewise, Randy Jones, the "cowboy" of the Village People, believed that the seventies witnessed gay men finally taking possession of their masculinity. The author of nycnotkansas.com felt relieved when gay men ditched "the effeminacy and corrosive bitchiness" that had so characterized gay life. Hanging around campy gay men had depressed him because it confirmed the notion that gay men either were or wanted to be women. He concedes that gay macho could be silly, but he believes that as a consequence of this shift, gay men "seemed to behave more decently toward each other."

But other gays were less sure. It's no accident that by 1979 some gays, including longtime gay activist Harry Hay, tired of the new gay masculinism, were coming together as "Radical Fairies" to reclaim their effeminacy. In San Francisco some gay Trotskyites protested by jeering at clones on Castro Street. They were a minority, for sure, but others began voicing their fears as well. One writer for the *Advocate* deplored the tendency of gay men to make themselves over into "ever more standardized packages." And a generational divide began to emerge as some gay teenagers came to think the Stonewall generation was synonymous with "unreflecting conformist machismo, with greed and consumption, with white supremacy and sexism."

While not hostile to the clone, Dennis Altman was nonetheless ambivalent, and argued vigorously against the strict dress codes prohibiting cross-dressing that some gay bars were adopting. He worried that the message behind gay macho might be "it's okay to be a fag provided you're also a man." Altman was not the only gay writer to question whether the normalization of homosexuality was being achieved through the continued stigmatization of effeminacy. Seymour Kleinberg believed that in refashioning themselves as specimens of masculine hardness, gay men were dressing up like the enemy. "Our old fears of our sissiness," warned Edmund White, "still with us though masked by the new macho fascism, are now located, isolated, quarantined through our persecution of the transvestite." And yet White, despite his apprehensions, also understood the embrace of macho as a "political act" in which gay men repudiated effeminacy as a form of internalized homophobia.

White was hardly the only gay man uncertain about the meaning of the macho turn. In *Faggots*, Larry Kramer's savage satire of gay life in the seventies, the narrator ponders the possibility that the macho look has taken hold because it's a way of "hiding" or "homogenizing." On the other hand, it occurs to him that maybe it's "a send-up *and* a turn-on." Gay macho operated in multiple registers, with its meaning shifting according to context. While it may have narrowed the parameters of acceptable masculinity in certain respects, it seems that in the sexual arena all that leather, denim, and butchness paradoxically helped to underwrite a softer masculinity, as gay men began to take up sexual practices such as anal receptive sex that had long been considered suspiciously feminine. Now gay men can behave like women, wrote Seymour Kleinberg, getting "gang-banged in the back room." Kleinberg was no fan of gay macho, but he admitted that it seemed to have achieved the decoupling of effeminacy and sexual passivity. Even very butch-looking men take the "passive" role, he noted, and the only way to discern a gay man's sexual tastes is from the handkerchiefs and key chains that hang from his back pocket. Writing about this shift, queer writer Guy Hocquenghem exclaimed, "Our assholes are revolutionary!"

DISCO WAS INSTRUMENTAL in the development of gay macho, but its leading gay performers positioned themselves differently in relation to it. In 1974, four years before the Village People made their presence felt on the charts, celebrity hairdresser turned headliner Monti Rock III put forward a gay disco persona that was emphatically effeminate. Puerto Rican Monti Rock was already something of a fixture on both *The Tonight Show* and *The Merv Griffin Show* when he began recording under the name Disco Tex and His Sex-O-Lettes. It was Bob Crewe, the veteran record producer and songwriter behind those Jersey Boys, the Four Seasons, who proposed that Monti Rock front a disco group. Disco Tex and His Sex-O-Lettes may have been the novelty act that critics pegged it for, but it included longtime pop music and R&B veterans with whom Crewe had worked. More importantly, in contrast to other acts that were recording danceable R&B without much thought to the emerging disco market, Crewe and Rock, both of whom are gay, quite deliberately set out to make a "disco" record. They even produced the album to sound as if it had been recorded in a club. Their collaboration is unusual in that it featured gay men in disco's first year actually making, rather than deejaying or remixing, the music.

Rock, who later described himself as "not your run-of-the-mill fruit," was so flamboyantly gay (resolutely limp wrists, multiple rings,

The campy cover of Disco Tex and His Sex-O-Lettes' 1974
album

and long flowing robes topped off with a feather boa) that coming
out would have been redundant. In his TV appearances his sexuality operated as a running gag for hosts and their sidekicks. His first
album, which shows Rock surrounded by swirling showgirls and looking more than a little like Liberace, was obviously designed to appeal
to a gay audience. The hit track off the LP, 1974's "Get Dancin',"
was the first record to be released as a promotional 10-inch single.
It was also among the first songs to break out of gay discos into the
mainstream, and its follow-up, "I Wanna Dance Wit' Cho," which
featured a Frankie Valli–like falsetto, performed well in discos. Rock
never again dented the disco market, but he appeared—considerably
butched up—as the loudmouthed Latino deejay in *Saturday Night
Fever*.

Like Disco Tex and His Sex-O-Lettes, the Village People were a novelty act, but with a macho twist. The group was the brainstorm of Jacques Morali, a gay Frenchman and Eurodisco producer. Morali was first introduced to disco in the early seventies through a hairdresser who worked for Cher and Elizabeth Taylor—a telling factoid that underscores the ways that homosexuality and disco circulated trans-atlantically. With his collaborator, the Moroccan-born lyricist Henri Belolo, Morali first penetrated America's disco charts with the Ritchie Family, a female trio that scored a hit with a discofied version of the show tune "Brazil."

Morali came up with the idea of the Village People in early 1977 after spotting future group member Felipe Rose dressed like an American Indian at one of New York's gay clubs. After seeing Rose again in another disco, and seeing other gay men in macho drag, he reportedly said to himself, "You know, this is fantastic—to see the cowboy, the Indian, the construction worker with other men around." After observing the macho men of New York's West Village, Morali decided that disco was ripe for an act that appealed to its core constituency: gay men. When first interviewed by *Rolling Stone* in 1978, Morali outed himself, and emphasized that as a homosexual he was committed to ending the cultural invisibility of gay men. "I think to myself that the gay people have no group," he said, "nobody to personalize the gay people, you know?" Detractors of disco often cite what literary critic Houston Baker called the "high-marketplace maneuverings" that made disco so commercially successful. But as the story of the Village People reveals, there was plenty of low-marketplace maneuverings and even personal passion that figured in the making of the disco juggernaut.

Glenn Hughes, the leatherman of the Village People, thought Morali was drawn to the idea of the Village People for another reason as well. Morali, he believed, was fascinated with gays who were appropriating "very strong, positive male American stereotypes." Hughes ventured that as a foreigner their producer was especially susceptible to the "whole mysticism attached to an 'American,' and here he's seeing it in bigger-than-life stereotypes." Randy Jones, the cowboy of the group, thought that Morali found it frustrating to be surrounded by the Village People, all of whom were attractive men, because he was not himself conventionally handsome. "I think that really deep in his heart he wanted to be what we were."

Morali sold the concept of the Village People—a cowboy, Indian, leatherman, hard-hat, cop, and sailor—to Casablanca Records before he had managed to even put together a credible group. For the group's first record, *Village People*, Morali and Belolo employed studio help and relied largely upon professional models for the cover shot. Pitched to a gay audience, the album featured paeans to well-known gay meccas— San Francisco, Hollywood, Fire Island, and Greenwich Village—and received play in gay discos. The only problem was that the producers were swamped with requests for live appearances of a group that didn't yet exist. They rushed to assemble a group that could perform on TV and at discos, and put together their second album.

For their second release, *Macho Man*, Morali and Belolo crafted multivalent songs that could be read one way by obtuse straights and another by those in the know. One would have thought that lines such as "Call him Mr. Eagle, dig his chains" from "Macho Man" might have been a tip-off, but apparently they weren't. "Macho Man" reportedly received a tepid response in many gay bars, but straight audiences, especially heterosexual men anxious to cop the macho style, could not get enough of it. Even bigger was "Y.M.C.A," which sold 4.5 million singles in the United States and 12 million globally. Powered by a sound that *Rolling Stone* critic Stephen Holden called a "goose-stepping pastiche" of Philly International disco, the Village People became America's "first gay-to-straight 'crossover' group," that is, the first (and only) disco act whose image and original following was gay but managed to cross over into straight discos. "They love 'em in Vegas and in tacky suburban dinner theatres in Midwestern shopping centers," reported ace disco promotion man Kenn Friedman.

As its audience shifted, Casablanca Records recalibrated the group's image and the Village People took to describing their act as a "male-image show." When *Rolling Stone* approached the Village People about a cover story, the paper was told it would have to sign a written agreement banning any discussion of the group's sexuality. That didn't happen, but the ensuing story revealed an organization anxious to rewrite the group's history. Suddenly, the Village People weren't really gay and their formation was simply a commercial gambit on Morali's part. "He's no dummy," said Belolo of his partner. "He had a concept about an album that could appeal to the gay discos. Because he knew that if your album was played in the gay discos, you had immediate sales." Group members (at least one of whom, the original lead singer Victor Willis, *is* heterosexual) refused to discuss their sexuality, except to say that they were not a gay group, but rather, as leatherman Hughes put it, "six very positive, male, energetic symbols," who would naturally attract both gays and straights. Another member, David Hodo, explained that the group disliked all labels—"black–white, straight–gay, disco–rock & roll." Emphasizing the group's indifference to politics, he sneered, "We're not Joan Baez."

If the Village People grew coy about their sexuality it was because, against all odds, they had achieved mainstream popularity. Morali never imagined that the group would cross over to straight audiences, but by 1979 the Village People were pop music's second-biggest "audio-visual package," after Casablanca's other big act, Kiss. Their outsized popularity did not endear them to critics, who complained that if disco was the "fast food of popular music," then the Village People were the Big Macs of the industry. Plans were under way for an $11 million movie, and the group was offered its own television show. In spring 1979 they embarked on a seventy-day, forty-five-city tour of the U.S. and Canada, and did fifteen days of TV promotion in Europe. The Village People were a global phenomenon, topping the charts not only in America and Europe but also in South Africa, Australia, and Israel. Not everyone was pleased with the group's supersized success. The militantly homophobic Anita Bryant reportedly sent President Carter a telegram asking him to deport Jacques Morali because of his corrupting influence on children.

Among gay people opinion was divided. Richard Dyer bemoaned the fact that the best-known gay disco act was responsible for such a "phallic form of disco." More typical was the criticism of gay activists who believed that the group's record label was "deliberately closeting the Village People to make the act 'safe' for straights." Even the *Advocate*, hardly a hotbed of radicalism, complained that the group had been transformed into "the Osmond Brothers from Oz." Dennis Altman began his book *The Homosexualization of America* with a dig at the group, which he said typified the new gay macho even if it "strenuously denied this identification and later abandoned the style to make it in Las Vegas." And yet as Andrew Kopkind pointed out, the group's lyrics made its homosexual themes an "open secret," certainly for those alive to the wink and nod. Even their movie, 1980's *Can't Stop the Music*, which offered viewers perhaps the most deracinated version of the Village People, features a Busby Berkeley–like dance number that emphasized the gay pleasures of the Y.M.C.A. And how could their song "Liberation" not conjure up gay liberation?

Although gay critics pounced on the group's newfound reticence, this was hardly the only problematic feature of the Village People. The Village People began as an effort to provide gays with masculine role models. A video of an earlier incarnation of the Village People (with seven members) performing "San Francisco" has not even a whiff of the camp about it. They really do resemble the men one might have met on Castro Street in 1978. However, by the time of "Macho Man" they had evolved into something far more predictable. Just as gay pop musicians from Little Richard to Elton John opted for clownish flamboyance rather than explicit homosexuality, so did the Village People, whose act became a campy caricature of homosexual style rather than an affirmation of the raunchy new macho. Group members boasted of "sticking our tongues in society's cheek," but onstage these macho men weren't sticking their tongues much of anywhere. Maybe this was the predictable effect of commercialism, that in order to get themselves on the Macy's float and aboard that navy ship, and in the hope of getting their image slapped onto kids' lunchboxes, they went along with the sexlessness that seems a precondition of gay male representation in pop culture.

Or perhaps there was no way in pop cultural terms to represent gay macho—which after all, was performative—without resorting to camp. Nonetheless, gay men couldn't be blamed for wondering if the Village People's macho burlesque was calling attention to the absurdity of normative masculinity or to the ludicrousness of gay macho. Clownishness was undoubtedly the path toward greater commercial viability, but producer Morali seemed reluctant to have the group go that way. Once criticism of the group became routine in the gay press, Morali shot back, "Look, make no mistake about it, I am the number one public relations man for the gay world." When Ken Emerson of *Rolling Stone*, who interviewed the Village People and their producers, observed that Morali didn't seem to understand how funny the act was, David Hodo agreed. In his view the only people with a sense of humor about the group were the Village People themselves. Although Felipe Rose complained that the group was treated like "slaves, dancing dolls," Emerson thought that they enacted their revenge by making clear the "ridiculousness of it all." If what the Village People proved was that "gay people could be as stupid and banal as anybody else"— the conclusion that critic Lester Bangs drew—one can understand why some gays might have felt just a bit queasy about them.

Disco's other popular gay icon, Sylvester, had been "in the life" since adolescence and had no qualms about proclaiming his queerness. When asked about his past, Sylvester emphasized how alien he had felt growing up in Los Angeles in a "black bourgeois family." Rather than elaborate, he told *Rolling Stone*, "let's just say I was the first test-tube baby." Although his professional career began at age seven with three years on the California gospel circuit, it was not long before he was rebelling against his family's respectable ways. By the time he was sixteen he was a part of the Disquotays, a group of cross-dressing black teens that his biographer Joshua Gamson describes as "a cross between a street gang and a sorority."

After leaving L.A. and moving to San Francisco, Sylvester hooked up with the Cockettes, an off-kilter theatrical troupe briefly famous for pushing the hippie embrace of androgyny into the realm of gender-fuck. The Cockettes pioneered a hippie-inflected drag in which the masculine and the feminine purposefully collided. Male Cockettes wore vintage women's dresses, but unlike conventional drag queens, they did so with their own untamed long hair and beards, Sylvester excepted. He performed in drag and told *Rolling Stone* that he was taking hormones to make himself busty. But from the beginning Sylvester was "among the Cockettes but never quite of them," as Joshua Gamson puts it. Race contributed to the disconnect. The Cockettes imagined themselves beyond all social categories, whereas Sylvester very much saw himself as working within the tradition of black entertainment. And in contrast to most group members, who were content with their underground notoriety, Sylvester yearned for the limelight. His performances, which were staged as interludes set off from the frenzied, shambolic performances of the Cockettes, were so different in tone that they were "like the reverse of comic relief." Before long he quit the group, re-emerging as Sylvester and the Hot Band, a bluesy rock outfit. However, his time with the Cockettes left its mark. While most drag queens were still doing Marilyn Monroe, Sylvester stretched drag's sartorial repertoire by developing multiple looks, from that of a twenties' classic blues singer to what comic Bruce Vilanch described as a "Vegas showgirl version of a voodoo priest."

Like the Pointer Sisters, with whom he sang before they became famous, Sylvester was fascinated by vintage American music. He was especially taken with the blues—not the raw Robert Johnson-style country blues favored by white rock fans, but the classic blues of Ethel Waters and Bessie Smith. And he idolized divas of the past—most of all Josephine Baker. In the fall of 1971, as he and the band set out for a nine-week engagement in New York, the *Advocate* declared that Sylvester was poised to become the first "big act to break out nationally with an up-front gay theme." But fame eluded him, except in San Francisco where audiences appreciated his stated objective—to "*destroy* reality." His label, Blue Thumb, which was having great success with the Pointer Sisters, tried to market him as the black David Bowie, but with little success. Rock critic Robert Christgau grew to appreciate Sylvester, but he wrote devastating reviews of the singer's early albums. Of his cover of a Billie Holiday song, Christgau wrote, "And people complain about Diana Ross," who had recently played Holiday in *Lady Sings the Blues*. With 1973's *Bazaar*, Christgau thought the Hot Band seemed to be "going macho," while Sylvester was "emulating the gospel ladies he grew up with." After all three albums tanked, Sylvester moved to San Francisco-based Fantasy Records, where he began working with veteran Motown producer Harvey Fuqua. Although his first record with Fantasy, 1977's *Sylvester*, had a few disco cuts, Sylvester still yearned to make a concept album about twenties' and thirties' Harlem. Band members remember him bringing to their rehearsals so many dusty recordings by obscure black women blues singers that they took to calling them his "Magnetta Washington" songs.

It was only in 1978, after attending *Billboard* magazine's Disco Forum, that Sylvester, tired of obscurity, resolved to transform himself into a disco diva. "Here were all these people putting out disco, making lots of money and becoming famous and everything," he later recalled, "so we thought 'why not?' We'll put it out and nobody will like it and *we certainly won't like it*, but we'll do it." Sylvester told the press that he began studying the genre and that he used what he had learned about disco—from its sound to its attitude—the next time he went into a recording studio. This is likely true, but Sylvester's success also owes a lot to Patrick Cowley, who was working at City Disco as a lighting technician, but also knew how to play the synthesizer. With his synthesizer wooshes, Cowley transformed Sylvester's breakout disco

Sylvester wearing gardenias in the manner of Billie
Holiday

hit "You Make Me Feel (Mighty Real)" from a gospel-fueled ballad into
a dance-floor scorcher.

Powered by that track and "Dance (Disco Heat)," both of which
were club hits, his next LP, 1978's *Step II*, went gold. That album garnered Sylvester three awards, including Top Male Vocalist, at *Billboard*
magazine's Disco Forum V. Onstage Sylvester was such an explosive
performer that most other performers looked "positively dowdy" by
comparison. Not Bette Midler, mind you, with whom he sang a Bob
Seger song in the 1979 movie loosely based on Janis Joplin's life, *The
Rose*. In San Francisco, Sylvester was an undisputed star. Mayor Dianne
Feinstein proclaimed March 11, 1979, "Sylvester Day," and that night

he performed at the War Memorial Opera House, backed by a twenty-six-piece orchestra and four singers.

Despite his talent, Sylvester never achieved anything resembling the crossover success of the Village People. Although "Dance (Disco Heat)" scaled the disco charts, it barely squeaked into the pop Top 20. He toured America and Europe and he appeared on TV, but his exposure was limited, likely because of his unapologetic homosexuality and his queer-sounding falsetto. When guest host Joan Rivers of *The Tonight Show* asked him if he wasn't in fact a drag queen, he replied, "Joan, honey, I'm not a drag queen. I'm Sylvester!"

Sylvester may have been gay America's leading disco star, but he could not have been more out of step with the new gay macho. After all, his idea of going "butch" consisted of "fifteen bracelets and hoop earrings and a man's haircut," hardly what it meant in seventies' gay San Francisco. When it came to gender, Sylvester really did destroy reality, as surviving video clips prove. In the video for "Mighty Real" he's a shapeshifter, appearing in two very different kinds of drag and, for maximum provocation, as a swishy man. But however much Sylvester flouted gender rules, he was hyperaware of them. With his male friends he used to joke about what constituted butch. After several years living under the regime of macho, Sylvester felt less inclined to joke about it. He began complaining about all the guys who thought their mustaches, muscles, and boots made them better than a sissy. The very same macho men who so annoyed Sylvester were, of course, the ones who rushed the dance floor whenever speakers blared his music. To Sylvester's biographer, this demonstrates how effectively the singer bridged the gap between the clones and the queens. "Everybody felt like he was speaking to them," recalled one of Gamson's gay informants. No doubt they did. But one wonders what happened when Sylvester ventured outside his turf, where he was just another unreconstructed queen in the clone world of the Castro?

Sylvester was a reluctant disco star as well. However much he enjoyed dancing to disco, Sylvester was a diva, and as such was dubious

"YOU MAKE ME FEEL (MIGHTY REAL)"

FEW DISCO SONGS have achieved the mythic status of Sylvester's sixteen-minute romp "You Make Me Feel (Mighty Real)." Although the track barely registered on the radio and barely cracked the American Top 40, it has come to epitomize gay disco. An unmitigated blast of men-RG, "Mighty Real" did not announce its homosexuality through name-checking familiar signifiers of gayness. There's no pumping iron or hanging out at the Y, but neither is there any old-school Judy Garland angst either. And yet the record was unmistakably queer. For one, Sylvester refused to mouth the usual pop platitudes. He didn't sing, "You kiss me / And it feels real good," opting instead for the far clumsier "Then you kiss me there / And it feels real good," a line that begs the question, Where's "there"? Still, that's not the biggest giveaway that one's in queer territory. The song's very premise, that a lover's touch or kiss provokes a feeling of realness, suggests the singer's familiarity with sexual illegitimacy, not a subject that would make sense to most straight men. And then there's the matter of Sylvester's falsetto. There is nothing intrinsically strange about falsetto vocalizing, especially in African American culture where it traditionally carried no connotations of effeminacy. But Sylvester's falsetto had the sibilant lisp of a sissy and the defiant shrillness of a don't-mess-with-me queen. When he feigned the heights of orgasmic pleasure, he produced italicized yelps and gasps so feminine they rivaled Donna Summer's. With "Mighty Real" gay listeners did not have to create a strained against-the-grain reading of the song or embark upon some complicated retranslation in which a diva's heterosexual desire became their own.

"Mighty Real" was breakneck-speed disco, powered by a galloping bass, cheesy synthesizer whooshes, and the breathy fabulousness of

Sylvester's vocal. Discographers sometimes credit "Mighty Real" with modeling the sound that became hi-NRG disco.

But if "Mighty Real" was the future of gay disco, it looked backward, too. Right down to its appropriation of the parenthetical, "You Make Me Feel (Mighty Real)" exists in dialogical relationship to Aretha Franklin's "(You Make Me Feel Like) A Natural Woman." When Aretha sings of being rescued from life's "lost and found," she conjures up the history of black women's sexual nullification and its reversal in the Black Power sixties. When Sylvester sings of the "disco heat" that makes him feel both sexually desirable and desiring, he evokes those heady post-Stonewall years when gays at last were able to experience on a dance floor the feeling of sexual realness long taken for granted by others. With both records what one hears is nothing short of "freedom time."

about what he once dismissed as "backup singers'" music. Initially, "Mighty Real" was nothing more to him than a forgettable ditty with throwaway lyrics—a song he tossed off in a matter of minutes. Weeks passed before he even committed its words to paper, and longer still before he understood its value. Once he conquered the world of gay disco, he was already plotting his exit. By the spring of 1979, he was proclaiming that disco was merely a means to an end, and that he was looking forward to singing "songs that I *really* like." Both Sylvester and his label tried to break him out of the disco market, but his only real success was as a disco/dance artist, particularly within the subgenre of hi-NRG which became so popular in white gay discos. He scored many more club hits and worked with a number of artists including Patti LaBelle and Sarah Dash of Labelle, but in 1988 he died of AIDS at age forty-two.

Despite his uneasiness about disco, Sylvester has emerged as its poster boy, the artist who embodies the genre's queer, black underground. When Sandra Bernhard wanted to convey the giddy exhilaration of a gay disco, the music she used was Sylvester's "Mighty Real." Even in disco's heyday, Sylvester received a good deal more respect than most disco artists. His falsetto could be as gratingly brittle as the falsetto wail of the Bee Gees, but rock critics, some of whom remembered him fondly from his brief time in the Cockettes, found him a vastly more appealing character than the Brothers Gibb or, for that matter, the Village People. Rock critic Simon Frith regarded him "a sexual utopian who seems, miraculously, to have made it." Always on the lookout for a rebel, rock critics, even those hostile or indifferent to disco, gave Sylvester the benefit of the doubt.

Discographers have showered Sylvester with attention, making him the subject of a weekend-long 2004 academic conference, which is more scholarly attention than any other disco artist—Donna Summer included—has ever received. To Walter Hughes, Sylvester not only stood "at the origin of the disco tradition," he also embodied the genre's upending of gender norms and conventions. When Sylvester sings "Mighty Real," Hughes argued, the identity he enacts "will never be permanent, fixed, or naturalized." Having fixed on Sylvester as the emblematic figure of queer, underground disco, scholars have been slow to register the commercial calculation and downright resistance involved in Sylvester's disco turn. At least Morali and Belolo, the masterminds behind the Village People, *liked* disco.

Sylvester notwithstanding, the biggest stars of gay disco were heterosexual African American women. Even though disco was powered in part by gay liberation, its deejays and dancers shied away from politically explicit music. Tellingly, Motown artist Carl Bean's 1977 gay anthem "I Was Born This Way" fell flat with gay men. By contrast, optimistic tracks such as Sister Sledge's "We Are Family," McFadden and Whitehead's "Ain't No Stoppin' Us Now," and Dan Hartman's "Relight My Fire," which invoked the righteousness of love, equality, and community but without reference to any specific group, were massively popular in gay discos. The preponderance of heterosexually themed disco has led at least one exasperated gay critic, John Gill, to lambast disco for its "heterosexual hegemony." And he is not the only one. Why should songs that are sung by straights and "make no mention of anything gay" enjoy the status of gay anthems, asks J. D. Doyle, the producer of the monthly radio program *Queer Music Heritage.*

Disco's queer critics have a point. Even a record cited by some music writers as the queerest of all disco songs, Loose Joints' "Is It All Over My Face?" is not explicitly gay. Like Sylvester's "Mighty Real," this record, with its mention of the unspecified but tantalizing "It," lent itself to more than one reading. Did "It" refer to the look of being turned on or to the telltale signs of a certain kind of quickie gay sex? The classically trained cellist and disco enthusiast Arthur Russell, who wrote this track, intended it to be "a hymn to cruising," but once remixer Larry Levan eliminated the male vocalists in favor of the female vocalist, "Is It All Over My Face?" became less discernibly gay. In fact, one of Russell's collaborators felt the remix "made it into a boring straight narrative . . . when it should have been a gay anthem."

But perhaps gay men preferred the opaque because it allowed them to "gay up" straight songs, making them over into anthems of gay lust and empowerment. A record such as South Shore Commission's "Free Man" had nothing to do with gay liberation per se until gay dancers hijacked its chorus for that purpose. "Dancing Queen" by Abba and "More than a Woman," recorded by both the Bee Gees and Tavares, were among the many songs that developed a queer meaning on a gay dance floor. Disco culture, which favored the evasive over the confrontational, preferred the oblique to something more explicit. Although camp was in some respects a casualty of the disco seventies, it was alive in gay men's appropriation and reworking of disco lyrics.

Gay disco was also diva-centric, a tradition that stretches back to Broadway musicals and even further to the opera, for at least one fairly obvious reason: they're singing about men. Discologists could be right that gays' love of divas also stemmed from identification with their narratives of pain, adversity, and resilience. However, it's worth noting that many of the biggest gay disco hits, such as the Weather Girls' "It's Raining Men," Cher's "Take Me Home," or Diana Ross's "I'm Coming Out," were anything but downbeat. It may be that in relying upon a diva to ventriloquize their emotionality, gay men achieved a feeling of control and play otherwise unavailable. Born of necessity—the larger record industry was hardly any less homophobic than other sectors of the culture—this approach allowed them to make the dance floor theirs, while Patti Jo demanded that her boyfriend "make me believe in you," Diana Ross reveled in a love hangover, and Evelyn "Champagne" King celebrated the delicious "shame" her lover engenders.

AS THE SEVENTIES gave way to the eighties, disco began to fall out of favor with just about everyone but its core audience. For gay men, especially New Yorkers, the early 1980s represented the years of disco's greatest fabulousness. When the disco industry constricted in the eighties, it hurt the gay men who made up the ranks of the major labels' promotional staff, but it had surprisingly little effect on the wider gay disco scene. Gay men were dancing before "disco became *disco*," as Andrew Holleran put it, and they were still dancing after the media proclaimed it dead.

In fact, in the fall of 1980, Manhattan became home to a new gay disco, more extravagant than all the others, including the storied Flamingo. The Saint occupied what had been Bill Graham's legendary rock venue, the Fillmore East, and before that Loew's Commodore Theater. Opened by Bruce Mailman, who owned the nearby New St. Marks Baths, from which the disco got its name, the Saint's renovation cost a staggering $4.2 million. The club featured an elevated 4,800-square-foot oak dance floor with a planetarium dome some 76 feet in diameter that hung 38 feet above the floor. The dome's porous skin meant that it looked solid when it was lighted from within and translucent when lighted from behind. In the dome's opaque surface the designers created an image of a diver. "It was like a three-D hologram," recalls Ian

Levine, a regular, "and it looked like he was going up and then he'd go *shoom* down to the ground, and all the lights would just *voom* from every direction." An enormous tower of lights that included a planetarium projector created all manner of special effects, including the image of the diver. According to one of Mailman's partners, the idea behind the club's design "was that there would be no points of reference." The club's sound was equally awesome, powered by thirty-two amplifiers and five hundred speakers.

News of the Saint spread quickly and Mailman began selling memberships even before its opening. Within two weeks, all three thousand memberships were sold. The Saint was so exclusive that even money did not guarantee membership. "To get one," recalls Mel Cheren, "you had to make an appointment and appear in person, so that the less-than-fabulous could be weeded out." The less-than-fab included all women. When a member asked to bring Bette Midler there, Mailman made it clear that his club would stick to a strict policy of "no women members." Mailman wanted all the A-list gays with perfectly chiseled faces and bodies who had made Flamingo their home. And he succeeded. For those A-listers lucky enough to snag a membership, life was organized around Saturday night. To Ian Levine, it seemed as if the point of it all was to "fuck yourself up senseless with drugs" on Saturday night, and dance until noon the next day, when you would retire to the nearby bathhouse. The rest of the week—from Monday until Saturday night—was recovery time and involved a strict regimen of healthy, no-fat foods and strenuous workouts. "They completely worked on their bodies like a temple," Levine marveled, "just to fuck it up on the weekend."

In contrast to some other discos, sex at the Saint was not relegated to the toilets or the backroom, but took place casually in the club's balcony. Despite all its glitz and glamour, the Saint, like its predecessors, was virtually unknown to the general public. Intensely tribal and highly exclusive, the Saint featured music that was unrelentingly hi-NRG. Some found this style hi-tech and antiseptic, but to others it proved irresistible. "The apotheosis of the underground dance experience" was the way one of its deejays described the club. To Rodger McFarlane, who later became the executive director of the Gay Men's Health Crisis, the Saint was not only the "headiest experience" he ever had, it was also the place "where I learned to love my brothers." The Saint quickly became the "It" disco, so popular that it drove both 12 West and Flamingo out of business.

Like other high-end gay discos, the Saint carried no vestiges of the old apprehensiveness and precariousness that had so characterized pre-Stonewall gay nightlife. More than that, the Saint was designed to make its members feel special, in a class by themselves. It turns out that they were, tragically so. What no one knew in those first few months at the Saint was that the men burning up the dance floor were, in the words of Rodger McFarlane, "dancing on the edge of our graves." Within months of the club's opening, some members began to die of a strange new disease, which, as Randy Shilts later wrote, "seemed to snipe vengefully at the top of Manhattan's ziggurat of beauty." So many of the club's regulars were dying of what came to be called AIDS that in those first months it was known as the "Saint's disease." In 1985 city officials temporarily closed the club.

Across America, gay discos began closing. Even in Ann Arbor, Michigan, where the rate of HIV infection was not high, the Rubaiyat, where I had deejayed, shut its doors. Apparently worried that AIDS would discourage straights and gays alike from disco dancing, the owner shuttered it and reopened it as a restaurant. Things developed differently at the Saint, which, in a bid to bolster its declining membership rolls, began serving liquor and finally permitted heterosexuals to become members. With heterosexuals on its dance floor, the space, which had once been a surging mass of men-RG, seemed to shrink. Explaining why its dance floor now seemed unable to accommodate the numbers of old, one club employee observed that in contrast to heterosexuals, "gay men don't mind being that close together."

When AIDS began decimating communities of men who had

danced together and loved together, sometimes for more than a decade, it was horrifying and terrifying. As the casualties mounted, the loss and the grief were almost too much to bear for those at the epidemic's epicenter. Going to the Saint meant facing all "the holes in the floor," as one regular put it. Some, unwilling to relinquish the freedoms of the past decade, resisted what seemed on the face of it common-sense warnings of public health officials, doctors, and other gays. People who counseled less sex, monogamous sex, or no sex—and all were advocated—found themselves in the early years of the crisis attacked as homophobic, and, when gay themselves, erotophobic. The Toronto-based gay newspaper *The Body Politic*, claiming that gay men were more likely to die in a car wreck than from HIV, opposed any and all efforts to close the bathhouses. Defending sexual freedom in the face of a sexual epidemic caused considerable outrage, particularly among those gays, most notably Larry Kramer, for whom it seemed proof that gay men really did value fucking over life itself. What none of the scolding critiques of gay male behavior sufficiently confronted was the social significance of sex for men whose sexuality had been rigorously policed in the years before Stonewall. Was there denial? Of course, particularly in the music, which offered no explicit commentary on the epidemic. Instead, as Walter Hughes argues, disco's celebration of "the pleasurable discipline of self-exhaustion" continued through the mideighties "almost as if to conceal the threat, to envelop it in a double consciousness that made it impossible to ignore the risk of which one was constantly aware." This was certainly the case with Miquel Brown's 1983 disco hit "So Many Men, So Little Time," written by longtime disco enthusiast and Saint patron Ian Levine.

Even if AIDS had not made itself known with the ravaging of the Saint's A-list regulars, it would be impossible to write about disco without reference to the epidemic that over the years has killed so many dancers, deejays, producers, and singers. Sylvester, Arthur Russell, Mel Cheren, Larry Levan, Dan Hartman, Patrick Cowley, Ray Caviano, Kenn Friedman, and Jacques Morali are just a few of the better-known figures who lost their lives to AIDS. Not even the mistress of the irreverent, Sandra Bernhard, was able to evoke the promiscuous thrill of the disco seventies without also evoking its melancholy end in her show *Without You I'm Nothing*. When the Pet Shop Boys in 1993 covered the Village People's 1979 rousing track "Go West," they transformed it into an elegy for all the gay men whose pursuit of a "promised land" led instead to their "saying goodbye." And, of course, AIDS has meant that disco classics such as "Never Can Say Goodbye" were transformed into songs of mourning.

To some commentators, the arrival of AIDS was like a biblical plague that offered all the proof needed that homosexuality was a sin and an abomination against nature. But even those who have absolutely no truck with the idea of AIDS as God's punishment find it hard to resist the moralizing imperative that the disease seems to encourage. Pop music historian Craig Werner, for example, is politically progressive, and yet he has argued that although the sexual freedom of gay disco culture "ostensibly celebrated the gay community as a whole, there were obvious problems—including the early stages of the AIDS epidemic—for individuals seeking relationships combining pleasure with long-term spiritual growth." Ignoring the fact that neither monogamy nor sexual moderation offers any guarantee against HIV, Werner's formulation pits sexual desire against spiritual growth. To him "hedonistic pleasure and communal aspiration" were on a collision course in gay disco culture. And yet to many gay men, the hedonism of the dance floor was nothing if not a communal aspiration. Queer theorist Michael Warner argues that the "phenomenology of a sex club encounter is an experience of being connected not just to this person but to potentially limitless numbers of people," and that's why, he has argued, "it is important that it be with a stranger." Novelist Edmund White is less interested in trumpeting the political value of anonymous gay sex, but he has challenged the widespread assumption that " 'anonymous sex' is somehow unfeeling or mechanical or merely lust-driven." It's a misapprehension, he thinks, that grows out of the heterosexual presumption that "friendship and sex are ideally all joined in the same person." In gay life, he argues, "these drives can be separated out," or at least often were in the precious years between Stonewall and the onset of AIDS, what writer Brad Gooch calls the "golden age of promiscuity." Although not, apparently for everyone. Mel Cheren recalls looking around the floor at Flamingo and counting "32 bed partners who had since become friends." These were the men, after all, "who took each other to a place that no one's ever been," to quote Diana Ross's song "Touch Me in the Morning."

That said, it is obvious that the compartmentalizing of friendship and sex in the seventies did happen, and it troubled some gay men. For them, anything less than having it all—sexual passion *and* emotional connectedness—involved settling for the same "lousy deal" that gays had always had. This sentiment informed two bestselling gay novels of the seventies, the aforementioned *Faggots* and *Dancer from the Dance.* With the onset of AIDS, this view crystallized and hardened as some proponents of monogamy went so far as to argue that a lifestyle constructed around cruising and one-night stands reflected nothing so much as gay self-hate. Condemnations of this sort provoked the countercharge that the advocacy of monogamy involved a pathetic aping of heterosexual ideals that was itself the result of internalized homophobia. In the end the debate about anonymous public sex came down to the following question: "Do we want to be more like the majority culture or do we want to retain our cultural distinctiveness?" This question, precisely, was creating fissures within two other groups—African Americans and women. It is a recurring and possibly irresolvable question, and one that helps shape whether one believes the seventies represented a golden age or the nadir of recent gay history.

The disco years transformed gay life in ways that we are only now in a position to appreciate. Whereas just years before gay men had fled their hometowns to live anonymously in big cities, now they were enjoying lives of hyper-visibility in San Francisco, New York, Los Angeles, and certainly greater visibility in other large American cities such as Miami, Chicago, and Dallas. Macho drag, which read "normal" to straights and queer to gays, worked well for men who were newly visible and newly vulnerable as they claimed for themselves what was sometimes dangerous urban turf. The macho turn was also inseparable from gay liberation, which challenged the dominant culture's pathologizing of homosexuality, and from disco culture, where gym-built bodies ruled and sexual assertiveness reigned. Not all the ways in which gay male culture changed in these years were unambiguously positive. Effeminate men and gays who longed for more lasting intimacy felt marginalized, and so did many gays of color as queer nightlife grew more racially segmented. *Dancer from the Dance* captures some of the ambivalence occasioned by this brave new gay world—particularly the exhilaration of brotherly oneness and the elusiveness of sustained emotional connectedness.

Disco revisionists, anxious to counter the usual depictions of disco as narcissistic and politically retrograde, have been drawn to Holleran's depictions of erotic anarchy. Hundreds of men packed together on a steamy dance floor feeling the libidinal charge of oneness is the stuff of disco revisionism. Yes, they argue, there was glitz and greed and tackiness in *mainstream* disco, but here in the gay/queer underground one finds disco's authentic self in all its noirish and subversive glory. Even Tim Lawrence and Peter Shapiro, who have written such supple and discerning chronicles of seventies' dance music, find themselves adopting a two-tier schema of "good" gay disco versus "bad" mainstream disco. Throughout *Love Saves the Day*, Lawrence draws a misleadingly fastidious distinction between Mancuso's Loft, which he discusses with hushed reverence ("a site not of foreplay but of spiritual communion," embodying a "new form of socialism") and the commercial disco scene, which he considers "driven by faddish, hedonistic fashion."

Yet hedonism was inextricable from the sexual intensity that made clubs like Flamingo and the Saint such unforgettable sites of disco oneness. Nevertheless, the idealization of gay/queer disco and the corresponding disparagement of mainstream disco has proven almost irresistible to discographers. Peter Shapiro contends that disco's commercialization not only erased the genre's gay roots but also portended the country's conservative shift. Likewise, Lawrence has argued that as disco gained a mass following, it began to "lose its queer quality." As a result of the pernicious influence of the mass media and celebrity-centric version of disco promoted by glitzy Studio 54, the dance floor reverted to "patriarchal heterosexuality."

This narrative of declension, whereby gays are sidelined by the disco tsunami they helped make, has some truth to it. But it fails to reckon with the centrality of commercialism to gay disco and gay culture more broadly. After all, the gay entrepreneurs who helped to turn disco into an industry wanted to turn a profit. The owners of 12 West were looking to build an empire around their disco. Jacques Morali and Kenn Friedman of Casablanca wanted the Village People to cross over. And gay artists were hardly shy about their commercial ambitions. Even Arthur Russell didn't object to Larry Levan's more commercial remixing of "Is It All Over My Face?" In 1975, as disco was beginning to cross over, the *Advocate* celebrated the fact that "the masses have turned on to what's been getting us off for the last four years." Indeed, critic Vince Aletti maintains that New York's disco aficionados "didn't want to remain underground. They were ready to be recognized." Aletti has waxed lyrical about the "underground idea of unity" that he experienced in New York's gay discos, but in an article published shortly after the release of *Saturday Night Fever* he was unequivocally enthusiastic about disco's widespread appeal.

If disco revisionists celebrate gays as disco's true underground—transgressive to their core—they invariably disparage as conformist and politically regressive the new audience that Aletti was looking to win over. The "quintessential mainstream disco experience," maintains Peter Shapiro, "was hearing 'Y.M.C.A.' six times in one night at the Rainbow Room of the Holiday Inn in Cedar Rapids, Iowa, while doing line dances with a bunch of traveling salesmen." Shapiro may be right, but if he is, it likely isn't because he (or any other discographer) knows what happened in that Rainbow Room. The research on the "mainstream" disco experience simply has not been done, partly because of its diffuseness, but perhaps also because discographers are so intent upon legitimating disco through its roots in the gay/queer underground. The upshot is that we don't know what those disco dancers in Cedar Rapids danced to, or with whom they danced, or how they danced. We don't know if "patriarchal heterosexuality" typified their dance floors or if some of the same breaching of social barriers that occurred in 12 West happened there as well. As the movie that threw the disco phenomenon into overdrive, *Saturday Night Fever* is often criticized for commercializing disco. *Fever* explored a different community of disco dancers, but as the following chapter shows, it was a much more complicated movie than discographers have made it out to be.

Saturday Night Fever

THE LITTLE DISCO MOVIE

How come we never talk about what we're feeling when we're
dancing together?

— *Tony to Stephanie in* Saturday Night Fever

*S*aturday Night Fever tells an American story, but from its incep-
tion the movie was a transatlantic undertaking. Its cast of
characters included British writer Nik Cohn, Australian-born
London-based music impresario Robert Stigwood, and his clients the
Gibb brothers, who were born in Britain and raised in Australia. The
making of *Fever* illuminates the transnational character of disco music
and culture. Although disco seemed like an American export, the reality
was more complicated. From the beginning disco music flowed along a
global circuitry, with hits often moving from the so-called periphery of
the music industry to its putative center. Moreover, one of the reasons
that disco became such a global phenomenon is that the sixties' discotheque never went away in much of Europe. Writing in 1976, British
music journalist Dave Godin recalled "how surprised visiting Americans were five years ago when they discovered that Brits would actually spend their nights listening and dancing away to recorded music
without a live act to entertain them."

By 1976, when *Saturday Night Fever* was in development, disco
music and culture was hardly confined to the cosmopolitan cities of

North America and Western Europe. The enormity of the disco market should have made Hollywood jump at the opportunity to get a piece of the action. But even after Paramount signed onto *Fever*, the studio looked down its nose at "the little disco movie." It took others, particularly non-Americans who were aware of the music's global reach and potential, to interest Hollywood in making disco a cinematic event.

Most of all it took the unflagging enthusiasm of Robert Stigwood, the British music mogul. Stigwood, who in his prime looked rather like a modish Oscar Wilde, enjoyed only patchy success in the music business until January 1967, when the Beatles' manager Brian Epstein surprisingly made him a joint managing director of his company, NEMS Enterprises. Epstein's decision was perplexing, especially given the terms of the deal, which gave Stigwood controlling interest in NEMS in exchange for half a million pounds. Friends and colleagues knew that Epstein was weary of the music business and was feeling emotionally fragile, but why, they wondered, would he partner up with Stigwood, of all people? Nat Weiss, an American lawyer who represented Epstein and the Beatles, thought Stigwood was "a real carnival promoter . . . a man who had two cents [to his name] but could run up a bill." Others, however, noted the Australian's "fabulous style" and his knack for spotting talent.

Epstein and Stigwood were soon at loggerheads over the latter's signing of a wannabe-Beatles group called the Bee Gees, and his lavish American launch for them. As for the Beatles, when they eventually got wind of Epstein's plan to effectively sell them to Stigwood, they mutinied. "We told Brian," recalled Paul McCartney, "that if he sold us to Stigwood, we would only ever record out-of-tune versions of 'God Save the Queen.'" Not long after Epstein's death in August 1967, the Beatles got rid of Stigwood with a £25,000 buyout that allowed him to depart NEMS with Cream, the Bee Gees, and a few of his other acts.

Stigwood quickly established his own label, RSO (Robert Stigwood Organization) Records. He then moved into the lucrative fields of concert promotion and theatrical production. His shrewd moves toward diversification made him, in the words of fellow rock manager Simon Napier-Bell, "the first British music business tycoon." So did his talent for spotting trends, which was so finely tuned that it was "like he had a pop gyroscope implanted in him." Stigwood pioneered rock musicals, producing a version of the hippie musical *Hair* for the London stage in 1968, and three years later the musical *Jesus Christ Superstar*. Seeing the money to be made from bringing rock musicals to the screen, he produced the 1973 film version of *Superstar* as well as the Who's 1975 rock opera *Tommy*.

Stigwood understood the theatrical and cinematic possibilities of popular music, but there was another reason that he was so keen to make a disco movie. In contrast to most American music executives, who never went to discos and found themselves blindsided by the upstart genre, he was well acquainted with it. Certainly Stigwood's lifestyle positioned him to see that disco, which he had first encountered among the "smart set and the gay set," could become a worldwide phenomenon. Disco's global potential reportedly struck him in January 1976, when he traveled on the maiden voyage of the Concorde from Paris to Rio. According to his business associate Freddie Gershon, Stigwood had seen disco happen in Europe, and he now saw it migrating "down the social strata" in places like Rio, which was "rough and very exotic, and [where] the music never stopped."

Five months later, *New York* magazine published Nik Cohn's "Tribal Rites of the New Saturday Night." A novelist and chronicler of popular culture, Cohn had some vague awareness that the hip scene was shifting. "There'd been a hit record called 'The Hustle,'" recalled Cohn, and its success "suggested there was a club culture . . . that wasn't being written up." Cohn was living in New York City, and he began frequenting Manhattan discos. At one of them he met a remarkable African American dancer who would serve as his guide to New York's disco nightlife. Tu Sweet often competed in amateur disco dance contests. In a feature about him, Cohn raved that this "Black Nureyev" had developed an athletic yet subtle "choreography all his own, filled with loops and dips, double takes, sudden freezes, ebbs and flows." To Cohn, he resembled nothing so much as "a most extravagant string bean, manufactured out of black elastic."

It was during his time with Tu Sweet that Cohn discovered 2001 Odyssey. The dancer had heard about a happening Bay Ridge disco, but he did not know how to get there. Nonetheless, the two of them set out in the dead of winter in an unheated car to find the club. Although they managed to locate Bay Ridge, they quickly became lost in what Cohn described as an urban wasteland. "There were automotive chop shops and nothing else except storage spaces with attack dogs." Driving around Bay Ridge, one could see "abandoned car seats, hubcaps, tyres, scattered by the side of the road," but no people. Finally Cohn and Sweet spotted some guys standing outside a building in "skintight disco shirts." As they pulled up, one of them walked over, stuck his head in the car and threw up on Cohn's pants. Cohn knew very little about Bay Ridge culture, but even he understood that this was not a propitious beginning. Chuck Rusinak, whose father owned Odyssey, recalls that Cohn "looked out of place—squirrelly guy with an old trench coat."

Cohn spent a couple of weekends feeling out of place at Odyssey before churning out "Tribal Rites of the New Saturday Night." Cohn's chronicle of the Bay Ridge disco scene, which was loudly billed as a "true story," ended up the cover story of *New York* magazine's June 7, 1976, issue. It focused on one memorable character, Vincent, whose slick dance-floor moves made him Odyssey's disco king. But it was the club's "thoroughly male dominated" sexual dynamics that most intrigued the writer. "Girls just kind of waited around this dance floor for male pleasures," he recalled years later. "When the Hustle came on the boys didn't face the girls, they faced forward in a military phalanx." "Tribal Rites" emphasized the club's sexual dynamics, which seemed more martial than hedonistic, more homosocial than heterosexual, and completely unromantic. Vincent's only real pleasure comes from commanding his "troops" on the dance floor as he "set the formations, dictated every move." As they performed the Odyssey Walk, the club's version of the popular Hustle, they swept "back and forth, across the floor in perfect unity, fifty bodies made one, while Vincent barked out orders, crying One, and Two, and One and Tap." To Cohn, Bay Ridge's disco dancers seemed like nothing so much as "a small battalion uniformed in floral shirts and tight flared pants."

Curiously, Cohn never explained how this martial version of disco developed. Did disco music, which to Cohn's ears sounded like "the same automaton chugging," encourage macho authoritarianism, or would the same sexual politics have obtained in a Bay Ridge rock club? And what distinguished a *disco* Saturday night from, say, a rock 'n' roll Saturday night? Cohn's wispy essay provides no clues. Moreover, Cohn's portrait of disco king Vincent amounts to little more than a sketch. Vincent is a sinister bully who one minute pledges his undying devotion to his mother and in the next fantasizes he's "a killer and a star" capable of reducing his adversaries to a "chaotic heap of bodies, dead and dying."

Cohn's essay was not the most arresting or illuminating piece about the new disco scene. And it turns out it wasn't even true. Twenty years after his story's publication, Cohn claimed to have been so ignorant of journalistic ethics and so "out of his depth" in Bay Ridge that he filed a fraudulent story. He defended his journalistic sleight-of-hand by advancing two other (quite contradictory) explanations. On the one hand, Cohn said, his status as an outsider made it impossible for him to penetrate the alien culture of Bay Ridge. On the other hand, he suggested that his lack of truthfulness didn't much matter because the rituals he observed at Odyssey were virtually the same as those that had prevailed among sixties' British Mods, about whom Cohn presumably knew something. (Perhaps he was also drawing on the movie *A Clockwork Orange*, since there is a whiff of Alex and his "droogs" in Cohn's essay.) The sensibility of both cultures, he later argued, was "that the rest of your life may be shit, but come Friday night the weekend is here and you're king of the night." Cohn said that there were models for the characters in "Tribal Rites," a group he dubbed The Faces, but, he admitted, "they were West London mods, circa 1965."

Cohn even claimed that Vincent was "a complete invention." However, if Odyssey regulars are to be believed, Vincent may have been the closest that Cohn got to the truth. According to them, there was a "real Tony Manero," a blond guy by the name of Eugene Robinson, who worked in a supermarket and was the club's hotshot dancer. Odyssey's deejay Ralphie Dee remembers him coming into the disco "with agents and lawyers" right after *Fever*'s release. According to another employee, Robinson even tried to sue Paramount Pictures. "I never saw him in any movies," says Dee, "but you can't blame the guy. Nobody thought [*Fever*] would ever be a cultural phenomenon."

Robert Stigwood was so taken with Cohn's article that it's unlikely he would have cared had he known it was fictionalized. Cohn contends that the very same day that *New York* magazine hit the newsstands, Stigwood, keen to acquire the film rights to his story, was wooing him. Still riding high from the success of *Tommy*, Stigwood told Cohn that he had just signed a three-film deal with heartthrob John Travolta, and was looking for appropriate vehicles for the actor. Cohn has said that he was perplexed by Stigwood's interest in his story. "I had no instinct when I was writing the article," he said, "that it was going to be anything." Even after signing the deal with Stigwood, he claims he was unsure if the film would ever be made. If by some miracle the movie materialized, Cohn figured it would be a "little film." However, according to writer Anthony Haden-Guest, Cohn not only harbored hopes of a film deal, he was actively pursuing one. He was already working with Stigwood's assistant, Kevin McCormick, on another movie project. Cohn gave a prepublication copy of his article to McCormick, who then passed it onto his boss.

"I see a hundred-million-dollar movie here," was Stigwood's excited reaction. He moved quickly, in part because he had already signed up Travolta to star in the film version of the retro-fifties' play *Grease*, which was set to begin filming in the spring of 1978. He may have seen big bucks, but at first Stigwood offered Cohn only $10,000 for the option rights. After another producer entered the picture, Stigwood came back with an unusually generous offer that suggests just how anxious he was to nab the rights. To secure the deal he offered Cohn the opportunity to write the first draft of the screenplay. Accounts differ, but at the very least Cohn walked away with a guaranteed fee of $90,000 for the first draft. Another account claims that Stigwood ponied up $150,000 for Cohn's screenplay and gave in to the writer's demand (unheard of at the time) for a percentage of the soundtrack royalties.

Even though "Tribal Rites" was the slenderest of stories, and Stigwood had no financial backing for it, he was confident that the film would get made. The success of the Bee Gees' shimmering single "You Should Be Dancing," which was blaring out of car radios and disco speakers all across America during the summer of '76, doubtless deepened Stigwood's conviction that a film about disco could be commercially viable. That summer he began laying the groundwork for the movie, arranging for John Travolta to undergo a tutorial with disco dancer Deney Terrio, placing his assistant Kevin McCormick as its executive producer, and meeting with director John Avildsen, whom he hoped to hire. Given the budgetary constraints within which Stigwood and McCormick were operating, it's likely that director Avildsen signed onto *Fever* before knowing that the film he had just wrapped—a low-budget movie starring Sylvester Stallone—was going to become an enormous hit. However, by Thanksgiving, when *Rocky* opened, Avildsen must have figured that his bargaining position vis-à-vis Stigwood and company had considerably improved.

Avildsen demanded that screenwriter Norman Wexler be brought in to write the script, even though Stigwood had already hired Cohn. Avildsen and Wexler had worked together on the critically acclaimed *Joe*, a 1970 movie that centered on a bigoted hard hat played by Peter Boyle. In her *New Yorker* review of *Joe*, critic Pauline Kael singled out Wexler for his "hip humor" and his skill at creating "virulent low-life dialogue with a demented lift." Wexler went on to make a bigger name for himself as one of the two writers responsible for the screen adaptation of *Serpico*, starring Al Pacino. Wexler, who was diagnosed as manic-depressive, received some unwelcome publicity when he was arrested and jailed in 1972 after making threats against President Nixon while on a flight from New York to San Francisco. His next two projects—screen adaptations of *Mandingo* and *Drum*—both of which dealt with slavery, were fairly disastrous, although *Mandingo* was a box-office success. Wexler wanted to indict slavery and racism, but his lurid depictions of plantation life made the films strangely campy. Despite Wexler's recent stumbles, Stigwood acceded to Avildsen's wishes and hired him.

As it happened, Avildsen was right to think that Wexler knew how to write the screenplay. While Wexler had graduated from Harvard (on scholarship), he had grown up working-class in Detroit, and it was ethnic, working-class America that fascinated him. When it came time to write the *Fever* screenplay, Wexler reimagined Vincent, his family, his gang, and his disco. Like Vincent, Tony sells paint in a hardware store, is the leader of his pack, and is a girl magnet. He dresses like a "cuigine" (a cocky womanizer) in tight flares, huckapoo shirt, dance shoes, and gold chains—with his hair short and blow-dried to perfection. But Wexler ditched far more than he took from "Tribal Rites."

THE BEE GEES enter the story in the spring of 1977, when they were working and living together in the same French château where Elton John had recorded his 1972 record *Honky Château*. The group had decamped there to mix a live LP and to begin work on a new studio album. At this juncture, *Fever* was well under way, but the Bee Gees were not on board. "The Bee Gees weren't even involved in the movie in the beginning," recalls Travolta. "I was dancing to Stevie Wonder and Boz Scaggs." Accounts differ, but it's been said that Stigwood turned to the Bee Gees after Scaggs backed out of a deal allowing the filmmakers to use "Lowdown" from his disco-ish 1976 hit album *Silk Degrees*.

Whatever precipitated the shift, the Bee Gees had barely settled in when Stigwood called them to say he had bought the rights to Cohn's story and needed songs for the soundtrack. He urged them to think of the soundtrack as their new studio release, and the Bee Gees agreed to give Stigwood four tracks—"How Deep Is Your Love," "Stayin' Alive," "Night Fever," and "More than a Woman"—that they had already written and recorded as demos. Stigwood asked if they could make them more "discoey." A fifth song, "If I Can't Have You," was written for another Stigwood artist, Yvonne Elliman.

However, just weeks before filming was to start, Avildsen reportedly rejected out of hand a Bee Gees-dominated soundtrack. By this juncture, trouble was brewing between Avildsen and Travolta. The director wanted to soften Tony's character, and Travolta wanted to play him warts and all. Avildsen also complained about the actor's weight and dance-floor moves. "Travolta's too fat. He can't dance, he can't do this, he can't do that," became his refrain. Stigwood's loyalty, unsurprisingly, was to his client, even though the director had just been nominated for an Oscar for his direction of *Rocky*—an award he later won. Stigwood fired Avildsen and hired John Badham, a capable but little-known director whose track record was largely in television.

Badham had no problems with the Bee Gees, who were already making a name for themselves as disco artists. The group's turn to danceable R&B in 1975 did represent a striking turnabout from their usual style. Until 1975, it was the Beatles, not the Stylistics, whom the Bee Gees seemed determined to emulate. Their shameless efforts to duplicate the sounds and the success of the Beatles had led the critical establishment to dismiss the group as the "original ersatz," to use Dave Marsh's brilliant phrase. Although the brothers harmonized beautifully, they had none of the Fab Four's cheekiness or verbal cleverness. In contrast to the Beatles, their ballad-heavy music was often mawkish. Critic Jim Miller got it right in 1968 when he argued, "never before has a rock group so intensely and consciously set sail on a sea of syrup." Listening to early Bee Gees, one hears echoes of earlier influences—particularly singers who specialized in multipart harmonies such as Neil Sedaka, the Everly Brothers, and Gene Pitney. But whatever the critics thought, the public had an almost inexhaustible appetite for the Bee Gees' brand of gooey pop, and they scored hits with "New York Mining Disaster 1941," "Massachusetts," "I Started a Joke," and "How Can You Mend a Broken Heart?"

By the time disco was taking shape in the States in the early seventies, however, the Bee Gees were stuck in a hitless drought. They fought and disbanded. Robin had a British hit, but Barry and Maurice made records that went nowhere. The group's first album after they reconciled was 1974's *Mr. Natural.* The legendary Ahmet Ertegun of Atlantic Records had suggested to Stigwood that the group work with veteran R&B producer Arif Mardin, who tried nudging them in a slightly more R&B direction. *Mr. Natural* flopped, but the Bee Gees signed up to work again with Mardin. Their friend Eric Clapton, who had recorded his most recent LP, *461 Ocean Boulevard*, at Miami's Criteria Studio, encouraged them to try it out. And Mardin suggested they listen to American R&B artists such as Stevie Wonder, who was turning out wonderfully funky rock-inflected R&B. He may have also mentioned the popular Scottish R&B outfit the Average White Band, a group Mardin had recently produced, and which one critic has cited as a prototype for the Bee Gees' blue-eyed disco-soul.

Main Course, their 1975 album, showed that they had been listening very assiduously indeed. The ballad "Fanny (Be Tender with My Love)" featured a key change that keyboardist Blue Weaver, a recent addition to the Bee Gees' backup band, later admitted was "a complete rip-off" of the recent hit "She's Gone" by the American rock and R&B outfit Hall and Oates. The Bee Gees' stuttering "ji, ji, ji" that opens "Jive Talkin'" sounds like a steal from Bowie's own "ch, ch, ch, ch changes." Ripped off or not, these tracks and several others revealed that the brothers were quick studies. They received considerable help from the staff at Criteria Studios, which had worked with lots of R&B acts, including the Average White Band. The house engineer, Karl Richardson, was very familiar with Miami's burgeoning disco scene, and he proved indispensable to the group. The Bee Gees were also working with some new musicians, not just Weaver, who had come on board a bit earlier, but also drummer Dennis Bryon and guitarist Alan Kendall. Geoff Wesley was scoring the brass section and playing keyboards. But then almost everyone was playing some sort of keyboard instrument in the new band. Some Bee Gees tracks had as many as six synthesizers, one electric piano, one regular piano, and a Hammond organ.

Main Course sounded nothing like the Bee Gees of old, not the least because of the album's falsetto vocals. Producer Arif Mardin remembers suggesting to Barry Gibb that he try injecting more energy into the track "Nights on Broadway" by taking his vocal up an octave. Unable to do so, Gibb began singing falsetto, and discovered, he later said, "that this voice was hidden back there." Although the brothers have sometimes spoken derisively of the group's falsetto vocalizing, Barry Gibb has also defended it on the grounds that the falsetto has long been a feature of rock 'n' roll. "I think if you go back far enough," he told an interviewer in 1998, "the first rock 'n' roll record I ever heard was "Little Darlin'" by the Diamonds, and that was falsetto."

The Bee Gees' makeover was part of a broader shift within British rock toward the new sounds of American R&B. Certainly the sixties offered many examples of British rock musicians' love of American R&B and the blues. This time around, though, the Brits weren't resurrecting black music from earlier decades, but were pursuing the new wave of R&B. Ex-Animals lead singer Eric Burdon moved to the States to "find out about blackness," and teamed up with the R&B band War, with whom he scored a top 10 hit "Spill the Wine" in 1970. By 1974 there were so many British rockers trying to incorporate the sounds of James Brown, Stevie Wonder, and the glossy soul coming out of Philadelphia that it was almost a trend. Jeff Beck spoke of Sly Stone's influence on his music and collaborated with Stevie Wonder on the Motown artist's 1972 LP *Talking Book*. In 1973, Humble Pie moved further in the direction of R&B with the help of the R&B vocal trio the Blackberries, who in earlier incarnations had been Ike and Tina Turner's Ikettes and Ray Charles's Raelettes. In 1974 Brian Auger of the Oblivion Express wrote the falsetto-driven, disco-ish Top 10 R&B hit "Happiness Is Just Around the Bend" for the American R&B group the Main Ingredient. The Average White Band, which included one of Auger's former band mates, drummer Robbie McIntosh, became momentarily famous in 1975 when they scored a number one hit with their disco-funk single "Pick Up the Pieces." And Eric Clapton was using female backup singers, one of whom, Yvonne Elliman, would later record the Bee Gees' song "If I Can't Have You" for the *Fever* soundtrack.

David Bowie got swept up in the craze for new-style R&B, too. In May 1974 he told a British interviewer that he wanted "a *really* funky" sound with his band, and he raved about two African American musicians he had hired. One of them, guitarist Carlos Alomar, had played with James Brown, jazz musician Roy Ayers, and the Main Ingredient. Bowie's infatuation with Philly-style soul stemmed at least in part from his time hanging out in Manhattan's emerging disco scene. From 1973 through 1974 he frequented discos like the Loft along with Mick Jagger, Carlos Alomar, and the guitarist's friend, the then unknown Luther Vandross, who would go on to sing backup and arrange vocal parts for Bowie. *Young Americans*, the record that marked his Philly turn, included his hit "Fame."

Unlikely though it seems, "Fame" came about when John Lennon, who was in the recording studio with Bowie, started tinkering with the guitar line from "Shame Shame Shame," the recent disco hit by Shirley and Company. "Fame," and the rest of the music on *Young Americans*, lacked disco's soon-to-be-ubiquitous four-on-the-floor beat, but it featured that proto-disco sound, right down to the falsetto. In a clever deflection, Bowie, who never bothered to appear authentically anything, took to calling his new music "plastic soul." When James Brown turned around and plundered "Fame," which owed more than a little to him, for his new single, "Hot (I Need to Be Loved, Loved, Loved)," he reversed the usual flow of appropriation.

The Stones had long worked and toured with American blues and R&B artists, including Billy Preston, so it is not surprising that they were seduced by this new music. They considered working with the B.T. Express and Jagger even toyed with the idea of covering Shirley and Company's "Shame Shame Shame." Although the Stones never recorded that song, their 1976 LP *Black and Blue* included the disco-ish "Hot Stuff," on which Preston played. Such was the R&B/funk influence that one British critic declared that Preston and Wonder "are among the most significant musicians of our time, and have out-stripped white rockers."

With even the Stones experimenting with disco, the Bee Gees' musical about-face was, if anything, predictable. They had always taken the well-trodden path. In an August 1975 interview, Barry Gibb explained the group's new direction by saying that "the main vein at the moment is soul—R&B and disco—so we've moved into that area." Only, he added, it was their intention "to do it better, if we can." Some people apparently thought that they had. When ex-Cream bassist Jack Bruce first heard *Main Course*, he reportedly telegrammed the Gibb brothers, with whom he was friendly, to tell them about this terrific new black band he had heard.

Initially the album's single, "Jive Talkin'," was shipped to British radio stations bearing only a blank white label, some say because of the group's unpopularity. Whatever the reason, *Rolling Stone* reported that only 20 percent of the deejays who listened to the label-less cassette were able to identify "Jive Talkin'" as a Bee Gees track. Mardin had engineered such an overhaul of the group's sound that only the most discerning listener would have guessed this was the Bee Gees. Mick Jagger was stumped when he heard the as yet unreleased *Main Course* at one of Robert Stigwood's parties. "That's fucking dynamite," said Jagger. "Who's that? Some new group you've signed up?" Although the album wasn't shipped with blank labels, Atlantic Records was careful to not include pictures of the Gibb brothers on the cover. "Atlantic didn't want black people to know the group wasn't black," claimed Al

Transatlantic Hot Stuff: Mick Jagger does the Bump with Stones' (and Beatles') collaborator Billy Preston, as Keith Richards looks on

Coury, the head of RSO Records. In the past it had been black artists whose pictures were kept off album covers so that whites would buy them, but disco was altering the dynamics of crossover.

When the Bee Gees left Atlantic Records for Stigwood's RSO Records, they were no longer able to work with Mardin. Richardson, engineer at Criteria Studios, thought that he and his friend, keyboard-ist and arranger Albhy Galuten, might be able to take up some of the slack from Mardin's loss, and they did. 1976's *Children of the World* featured the infectious single "You Should Be Dancing," which topped the disco chart for seven weeks and proved a major hit on both the pop and R&B charts. Even with the Bee Gees' increasingly strident fal-setto, the album's highlights were pop confection of the highest order. With a staggering eighteen tracks of various kinds of drums, "Danc-ing" achieved what engineer Richardson called a "Wall of Percussion." *Children* worked well enough that when the Bee Gees headed off to the Château D'Hérouville in the spring of 1977, so did Richardson and Galuten.

Over the years the Bee Gees have given divergent accounts of how long it took them to write the five songs for Stigwood's soundtrack. Maurice Gibb once claimed that they wrote the entire musical score of *Saturday Night Fever* in several hours. "We spent as much time at the premiere party as we did in composing the music!" On another occasion, brother Robin said, "If we had known Travolta would make such a good job of it, we wouldn't have knocked out any old rubbish and sung in those stupid voices." But Barry Gibb has said that the group actually spent four to five weeks working on the songs that ended up on the soundtrack. Richardson, Galuten, and the Bee Gees spent even longer refining the sound with overdubs. They also experimented, quite successfully, with what may be the first ever drum loop. It was Galuten who came up with the idea after the Bee Gees' drummer was forced to return to England to look after his ailing father. Bryon had already completed the drumming on "Night Fever," but they were being pressured to finish the other tracks. After trying a primitive drum machine and quickly abandoning it, Galuten suggested that they take a particularly good bar from "Night Fever" and make a drum loop of it. He and Barry Gibb selected the bar, and then Richardson and Galuten went through a laborious effort to construct the loop, which they then used for "Stayin' Alive" and "More than a Woman." The group grew so attached to this loop, which sounded "insistent" without also sounding machinelike, that they recycled it on other tracks, including Barbra Streisand's "Woman in Love."

The cast and crew didn't hear the Bee Gees' songs for the *Fever* soundtrack until they were three weeks into what was turning out to be a very fraught film shoot. "We thought we'd fallen into a bucket of shit," recalls camera operator Tom Priestley. Faced with upward of fifteen thousand Travolta fans anxious to catch a glimpse of the filming going on in their streets, the crew resorted to posting fake call sheets and took to filming at 5:30 in the morning. Then there were the locals who tried to firebomb the Odyssey—their way of negotiating for a piece of the action—for jobs and payoffs. But when the cast and crew

THE BEE GEES' "STAYIN' ALIVE"

THE BEE GEES started out such adept pillagers of pop music that years before they even took a stab at disco, critics were dismissing them as rank imitators. Music critic Jim Miller wrote scathingly of the Bee Gees' preoccupation with "sounding pretty," but he was less bothered than most critics by their habit of plundering quality riffs and rhythms. In a lengthy review of a 1968 Bee Gees album, Miller cited American composer Ned Rorem, who had said of the Beatles, "Genius doesn't lie in not being derivative, but in making right choices instead of wrong ones." Miller thought it time that the Bee Gees' "capacity of occasionally making the right choices" be acknowledged.

Certainly, by the midseventies, the Bee Gees were making even more "right choices." Take the song "Night Fever." It turns out that the Bee Gees' keyboardist, Blue Weaver, had always wanted to play a disco version of the Percy Faith Orchestra's "Theme from *A Summer Place*." (Yes, this was the schlocky sixties' hit that British critic John Peel thought he had heard in Barry White's early disco hit "Love's Theme.") One day Barry Gibb overheard Weaver on a string synthesizer trying to make over the song. Gibb asked what he was playing, and when Weaver replied, "Summer Place," he corrected the keyboardist. It wasn't Percy Faith's tune, but rather a new song, which was already taking shape as Gibb sang a riff over it. "Night Fever" showcases the Bee Gees' well-honed talent for appropriation, but it also, oddly enough, proclaims it. Right there, in the middle of the song, are these curious lines, "If it's somethin' we can share / We can steal it." Maybe by the time of *Fever*, the Bee Gees were big enough to brag about their musical kleptomania.

"Stayin' Alive" is also brilliantly cobbled together from bits of other songs. Its guitar riff borrows from the clavinet riff that powered Stevie

Wonder's smash record "Superstition." The middle of the song contains a less recognizable appropriation from "I Feel the Earth Move" by Carole King. And the Spencer Davis Group's midsixties' record "Somebody Help Me" likely provided a crucial line for this song that was, in Barry Gibb's words, about "people crying out for help." But, lyrically, "Stayin' Alive" is mostly memorable for the lines "We can try to understand / The New York Times' effect on man." Presumably they were trying to fit in a reference to the city and convey something about upward mobility. (Maybe some-one told them about the New York Times on the doorstep of Stephanie's apartment building?) But these are such inelegant, head-shaking lines that for years critic Dave Marsh, eager for more class-conscious lyrics, misheard them as "We can try to understand / The New York Times don't make a man."

Nonetheless, "Stayin' Alive" has much to recommend it. Beatles pro-ducer George Martin noticed that the Bee Gees arranged their vocals to come in before the bar line, which kept the song surging ahead. And there was a tension, added Martin, between the song's "macho" lyrics and the group's "almost feminine voices."

Ah, feminine voices. There is no way to write about "Stayin' Alive" without addressing the Bee Gees' falsetto. When it came to falsetto vocalizing, the brothers departed from the usual script. R&B groups such as the Stylistics that employed the falsetto almost always made sure that it was counterbalanced by deeper, more resonant voices. Even Marvin Gaye's full-throttle falsetto on the disco hit "Got to Give It Up," boasted a male chorus hitting deeper notes. On 1975's Main Course, when he was just beginning to employ a falsetto, Barry Gibb had used it strategically, a phrase or so here or there. But by 1976 the Bee Gees were pioneering a different approach—a collective falsetto scream that, as critic Rob-ert Christgau observed, sounded rather too much like "mechanical mice

with an unnatural sense of rhythm." The Bee Gees had always specialized in close harmonizing. Perhaps this was the one piece of their former
sound that they refused to abandon, even if it did mean going against the
usual terms of falsetto engagement.

This proved to be an audacious move, and one that the group clung
to even after abandoning disco. Audiences in the sixties had accepted
falsetto—in the Beach Boys, the Four Seasons, the Miracles, the Righteous Brothers, and Crosby, Stills, Nash and Young, whose "Marrakesh
Express" comes close to rivaling the Bee Gees in shrillness. And no one
had raised a fuss about those falsetto "ooohs" of the Beatles channeling
Little Richard channeling Ruth Brown. But the 1970s witnessed a flood
of falsetto—not just so-called "sissy soul," but among rockers, including Mick Jagger and David Bowie. Perusing the criticism of the day, one
finds reviewers sometimes evaluating falsetto vocalists not just on the
timbre of the voice but on the persuasiveness of their masculinity. Falsettos were "virile" or, by contrast, "flaccid" and "wimpy."

of *Fever* heard the Bee Gees' music "it changed everything," recalls
Priestley. Karen Lynn Gorney, who played the female lead, thought
they were "monster hits" the first time she heard them. Suddenly the
cast and crew began to entertain the possibility that the film might
succeed.

Saturday Night Fever owed much of its success to the Bee Gees'
music, but this music had a much more conventionally pop structure
and sound than lots of the records, particularly the Eurodisco, being
played in many clubs. Likewise, the dance floor in *Fever* departed from
what one would have found in clubs. Discos did not use dry ice or any
other technique to envelop dancers in smoke, as screenwriter Wexler pointed out to an unyielding Badham. More importantly, Tony's

Skittishness about the falsetto was hardly limited to critics. When David Bowie released *Young Americans*, many Ziggy-period loyalists criticized him for "going disco." Critic Lester Bangs reported that some fans felt he had turned them into "veritable women" by going "black" in his music, perhaps because the new R&B was seen as too soft, almost neutered. If true, it's curious that Bowie's falsetto-powered disco, and not his cross-dressing, declarations of bisexuality, and gay-themed lyrics provoked this response. But then again "Young Americans" italicized the shift as Bowie sang lines such as "Just you and your idol singing falsetto about / Leather, leather everywhere, and not a myth left from the ghetto."

As for the Bee Gees and "Stayin' Alive," their falsetto is so manic and excessive one almost marvels at it. However, repeated listening— of which there has been much in my life—suggests that perhaps they would have been better off if they had stuck with their inspired plagiarizing and sung it like the Stylistics.

Bogarting, floor-clearing solos went against the communal, democratic ethos of disco. Maria Torres watched *Fever* with about fifteen other amateur disco dancers and remembers that they were all perplexed by the movie's representation of disco dancing, particularly Tony's moves, which didn't resemble what was happening in the clubs. This wouldn't have much mattered had it not been for the disco newcomers who tried to replicate Tony's freestyle moves, and in the process, she says, "really killed the ambience" at some clubs.

However, in other respects *Fever* has an aura of authenticity about it, much of it stemming from the fact that the producers filmed in Bay Ridge's own 2001 Odyssey. For another, the producers included club regulars rather than relying entirely upon Broadway dancers. Then there

At the disco New York New York, January 1979. L–R: music mogul Robert Stigwood, TV journalist David Frost, and three of the Brothers Gibb—Andy, Maurice, and Robin

was the look of Odyssey, which had the tarted-up but tired appearance of so many discos, most of which had been cheaply converted to take advantage of the disco boom. In its previous incarnation, Odyssey had been the 802 Club, a nightclub for couples. On any given weekend night the lineup there might include an Italian American singer such as Jerry Vail, a band, a comic, and a stripper or belly dancer. Owner Charles Rusinak also took risks, as when he hired transsexual entertainer Christine Jorgensen, a gambit that garnered "a lot of notoriety and publicity" for his club. By the early seventies, however, the 802 was fading, just like the comics and crooners who had once sustained all the cheesy nightclubs like it. When the owner's son, a college student who loved disco, suggested they switch formats, Rusinak did not hesitate. The club's disco transformation required very little work, just some Mylar for the walls and big, multicolored plastic balls that hung from the ceiling to "give the illusion that you were out in space." Although deejay Chuck Rusinak installed a stainless steel metal floor like one he had seen in a Montreal club called the Limelight, Odyssey (like most discos) had a saggy, worn look to it. Deejay Ralphie Dee recalls feeling "amazed" by the size of Odyssey, but concedes that it was something of a "dive." (The snazzy dance floor with its multicolored lights was installed for the movie.)

Dive or not, 2001 Odyssey was one of Brooklyn's two hottest discos, and people dressed up to go there. In those days, dressing up could be done cheaply. "Quiana shirts were, like, $10 a piece," recalls deejay Dee. "You'd buy one with a print, one solid." The guys "wore suits, not because they had to," he says, "but because they wanted to." For their part, the girls, who usually came in packs of three or four, often wore Lycra body suits under either a skirt or skintight jeans—and always with heels. Ed Cermanski, keyboardist with the disco group the Trammps, recalls Odyssey as very unlike Studio 54; it was all about "guys coming to meet girls." Odyssey was a singles club, but what sex there was, and there was plenty of hooking up, happened in cars, although perhaps not in the sort of car Tony and his gang used, and perhaps not much during the summer of 1977 when they were filming.

Norman Wexler's screenplay captured the Odyssey scene with few missteps. However, Wexler did have Tony and his crew riding around in a beat-up Chevy Impala. During filming the disco's regulars let the director know that they wouldn't be caught dead in such a junker. By that point, however, the production crew had acquired two identical, sad-sack Impalas and the film's budget was so negligible that they could not afford two more cars, much less the late-model cars needed.

Nor would many Odysseys regulars have been going at it in parked cars that summer. This was the summer that the serial killer Son of Sam transformed making out in cars into a high-risk activity. His attacks on young, often disco-going couples, sometimes as they were necking in parked cars, put the city, especially the outer boroughs where the killer roamed, on edge. In fact, that July, as they were filming, the killer struck a man and a woman who earlier that evening had been dancing at Jasmine's, another Bay Ridge disco. He shot the couple, killing the woman and seriously injuring the man, on the shoreline in Benson-hurst, an area from which one could see the lights of the Verrazano-Narrows Bridge—the bridge that looms so large in the lives of Tony and his gang.

But Wexler got much more than he missed. His script had every-thing that "Tribal Rites" lacked: full-bodied characters, narrative ten-sion, and a much-needed plot. Wexler transformed Cohn's sullen sociopath, Vincent, into a character by turns cocky and vulnerable. At night, Tony Manero commands the dance floor and the women who swoon over him. Even though his job in the neighborhood hardware and paint store is unglamorous, he at least feels competent there. However, inside the modest Bay Ridge house where he lives with his family—his God-fearing mom, unemployed construction-worker dad, grandmother, and little sister—Tony feels beleaguered. His father belittles him and his mother compares him frequently and unfavor-ably to his older brother, Frank Jr., a Catholic priest. Theirs is a claus-trophobic world that clings to tradition—spaghetti dinners, Catholic orthodoxies, and straight-up male dominance. Tony is clearly the black sheep of the family, but he doesn't come on like a big-time rebel. He wears a crucifix around his neck, works a nine-to-five job, and judges women "nice girls or cunts."

When he is not working or being hassled by his parents, Tony hangs out with his buddies, cruising the streets of Bay Ridge, dancing at Odys-sey, screwing girls in the back seat of his friend Bobby's car, and top-ping it off with some daredevil gymnastics on the Verrazano-Narrows Bridge. At the movie's start, Tony's idea of the future extends no fur-ther than "tonight." When he ponders his prospects, he thinks about flashy threads, girls, and dance contests. He may live within minutes of Manhattan, but it's another world, completely outside his orbit.

However, events conspire to upend Tony's aim-low approach to life. First, his brother returns home to break the news that he's quitting the priesthood. His announcement devastates their parents, but it enables Tony to see himself as something other than the perennial screw-up within his family. Then Tony spies a new girl on Odyssey's dance floor. Stephanie is not your typical Bay Ridge girl eager to fawn all over Tony. Like Tony, she knows her way around a dance floor. But Stephanie is a career girl, and she yearns to extend her accomplishments to other sites of power. She still lives in Bay Ridge, but she is Manhattan-bound. Stephanie is not immune to Tony's good looks and dance-floor prowess, but she finds him small-minded, and his prospects depressingly dead-end. When Tony, anxious for a romantic involvement, suggests that they partner for an upcoming Odyssey dance contest, she agrees, but without any apparent enthusiasm. "You're a cliché," she tells him early on. "You're nowhere on your way to no place." Tony finds Stephanie stuck-up and affected, and he dislikes feeling that she holds all the cards. But she appeals to that part of Tony that daydreams about another kind of life. Over time he begins to see Bay Ridge through her eyes, as a close-minded place filled with people going nowhere. For her part, Stephanie is forced to admit that Tony, who has criticized the falseness of her Manhattan life as so much "bullshit," has a point.

The movie climaxes on the night of the dance contest. When the judges award the top prize to Tony and Stephanie, who danced far more romantically than athletically, rather than to the more deserving Puerto Rican couple, Stephanie is thrilled, but Tony is outraged at the undisguised racism of their selection. He hands over the $500 award to their stunned rivals and drags Stephanie out of the club, vowing never to return. The evening deteriorates further when Tony forces himself on Stephanie, who escapes by kneeing him in the groin. Tony and his gang regroup, accompanied by Annette, the young woman Tony has rejected. As she has sex with two of his buddies in the back seat of the car, in what seems like a gang bang, Tony simmers. Events spiral further out of control when his hapless friend Bobby, desperate that he has no recourse but to marry the girl he's knocked up and hurt that no one understands his pain, ventures onto a girder of the Verrazano-Narrows Bridge. Unlike the others, Bobby is not a veteran of bridge acrobatics, and, with a crazed look, he fools around recklessly while the others watch in horror. As Tony tries to rescue him, Bobby falls from the bridge in what Tony later characterizes to the police as "taking your life without taking your life." After walking away from his gang, Tony rides the subway until dawn. Contrite and humble, he shows up at Stephanie's building. Although she's reluctant to let this "known rapist" inside, she finally relents, and for the first time they talk seriously about his future. He resolves to follow her into Manhattan—not, it would seem, as her lover (he knows he has blown her trust), but as her friend. Curiously for a movie marketed as a celebration of disco, *Saturday Night Fever* suggests that getting ahead (as opposed to "stayin' alive") requires abandoning disco.

SATURDAY NIGHT FEVER was released a little more than a week before Christmas 1977, a mere eighteen months after Cohn's article appeared. Production moved briskly for a number of reasons, not least because the specter of disco crashing hung over the movie, especially at Paramount, whose executives expected little from *Fever*. Even the Bay Ridge locals were dubious about the movie's commercial prospects. "It looked like such a low-budget film," recalls Alex Marchak, a club regular and movie extra. *Fever* was low-budget, so much so that its biggest expenditure besides actors' fees was its $15,000 multicolored lighted dance floor. But with Travolta's knockout performance, the riveting dance sequences, and irresistible music, there was no stopping it. A runaway hit, *Fever* ended up grossing more than $100 million in the U.S. and $300 million worldwide.

Within weeks, the *Fever* soundtrack, which was released before the movie, had pulled off the unlikely feat of dislodging Fleetwood Mac's *Rumors* from its position atop the charts where it had been perched, seemingly impregnable, for half a year. For well over six months, from December 1977 through June 1978, the Bee Gees ruled the charts. "How Deep Is Your Love" went gold in mid-December 1977, "Stayin' Alive" reached platinum in March, as did "Night Fever" in May. That same month, Yvonne Elliman's Gibb-penned song "If I Can't Have You" reached gold, and Andy Gibb's "Shadow Dancing," which his brothers wrote and sang on, went platinum. Moreover, the Bee Gees-dominated *Fever* soundtrack ruled both the pop *and* the R&B charts. Eventually it sold thirty million copies worldwide, making it the biggest-selling album of all time, a record it held until Michael Jackson's *Thriller* surpassed it. Ultimately, the Bee Gees' success rivaled that of the other British group whose fame they had always envied.

At the time of its release, critics were mixed about both the movie and its music. *Variety* called *Fever* "vulgar . . . the worst in teenage exploitation rehash." Gene Siskel, by contrast, raved about it. Few critics were immune to the pleasure of watching the kinesthetic Travolta. Film scholar Marsha Kinder thought Travolta and his "stylized sensuality" exploded on the screen, but she faulted the movie's depiction of working-class Italian American Brooklyn as cartoonish. The *New York Times*'s reviewer Janet Maslin found Travolta "deft and vibrant."

On December 12, 1977, John Travolta, with a friend, navigates his way past the press to attend a party to celebrate *Fever* at New York's Tavern on the Green

For the most part, Maslin thought that the music and movie moved "with a real spring in its step." Robert Christgau called the Bee Gees' songs "pop music at a new peak of irresistible silliness." Even Stephen Holden, who usually panned the Bee Gees, maintained that not since the time of Glenn Miller had the "dreamy and aggressive impulses of pop . . . meshed so seamlessly to stamp an era." Vince Aletti gushed over the soundtrack, particularly the Bee Gees' contributions. He noted the Gibb brothers' "peculiarly piercing falsettos," but he judged the "elusiveness and terse delivery" of their pop-disco "thrilling and perfect." Aletti believed the soundtrack, which he called a "rich selection of American disco," might banish the "formula commercialization"—the copycat product—that had plagued the first disco boom. Although he doubted that the *Fever* phenomenon would "put an end to DISCO SUCKS buttons," he was upbeat, arguing that its commercial success had already given disco a newfound respectability.

However, within about a year of *Fever*'s release, opinion about the movie and its music began to shift to a more skeptical register. Vince Aletti's hopes that *Fever*'s success would bring about a critical turnaround for disco were misplaced. It was punk—low-grossing and nose-thumbing—that was snagging all the critical acclaim and respect. And, of course, Bruce Springsteen, whose sincerity, substantiality, and heroizing of the working class stood in such sharp contrast to disco's synthetic fluff. Critic Andrew Kopkind did not attack the movie or its soundtrack, but observed that the Bee Gees, in crossing disco over and moving it out of its "subcultural ghettoes," had done for disco what Elvis Presley had done for black rhythm and blues. He also advanced a related argument that would prove influential. *Fever*, he argued, "made disco safe for white, straight, male, young, and middle-class America."

Decades later, when disco finally began to get some respect from scholars and critics, *Fever* remained beyond redemption, blamed for transforming what had been an urbane, underground, illicit activity into an industry geared to the biggest and blandest demographic. *Fever* wasn't real disco, it was argued; it was blow-dried, processed, polyester disco. And even though the Bee Gees had been making disco before many others, they were mere disco arrivistes who peddled "whitened-up blown-dry hetero-pop." According to this narrative, everything that had been transgressive about disco was lost as legions of uptight, white-bread suburbanites decked out in *Fever* drag began crowding into newly opened plastic discos. With its lockstep, line-dancing tough guys and the sexually submissive young women who worshipped them, *Fever* "repatriated" disco to hetero America, and in the process ended up killing what was original and thrilling about it.

Saturday Night Fever mainstreamed disco, but it was hardly the exercise in racist, patriarchal propaganda that subsequent revisionist analyses have taken it for. The movie lured all kinds of people, including sexist hyper-macho guys, onto the dance floor, but if anything the movie seeks to expand, not constrict, the parameters of masculinity. *Fever* reveals the city's postindustrial turn, shifting sexual landscape, and upended gender and race rules. Beginning with the famous opener of Tony Manero, paint can in hand, looking sharp as he struts down the street to the strains of "Stayin' Alive," the movie establishes that Bay Ridge, which looks like it's caught in a fifties' time warp, has not escaped the changes of the sixties and their aftershocks.

Even without "Stayin' Alive" blaring away, the audience can tell by the way Tony "uses his walk" that he's a "woman's man." However, Tony isn't quite like the ladies' man of old. Although he is meant to be rushing back to the hardware store with a desperately needed can of paint, Tony takes the opportunity to shop. In a close-up, Tony stops in front of a shoe store and lifts his foot so that his shoe is parallel to—and almost the mirror image of—the one in the shop window. Satisfied that he is decked out in the latest, coolest footwear, he saunters down the street. He makes a couple of passes at women and grabs two slices of pizza that he hoovers down Brooklyn style as a sandwich, before his head is turned by a shirt in the window of a men's clothing store. It's expensive—$27.50—but Tony gives the owner five dollars on layaway. *Saturday Night Fever* may be the first Hollywood movie to feature in its opening scene a male protagonist consumed with consuming. It signals that Tony, macho and heterosexual though he is, is not old-school.

Saturday Night Fever returns to the theme of masculinity in scene after scene—a preoccupation that may reflect Stigwood's fascination with disco's challenge to normative masculinity. According to Freddie Gershon, Stigwood was fascinated by the way that disco was challenging conventional norms, as men who five years earlier would have worried about stepping onto a dance floor lest they appear "effete" were now turning into veritable "peacocks." Certainly the film drives home the point that Tony's masculinity, in contrast to that of his father, is highly self-conscious and self-consciously performative. First and foremost, Tony dances. And unlike his father, who seems indifferent to his own appearance, Tony is fastidious, covering up his shirt with an oversized napkin at dinner, and complaining when his hair gets mussed. When we first see Tony return home from work, he ducks upstairs to his bedroom where he prepares for that night's conquests. Dressed only in his briefs, he primps in front of the mirror, daydreaming of the dance floor, and moving to the music in his head. These were not the only scenes of a scantily clad Travolta, and director Badham remembers them bringing the movie "all kinds of hassle" from those made uncomfortable by the display of so much male flesh.

Finally, although Tony is contemptuous of women who desire him ("you make it with some of these chicks and they think you have to dance with them"), he is noticeably hesitant around the upwardly mobile Stephanie. He asks if he can walk her home, and backs down when she insists on walking home alone. When she brags about the actors and musicians she has met through her job at a public relations firm, Tony turns shy and bumbling, feigning knowledge of Manhattan nightspots and the celebrities who frequent them. Most tellingly, he is the one who makes himself vulnerable when he blurts out, "How come we never talk about what we're feeling when we're dancing together?" Tony is the one who insists, as a girl might, that they talk about their "feelings."

The anxiety and insecurity that characterizes Tony's relationship with Stephanie is by no means aberrational. It courses through the film as a whole, driving it as surely as the Bee Gees' soundtrack punctuated by those "helpless cries." There's Tony's anxiety about his future, which kicks in about midway, largely as a result of his connection to the aspirational Stephanie. Early in the movie, Tony's boss rejects his request for an advance so he can buy that layaway shirt. When he lectures Tony on the prudence of saving for the future, Tony replies, "Fuck the future." The owner's riposte—"You can't fuck the future. The future fucks you"—means nothing to Tony at this juncture in the film. Later, after he's been fired and returns to the hardware store only to find his boss eager to have him back, Tony rethinks his relationship to the future. As his boss reels off how long his other employees have been with him, Tony newly understands his older coworkers' sadness and sense of defeat. His boss means to impress upon Tony what a good, secure job he has, but the nineteen-year-old sees his future in these resigned men who have long since given up on themselves.

Tony's family life has its share of anxiety and dread, too. Tony's father, Frank Sr., has been out of work for seven months, and it has taken its toll not only on the family's finances but also on his relations within the family. Cooped up in the house, his father is a menacing presence. During one particularly memorable scene around the dining-room table, Frank Sr. smacks Tony's head, which elicits Tony's famous complaint about his dad hitting his hair. Tony's remark, and the family's punch-fest that elicited it, provides some comic relief in an otherwise bleak scene in which the mother threatens to get a job, and upbraids and even slaps Frank Sr. for hitting Tony. Frank Sr., looking at her in wounded disbelief, quickly makes the connection between his being out of work and her disrespect of him. "You never hit me before or talked back to me," he mutters. And there's the anxiety and shame caused by Frank Jr.'s abrupt departure from the priesthood, for reasons that remain murky. The question of why he quit the priesthood hangs over the family. Frank Jr. figures that his parents' dread of talking about his disenchantment with the Church stems from their fears that he might have tired of celibacy.

But the Maneros hardly have a corner on anxiety in this movie. The boys in Tony's gang don't often talk about the larger world, but they are not oblivious to the uncertainties that postindustrial New York holds for their kind. For the most part, though, they focus on the Puerto Ricans and gays infringing on their turf. Odyssey is their refuge from worry, although it, too, can serve as a reminder that the neighborhood is changing, that outsiders are now a visible presence. When the club's deejay, played by Monti ("Get Dancin'") Rock III, segues into a salsa-inflected disco record, Tony storms off the floor and confronts him for playing "spic music."

Tony and his gang are also caught in the flux caused by feminism and the sexual revolution. Cohn's story treated Odyssey as if it were a backwater immune to any force but its own backwardness, but Wexler's script emphasizes the instability caused by the culture's changing gender and sexual conventions. Throughout the film, we see the characters brought up short when old-fashioned social conventions are tossed aside. Annette, who is desperate to snag Tony, can't believe that Tony won't light her cigarette, even when he's lighting his own. Tony himself is surprised when Stephanie stops him from walking her home. And he is appalled when Annette, condoms in hand, has the temerity to tell him they can now make it. For that matter, Frank Sr. is incredulous when Tony starts clearing the dining-room table after supper. "Girls do that," he sneers.

But what girls do and don't do is up for grabs, even at the Odyssey, where at least some of the girls are refusing to wait patiently for guys to ask them to dance. Annette (Donna Pescow), Connie (Fran Drescher), and Doreen (Denny Dillon) all pursue Tony. Annette is pathetic and Doreen ridiculous, but Connie is a live wire, with nothing of the doormat about her. "Are you as good in bed as on the dance floor?" she asks him. Critics of the movie have emphasized the patriarchal quality of the club, and Tony and his crew do behave as if they own the place. There is plenty of misogyny in this movie, which features Stephanie's near-rape and a gang bang of the very wasted Annette. The men often take women's sexual forwardness as permission to be sexually callous, even abusive. It's a culture in which men are trying to hold onto masculine privilege, but losing it steadily. Although it takes a while for the film to make its position known, and though it never turns preachy, *Fever* does have a message: preordained social hierarchies, be they rooted in race or gender, are toxic. As if to underscore the unlivability of the old order, there is Bobby, dead at the bottom of the Narrows, survived by his pregnant girlfriend; the gang rape and the attempted rape; and Tony's squabbling parents.

Tony is such a compelling character, at turns vulnerable and hard, naïve and street-smart, that it's not until the final scene in Stephanie's fashionable, brick-exposed Manhattan apartment that the gender reversal at the heart of the movie becomes obvious. By this point, we have already seen that Stephanie's desk job affords her perks that Tony's job lacks. She can take time off and enjoy long lunches with clients, and one imagines her employers encouraged her to take those college classes at the New School. In the movie's final minutes we see the disparity in their circumstances. Shattered by the events of the previous night, Tony tells Stephanie he's had it with his life—his gang, the neighborhood, everything—and, like her, he's moving to Manhattan. When she asks him how he plans to support himself, he shrugs and says he'll find something to do. She presses the issue, and he begins to get testy. "What did you do? You couldn't do nothing," he says defensively. "I could type when I came in," she says.

A decade earlier, before the worst effects of deindustrialization were felt, blue-collar, union jobs were plentiful, and a white working-class man like Tony would have had more marketable skills, or a father who could get him a good-paying job. By the midseventies, with the ascendance of the service sector, the Frank Sr.'s of New York were getting laid off, and the job market favored the Stephanies of the city—young, ambitious working-class women with pink-collar skills and dreams of making it. But, as Tony reveals during their early morning talk, his desire to move into Manhattan isn't rooted simply in the materialistic. "Maybe we could be friends," he asks Stephanie tentatively. "Could you stand being friends with a girl?" she asks sarcastically. *Saturday Night Fever* isn't *My Fair Lady* with Tony as Eliza Doolittle and Stephanie as Professor Higgins, but it suggests a shift in power relations between the sexes, one not predicated upon the old sexual bargain. By the movie's end Tony Manero, while not yet a sensitive New Age male, has renounced his tough-guy, trash-talking misogynist past.

In contrast to most scholars and critics, feminist cultural critic Barbara Ehrenreich grasped that the movie was intended as a critique of masculinity. What she objected to was the way in which *Fever*, and a host of Hollywood movies, represented working-class masculinity as stunted and regressive. Like *Bloodbrothers* and *The Wanderers*, *Fever*, argued Ehrenreich, locates traditional masculinity in the working class, and then depicts it as a dead end. Hollywood rendered machismo lower-class and then banished it, she wrote, "like undershirts, Vitalis, and plastic furniture coverings." Ehrenreich's analysis of *Fever* works up to a point. After all, judging by Tony's dad and his gang, Bay Ridge is an entrenched bastion of male chauvinism. But the movie doesn't idealize Manhattan as the promised land. Tony sees through Stephanie's bullshit—her disparagement of her roots, scrapping of her accent, and romanticizing of all things "refined."

The film also emphasizes the compromises that Stephanie has had to make to get there. As the film shows, and as nonjudgmentally as possible, no one knows better than Stephanie the price she's had to pay to keep her job at a Manhattan PR firm. It's not just that she apparently had to put out sexually to maintain a position at the bottom of the business; she is still having to put up with her one-time boyfriend, a supercilious record producer who helped her learn the ropes at work. We meet him only briefly as Tony helps Stephanie move into the apartment the producer is passing on to her, and he is smug and censorious. He criticizes her reading choices and admonishes her for saying "super," a word that marks her as unhip. All along the film has viewed much of Stephanie's relentless effort at self-improvement skeptically, but this scene underscores powerfully and poignantly that the terminal trendiness of swinging Manhattan can be as parochial and close-minded in its way as the customs and conventions of Bay Ridge.

Fever takes on racism as well as misogyny. Although *Fever* featured few people of color, its message was unambiguously antiracist. Indeed, Nile Rodgers of the disco group Chic considered *Fever* sheer "genius" for the way it dealt with racism. African American Rodgers grew up in New York and was familiar with the Tony Maneros of the city. "We used to call these Italian guys 'hitters,'" he says. But *Fever* shows us a hitter being transformed into "an open-minded, broad-thinking human being." Yes, Tony has "contradictions in his world and in his life," but, Rodgers notes, "through music and dance he's transformed."

Saturday Night Fever offers no systematic critique of homophobia, and it makes no effort to dislodge conventional notions of male homosexuality. The movie's only identifiably gay characters—the two "fags" the Faces hassle, are predictably swishy, not macho. Indeed, on its surface *Fever* operates in a heterosexual register. The dancing and the sex are undeniably heterosexual, aggressively so. And yet homosexuality is never entirely sidelined or silenced. Whether it's in the casual homophobia that courses through the movie—the confrontation with the gays or the description of bisexual David Bowie as a "fag" or a "half-fag"—the pop cultural references, or the subplots that circle suggestively around it, homosexuality keeps rising to the surface, just as was happening in the larger culture. *Fever* treats it glancingly and usually obliquely, but it is hardly negligible. Take the scene of nearly naked Tony strutting down his hallway, shouting "Attica, Attica." We know Tony worships Al Pacino (a *Serpico* poster hangs in his bedroom) and is thrilled that one of the Odyssey girls likened him to Pacino. But why is Tony imitating Pacino playing Sonny, the gay bank robber in *Dog Day Afternoon*, and not one of Pacino's many straight characters? And if the filmmakers really wanted to heterosexualize disco, why did they choose that well-known gay celebrity Monti Rock III as the movie's deejay? Although Rock plays the role straight, his assistant for much of the movie is a surprisingly butch-looking woman.

Even more intriguing is the filming of Travolta, who twice appears in nothing but his snug black briefs. Hollywood was famously skittish about male nudity. Confronted with male flesh, most filmmakers settled for artful suggestiveness. But *Fever* offered a lot more than a glimpse of Travolta's body. The camera celebrates his body, moving so slowly and lovingly over it that these scenes could almost be mistaken for soft-core gay porn. The first scene of the almost nude Tony contained such a homoerotic charge that the movie's production designer decided to "cool things off" by hanging a poster of *Charlie's Angels* star Farrah Fawcett by Tony's mirror. Lest the audience think there was something too queer about the scene, the camera briefly focuses on the voluptuous Fawcett.

Then there's anxious Bobby in ludicrous platform shoes. Bobby is outwardly heterosexual, but he isn't like the other Faces. He is wimpy. Even his friends call him a "punk," a term often applied to gays. In fact, he looks more than a little like the "fags" on the playground. And though we know Bobby has had sex with at least one woman because he's gotten her pregnant, unlike the others he seems uninterested in women. Although Bobby provides the car that serves as the gang's mobile bedroom, he never takes a girl there himself. Instead, Bobby worships Tony. He hangs on his every word, and lends him his prized car in the hope that Tony might actually call and talk with him about his predicament. Just before he falls from the bridge, the heartbroken Bobby looks at Tony, who is trying to help him to safety, and, sobbing, says, "You said you'd call me, Tony. You never called me." Bobby, who here sounds more like a brokenhearted girlfriend than a pal, is not presented as gay, but his love of Tony, like Plato's for Jim in *Rebel Without a Cause*, is barely disguised.

Perhaps *Fever*'s flirtation with homosexuality reveals the difficulty of achieving a thoroughly heterosexual makeover for disco. Maybe disco couldn't be entirely shorn of its roots in the gay underground. After all, Stigwood was the movie's presiding force and the filmmakers drew on at least two people who were figures in the world of gay disco—Monti Rock III and Lester Wilson, the black choreographer who taught Travolta his dance routines. Quite possibly other crew and cast members were part of this scene as well. In any case, disco's disregard of convention seems to have rubbed off on the cast and crew, whose last bit of filming made explicit the movie's subtextual queerness. According to journalist Sam Kashner, at the end of the shoot the cast and crew decided to wind up some visiting executives from Paramount, who everyone knew to be less than keen on *Fever*. "Travolta and members of the crew filmed a mock wedding at the disco—for laughs—with John dressed as the bride and one of the grips appearing as the groom," Kashner writes.

Although homosexuality works subtextually rather than explicitly in *Fever*, even at the time the film generated anxious responses. There were the complaints about male nudity, and there were those who thought it transformed Travolta from the dim but adorable Vinnie Barbarino of *Welcome Back, Kotter* into the narcissistic, effeminized "Revolta." Tony may have danced athletically and behaved like a pussy hound, but some found him suspiciously soft. Tellingly, in "Pretty Boy," singer-songwriter Randy Newman made a poseur who "looks just like the dancing wop" the target of a street tough's rage. For some, the Bee Gees' falsetto squeal consolidated their apprehension that *Fever*, like disco more broadly, was suspiciously unmasculine. It didn't matter that the Bee Gees were hairy-chested guys who sang hetero love songs; their falsetto front and gooey sentimentalism feminized them.

Critic Stephen Holden was no homophobe, but to him the success of the Bee Gees (and disco more broadly) unpleasantly revealed how much had changed since the 1960s. The Beatles, Holden argued, embodied a "non-bureaucratic world of hippie individualists," whereas the Bee Gees' "global village would be a junior high of androgynous, conformist goody-goodies: a world with no violence or sex, only puppy love, and every toy in creation." The Bee Gees left themselves open to the charge that their music was cloyingly sentimental (that glee-club vocalizing!) and that they were sexless and their androgyny bland, but Holden's far-ranging indictment is about a deeper change—the waning influence of artistically driven rock, with its renegade, rolling-stone masculinity, and the reassertion of consumable, girl-friendly pop.

Fever became a lightning rod for people across the political spectrum, but the movie offers us a richer portrait of the disco seventies than critics and discographers have granted it. Its soundtrack may be all pop sheen, but the film is gritty and surprisingly bleak as it chronicles the prejudices, anxieties, and all-around unsettledness of those times. Disco is often criticized for being either apolitical or politically regressive, and yet, as Nile Rodgers argues, *Fever* was full of "politically, socially relevant stuff," as much so as punk. To this day *Fever* is remembered for its fashions—the platforms, polyester, and blow-dried hair—John Travolta's moves, and the Bee Gees' signature falsetto, all of which operate as a kind of shorthand for the ludicrousness of the 1970s. What happened? How did its critique of racism and sexism, and its subtle queering of Tony's Bay Ridge world, come to be so forgotten?

6

One Nation under a Thump?

DISCO AND ITS DISCONTENTS

Disco's so *straight.* It's something Nixon would approve of.
                                    —*KOME radio DJ Dennis Erectus*

Even before the release of *Saturday Night Fever* in late 1977, disco was a proven cash cow, generating substantial profits for both record labels and club owners. Just before the movie's release, a leading executive at the disco-dominated Casablanca Records boasted that the revenue from the disco economy was so great—$4 billion, he bragged—that it was surpassed only by that of organized sports. Adding to disco's trendiness was the opening in April 1977 of Studio 54, Steve Rubell and Ian Schrager's glam palace of a disco. Studio 54, which was reportedly meant to be a white, Hollywood version of the fashionable black Manhattan disco Leviticus, was located on 54th Street near Eighth Avenue in a distinctly unchic part of the city. Originally built as an opera house, the theater had last been used by CBS as a TV studio. With its celebrity regulars, 5,400-square-foot dance floor, and state-of-the-art sound and lighting systems, 54 became the country's happening disco. And that was its selling point. For non-celebrities, just getting inside the place was meant to be its own reward. For that matter, even celebrities were sometimes left cooling their heels on the sidewalk.

Mel Cheren, whose West End Records office was located next door to the midtown Manhattan club, claims that Rubell was so anxious that the club exude an aura of exclusivity that he and his infamous doorman Marc Benecke often kept mobs of desperate people waiting outside even when only a few hundred partied on the inside. "They wouldn't let anyone in," recalls one regular. "And then they'd say, 'You, all right *you*, in the back, you can go in.'" At 54's first anniversary bash, a throng of desperate revelers "hell bent" on getting in shattered a plate-glass window. Rubell finally relented and allowed several hundred people in, but in no time the crowd outside was just as thick as before.

54 became such a celebrity magnet (Mick and Bianca Jagger, Truman Capote, Calvin Klein, and Andy Warhol were just a few of the regulars) that it was forever turning up in the style sections and gossip columns of glossies and newspapers. *Village Voice* gossip columnist Michael Musto joked that 54 "was not just the be all and end all, it was the be-there-or-end-it-all." Rubell even branded the club by selling Studio 54 Jeans—on the market only long enough to generate a buzz. Rubell's interest in "fabulosity" (and handsome young men) rather than in wealth made for an eclectic dance floor. "This is the nightclub of the future," gushed Truman Capote. "It's very democratic. Boys with boys, girls with girls, girls with boys, blacks with whites, capitalists and Marxists, Chinese and everything else—all one big mix!" However, anyone expecting one big mix quickly discovered that 54 was anything but democratic. Drama critic Frank Rich recalled going there as a "peon," and feeling that "the real action, not all of it appetizing, was somewhere in the dark periphery, out of view—and kept there, to make you feel left out."

Within two weeks of 54's debut, another glitzy midtown disco, New York New York, opened. Its owners imagined that they would be competing with 54 for the same clientele, but they quickly had to ratchet down their expectations and adopt a relatively casual door policy. Writer Vita Miezitis characterized its clientele as a mostly straight, interracial crowd, but from so many foreign countries that at times the disco "resembled the United Nations Plaza around lunchtime." A year later, in June of 1978, the $2 million Xenon, billed as the "ultimate

197

ONE NATION UNDER A THUMP?

discotheque," opened its doors. Even though few of its flashing lights worked, the paint on its walls hadn't yet dried, and its liquor license had not yet been issued, its owners went ahead with its launch. Xenon boasted a $100,000 sound system and a $90,000 spaceship designed by Douglas Trumbull, an Oscar nominee for his special effects on *Close Encounters of the Third Kind*. However, when the "Big Moment" arrived at 1 a.m. and the 8,300-pound "mothership" descended from the ceiling, it barely registered because so few of its lights were working. Xenon also offered "playpen areas," where people could lounge on huge couches or play electronic games or work the pinball machines. Despite its disastrous opening night, the club managed to win back much of the glitterati. Manhattan also boasted quite a few important black-oriented clubs, including the aforementioned Leviticus and Le Martinique. Disco's influence was so great that it also spilled out into the streets of New York. Reminiscing about the summer of 1977, filmmaker Spike Lee says it was the moment that "disco hit, and all over the city there were block parties and D.J.'s hooking up turntables to street lamps."

But as popular as disco already was, *Saturday Night Fever* threw it into manic overdrive. A year after its release, there were one thousand discos operating in New York's metropolitan area. No longer a primarily urban experience, disco laid claim to suburban America. Journalist Andrew Kopkind's assertion that all of Nassau County (on Long Island) was now "lining up for disco lessons" was only a touch hyperbolic. It wasn't just the greater New York metropolitan area that fell under the sway of disco. Critic Stephen Holden, never a disco fan, observed that *Fever* "seduced Middle America back onto the dance floor." Writing in *Rolling Stone*, he maintained that "Travolta showed that it was okay for a guy to shake his booty on Saturday night." Soon it wasn't unusual to see that one's local Arthur Murray Dance Studio was now the Arthur Murray Disco Dance School.

By the end of 1978, a year after *Fever*'s release, there were somewhere between fifteen and twenty thousand discos operating in America, double the number just three years earlier. The vast majority of them were makeshift spaces with mediocre sound systems, especially those in hotels and motels. All across America, supermarkets were converted into discos, and bars and clubs that had featured rock bands were being made over into discos, leaving fewer and fewer performing venues for rock musicians. Disco's partisans have argued that this shift benefited audiences that were now spared listening to "the local rock band play third-rate versions of old hits."

Yet as plenty of musicians maintained at the time, disco's takeover of club space had more to do with economics. The business magazine *Forbes* revealed that discos, if done right, yielded enviably fat profit margins. By way of example the magazine cited one Washington D.C. club, Tramp's Discotheque. Marketed as a user-friendly disco ("the disco for people who don't like discos"), it boasted an average annual gross of just under $1,000,000, of which $400,000 was sheer profit. Its owner Michael O'Harro quickly branded his disco, selling Tramps cigarettes, T-shirts, and necklaces, and began plotting to make another of his ventures "the McDonald's of disco."

As it turned out, O'Harro did not become the Ray Kroc of discotheques, but he did write a $75 manual, *Disco Concepts*, which was meant to initiate the inexperienced disco entrepreneur into the finer points of setup and management. There was enough interest in this subject that he managed to sell a thousand copies of his work. It was club owner Thomas Jayson who came the closest to franchising his disco into the McDonald's of the glitterball world. Jayson's goal was to bring disco to the American shopping center, and by 1978 his first disco, 2001 Club, had spawned ten franchises. A year later he claimed to have two hundred applications on file for the six new franchises he would be granting. Jayson made sure that his franchises were "geared like IBM" in that "once you're involved with us, we'll provide you with the specifications right down to the macramé wall hangings." If he reached his goal of one hundred and fifty franchises by the early eighties, noted journalist Jesse Kornbluth, Jayson's company would effectively be the "entertainment equivalent of a fast-food restaurant."

Even radio deejays, at first none too keen to play tracks whose popularity stemmed from club play, began to cater to the disco market. Before the emergence of all-disco stations, disco enthusiasts had relied on R&B stations, but there were always quite a few disco tracks that these stations never played. Recognizing an opening, the ownership of New York City's WKTU, a mellow rock station with negligible ratings, switched gears in the summer of 1978 and converted to disco. Within nine months, WKTU was the city's number one station. (Madonna seems to reference the station in *Confessions on a Dance Floor*, albeit with the rejiggered call letters of KUNT.) Its turnabout had a catalytic effect on radio. "When I was in New York," recalled Ed Boyd, then the vice president and general manager of Los Angeles' KIIS–FM, "you literally couldn't go anywhere without hearing WKTU." Within no time KIIS became an all-disco-all-the-time station, and many others such as Boston's WBOS and Detroit's WLBS followed suit. By 1979, there were two hundred all-disco radio stations nationwide, including two twenty-four-hour stations in Los Angeles. Even people seemingly out of range of disco radio stations developed disco fever. Investigators of the 1978 mass suicide at Jonestown in Guyana discovered that the children had written down the names of recent disco hits in their notebooks.

Television ramped up its disco programming as well. *American Bandstand, Soul Train*, and *Solid Gold* had always included disco, but by 1979 rock stalwarts *Don Kirshner's Rock Concert* and *Midnight Special* were featuring it. TV hosts Dinah Shore and Merv Griffin often invited disco artists onto their shows. And in 1979, Griffin became the producer of *Dance Fever*, whose host, Deney Terrio, had helped coach Travolta in the early stages of his preparation for *Saturday Night Fever*. Even *Sesame Street* went disco when the Muppets, with permission from the Bee Gees, put out *Sesame Street Fever*.

Kevin McCormick, *Fever*'s executive producer, isn't exaggerating when he says that the movie "institutionalized disco." And not just in America. Disco was never simply an American phenomenon, and *Fever* extended and deepened disco's global reach. In Brazil, where disco had thrived for some years, *Saturday Night Fever* was such a blockbuster that its extended run kept the highly praised Brazilian film *Doramundo* by director João Batista de Andrade, which had been slated for showing at the same chain of theaters, off the screen. After *Fever*'s release there, Brazilians began to use neologistic verbs and nouns from the root "Travolta"—*travoltar* (to travolt), *travoltice* (travoltage)—to describe the condition of disco fever.

England, France, and Germany gained even more discos. France alone had 3,500 clubs. England's vibrant disco market was served for the most part by working-class ballroom chains owned by Mecca and Top Rank. Disco became big business early on in Japan, too. Although most discos were small-scale, the country did have a couple of 3,000-plus-capacity venues. Disco was so popular there that in 1974 forty deejays traveled to America to study disco culture. Even after being taught the American style of no-talk deejaying, the Japanese deejays continued to talk along to the music, apparently a necessity given the shyness of their audience. Although a journalist with Tass, the official Soviet press agency, wrote disparagingly of New York discos as "havens of decadence and loneliness," the Voice of America claimed that its hour-long, Saturday-night disco program was proving unexpectedly popular. In the fall of 1978 the newspaper of the Young Communist League reported that discos were "growing like mushrooms" in the USSR despite the shortage of equipment and American records, which were black-market items. As a consequence, Russian clubs tended to rely on live bands playing disco hits. One of the most popular clubs drew 40,000 customers during a four-month period. Discos were a feature of many African countries, too. About South African clubs, David Robert Lewis recalls they were mostly "cocaine dens with disco balls and mirror ceilings."

By 1979 some of the biggest disco producers were Italian, French, German, and British, although many disco performers continued to be American. One exception was Abba, the Swedish group whose victory with "Waterloo" in the Eurovision Song Contest marked the beginning of the group's massive popularity in Europe. By the time "Dancing

Queen" topped the American pop chart in April 1977, Abba had already conquered the rest of the world's dance floors. As critics (and fans) Simon Frith and Peter Langley noted, Abba may have had a flair for the sartorially uncool, with the women dressed in "authentically fiery caftans four sizes too big" and the guys in "poncy zippered one-piece suits in nylon," but they got over through their supernal grooves.

Disco was such a juggernaut that it really did seem as if it might succeed in shoving rock 'n' roll to the margins of American popular music. Anticipating massive demand for disco records in the winter of 1978, Columbia Records went so far as to invest millions in a new manufacturing complex. Although most record company executives and staffers despaired at the thought that disco might supplant rock, they also suspected it might be their best way to survive the recession that was hammering the record industry. Columbia's hunch seemed reasonable. After all, at the twenty-first annual Grammy Awards in February 1979, disco performers, with the Bee Gees in the lead, snagged eight of the fourteen awards. That same month, nine of the country's Top 10 records were disco. By the summer of 1979, disco records constituted a potent 40 percent of all chart activity. By 1979, Chic alone had racked up $50 million in sales for its label Atlantic Records. Everyone from Broadway belter Ethel Merman and folkies Janis Ian and Joan Baez to the Percy Faith Orchestra was churning out disco records. When Rod Stewart scored the biggest hit of his whole career with "Do Ya Think I'm Sexy?," Ray Caviano, who had his own custom disco label at Warner Bros. Records, bragged to a reporter that he and his staff were going to "disco-ize" the company's entire, mostly disco-hating staff.

The press was full of stories about the disco tsunami flooding America. In April, that bastion of capitalism, *Fortune* magazine, ran a disco feature, and six weeks later the socialist newspaper *In These Times* published a critical forum on the meaning of disco. To rock critic Tom Smucker, who contributed to the *ITT* forum, the left-wing paper's hand-wringing about it was amusing. "It's a little late to debate the merits of disco music," Smucker observed, "as if it were something

Twenty-year-old Caroline Kennedy in the arms
of actor/model Sterling St. Jacques at Studio 54,
December 1977

that we could think out of existence if we want to." *Rolling Stone* was never enamored of disco, but that April it caved in to advertisers and put out a special disco issue with a number of surprisingly evenhanded articles. That same month, *Newsweek* summed up the feeling of many with the title of its cover story: "The Disco Takeover."

Disco's conquest of America occurred against a backdrop of diminished possibilities. No longer able to count on cheap and bountiful energy, plentiful jobs, and military invincibility, Americans approached the indignities of the late Carter years with a kind of angry bewilderment. How had the American Goliath managed to lose South Vietnam to a rag-tag army of Communist peasants? Did the ignominious fall of Saigon to the Viet Cong in 1975 mean that the 58,159 American soldiers who had died there did so in vain? Losing the war was bad enough, but America's standing throughout the world seemed at a nadir. How had we come to be at the mercy of the OPEC oil producers' cartel, whose price hike during the summer of 1979 caused severe shortages and long lines at gas pumps? How had America come to be outmaneuvered by nations whose economic success we had nurtured and subsidized? How was it, asked many, including musicians Bruce Springsteen and John Mellencamp, that in the Northeast and the Midwest so many factories—from textile and steel mills to automobile plants—now stood shuttered? And what would happen to all the laid-off factory workers whose mornings were now so empty that they had given in to the temptation of watching morning TV and consuming two breakfasts rather than hunting for jobs? Was slinging burgers at McDonald's the best they could hope for once the unemployment checks came to an end?

Americans, accustomed to supersized cars and toasty houses even in subzero temperatures, found themselves reduced to driving tinny, subcompact cars and to bundling up in sweaters and down jackets to survive the 55-degree temperature of their own homes. To make matters worse, Jimmy Carter seemed to blame Americans, not his own micromanaging governance, for the "crisis of confidence" afflicting the country. In what became known as his "malaise speech," President Carter upheld the values of "hard work, strong families, close-knit communities and our faith in God," and lectured that "too many of us now tend to worship self-indulgence and consumption." And then, on November 4, 1979, the U.S. experienced the final humiliation. When Americans learned that Iranian militants had seized the American embassy in Tehran and had taken approximately seventy Americans hostage, it seemed to be incontrovertible proof of the country's loss of prestige. "I'm as mad as hell and I'm not going to take this anymore," as the character Howard Beale in the 1976 film *Network* put it, described the exasperation of many Americans.

Certainly, for some Americans, the feeling of beleaguerment was compounded by the ways in which feminism, gay rights, and civil rights were changing the national landscape. By the midseventies a sizable number of onetime liberals, dubbed neoconservatives, were joining with longtime conservatives to mobilize "Middle America" against abortion rights, affirmative action, school busing, sex education, the Equal Rights Amendment, welfare, and "criminal-coddling" civil liberties. In 1977 singer Anita Bryant, best-known as the sunny spokeswoman for Florida's citrus industry, became the public face of another organization: Save Our Children, which sought to repeal the recently enacted human rights (read, gay rights) ordinance in Dade County, Florida. Bryant was an ally of veteran conservative Phyllis Schlafly, whose Stop the ERA movement managed to erode the groundswell of support for the Equal Rights Amendment. Alan Bakke, a white applicant who was twice rejected by the medical school at the University of California, Davis, persuaded the Supreme Court (and many Americans) that he had been victimized by affirmative action policies that condoned "reverse discrimination" against whites. The Supreme Court also upheld the Hyde Amendment, which banned federal funding of abortion, and many states passed legislation restricting women's right to abortion. Supporters of gay rights could celebrate the November 7, 1978, defeat of Proposition 6 in California, which would have banned gays and lesbians (and supporters of gay rights) from working in California's public schools. However, the assassination three weeks later of San Francisco city supervisor Harvey Milk, among America's first elected gay officials, and his ally mayor George Moscone, and the subsequent verdict of manslaughter for the man who killed them, seemed a depressing indicator of the entrenched resistance to gay rights.

To some, disco's "takeover" was further evidence of the corrosive influence of permissiveness. Historian Gillian Frank points out that by 1979 the evangelical right was going after disco. He notes that in her June 1979 newsletter to her supporters, Anita Bryant warned that homosexuals were "producing [disco] records with double meanings . . . then having 'straight' children buy them." Earlier that spring TV evangelist Jerry Falwell appeared before 8,000 flag-waving supporters to denounce "President Carter, homosexuality, pornography, television comedies, abortion, discos, divorce and sex education." Indeed there was such a groundswell of anti-disco sentiment that a vice president of ABC Radio emphasized to advertisers that, in contrast to disco, contemporary rock stations offered wholesome family fare. It should hardly come as a surprise that Ronald Reagan, who promised a "new morning in America"—that is, a return to traditional values—defeated Carter in a lopsided victory in November 1979.

In the end, the people who organized most effectively against disco were not religious conservatives but deejays employed by classic rock or album-oriented rock (AOR) stations. Perhaps the first rock deejay to make discophobia a part of his shtick was Dennis Erectus of KOME in San Jose, California. According to *Village Voice* writer Frank Rose, Erectus would put on a record, "play a couple of bars, then crank the turntable up to 78 rpm (especially effective on 'Macho Man'), grind the needle into the vinyl, play sound effects of toilets flushing or people throwing up, and follow it up with the searing guitar chords of Van Halen or AC/DC." His audience couldn't get enough, and other deejays began to copy him. Two deejays at Detroit's WWWW formed an anti-disco vigilante group called Disco Ducks Klan. They were laying plans, which were later aborted, to wear white sheets onstage at a disco that was switching back to rock. At their next job, at AOR station WRIF, they performed on-the-air "electrocutions" of disco lovers whose names and phone numbers had been sent to the station by members of the "intelligence" arm of DREAD (Detroit Rockers Engaged in the Abolition of Disco).

The best-known purveyor of discophobia was twenty-four-year-old Chicago deejay Steve Dahl. Like many others in the AOR world, Dahl believed that disco was creating a "cultural void," the prescription for which was his kind of classic rock. Dahl's opposition to disco hardened when WDAI, the AOR station where he worked, fired him several days before Christmas when it switched to a disco format.

Dahl was soon deejaying at another rock station, WLUP. If Dahl's listeners didn't know that disco was associated with gay male culture, they did after listening to the deejay, who always made a point of lisping the word disco. But Dahl went further than on-air rants and parodies of Stewart's "Do Ya Think I'm Sexy?" Like the WRIF deejays, he organized an "antidisco army . . . dedicated to the eradication of the dreaded musical disease known as DISCO." When Van McCoy, of the hit single "The Hustle," died, Dahl memorialized him by destroying his record on air. He also encouraged one hundred contest winners for a Village People concert to "write DISCO SUCKS on marshmallows and . . . to throw [them] at the group." When a disco in Linwood, Indiana, a suburb of Chicago, ditched disco for rock, Dahl called on his "army" to join him in celebrating. Almost 5,000 of his troops showed up, and the police were called in to keep the peace. Dahl staged a number of such events and by late June he had amassed such a force—reportedly 10,000 card-carrying members—that WLUP had to hire two people to handle the mail.

These incidents were a prelude to Dahl's main event. Disco Demolition Night was held on July 12, 1979, at Comiskey Park, during a double-header between the Chicago White Sox and the Detroit Tigers. Dahl planned the event with the son of the White Sox's owner, Mike Veeck, who was the sports broadcaster at WLUP. For weeks leading up to the game Dahl had promised that fans showing up with disco records in hand would be admitted for a mere 98 cents. That evening over 70,000 people descended upon the ballpark. So many Dahlites showed up with records—reportedly 10,000—that regular ticket-holders were denied admission. Not all Dahlites could be accommodated either. The stadium could hold only 55,000, leaving the rest on their own. According to news stories, upwards of 15,000 people milled around outside the stadium and another 10,000 were stuck in traffic on the Dan Ryan Expressway as they tried to get to the park. Even before the intermission between the games, pandemonium threatened. By the fifth inning the field was strewn with records that Dahlites threw, often at the players. During the intermission, Dahl, who was decked out in military fatigues and an army helmet, drove onto the field in a military-style jeep. Next to him sat a blond bombshell, a model named Lorelei who often appeared in WLUP's ads. Then an enormous crate filled with what was said to be 50,000 disco records was placed in center field. After setting off fireworks in front of the crate, Dahl detonated a fireworks bomb inside the crate that sent shards of the exploded records flying. As if on cue, 7,000 fans rushed onto the field, starting bonfires, tossing firecrackers into the stands, and destroying turf, batting cages, the pitcher's mound, and, of course, records. "Oh, God almighty, I've never seen anything so dangerous in my life," recalls Rusty Staub, who played for the Detroit Tigers. The rioting lasted about half an hour until the arrival of the tactical force of the Chicago Police Department. At the end of it, thirty-nine people were arrested, several were injured, and the White Sox had to forfeit the game.

The day after Disco Demolition, Chicago's dedicated disco station, WLUP, played Donna Summer's "Last Dance" for twenty-four hours straight, then pronounced disco dead and started spinning Top 40 rock songs. Interviewed by *Rolling Stone* after the riot, Dahl revealed that he had been talking with radio programming consultant Lee Abrams about a "national hook-up . . . to blow up disco records all over the country."

By the summer of 1979 the sentiment against disco was so strong in certain segments of the American population that rock radio's paroxysms of discophobia were believed to be spontaneous outbursts. But as *Village Voice* reporter Frank Rose revealed in late 1979, radio's crusade against disco turned out to have been orchestrated. Spearheading the campaign were two radio consultants, the aforementioned Lee Abrams and his colleague Kent Burkhart, who had a hunch that the backlash against disco might prove as lucrative as disco itself. Between them, the two men had accounts with forty-odd country, Top 40, and disco stations and fifty-three AOR stations, including Dahl's WLUP. That summer they advised disco stations to switch formats, and they counseled all their clients to campaign against disco. It wasn't just the increased listenership generated by the discophobia of Dahl and others that led them to encourage stations to pursue an anti-disco crusade. Abrams and Burkhart had consulted yet another consultant, John Parikhal of Toronto, who had conducted attitudinal research on discophobia. What he discovered through his focus groups was that most people in these groups were fairly neutral about the genre until one or two disco haters began ranting, at which point the group would turn decisively anti-disco. The groups reached a consensus: "disco was superficial, boring, repetitive, and short on 'balls.'" After consulting with Parikhal, Abrams managed within a week to convince sixty radio stations to appeal to their base by launching anti-disco campaigns.

Rock radio's assaults on disco solidified its stigmatization, but the evidence suggests that listeners were beginning to sour on disco even before Disco Demolition. Despite the fact that 1979 witnessed some terrific disco records, including McFadden and Whitehead's "Ain't No Stoppin' Us Now," Chic's "Good Times," Sister Sledge's "We Are Family," Donna Summer's "Hot Stuff" and "Bad Girls," and Michael Jackson's "Don't Stop 'Til You Get Enough," record sales were down. In fact, "Disco Rules, But Where Are The Big Sales?" was the headline in the May 1979 issue of *Billboard* magazine. Within the music industry the consensus seemed to be that disco artists were capable of generating healthy 12-inch single sales but not the much more lucrative LP sales. In the summer of 1979, Britain's *Melody Maker* weighed in on the downturn in sales and suggested that disco's lack of star power prevented it from selling much of anything except 12-inch records. The all-important Arbitron ratings of American radio stations also indicated a leveling off of consumers' interest in disco. New York's WKTU slipped badly in the ratings that spring. Writer and humorist Fran Lebowitz, that keen observer of New York life, had predicted as much a year earlier, when she pronounced disco "over" to an "incredulous" journalist from Warhol's disco-besotted *Interview* magazine.

Disco may have lost its sparkle, and it may have been under siege, but the way in which it collapsed was nonetheless remarkable. Within a year of having virtually owned the Top 10, "disco was so officially over," recalls Mel Cheren of West End Records, "that the word itself ceased being used by the mainstream media except as a pejorative." Far from becoming discofied, as disco's boosters predicted, Warner Bros. and other major record labels dumped their disco divisions. In February 1980, *Billboard* reported that American radio had adopted a "virtual ban" on disco as a format. WDAI, the station that had fired Dahl, not only ditched disco in favor of "adult rock" but also changed its call letters so listeners would no longer associate it with the discredited genre. Had the organizers of the Twenty-First Grammy Awards known that disco would crash, they wouldn't have bothered to establish a special category for disco to prevent another runaway year for it at their awards ceremony. In spring 1980, Gloria Gaynor's 1979 hit "I Will Survive" won the first *and* the last award for Best Disco Recording. The category only lasted that single year. By 1980, artists who had made their name with disco were busily making themselves over into anything but. The Village People came on like foppish British New Romantics, Chic announced their "exit" from disco, Donna Summer tried to reposition herself as a rock 'n' roller, and the Bee Gees went into artistic freefall.

How did disco, which had seemed to be on the brink of pop music hegemony, fall into such disrepute that by the end of 1980 even its name was banished in favor of the neutral-sounding "dance music"? The consensus among historians and discographers is that the backlash against disco reflected anger and frustration with America's changing sexual and racial rules. Discophobes might not be able to "bomb bomb bomb Iran," as Vince Vance and the Valiants urged in 1979, but they could demolish disco, the music of outsiders—racial minorities and gays. Even some punk rockers opposed disco on grounds that seemed suspiciously nonmusical. *Punk* magazine even printed a cartoon portraying lisping, limp-wristed "faggots" as disco's core constituency. So straightforward was the prejudice against disco's partisans that several rock critics, including Dave Marsh, noted the undercurrents of racism and homophobia in the disco backlash.

Radio consultant John Parikhal found that homophobia rather than racism came up time and again in his focus groups. However, he explained to journalist Rose that on matters of race, Toronto was not the best guide to American attitudes. Certainly the "decidedly racist" mail sent to *Rolling Stone* in response to its disco coverage, and the hostile fan reaction to Prince when the Rolling Stones chose him as an opening act for their 1981 tour, underscore the racial bigotry and sexual intolerance alive in the rock world. At the Los Angeles Coliseum, Prince and his band the Revolution found themselves subjected to vicious booing and a veritable "hailstorm of beer bottles" from rock fans who had never heard of him and quite liked it that way. They were forced from the stage after only twenty minutes. The undertow of racism in all this is a tad surprising, given rock's origins in fifties' R&B. Rock fans' possessive investment in the whiteness of rock music owes a lot to the "narrowcasting" practices of AOR stations that targeted white males between the ages of thirteen and twenty-five whose appetite for Led Zeppelin, Aerosmith, and others of that ilk seemed insatiable. Critic Ken Tucker went so far as to claim that AOR programming amounted to "institutionalized racism and sexism." Black musicians were critical to the formation of rock and key players in its history, but that wasn't the way that KSFX, a San Francisco FM station, narrated the history of rock. Writing about the station's version of rock history from 1965 to 1980, critic Greil Marcus noted that only three of the almost two hundred segments of the program acknowledged even one black musician—predictably enough, Jimi Hendrix.

By the late seventies rock fans understood their music to be implicitly (if not explicitly) white, and pretty much all music by black musicians to be disco. This appears also to have been the case at New York's *Punk* magazine, whose inaugural issue included a mission statement declaring disco "the epitome of all that is wrong with Western civilization." By contrast, punk was breaking the mold, claimed the magazine's publisher Legs McNeil, as it shifted rock music away from an outmoded and undesirable emulation of black culture. To journalist Marc Jacobson, it seemed that for McNeil and his crowd punk represented the assertion of "all things white, teenage and suburban."

It is easy to depict discophobia as a by-product entirely of the conservative turn. Certainly, for some, disco's hegemony was yet another affront—further evidence of the growing power of racial and sexual minorities and the shrinking power of white straight men. However, the backlash against disco is by no means entirely reducible to straightforward racism and homophobia. After all, some African Americans objected to disco on the grounds that it bleached R&B to such an extent that the music became soulless. Likewise, some gays loathed disco. By 1978 even some of the genre's earliest enthusiasts had concluded that, with the absolutely generic disco that record companies were cranking out, much of it did suck. Contributing to the glut of subpar music was the disco label Salsoul Records, which almost tripled its number of releases between 1977 and 1978. Salsoul was not putting out more records because there was suddenly so much good disco around, but because the label was preparing for a distribution deal with CBS Records and needed to release a certain number of records. One Salsoul executive admits that the label "ended up releasing inferior garbage." The majors were just as shameless as they frantically discofied artists and songs in a desperate bid to keep the disco phenomenon going. By the summer of 1978 it was clear to deejay Michael Gomes that disco was "fast approaching a critical state" largely because the disco "formula is so well known" and so easy to imitate.

Indeed, the growing emphasis upon a record's mixability worked to the detriment of everything else in the song, particularly its lyrical content and rhythmic inventiveness. The appearance of the *Disco Bible*, a newsletter for deejays that assessed disco records in terms of their beats per minute so as "to ensure a totally smooth music flow," both reflected and encouraged disco's sonic predictability. Deejays, especially younger ones, came to rely upon the *Bible*'s "printed sheets of dot matrix with lists of beats per minute from slow to fast." Increasingly, those dee-jays who failed to follow the new bpm regime found themselves out of work. To longtime deejay Bobby Guttadaro, these changes emblem-atized nothing less than the "fall of the vinyl empire." In December 1978, Andrew Holleran, the novelist who had written with both affec-tion and sardonic bite about the earliest gay discos, decried the "terrible uniformity of beat and style" that now characterized disco. The music being cranked out for the mass market—"fast, mechanical, monoto-nous, shallow stuff"—was, he contended, "light-years away from the old dark disco, which did not *know* it was disco, which was simply a song played in a room where we gathered to dance."

The romanticizing of the "old dark disco" and the disparagement of what Holleran derisively called "roller rink disco" exaggerates the won-drousness of the old and the awfulness of the new. Of course, original scenesters—be they the first hippie rockers at the Avalon Ballroom, the earliest punk rockers at CBGB, or the first dancers at the Loft or the Tenth Floor—can almost always be counted on to cast the virgin days of a scene as a golden age after which everything turned to commer-cialized crap. There is no doubt that as disco became Disco, producers, musicians, and labels scrambled to exploit the craze. That said, there is nothing dark about such early disco hits as MFSB's "Love Is the Mes-sage," the O'Jays' "I Love Music," or Shirley and Company's "Shame Shame Shame." And, for that matter, 1978 offered some arresting disco among the dreck—the Stones' "Miss You," Chaka Khan's "I'm Every Woman," Sylvester's "(You Make Me Feel) Mighty Real," and the Bee Gees' *Fever* songs, at least until they were played to the point of exasperation.

Yet the fact that disco was accumulating critics from within suggests the trickiness of generalizing about its many detractors. Indeed, what is most striking about the anti-disco backlash is what a dependable lightning rod disco had become for Americans' multiple discontents. For example, "disco sucks" was perhaps the one thing that progres-sives and conservatives could agree upon. For many on the left, disco was the final nail in the coffin of the sixties—all the proof needed that commodification had transformed pop music from a site of counter-cultural rebellion into triviality and acquiescence. "There is something sleazy about the ease—no, the desire—of many disco stars to toady up to the worst creeps in the music industry," argued left-winger Bruce Dancis. By way of example he cited the Bee Gees, who had appeared wearing proper suits and ties on the cover of *Fortune*. For the right, by contrast, disco represented not political quiescence but rather the con-tinuation of the sixties' hedonism and all-around depravity. For many, irrespective of where they positioned themselves on the political spec-trum, disco wasn't art. "No auteurs in disco," went the criticism, "just calculated desiccating machines." The complaints of rock 'n' rollers, whatever their politics, that disco was mass-produced rather than artis-tically driven assumed that rock music, despite its own considerable commercialization, had, as critic David Buxton put it, "retained artisa-nal status."

Even the hardcore discophobia of Steve Dahl and Dennis Erectus is more complicated than disco's critics and historians have acknowl-edged. Discographers have emphasized discophobes' hostility towards outsiders—in particular gays and African Americans. But the rhetoric of discophobia suggests that anti-disco rockers were also critical of what they saw as disco's perceived innocuousness and conventional-ity. "Disco's so *straight*," complained Erectus to journalist Frank Rose in 1979. "It's something Nixon would approve of." Disco's ubiquity—on the radio and TV, in the bar, at the mall, the wedding party, and prom—proved that it was plastic music for plastic people. It is true that by 1978 disco, unlike rock, was a cross-generational phenomenon. As "everyone's music," disco had no currency. As Joyce Trabulus, who managed Donna Summer and Kiss and was married to Neil Bogart of Casablanca Records, contends, disco just reached too deep into Middle America to retain any semblance of trendiness. "Once it became, you know, Uncle Herman from Great Neck was doing the *Saturday Night Fever* thing, you thought, 'No, I think I need to find something else.'"

The taint of uncoolness that attached to disco by late 1978 practically required disavowal.

But it was not just disco's bland cross-generational appeal that alienated. After all, discophobia suggests that fear as well as loathing was at work. Radio consultant Parikhal noted that discophobic rock fans felt intimidated by the highly sexed (and, one might add, female-centered) quality of disco and by the physical and sartorial demands of glitterball culture. Certainly this was true of deejay Dahl, who told one interviewer at the time, "You have to look good, you know, tuck your shirt in, perfect this, perfect that." Dahl's views have remained remarkably consistent. Years later he recalled having felt angry about the way that disco clubbers were "seemingly making it harder for you to measure up." As homosexual style—machine-sculpted body, fastidious grooming, and fashion-consciousness—increasingly became masculine style in what now looks like the beginnings of metrosexuality, some heterosexual men resisted. That they should target disco, which, after all, was an engine of this change, is hardly surprising. In heterosexual terms, the rebel rocker seemed to be losing ground to the domesticated male who would not only dress up and muscle up, but would also shake his booty—for his woman. For these reasons, disco, in many ways associated with the illicit, nonetheless came to be understood as square.

Moreover, disco was not just forcing straight men to tuck in their shirts and leave behind the casualness of sixties' style, it required that they *move*, especially scary for dance-phobic white men. There was no playing air guitar on a disco dance floor. Even male artists whose music was played in discos could find the dance floor an utterly intimidating experience. Stephen Morris, the drummer of New Order, recalls going with his bandmates in 1980 to the New York dance clubs, but never dancing because, "It takes ecstasy to make a white man dance."

Attacked for being both too gay and too straight, too black and too white, oversexed and asexual, leisure-class as well as leisure-suited (loser) class, disco represented anything but a stable signifier. Its ability to arouse such disparate responses meant that disco was fair game for all manner of scapegoating. The butt of late-night comics, music critics, screenwriters, radio deejays, and pundits, disco ranked among the biggest embarrassments of the 1970s.

Disco's demise happened almost in a blink. Travolta's *Fever* dance routines were already being spoofed as early as 1980, in the hit movie *Airplane.* The Bee Gees, John Travolta, Chic, Gloria Gaynor, and Donna Summer—those names were now rarely heard unless as part of a joke. Unlike sixties' rock, which instantly became "classic rock" and a mainstay of FM radio, seventies' disco was banished from the airwaves except as an April Fool's Day joke. Chic were hardly one-hit disco wonders, with a string of disco hits including "Le Freak," the all-time top-selling single for Warner/Electra/Asylum, but after disco crashed the group could not get any further traction with their record company or with consumers. Chic limped along until 1983, after which guitarist Nile Rodgers and bassist Bernard Edwards had the good sense to move entirely into production. Rodgers produced David Bowie's 1983 album *Let's Dance,* and he maintains that the former glam rocker told him that when people learned he had chosen Rodgers as his producer, their jaws dropped. "You mean you are going to do an album with a disco producer?" they asked. Rodgers always felt there was "an underlying tone of racism" in such responses. And when Madonna began to make waves she was frequently sneered at by critics who considered her a "little disco tart," as she once put it. Disco remained so thoroughly disreputable that in 1993 the Bee Gees were still making fun of their biggest hit record. Barry Gibbs revealed that he wanted nothing so much as to dress up "Stayin' Alive" in a "white suit and gold chains and set it on fire." The ridicule lasted well into the nineties, with comics such as Chris Rock mocking disco, and Chevrolet trying to sell its macho Camaro Z28 with the line, "If everyone owned one, maybe we could have prevented disco."

However, something curious happened on disco's way to the pop music morgue. Yes, it was largely banished from the airwaves, many of its artists struggled to shed their one-time disco identity, and many, many discos closed their doors, especially in smaller cities and towns. However, the 1980s hardly marked the end of disco. It was just that disco then went by that blandest of appellations, "dance music." Rock 'n' rollers who thought that they had beaten back disco and "cued up 'Stairway to Heaven' one more time," as critic Jon Pareles put it, discovered that theirs was in many respects a Pyrrhic victory. Disco's crash at the end of 1979 had little effect on gay disco-goers in big cities. "The death of disco! *Jeez, I missed that one!*" was remixer Tom Moulton's reaction. Deejay Michael Gomes remembers, "We still went out, and we still had music. *We didn't miss a beat!*" Many would argue that disco's peak years, at legendary gay clubs such as New York's Paradise Garage and the Saint, were in the early eighties.

I was deejaying in the years after disco's collapse, from 1980 until 1985, and in many respects little had changed, at least in Ann Arbor, Michigan. In many quarters, like hip Schoolkids' Records where I sometimes shopped, disco still sucked. But long-playing 12-inch singles were still available, even if all vestiges of disco packaging—pictures of platform shoes and disco balls, for example—were gone, replaced by new wave-inspired graphics. As before, I read about new tracks in *Billboard* and the *Village Voice*, whose senior pop music critic Robert Christgau had always been open-minded about disco. On my weekly trips to Kendricks' Record Shop in Detroit, musician Ronń Matlock, whose day job was clerking at the store, played me the latest dance tracks. The Rubaiyat where I worked and the Motor City discos where I danced remained packed, often surpassing the occupancy limits mandated by the fire department. Radio deejay Electrifyin' Mojo of WGPR continued to broadcast both black and white artists usually ignored by R&B radio. Although the Rubaiyat closed sometime around 1985, it was hardly the end of disco or, to use its alias, "dance music." About the same time, Ann Arbor's major venue for rock bands, the Second Chance, closed and reopened as the Nectarine Ballroom—a dance club.

In fact, if disco had died, it was not immediately obvious from the pop charts of the 1980s. Madonna, Michael Jackson, and Prince—arguably among the biggest pop stars of the 1980s—made music that many would argue was disco in all but name. The Rolling Stones continued to have dance-floor hits with "Emotional Rescue" and "Start Me Up," and Jagger collaborated with the Jacksons on "State of Shock." Even rockers not normally associated with disco cozied up to the dance floor. Paul McCartney worked with Michael Jackson on "Say Say Say," and Grace Slick of the Jefferson Airplane/Starship sang backup on Rick James's "69 Times." Even that echt rocker Bruce Springsteen issued 12-inch dance singles of his 1984 hits "Dancing in the Dark" and "Cover Me."

Rap figures in disco's afterlife as well. Usually treated as disco's polar opposite, there's no denying that as rap evolved it put considerable distance between itself and disco. Hip-hop's evocation of the "real"—i.e., the street—its reconfiguring of black masculinity as tough, hard, even violent, and its embrace of outsize personalities operated in stark contrast to disco's escapism, elevation of the feminine, and facelessness. However, as posters for early hip-hop events, advertised as "disco," suggest, the line between disco and early hip-hop was initially porous. In fact, the earliest rap was danceable party music, as Missy Elliott reminded listeners in "Back in the Day," and it often relied upon disco records for its backing tracks. The first rap record to hit the charts, 1979's "Rapper's Delight" by the Sugar Hill Gang, adapted the rhythm track of Chic's "Good Times." *Village Voice* music critic Carol Cooper was perhaps the first to note the ways in which this appropriation shaped the sound of early hip-hop. Bernard Edwards's "percussive, attitudinal bass line," she argued, "dictated the cadence and the timbre of rappers' rhymes for the next three years." Chic keyboardist Raymond Jones acknowledges that rap's "macho nature" is often contrasted to disco's "fruitiness," but he correctly points out that "if disco had sucked in such a major way, hip-hop would not have stepped in and appropriated it."

More remarkable still was how deeply disco penetrated punk and new wave, which were not even remotely disco-friendly at first, especially in the States. Like disco, punk and new wave broke with the sixties' ethos of authenticity, particularly its elevation of all things natural. But punk and new wave's penchant for fitful rather than groovy rhythms, unsoulful vocals, choppy, harsh-sounding guitars, and the sonically stripped-down made their incorporation of disco sounds and techniques unlikely. Given this spiky relationship, it's not surprising that the earliest dance-rock hybrids were often spoofs of disco. Ian Dury and the Blockheads' 1978 single "Hit Me with Your Rhythm Stick," which ends with Dury screaming "hit me" again and again, seems to poke fun at all the masochistic slaves to the disco rhythm. The B-52s' "Rock Lobster," another of the first new wave tracks to be played on disco dance floors, did not quite mock disco. But had the band not presented *itself* as a joke, with everyone decked out in thrift store retro-wear and the women in beehive wigs, their blend of new wave, disco, and surf music might not have gone over as well with the rock crowd.

Blondie's 1978 track "Heart of Glass," which the band soon dubbed "The Disco Song," also received considerable play in discos. Blondie might not have recorded a disco track were it not for their producer, who urged them to discofy one of their earlier songs, the reggae-tinged "Once I Had a Love." Like most dance-floor excursions by punk and new wave bands, "Heart of Glass" dispensed with disco's sweet strings, sweeping brass, and romanticism. In their place were guitars, piano, synthesizer, and frosty cynicism summed up by the line, "Once I had a love and it was a gas / Soon turned out to be a pain in the ass." Blondie front woman Deborah Harry used an archly cool voice. The video, shot at Studio 54, shows band members fiddling with disco balls as if to underscore that the whole episode was nothing more than a prank. Drummer Clem Burke has said that the skipped beat in the record's instrumental bridge was meant to "screw people up when they're on the dance floor."

No matter how ironically the band played "Heart of Glass," many of their fans saw their disco turn as a crass sellout of punk principle.

But then, to many punks, disco epitomized loathsome commercialism. The resulting backlash did not deter Blondie from collaborating with Eurodisco's Giorgio Moroder on the hit single "Call Me," for the soundtrack to *American Gigolo*. Although Blondie was never known for its earnestness, its 1980 dance-floor tracks, the reggae-inflected "The Tide Is High" and the hip-hop-influenced "Rapture," seemed as "real" as anything the band did.

Johnny Lydon's band Public Image Ltd. never garnered as much disco play as Blondie or the B-52's, but their music was arguably more important in shaping the post-punk soundscape. The band's 1978 promotional video for the irresistibly danceable "Public Image" shows John Lydon moving his body rhythmically to the music rather than lunging about the stage in his trademark Hunchback of Notre Dame impersonation. It also features a disco-ish beat, sonorous bass, and ex-Clash guitarist Keith Levene's jangly, soaring riffs. This sound went a long way toward establishing the aural template of U2, Joy Division, and many other bands. It is no wonder that music journalist Simon Reynolds begins his provocative history of post-punk, *Rip It Up and Start Again*, with Lydon and Public Image Ltd.

For no-wave artist James Chance, who fronted the Contortions, disco was also something of a lark, at least at first. The unpolished, atonal, non-electronic, minimalist music of no-wave is a far cry from the glossy sounds of Donna Summer, but in 1978 Chance was approached by Michael Zilkha, the cofounder of the New York indie record label ZE, about cutting a disco record. "It doesn't have to be a *commercial* disco record," Zilkha assured him. "Just do whatever *your* idea of disco is." A provocateur, Chance began to warm to the idea of going disco if only to mess with people's minds. He told one journalist, "I've always been interested in disco. I mean disco is *disgusting*, but there's something in it that's always interested me—*monotony*." He continued, "It's sort of jungle music, but whitened and perverted. On this album I'm trying to restore it to what it *could* be. Really primitive." The idea of racial primitivism, which Chance toyed with in his "disco" group James White and

PUBLIC IMAGE LTD.'S "FODDERSTOMPF"

"FODDERSTOMPF" WAS A 7-minute 46-second prank meant to cause maximum offense. The track grew out of PiL's recording sessions for their first album, 1978's *Public Image—First Issue*. Looking for a way to meet their contractual obligation to Virgin Records—thirty minutes of music—and coming up short by almost eight minutes, PiL hit on the idea of recording a long and obnoxious song to finish off their album. The cut consisted of little more than their screeching like Terry Jones, Monty Python's spam-serving waitress, over an unchanging, thunderous funk bass line set to a snare-heavy disco beat. The band made no bones about their dodge. In fact, you can hear Jah Wobble talking in the background about wanting to complete the record with minimal exertion, which, he notes, "we are now doing very suc-cess-fully." At various points, band members talk about going out for cigarettes, mumble about the song's tediousness, and urge listeners to be boring. Listeners who persevered to the end were told that they were as "sad" as the band churning out the dreck.

The cut was guaranteed to piss off their record label as well as Sex Pistols fans unprepared for music that so violated punk's conventions of speed and economy. Like other punks in this Disco Sucks period who were experimenting with danceable sounds, PiL gave themselves an out: "Fodderstompf" was a spoof of disco, perhaps even of Donna Summer's "Love to Love You Baby." Its German-sounding title alone suggested inferior material, stomping beat, "stumpf" (meaning numb or blunt), and perhaps the German penchant for the mechanistic, as in Kraftwerk and Giorgio Moroder, a.k.a. the Munich Machine. As for the lyrics, the whining cries of wanting "to be loved" mocked disco's faith in the restorative power of love ("Love's Theme," "Love Train," "Love Is the Message," "I Love Music," etc.).

Designed to be offputting, "Fodderstompf" proved unexpectedly compelling, even to those it apparently meant to disparage. Legend has it that the song ended up being played at Studio 54 where dancers would scream along with its manic chorus, "We only wanted to be loved!" Over the years critics and fans have rhapsodized about the song's bass line, which bassist Wobble admitted was in its own way "as mental as Funkadelic." (George Clinton's P-Funk crew likely influenced PiL, but "Hydraulic Pump," the 1983 collaboration between P-Funk and Sly Stone, sounds surprisingly like "Fodderstompf.") Moreover, far from being a one-off, "Fodderstompf" prefigured PiL's embrace of dance music, particularly its pursuit of "the studio-as-instrument methodology." Their next LP, 1979's critically acclaimed *Metal Box*, found the band further developing their "anti-rock & roll." Soon Lydon was shocking former fans with the news that the only music he really liked was disco, and that PiL was a dance band.

So how did these punk rockers become disco converts? Reggae was certainly one route into dance music. All the members of PiL were "total dub fanatics." Like descriptions of gay disco, Lydon's characterization of London's reggae clubs emphasizes the high-volume bass, whose physicality, he writes, "just left me gobsmacked." However, reggae was not punks' only way in to disco. Lydon and his friends had been going to gay bars for years to avoid what he calls "boot boy harassment" and because these underground clubs "always had the best records." Although many punks hated disco, it turns out that others merely posed as disco haters. During his punk days Lydon slagged off dance music, but in the late 1990s he admitted that he had "loved disco" and saw "no shame at all in admiring the Bee Gees and being a Sex Pistol." Although he was never an Abba fan, it turns out that two other Sex Pistols—Sid Vicious and Glen Matlock—were. Indeed, Matlock's original riff for the Pistols' song "Pretty Vacant" drew upon an unlikely source: Abba's "SOS." And in the States, not all punk rockers were disco haters either. Back in 1975, "Lady Marmalade" and "Shame Shame Shame" were part of Blondie's repertoire, and the band often hung out at a gay disco called Club 82. All of this raises the possibility that at least in certain sectors of the punk world, "Disco Sucks" was little more than a pose adopted as a matter of commercial positioning.

the Blacks, was, of course, antithetical to the original thrust of disco as sophisticated music. Although their record "Contort Yourself" saw limited club play, it helped to spark the so-called mutant disco movement, whose participants included those riot grrrl precursors the Bush Tetras, whose "Too Many Creeps" was a hit in some dance clubs.

There were artists, however, whose forays into disco were not ironic or parodic exercises, but who set out to bring together the repetition, production techniques, and the rhythmic intensity of disco with rock's greater lyrical heft. Some of the key American players include Prince, Bernie Worrell of P-Funk, Nona Hendryx (formerly of Labelle), Bill Laswell of Material, Was (Not Was), and Talking Heads.

In Britain the resistance to dance music was never as strong as in America, which may explain the ease with which the Clash, exemplars of politically oriented punk, made 1980's disco-ish "The Magnificent Seven." It also helps to explain the rapid proliferation of dance-oriented acts there—Cabaret Voltaire, Pete Shelley, the Human League, Gary Numan, Depeche Mode, Culture Club, Bronski Beat, Soft Cell, Gang of Four, Joy Division/New Order, Killing Joke, the Eurythmics, and Duran Duran.

Certainly the path that British bands took to the dance floor tended to be less circuitous and apologetic than that of their American counterparts. British bands were often gleeful in their flouting of rock conventions as they ditched guitars, the most sacrosanct of rock instruments, for the synthesizer, which rockers regarded as a somewhat effeminate instrument. For some British bands, making the dance turn involved rejecting rock out of hand, or at least saying so. The pioneering synth-pop band the Human League opened their song "Dance Like a Star" with the announcement that the cut was for "all you big heads out there who think that disco music is lower than the irrelevant gibberish and tired platitudes that you try to impress your parents with."

So what changed in the transition from disco to dance music? Some writers contend that queerness was the real casualty of disco's so-called death. Mel Cheren argues that what separated the new dance music being made by Michael Jackson, Prince, and Madonna was that their music was not identified with "urban gay men." In all other respects, he judges eighties' dance music absolutely indistinguishable from disco: mindless lyrics, unchanging beat, and musical homogeneity. By successfully shedding its association with queers, Cheren argues, dance music was reclaimed by the "same forces that had run things for decades: White, straight, mainstream, largely homophobic."

Yet even assuming that the forces of white, patriarchal, heteronormativity killed off disco, it is far from obvious that a pop landscape dominated by Madonna, Jacko, and Prince represented anything like a return to red-blooded, white, hetero, masculine power. Moreover, the idea that disco's collapse and subsequent reconfiguration as dance music was primarily about dequeering the genre ignores the significant differences that exist between disco and dance music. For one, eighties' dance music boasted actual personalities along with the usual anonymous artists—the Cherrelles, Shannons, and C-Banks. Madonna's seductive but top-girl personality, Jackson's apparent guilelessness and curious paranoia, and Prince's routine nose-thumbing and preternatural musical talent provoked genuine interest. The Village People, the Bee Gees, Donna Summer, and Barry White may have sold enormous quantities of disco records, but the cult of personality never attached itself to them. Indeed, once the disco market weakened, the record industry came to think that the facelessness of so many of disco's hit-makers contributed to the genre's demise. Ray Caviano of Warner Bros. had bragged to the press that "thirty-five percent of all disco records are a figment of some producer's imagination," as though this was somehow a good thing. However, the fact that disco was so much a producer-driven medium proved a stumbling block for most listeners, who were still drawn to personalities. Disco booster Vince Aletti, who for a time worked with Caviano, believed that the company's difficulty in signing anything but one-hit wonders proved financially disastrous in another respect. The fact that so many of these artists released 12-inch records that had a short shelf life "meant that they cost the company a lot of money and didn't end up leading us anywhere."

The producer-centric quality of disco encouraged facelessness, but so did the tendency of record labels and producers to treat disco artists as interchangeable and ultimately disposable. Record companies were much more apt to promote rock musicians rather than disco artists as personalities worthy of feature articles in the music and mainstream press. While it's true that bland individuals such as Gloria Gaynor and Barry White dominated the genre, disco nevertheless had some genuine personalities. The fierce women of Labelle, the sexually provocative Grace Jones, the offbeat Dr. Buzzard's Original Savannah Band, the volatile Chaka Khan, the cheeky Sylvester, and the coolly ironic Chic—all of them could have been promoted and cultivated as personalities, but the majors skimped on disco artists. And with the rock press focused on its own kind, there were few media outlets, outside of *Jet* and *Ebony*, left for feature stories about disco's mostly black artists.

Moreover, largely as a result of MTV, which began broadcasting in the summer of 1981, some eighties' dance music artists were able to cultivate their visual appeal. Dance music and the video format, both of which presumed that pop music was an act, should have cozied right up to each other. After all, as Jon Pareles notes, what had seemed artificial in the disco era—a diva lip-synching over prerecorded music for a so-called "track date" in a club—became business as usual with MTV. But

"No black performer since Little Richard had toyed with the heterosexual sensibilities of black America so brazenly," wrote critic Nelson George of Prince, pictured here in 1985

MTV resisted playing videos by dance artists, perhaps because it targeted as its core audience rock fans, presumably attached to notions of rock 'n' roll realness and leery of disco's artifice. Instead, MTV's first roster was drawn largely from the ranks of the usual AOR suspects—REO Speedwagon and Styx—and the newly rehabilitated rocker Rod Stewart singing "She Won't Dance with Me," a song that deployed rock clichés stretching back to the fifties. Yet British artists, who were accustomed to making music videos for promotional purposes, turned out to have an advantage over American groups. MTV began to turn to British musicians like Peter Gabriel, whose 1982 video for the danceable "Shock the Monkey" was head and shoulders above the usual MTV fare. Soon post-punk British bands, like the stylish Duran Duran, who were experimenting with dance grooves, became such a presence on MTV that some declared it the second British Invasion. Yet through the early 1980s MTV's roster was virtually lily white. (Incredibly, among the first "rap" videos the network broadcast was white comic Rodney Dangerfield's "Rappin' Rodney" in 1983.) The same year, Michael Jackson broke MTV's de facto color line with *Thriller*, and the LP's "Beat It," "Billie Jean," and "Wanna Be Startin' Somethin'" dominated the pop, R&B, and dance charts. Prince quickly joined Jackson (and Madonna), and the three proved among the network's most savvy, telegenic, and popular performers.

Much eighties' dance music also diverged sonically from the disco that knew it was disco, to borrow Holleran's phrase. Hi-NRG remained classic disco, hewing to its fundamentals, albeit at an ever-racing beats-per-minute clip. But as Eurodisco became the canonical disco sound, the rest of dance music became, in the words of Vince Aletti, "less and less disco and more and more freaky." Dance music producers and artists often abandoned the straight 4/4 thump for an even harder-hitting, on-the-one funk thwack, or opted for an electronically produced beat that often skittered. They played with more varied tempos and largely abandoned the sweet lushness—those swelling strings and brass that characterized so much disco. Instead, eighties' dance music pursued a sparer sound built upon heavy bass and synthesizers. In fact, Mel Cheren's record label, West End, began releasing minimalist tracks such as Taana Gardner's "Heartbeat," the Peech Boys' "Don't Make Me Wait," and Loose Joints' "Is It All Over My Face" which exemplified the aural shift away from disco qua disco.

There was also less homogeneity in dance music than in the late seventies' disco it superseded. In theory, a deejay in 1983 might play a set that included Afrika Bambaataa's electro-funk cut "Looking for the Perfect Beat," George Clinton's "Atomic Dog," Madonna's "Lucky

Star," Talking Heads' "Burning Down the House," and the Human League's "(Keep Feeling) Fascination." However, you likely would have had to visit a number of clubs to hear such a set. By 1978 the ecumenical approach of the first disco deejays, who delighted in unlikely juxtapositions, had already given way to specialization—Eurodisco, pop disco, and funk disco. Unsurprisingly, naming only encouraged more naming, so that by the eighties ever more minute subgenres of dance music were proliferating at a dizzying rate. Hi-NRG, house, freestyle, garage, techno (a.k.a. electro or electronica), rap, and varieties of funk represent only a sliver of the microgenres within dance. Although some clubs, such as New York's Mudd Club, the Roxy, and the Funhouse, encouraged musical conversations between uptown black and Latino kids and downtown white kids, this was not the norm. As Carol Cooper notes, "gay discos, black mainstream clubs, fashion-trend dens, 'new wave' discos, and hip-hop parties all squared off against one another during the early eighties." The result was the kind of balkanization that plagued radio in this period.

However, even those creating new microgenres were sometimes unaware that the music they spun was becoming named and codified. Take "house" music, which Mel Cheren describes as Paradise Garage music "on a budget," because it did not feature disco orchestras such as MFSB or Salsoul but rather relied upon cheap drum machines and reel-to-reel tape edits, and eventually computers. Chicago deejay Frankie Knuckles, Larry Levan's one-time collaborator, whose choice of music and remixes inspired the term "house," did not even know what the term meant when he first encountered it around 1981. "We came to this stoplight, and there was a bar on the corner with a sign in the window saying, 'We play house music,'" he recalls. When Knuckles asked his friend what house music was, he was told, "All the stuff that you play at the Warehouse!"

Ann Arbor, Michigan, was hardly a dance music wasteland, but I had no idea that the music I was playing was called anything but disco or dance. I was dimly aware that increasingly the music involved more synthesizers and drum machines, often offered little by way of melody, and that its structure often seemed even more arbitrary than that of a classic disco track. However, I did not know that Shannon's hit record "Let the Music Play," which I played faithfully for a couple of months, was part of a new genre called "freestyle" or "Latin freestyle." Nor did I know that Kano's "It's a War" was Italo-disco. This relentless splintering and mutating of eighties' dance music was at odds with seventies' disco, whose aims were more expansive (and expansionist) than preciously particularistic.

In other ways, however, the new dance music followed in disco's footsteps. For one, it was more sexually explicit, and sometimes even queerer than classic disco. For British bands, in particular, dance music became the occasion for flamboyantly androgynous self-presentation. While the musicians in question were not always gay, it was not obvious from their appearance, which leaned heavily towards the pretty-boy and the foppish. Singer Philip Oakey of the Human League, for example, was known for his dramatically lopsided haircut, eye makeup, and lipstick. Although Oakey was heterosexual, the band nonetheless enjoyed what he characterized as a "massive" gay fan base. Oakey was hardly the most gender-bending of the lot. Martin Gore of Depeche Mode performed in a leather skirt, and in the song "People Are People" the group tackled racism and homophobia. Boy George of Culture Club may have projected cuddliness and have identified as bisexual, but he was widely assumed to be gay. Andy Bell of Erasure made no bones about being gay, nor did Jimmy Somerville of Bronski Beat whose "Smalltown Boy" evoked the pain of having to leave behind one's provincial hometown to escape homophobia. In the context of the health crisis just unfolding in gay communities, Soft Cell's 1981 cover of Gloria Jones' soul nugget "Tainted Love" seemed undeniably about something scarier than a failed love affair.

Then there was Frankie Goes to Hollywood, a group that ditched homo-cuddliness entirely. What kind of sexual advice Frankie was dispensing in their 1984 hit single "Relax" was obscure, but with Holly

Johnson and Paul Rutherford dressed in leather fetish wear, ads for the group proclaiming, "all the nice boys love sea men," and the song's video, which was set in a gay bar, the record was clearly about queer sex. Working with producer Trevor Horn of the Art of Noise, Frankie successfully merged hi-NRG with a "rock edge." Americans were less over-the-top androgynous than the British, although neither crotch-grabbing but elfin Michael Jackson or Prince (he of the curious back-side revealing pants) could be said to have presented themselves as conventionally masculine or heterosexual.

If anything, the disco-rock hybrid that comprised so much eighties' dance music built upon and extended the (mostly) implicit queerness of seventies' disco. Something similar happened in relation to women. Disco divas often demanded that their pleasure be taken into account, but the women heating up the dance floor in the eighties proclaimed their control. Influenced in part by David Bowie, Madonna presented herself quite deliberately as "feminine and masculine at the same time," a move that led some to denounce her as "unladylike." Janet Jackson bragged of calling all her "own shots" in "Control." Grace Jones turned decisively mannish as she instructed her lover in the not-so-fine points of anal sex to "pull up to my bumper baby / in your long black limousine." Annie Lennox, with her crew cut and mannish suits, came across as such a top that she was primarily sexy to those harbor-ing fantasies of submission. Lennox not only impersonated Elvis at the Grammys but played both the betrayed female and the man who kisses her in the video for "Who's That Girl?" In the clever "Come Again," the Au Pairs sent up politically correct heterosexual sex in what amounted to a "Satisfaction" for the eighties. The song at last reaches a climax as female vocalist Lesley Woods taunts her male lover after many minutes of foreplay, "Is your finger aching?"

To pop music critic Barry Walters, the utopian promise of this music was that "it didn't matter if you were a boy or a girl, black or white, gay or straight." Architects of this new pop made music that he called "deliberately impure," the better to confound audiences' expectations about what any particular group might sound or look like. Before long, it provoked a backlash, although nothing so dramatic as what had greeted disco. Rock critics dismissed Madonna as a "prefab disco prima donna," and they were excessively harsh in their judgments of what they derisively called "English haircut bands"—groups such as the Human League, ABC, and Soft Cell. Frequently criticisms of these British bands recycled those made of disco just a few years earlier— that is, that they prioritized style over substance and the synthetic over the real—criticisms that seemed to reflect a vague squeamishness about soft masculine self-presentation.

By 1985 enough American music journalists were assailing this new pop music that some thought it constituted a full-fledged back-lash, which critic Simon Frith dubbed the "New Authenticity move-ment." Those weary of all the gender-bending and sexual ambiguity could take refuge in the music of Bruce Springsteen and the new cat-egory of "indie rock." As Simon Reynolds argues, indie rock, which took shape during this period with bands such as the Jesus and Mary Chain, embraced the very sounds that most of the above-mentioned dance artists had spurned—"scruffy guitars, white-only sources, weak or 'pale' folk-based vocals, undanceable rhythms, lo-fi or Luddite pro-duction." By the mideighties rap was increasingly presenting itself as the authentic voice of the streets. Although rap arguably emerged out of disco, over time it cultivated a distinct heaviness and a machismo in direct, and sometimes conscious counterpoint to the perceived trivial-ity and female-dominated quality of disco. Cultural critic Touré even claimed that hip-hop culture "was built to worship urban black male-ness: the way we speak, walk, dance, dress, think."

Writing about the state of popular music in 1994, Barry Walters claimed, " 'real' rap now avoids uptempo cuts (too disco, too gay), love songs (too soft, too feminine), rock samples (too pop, too white)." Rock was just as hidebound. " 'Real' rock now avoids melody (too accessi-ble, too universal), dance rhythms (too black *and* too gay), intricate arrangements (too sensitive, too girly)." For Walters, the salvation for

American pop was Europop, which was forging a "new world disco ... without a door policy." But he did not hold out much hope that U.S. audiences would be lining up outside this global disco where deejays would spin the records of 2 Unlimited and Ace of Base.

The dance music that got the ear of the American rock crowd in the nineties was techno—the music that powered Ecstasy-fueled raves. Techno's roots were in black Detroit, but it migrated to Britain and continental Europe where it became enormously popular before recrossing the Atlantic. Techno's metal-like fierceness—the result of the synchronizing of layer upon layer of electronic sound—managed to attract young white rock crowds in the States, which may be one reason some music business insiders believed techno could turn around slumping rock sales. Suddenly even veteran rockers wanted to hire remixers to do techno versions of their songs. Techno enthusiasts were often careful to distinguish their music from what one writer called "mostly witless disco." As *Rolling Stone*'s Mike Rubin pointed out, most electronic artists actively "shunned dance music's roots, preferring to treat disco like a five-letter word." Techno produced a number of popular acts, including Prodigy, the Chemical Brothers, and Moby, but it never became the next big thing. Soon the industry renamed it electronica so that "people would buy it without thinking of words like disco or techno," observed critic Ed Ward.

Rap boasted outsized beats, too, but the more commercially successful it became the more aggressively it policed its borders to guard against interlopers and so-called sellouts. As a consequence, groups such as P.M. Dawn that were uninterested in black macho or in upholding purist notions of black music came under attack, sometimes literally. MC ("U Can't Touch This") Hammer, who became a superstar by purveying dance-friendly hip-hop, saw his career founder when he gained mainstream success (and started wearing harem-style trousers), which led other rappers to ridicule him as a sellout. In some sectors of the hip-hop world hook-friendly, crossover rap was seen as commercial fodder that threatened to "emasculate" the genre.

Despite these counterblasts of "realness," on the twentieth anniversary of *Saturday Night Fever* it seemed at last as if disco might be able to be unapologetically disco. After all, critics and scholars were finally beginning to give disco its due. Jon Pareles noted that the genre's studio manipulations—the multiple remixes, the use of tape loops and eventually drum machines and synthesizers—were now utterly routine as electronic technology became naturalized. "Disco," he perceptively observed, "once mocked for being shallow and synthetic, has turned into roots music." Rock superstars U2 had already edged toward dance music with 1991's *Achtung Baby*, but their 1997 techno-inflected CD *Pop* was such a giddy assemblage of loops and samples that *Rolling Stone* entitled its rave review "Disco Inferno." Two years later *Rolling Stone* devoted a lengthy (and loving) feature to what it called the "Nineties Rhythm Revolution." Meanwhile, 1998 witnessed the arrival of two glitterball movies—*The Last Days of Disco* and *54*—and a year later the theatrical production of *Fever* made its Broadway debut at about the same time that British audiences fell headlong in love with the Abba-powered *Mamma Mia*. Finally, on June 29, 1999, twenty years after Disco Demolition, Chicago's other ballpark, Wrigley Field, hosted a "70s Night" that featured a mini-concert by the Village People, who received a standing ovation. Still, disco's comeback didn't quite make it, as most of America chose to keep its boogie shoes in the closet.

At the millennium, disco in America was a paradox. Millions of Americans were dancing to music whose popularity seemed predicated upon both its sonic proximity to disco and its long-armed distance from it. It was almost as if "don't ask, don't tell" was the unspoken law of the land on America's airwaves and dance floors. Fans looking for music that was unrepentantly disco—music unafraid to bear that name—had to look to the rest of the world. In America the case against disco seemed open and shut.

Epilogue

Do It Again

When I began working on this book I assumed that disco would continue to be influential without ever being culturally rehabilitated. Yet it now seems as if there is a shift in our soundscape that may prove me wrong. Actually, I don't know if it's a cultural shift or a cultural blip we're experiencing, but one thing's for sure: disco *is* back. Okay, my evidence is ridiculously fragmentary, starting with the sounds of my neighborhood. For the past five years I have lived on a busy street not far from downtown Los Angeles. Several times a day I hear snatches of songs—almost always rap or Latin ballads—blasting from passing cars. But last week it was a laserbeam "pWOOoooOooo" repeated at three-second intervals, and anchored to a thump-like beat that was rocking the street. I would know that sound anywhere, and if you were alive in 1979 and between the ages of five and fifty-five you would remember it, too. It was the sonic tick that made Anita Ward's "Ring My Bell" among the most recognizable and irritating disco cuts of all time.

About the same time that "Bell" earwormed its way once again into my consciousness, I came across an article in *Time Out London* heralding disco's revival. One of the deejays interviewed, Luca C of the monthly Spangles party, actually bragged of spinning only "real disco" rather than techno or house. Several months earlier KCRW, L.A.'s best-known public radio station, named the veteran host of its electronica/dance music show "Metropolis" its next program director and the new host of its influential "Morning Becomes Eclectic," a show that had always leaned toward indie rock. Then last month *The New Yorker*'s Sasha Frere-Jones devoted a column to the woman who may or may not be the next Madonna, Lady Gaga. The latest pop sensation is besotted with the seventies, disco, and Studio 54, going so far as to trick herself out as a disco ball. Frere-Jones links Gaga's ascent to what he considers the "sea change in pop, away from hip-hop and back towards disco." Indeed, he suggests that the U.S. is finally catching up to Europe, where disco has presided over the charts for some time.

I am a historian, not a pop music prognosticator, but it seems as if we may have reached the last days of discophobia. So what happened to nudge the culture toward an acceptance of disco? Factors surely include the resurgence of rhythm in nineties rock and the return of danceable rap, both of which succeeded in getting the normally dance-averse moving. Hip-hop helped to destigmatize disco in other respects, too. Rap positioned itself against disco fluff, but it nonetheless followed disco's approach to making music, one in which a record is put together rather than simply captured, as supposedly happens in rock music. Rock's preference for the spontaneous and the natural has exerted a powerful pull over the decades. Even though MTV broadcast videos that inevitably underscored the artificiality of it all, the network tried to keep one foot in the keeping-it-real camp with its *Unplugged* series. Certainly the ethos of authenticity persists in many quarters. Yet the splicing, mixing, and remixing that was pioneered by disco and taken up by rap now represents business as usual.

The frankly appropriative method of rap—its manic sampling—has also proven critical to disco's acceptance. Disco, like rock, often made over classics in its image. Eddie Floyd's soul gem "Knock on Wood" was hardly the only hit record discofied. But rap's method of sampling, at first disparaged as evidence of its unoriginality, is simply part of today's pop music universe. The stitching together of samples from unpredictable sources, such as Kanye West's use in "The Glory" of Laura Nyro's "Save the Children," is recognized as part of rap's genius. It has spawned the phenomenon of the mashup, where unlikely records such as Blondie's "Rapture" and the Doors' "Riders of the Storm" are joined together, sometimes with bracingly fresh results. Indeed, there are clubs that devote whole nights solely to mashups. This culture of musical recycling permeates all genres. Jazz standards (even Billie Holiday's protest song "Strange Fruit") are routinely remixed, and rockers cover seventies' disco records. Today, every song is a track waiting for its makeover.

Punk's DIY ethos is usually credited with democratizing popular music, but disco promoted a more participatory approach to music-making, too. From the moment that Tom Moulton remixed Gloria Gaynor's first disco tracks, records became caught up in a never-ending process of recycling. YouTube's endless offerings of remixes and covers are in many ways the legacy of disco's project of splintering and re-assemblage. Indeed, at the same time that some theorists of postmodernism were proclaiming punk the epitome of the po-mo, disco was cheerfully dismantling popular music in ways quite consistent with the concept's practice.

Certainly the shift in thinking about technology has helped to destigmatize disco. Arguments about disco's soullessness have fallen flat in a climate in which technology and emotional expressiveness are no longer considered automatic antagonists. Perhaps more to the point, technology has transformed ways of listening. Carefully tended record collections, delivered by megawatt amps and monster speakers that promise audio fidelity, have given way to eclectic playlists listened to on miniaturized components that offer the convenience of portability and the pleasures of heterogeneity. Digitally downloaded music may sound tinny to some, but audio quality has been trumped by the thrill of access.

Inevitably, these technological shifts have encouraged listeners to disregard national boundaries. The result is that it's not uncommon for music mavens to count among their favorites musicians as disparate as, say, Afrobeat's Femi Kuti, the French electronic duo Daft Punk, American singer-songwriter Fiona Apple, and British classic rockers Led Zeppelin. Increasingly musicians themselves defy easy categorization as they move promiscuously across genres. For example, the British duo Goldfrapp have had their greatest success on the dance charts, but they have explored a number of genres, including ambient, electronica, glam rock, and, most recently, folk. The 2009 *American Idol* near-winner, Adam Lambert, is a proud generalist committed to a multigenre approach that includes glam rock, dance, funk, and electronica. In the current pop music universe that values breadth over depth, hybridity over purity, disco is no longer a corrupting influence but another strand of our recombinant pop world.

The fading away of discophobia is of course inextricably bound up with larger cultural and political transformations. Although Barack Obama's election does not prove that America has magically entered the realm of the postracial, it does suggest that our increasingly multiracial country has begun to move away from the racial caricatures that have shaped our political discourse. So does the unprecedented election of a black mayor in Philadelphia, Mississippi, the site of the brutal 1964 murders of civil rights workers James Chaney, Michael Schwerner, and Andrew Goodman. After all, it was only a little more than twenty years ago that a political advertisement featuring furloughed black prisoner Willie Horton helped to put George H. W. Bush in the White House.

Feminism, as incandescent an issue as any in the polyester era, still provokes opposition, especially when it comes to abortion rights, but parts of its agenda are so deeply ingrained in our culture as to make any significant rollback politically difficult. And just as Gloria Steinem predicted, feminism has transformed men as well as women. While John Lennon's decision in the seventies to become a house-husband was seen as peculiar, no one has even raised a disapproving eyebrow about Chris Martin of Coldplay urging men to get involved in diaper-changing.

As for gay rights, the opposition to gays and lesbians serving in the military, entering into civil unions, and even into marriage, has diminished, and will continue to do so because "young people just can't see the problem," as *New York Times* columnist Gail Collins rightly observes. Even the Republican Party, which for decades reliably deployed gay rights as a wedge issue, now finds itself casting about for other issues to motivate its base.

Disco's resurgence—both in its classic and contemporary manifestations—may be related to broader political shifts, but are the waves of nostalgia for seventies' disco in any way driven by a longing for the cultural and social transformations discussed in this book? Hollywood's revisiting of the Disco Years bears only a faint resemblance to my account of the era. In 1998's *The Last Days of Disco*, the lone homosexual turns out to be passing himself off as gay to discard unwanted girlfriends. Released that same year, Mark Christopher's *54* was originally about a love triangle involving two men and a woman, all employees at the glitzy New York disco. However, after test screenings reportedly turned up negative responses, studio executives gutted the movie, leaving Steve Rubell as the only significant gay character. But if these movies (and 1997's *Boogie Nights*, another "seventies" movie) sideline disco's core constituency and play on well-worn themes of innocence turned to decadence, they also hint at the extrafamilial bonds that disco culture engendered. Curiously, the movie that best conveys the tremors of the era is the silliest of the lot. 2008's *Mamma Mia*, with its improbable armies of Abba-singing women, and its protagonist, a wistful but not unhappy middle-aged woman who has lived a lusty and independent life, conjures up the feminist struggle for connectedness and autonomy, albeit in a spirit of exuberance not always apparent in seventies' feminism.

Gay men may be marginalized in the most popular expressions of disco nostalgia, but they, nonetheless, have played a prominent role in reviving disco. From the beginning the Pet Shop Boys, one half of whom—Neil Tennant—is openly gay, identified as a disco group. They did so, says Tennant, "to try and change [its] connotation from a dirty word into something contemporary and innovative." They did this through marrying the rhythmic pleasures of disco to the lyrically arch and enigmatic in what Tennant called an "uneasy hybrid." The Boys were not the first to take this sort of approach (think of Talking Heads, Was (Not Was), Joy Division, and Soft Cell), and, more to the point, they were not the last. Ironically, it's not uncommon today for artists going against pop blandness and sexual conformity to treat disco, once derided as the aural equivalent of fast food, as if it is almost the taproot of authentic transgressiveness. For example, in her hit record "Poker Face," Gaga sings of how she fantasized about women while having sex with her boyfriend. More recently, Hercules and Love Affair, whose record company describes the group's members as a "pansexual mix," have recycled the sounds of old-school disco (right down to the horns), but with unusual sonic twists and lyrics that unsettle. The band's 2008 song "Raise Me Up" may begin nostalgically, but as a reviewer for England's *Guardian* notes, it moves away from "touchy-feely warmth to queasy unease to deep melancholy," as guest vocalist Antony Hegarty sings of having "the life danced right out of me." In the end, for many gay listeners disco may be a camp affair, but the wistfulness for what might have lasted and the sorrow about what happened next will likely cling to it for some time.

And what about America more broadly? What does it mean that disco has become the music of choice at weddings, bar mitzvahs, church dances, and fundraisers? Why is it that when one shops at Trader Joe's or Lowe's Home Improvement or any number of other stores, it's disco that one often hears? What is it about disco that makes the bands Panic! At the Disco, Slum Village Disco, and Disco Biscuits want to incorporate it in their names? It would be gratifying to argue that when wedding parties get down to the strains of the Village People's

"Y.M.C.A." they're responding to the vestiges of its subversiveness. Yet it seems to me that as classic seventies' disco washes over the culture once again it is largely emptied of such traces. If disco has become America's go-to party music, it likely has little to do with the way the records were once used or what they are actually about. Classic disco exists as silly fun that gets people up onto their feet and dancing. It can be played and listened to uncritically and it can be indulged in by would-be hipsters through the self-protective stance of irony. Above all else, it is safe music that crosses generational and racial lines in ways that much rock and rap don't.

Pop music is full of unlikely turnabouts, but surely disco's history—its shift from hot to safe music—is among the strangest. The hotness of seventies' disco doesn't just refer to its raunchiness or its rhythmic drive; it also signifies its politically incendiary quality. It is easy enough to lose sight, when spelling out the letters to "Y.M.C.A." at this season's wedding parties, that thirty-five years ago disco was the opportunity for people—African Americans, women, and gays in particular—to reimagine themselves and in the process to remake America.

NOTES

INTRODUCTION: PLASTIC FANTASTIC

page

xvi   The "Me Decade": Tom Wolfe's influential 1976 essay, "The 'Me Decade' and the Third Great Awakening," appeared in *New York* magazine, August 23, 1976, 26–40. Wolfe traced the Me-ness of the seventies to the sixties' counterculture and the new left, and plenty of conservative writers have indicted the seventies for exacerbating the unruliness and permissiveness of the sixties. "A slum of a decade," is Michael Barone's harsh verdict on the 1970s (Barone, "Commentary," *Real Clear Politics*, at http://www.realclearpolitics.com/Commentary/com-1_30_06_MB.html). Writers on the left are often no fonder of the Disco Years, but they emphasize the discontinuities between the two decades. To them, the seventies represented navel-gazing, self-indulgent identity politics. For one incisive critique from the left, see Jesse Lemisch, "Angry White Men on the Left," *New Politics* 6, no. 2, Winter 1997.

xvi   "After the poetry": Robert Vare, "Discophobia," *New York Times*, July 10, 1979, A15.

xvi   It is a measure: Edward D. Berkowitz, *Something Happened: A Political and Cultural Overview of the Seventies* (New York: Columbia University Press, 2006).

xvi Its leading record: Schoolkids' Ann Arbor was originally part of a co-op started by Eric Brown in Athens, Georgia. The store's name doubtless was derived from its clientele of college students, but it may also refer to issue 28 of the British counterculture magazine *Oz*. This issue, *Schoolkids OZ*, was targeted in a well-publicized obscenity case.

xvii flytrap: Conversation with Bette Skandalis, 2000.

xxi Jheri-curled: The loosely curled style, which was popularized by Michael Jackson and Rick James, was popular in black communities from the late seventies through much of the eighties.

xxii "rigid correlation": Ralph Ellison, *Shadow and Act* (New York: Random House, 1964), 252.

xxii Revisionist histories: Admirable histories of the seventies include: Andreas Killen, *1973 Nervous Breakdown: Watergate, Warhol and the Birth of Post-Sixties America* (New York: Bloomsbury, 2006); Berkowitz, *Something Happened*; Beth Bailey and David Farber, eds., *America in the 70s* (Lawrence, KS: University Press of Kansas, 2004); Bruce Schulman, *The Seventies: The Great Shift in American Culture, Society, and Politics* (New York: Free Press, 2001); Peter N. Carroll, *It Seemed Like Nothing Happened: The Tragedy and Promise of America in the 1970s* (New York: Holt, Rinehart and Winston, 1982).

xxii "long sixties": See, for example, Arthur Marwick, "1968 and the Cultural Revolution of the Long Sixties," in Gerd-Rainer Horn and Padraic Kenney, eds., *Transnational Moments of Change* (Lanham, MD: Rowman & Littlefield, 2004); Fredric Jameson, "Periodizing the 60s," in Sohnya Sayres et al., eds., *The 60s Without Apology* (Minneapolis: University of Minnesota Press, 1984).

xxiv Giorigo Moroder . . . possibilities of technology: see http://www.soundonsound.com/sos/mar98/articles/giorgio.html.

xxiv "the sex appeal": Walter Benjamin, *The Arcades Project* (Cambridge, MA: Harvard University Press, 1999), 8. Benjamin began it in Paris in 1927 and was still working on it when he fled the Nazi occupation in 1940.

xxiv Years later: For a smart critique of the reverence with which today's clubbers treat the 1970s' underground disco scene, see Simon Reynolds, "Disco Double Take," *Village Voice*, July 10, 2001.

xxv "beige": Nelson George, *The Death of Rhythm and Blues* (New York: Plume, 1989), 157–9.

xxv "mush of vacuous": *New Musical Express* quoted in Simon Frith, *Sound Effects* (New York: Pantheon, 1981), 22.

xxv "X-rated disco": Robert Fink, *Repeating Ourselves* (Berkeley: University of California Press, 2005), 42.

1 I HEAR A SYMPHONY

1   The major labels may: For contemporaneous accounts of the countercul-
ture and sixties' rock, see Robert Christgau, *Any Old Way You Choose It*
(Baltimore: Penguin, 1973); Richard Goldstein, *Goldstein's Greatest Hits*
(Englewood Cliffs, NJ: Prentice-Hall, 1970). Recent accounts include Fred
Goodman, *The Mansion on the Hill* (New York: Times Books, 1997); Joel Sel-
vin, *Summer of Love* (New York: Penguin, 1994); Alice Echols, *Scars of Sweet
Paradise: The Life and Times of Janis Joplin* (New York: Metropolitan Books,
1999).

1   Six years later: One could also point to the eagerness with which some major
labels would soon go after new wave.

2   "party music": Vince Aletti, "Discotheque Rock '72: Paaaaarty!" *Rolling
Stone*, September 13, 1973, 60.

2   "hot dance club": Tim Lawrence, *Love Saves the Day: A History of American Dance Music Culture, 1970–1979* (Durham, NC: Duke University Press,
2003), 147.

2   Discos were not nearly: Although some critics, such as Arnold Shaw, differ-
entiate between R&B and soul, throughout this book I use the terms inter-
changeably, largely because they were not generally treated as distinct in the
period I am writing about. The terms "black" music and "urban contemporary" came into general usage in this period as well, and on occasion I do use
those terms, although I don't believe that music is best understood by way
of racial categorization.

2   "shocked": Lawrence, *Love Saves*, 113.

3   By 1971: Arthur Kempton, *Boogaloo: The Quintessence of American Popular
Music* (New York: Pantheon Books, 2003), 298.

3   Yet even with: Fans of rock music could read *Rolling Stone, Crawdaddy,
Creem*, and *Circus*, whereas fans of soul music had to look for the occasional
article on R&B in the rock press or in black-oriented magazines like *Jet*.

4   Steady disco play: John Lombardi, "Barry White," *Rolling Stone*, August 28,
1975, 54. See Lawrence, *Love Saves*, 142–3.

4   White's "Love's Theme": The Wall of Sound was the term used to describe
producer Phil Spector's signature sound of densely layered instrumentation.
Spector called it "a Wagnerian approach to rock & roll: little symphonies for
the kids." http://en.wikipedia.org/wiki/Wall_of_Sound.

4   "stunningly dull": John Peel, "The Things You Find in Groove City," *Sounds*,
January 26, 1974, 13.

4   "white soul conservative": Robert Christgau, *Christgau's Record Guide* (New

York: Ticknor and Fields, 1981), 418. He used the term in relation to Barry White's critics.

5   "as a people": Wonder quoted in Chris Welch, "Hah—The Boy Is Getting Militant!" *Melody Maker*, February 10, 1973, 17.

5   "anything quite": Lester Bangs, *Psychotic Reactions and Carburetor Dung* (New York: Knopf, 1987), 152–3.

5   "We have a crying need": John Peel, Review of Eddie Kendricks's "Keep on Truckin'," *Sounds*, October 13, 1973, 31.

5   "Afro-Latin in sound": Aletti, "Discotheque Rock," 60.

5   "the new genre": Quoted in Peter Shapiro, *Turn the Beat Around: The Secret History of Disco* (New York: Faber and Faber, 2005), 152.

5   Certainly that was true: Mike Flood, "Captain Fantastic," *Sounds*, November 9, 1974, 8. John said that the record had secured the number one spot in New York City but had yet to break out nationally.

6   By 1974: PIR said that the acronym MFSB stood for family (Mother, Father, Sister, Brother), but insiders knew it meant "mother-fuckin' son-of-a-bitch," as in "he played his ass off." John A. Jackson, *A House on Fire* (New York: Oxford University Press, 2004), 115.

6   While Barry White's: Nelson George, *Top of the Charts* (Piscataway, NJ: New Century Publishers, 1983), 162. I have used the record charts of both *Billboard* and *Record World*.

6   "lush fluidity": Disco deejay Michael Gomes thought it marked a break from Motown. See Lawrence, *Love Saves*, 122–3.

6   "tropical funk": Jon Pareles and Patricia Romanowski, *The Rolling Stone Encyclopedia of Rock & Roll* (New York: Rolling Stone Press/Summit Books, 1983), 298.

7   "bubblegum funk": Joe McEwen, "KC and the Sunshine Band," in Dave Marsh with John Swenson, eds., *The Rolling Stone Record Guide* (New York: Random House, 1979), 201.

7   The success of white: This is one of Nelson George's many criticisms of disco. See his useful *The Death of Rhythm and Blues*.

7   "the total black experience": Shapiro, *Turn the Beat*, 151.

7   "He sounds black": Ianthe Thomas, "Spinning Crossover Music to the Crossover Culture," *Village Voice*, December 12, 1977. Crocker, who died in 2000, was African American.

7   "your mother will": Mike Flood, Review of Hues Corporation, *Sounds*, December 14, 1974, 15.

7   "still exciting": Rob Mackie, "A Lesson in Streetology," *Sounds*, October 20,

1973. For another example see Charles Shaar Murray, who in his column, "Singles," praises Betty Wright's "Clean Up Woman" and compares it favorably to the "plastic imitation [funk] that's getting churned out by the ton at this juncture in time." See *New Musical Express,* June 30, 1973, 13.

7   "black people are just": "Elton John Talking to Jerry Gilbert: Mr. Spaceman and The Eggplant," *Sounds,* January 13, 1973, 15.

7   "What happened to the days": Quoted in Frith, *Sound Effects,* 22. There are many such reactions in both the British and U.S. music press. A British reviewer, writing of Harold Melvin and the Blue Notes, emphasized the tension in their music "between Soul and Schmaltz." See *Melody Maker,* February 17, 1973, 26. Another writes that the Stylistics "have finally crossed the line that separates fragile, floating soulfulness from effete schmaltz." See *Melody Maker,* February 24, 1973, 25. American critic Robert Christgau, by contrast, argued that *Shaft* proved that "not only do black people make better pop-schlock movies than white people, they also make better pop-schlock music." See Christgau, *Record Guide,* 173.

8   "People would kill a DJ": Mel Cheren as told to Gabriel Rotello, *Keep on Dancin': My Life and the Paradise Garage* (New York: 24 Hours for Life, 2000), 148.

8   In Detroit: Author interview with Marty Ross, January 31, 2009.

9   Moulton's remixes: Up until this point, the single had been produced on a 7-inch record at 45 rpm. These new extended-play singles were 12-inches in diameter and usually, although not always, at 33 rpm.

9   In an era of primitive: See Cheren, *Keep On,* 151–2. According to Cheren, Moulton also made the serendipitous discovery that spreading the grooves of a single song on a 12-inch record produced a "sharper, cleaner and hotter" sound. Cheren takes credit for another disco innovation—putting on the B-side of a single an instrumental version of the song on the A-side. See Cheren, *Keep On,* 119–20. However, several years earlier, in 1970, James Brown had put an instrumental version of "Hey America" on the B-side of that single. See "Discography," *James Brown: Star Time,* Polydor Records, 1991, CD boxed set booklet, 56.

9   By looping back: See Lawrence, *Love Saves,* 148–9, for Moulton's mixing techniques.

10 "I don't sing much": Ibid., 148–9.

10 Veteran R&B singer: Ibid., 263–4.

10 "it wasn't the way": This is Moulton's memory of their reaction. See ibid., 146.

10   Mindless, repetitive, formulaic: See Walter Hughes's provocative essay "In the Empire of the Beat: Discipline and Disco," in Andrew Ross and Tricia Rose, eds., *Microphone Fiends: Youth Music, Youth Culture* (New York: Routledge, 1994).

10   The fact that many: This seems to be what R&B music writer Nelson George was getting at in his groundbreaking book *The Death of Rhythm and Blues,* which blames disco for defunking or whitening R&B. He identifies club deejays as the "real movers and shakers of disco," and argues that they whitened the music because they frequently were gay men whose taste, like that of other disco fans, was characterized by "a feeling of pseudosophistication." George also targeted sellout black musicians who churned out "beige music," their bourgie black fans, and the recent consolidation of the record industry, a shift that encouraged crossover success at the expense of funky R&B. See 157–9.

10   "the most artificial": Chuck D quoted in Simon Reynolds, *Generation Ecstasy: Into the World of Techno and Rave Culture* (New York: Routledge, 1999), 13.

11   The idea that disco: Disco is so often treated as gay that its roots in R&B are sometimes obscured. Disco insider Mel Cheren makes the point that disco's earliest producers and musicians were not gay, which is, for the most part, true. See Cheren, *Keep On,* 115. At the same time, most histories of R&B or soul music—including the excellent ones listed here—either downplay or ignore disco or treat it as a species alien to black musical traditions. See George, *The Death;* Guthrie Ramsey Jr., *Race Matters* (Berkeley, CA: University of California Press, 2004); Marc Anthony Neal, *What the Music Said* (New York: Routledge, 1999); Rickey Vincent, *Funk: The Music, the People, and the Rhythm of the One* (New York: St. Martin's Press, 1996); Gerri Hirshey, *Nowhere to Run: The Story of Soul Music* (New York: Penguin, 1984), 351.

11   Yes, disco staked out: On the importance of sweetness to African American pop music, see Robin D. G. Kelley, "A Sole Response," *American Quarterly* 52, no. 3 (2000): 537. In this essay, a review of Brian Ward's *Just My Soul Responding,* Kelley argues that Ward's ready identification of "white styles" and "black styles" of music-making runs counter to the author's explicit critique of racial essentialism in popular music. Kelley is especially critical of Ward's tendency to associate a "sweeter" vocal tradition with whites and to limit his definition of the "black elements" of pop music to the blues. Kelley contends that the sweet vocal and instrumental tradition stretches back quite a ways, and is present in the work of Billy Eckstine, Sarah Vaughan, Ella Fitzgerald, and Lester Young, to name but a few.

11   Disco, and the music: Theorists of rap music have written of the way in which it contests and resists forces of social domination through a "hidden" transcript that operates very often in a disguised, coded form. While this is doubtless true of some rap, quite a lot of rap music seems anything but reticent about its views of the police, the media, and politicians. See Tricia Rose's important study *Black Noise* (Hanover, NH: Wesleyan University Press, 1994), 100–1.

11   "hidden transcript": See James C. Scott, *Domination and the Arts of Resistance: Hidden Transcripts* (New Haven: Yale University Press, 1992).

12   Disco's history: Even a question as straightforward as when music critics first become aware of this new music has eluded discographers. According to most discographers, it was Vince Aletti, in a September 1973 *Rolling Stone* article, who identified the music that would come to be called disco. However, my research shows that even before Aletti's essay appeared, British music critics were already using the term "disco" and were cognizant of a shift within American R&B. And the British music press was full of ads for disco equipment and disco deejays, and mentions of disco-goers. See Martin Hayman's review of Steely Dan's *Countdown to Ecstasy* in *Sounds*, August 18, 1973, 44. In it he describes their music as having a "heavy discopop groove." In a review of Earth Wind and Fire's "Head to the Sky," Hayman describes the group as "mid-paced disco fodder with a touch of class." See his review in *Sounds*, October 13, 1973, 30.

12   "You probably haven't": Hirshey, *Nowhere to Run*, 189.

13   "beat on a bloody": Ibid., 186. Pop critic Don Charles Hampton argues that what we think of as the Motown beat was, in fact, pioneered by the Four Seasons and their producer Bob Crewe in songs such as "Sherry" and "Big Girls Don't Cry." See http://popculturecantina.blogspot.com/2007/10/bob-crewe-part-two.html.

13   "Now it was the standard": Ibid., 184.

13   Critics have often: There are important exceptions, including Robert Christgau, John Peel, David Marsh, Penny Valentine, Robin Katz, Vince Aletti, Tom Smucker, Russell Gersten, Charles Shaar Murray, Simon Frith, and Greil Marcus, who took R&B/soul artists seriously. America's premier rock paper, *Rolling Stone*, covered black musicians, but focused on Jimi Hendrix (while he was still alive) and those, such as Little Richard and Chuck Berry, whom it regarded as roots musicians. One angry letter writer to the paper contended that black musicians were more likely to turn up in the paper's obituaries than in its reviews or news sections. See Letter to the Editor, *Rolling Stone*,

May 9, 1974, 16. As David Morse argued, rock critics sometimes treated black musicians like dinosaurs, "precursors who, having taught the white men all they know, must gradually recede into the distance." Morse quoted in Iain Chambers, *Urban Rhythms* (New York: Macmillan, 1985), 117. Jazz critic Ralph Gleason, who was *Rolling Stone*'s senior editor, did not think that black musicians needed to lumber off into the distance, but he counseled them (everyone from the Four Tops to James Brown) to abandon the whole "Ed Sullivan trip, striving as hard as they can to get on that stage and become part of the American success story." He urged them to begin taking their cues from anti-establishment hippie groups such as the Jefferson Airplane. Quoted in Charles Shaar Murray, *Crosstown Traffic: Jimi Hendrix and the Rock 'n' Roll Revolution* (New York: St. Martin's Press, 1989), 79. In the pages of *Rolling Stone*, Motown acts came in for the lion's share of criticism. The paper's usual R&B critic in its early years, Jon Landau, soon to be manager of Bruce Springsteen, argued that the Supremes were "totally committed to show business values and lost their soul long ago." Jon Landau, "Soul '67," *Rolling Stone*, February 24, 1968, 18. See also Jon Landau, "Rock 1970," *Rolling Stone*, December 2, 1970, 43.

13   "so much more popular": Peter Guralnick, *Dream Boogie: The Triumph of Sam Cooke* (New York: Back Bay, 2006), 250.

14   And he went so far: See Gerald Early, *One Nation Under a Groove,* rev. ed. (Ann Arbor, MI: University of Michigan Press, 2004), 187. See also Suzanne Smith, *Dancing in the Street* (Cambridge, MA: Harvard University Press, 1999), 164. The subsequent success of "Shotgun" on the pop charts revealed the trickiness of these racial categorizations, especially at a time when young whites were thirsty for hard-driving, gutbucket soul.

14   But if Gordy was: This is Early's argument in *One Nation*. When the Motown Revue hit the South in 1962, its bus was shot at and its performers and crew faced Jim Crow conditions, but as a result the racial barriers became more porous. See Early, *One Nation*, 104.

14   Of the 537 singles: Kempton, *Boogaloo*, 262.

14   "a metaphorical theme": Early, *One Nation*, 104.

14   Two qualities distinguished: Disco historian Tim Lawrence describes this gospel device as the "sweeping and apparently decisive end to a song that is instantaneously followed by the piecemeal reintroduction of the instrumental and vocal parts." See Lawrence, *Love Saves*, 112–3. As regards the song's percussion, Lawrence points out, the sound remained more snare than bass or kick drum. See ibid., 120.

15   Many of the black musicians: See Jackson, *A House on Fire*, and Shapiro, *Turn the Beat*, 143–5. PIR was meant to be the Motown of the seventies, and Gamble and Huff's ambitions became more realizable after they struck an independent production deal with Columbia Records' president, Clive Davis. Although the financial arrangement with Columbia was not especially generous, it provided Gamble and Huff with the capital they needed to make an impact, and it gave Columbia a firmer foothold in R&B.

15   "The Philly sound": Montana quoted in Lawrence, *Love Saves*, 119.

16   "brassy and up": Jacobson quoted in Shapiro, *Turn the Beat*, 152.

16   Thom Bell was a key: Terry Gross's interview with Bell is at http://www.npr .org/templates/story/story.php?storyId=6181419.

16   The Stylistics lead: See David Bertrand Wilson's review, http://www.warr .org/odd70s.html#TheStylistics.

16   "hissing hi-hats": Shapiro, *Turn the Beat*, 145.

17   "Motown used four-four": Lawrence, *Love Saves*, 120.

17   That pattern: Thom Bell has also said that Young's drumming on "The Love" "started that whole disco thing." Jackson, *A House on Fire*, 154.

17   "comparatively ornate records": Dave Marsh, *The Heart of Rock & Soul: The 1001 Greatest Singles Ever Made* (New York: Da Capo, 1989), 5.

17   "scream at the end": Albert Goldman, quoted in Hirshey, *Nowhere to Run*, 261.

17   "a little beyond": Cliff White and Harry Weinger, "Are You Ready For Star Time?," *James Brown: Star Time* booklet.

17   "Everything came out": Fred Wesley is the speaker here. See http://www .downbeat.com/jamesbrown.asp.

17   "rhythmic elements": Vincent, *Funk*, 37–8.

17   "the horns played": Robert Palmer, "James Brown," in Jim Miller, ed., *The Rolling Stone Illustrated History of Rock and Roll* (New York: Random House, 1980), 140.

17   "choked his guitar": Palmer, "James Brown," 140.

18   "crawling the floor": Guralnick, *Dream Boogie*, 145.

19   "trying to do a sophisticated": James Brown with Bruce Tucker, *Godfather of Soul* (New York: Thunder's Mouth, 1990), 245.

19   "the blahs": The cover of Funkadelic's *Uncle Jam Wants You* includes a bottom banner that reads, "Rescue Dance Music from 'the blahs.'"

20   "I can see the disco": "Get Up Offa That Thing" lacked the sharp-edged quality of Brown's funk experiments, but that and the 4/4 cymbals were Brown's only concessions to the disco sound.

20 "exploring the alien": Christgau, review of *Get Up Offa That Thing* in Christgau, *Record Guide*, 62.

20 "inspiration, contemplation": Brian Ward, *Just My Soul Responding* (Berkeley, CA: University of California Press, 1998), 265. Interestingly, in contrast to disco producers, Brown never really took advantage of the possibilities of remixing his tracks. Conversation with Charles Kronengold, February 2008.

21 Brown's problem: Correspondence with Charles Kronengold, January 31, 2008. For an extended discussion of Brown's music and why he might have segregated the funky from the sophisticated, see my article "The Land of Somewhere Else: Refiguring James Brown in Seventies Disco," *Criticism* 50, no. 1 (Winter 2008).

21 "Disco music": See http://www.discomusic.com/forums/disco-music-70s-80s/26199-disco-music-funk-bow-tie-fred.html.

21 "bridge the gap": Clinton quoted in John Abbey, "We Have Lift-Off!," *Blues and Soul Review* 199 (June 29, 1976): 4.

21 "Family Affair" featured: Some have said that drum machines were only used at the very tail end of disco, and this seems to be fairly accurate. However, the idea persists that disco was produced by machines. Timmy Thomas's R&B record of late 1972, "Why Can't We Live Together," which featured a primitive drum machine, did lead some other artists to follow suit. John Peel was perhaps the first critic to notice their use. Peter Shapiro's discussion of disco percussion and the drum machine is excellent. See Shapiro, *Turn the Beat*, 98–9.

22 "repetitious part": See James Brown and Marc Eliot, *I Feel Good: A Memoir of a Life of Soul*, rev. ed. (New York: NAL, 2005), 195. Other sixties' soul men were critical of disco. Although Curtis Mayfield helped to pave the way for disco, he claimed that it left him "flat wondering what the hell to do and even how to do it" because it was so "monotonous." See "A Lasting Impression: The *Rolling Stone* Interview with Curtis Mayfield," *Rolling Stone*, October 28, 1993, 66. A number of R&B critics and historians of R&B have criticized disco, too, including Rickey Vincent. See Vincent, *Funk*, 23.

22 "P-Funk for passives": Kempton, *Boogaloo*, 405. Some writers hail P-Funk as the apotheosis of blackness. For example, Cornel West writes that George Clinton's "technofunk unabashedly exacerbates and accentuates the 'blackness' of black music, the 'Afro-Americanness' of Afro-American music . . ." See West, *The Cornel West Reader*, new ed. (New York: Basic Civitas Books, 2000), 479. However, the P-Funk sound was forged in part through the group's connection to Detroit's largely white acid rock scene. "We was too

white for the blacks, and we was too black for the whites," recalls band leader Clinton. "You had to be, like, a freak to be into them," according to P-Funk's album cover artist, Ronald "Stozo" Edwards. Both quotes from David Mills et al., eds., *George Clinton and P-Funk: An Oral History* (New York: Avon, 1998), 73. Of course, the acid rock scene that P-Funk took part in didn't exist in a bubble. Those groups had been influenced by black musicians, especially blues artists, which demonstrates the trickiness of racially based musical categorization.

23 Specifically, it means: Other writers and scholars have criticized the tendency to privilege as authentically "black" music that is raw and unadorned. That list includes Brian Ward (albeit somewhat inconsistently) in his magisterial *Just My Soul Responding*, 262–6; Steve Perry, "Ain't No Mountain High Enough: The Politics of Crossover," in Simon Frith, ed., *Facing the Music* (New York: Pantheon, 1989); Ingrid Monson, "The Problem with White Hipness: Race, Gender, and Cultural Conceptions in Jazz Historical Discourse," *Journal of the American Musicological Society* xlviii, no. 3 (Fall 1995); Ann Powers, "Pop Diva, Soul Sister," *Los Angeles Times*, January 28, 2007; Susan McClary, *Conventional Wisdom: The Content of Musical Form* (Berkeley, CA: University of California Press, 2000); Alice Echols, " 'Shaky Ground': Popular Music in the Disco Years," in *Shaky Ground: The Sixties and Its Aftershocks* (New York: Columbia University Press, 2002). Hugh Barker and Yuval Taylor return to this theme again and again in their wonderful *Faking It: The Quest for Authenticity in Popular Music* (New York: W. W. Norton, 2007).

23 For example, Houston Baker: See Houston Baker, "Hybridity, the Rap Race, and Pedagogy for the 1990s," in Andrew Ross and Constance Penley, eds., *Technoculture* (Minneapolis: University of Minnesota Press, 1991), 198. See also Mills et al., eds., *George Clinton*, 93.

23 "the heartbeat": Charles Kronengold, "Exchange Theories in Disco, New Wave and Album-Oriented Rock," *Criticism* 50, no. 1 (Winter 2008).

23 Hayes favored lush: Procul Harum's "A Whiter Shade of Pale" had broken the mold for Top 40 radio in 1968.

24 "to make soul music": Ed Ward, Geoffrey Stokes, and Ken Tucker, *Rock of Ages: The Rolling Stone History of Rock & Roll* (New York: Rolling Stone Press, 1986), 503.

24 "walk out onto the studio": http://www.memphisflyer.com/memphis/Content?oid=oid%3A20913.

24 "real deep into a listener's": Hirshey, *Nowhere to Run*, 354.

24   Indeed, Denise Chapman: Lawrence, *Loves Saves*, 263. Hayes also covered "Windows of the World" and "The Look of Love."

25   "dull, enervated": Russell Gersten, "Record Review," *Rolling Stone,* January 20, 1972.

25   "the *native* sensuality": Mark Vinig, *Rolling Stone*, January 3, 1974.

25   "black Muzak": Vince Aletti, *Rolling Stone*, January 7, 1971.

25   "what's next": Ertegun quoted in George, *The Death*, 93. R&B critic George seconds Ertegun, and contends that whites tend to cast themselves as upholders of musical tradition much more so than blacks, who are in a "constant flight from the status quo" (107).

25   "That's putting me": Wonder quoted in O'Connell Driscoll, "Stevie Wonder in New York," in Jann Wenner, ed., *Twenty Years of Rolling Stone* (New York: Straight Arrow Press, 1987), 254.

26   "whitening process": Gamble quoted in Michael Watts, "Working in a Soul Mine," *Melody Maker*, March 17, 1973, 15.

26   "green": Gamble quoted in Shapiro, *Turn the Beat*, 143.

26   "cannot really hear": Jackson, *A House on Fire*, 135.

26   For starters, he made: It wasn't at all unusual in the fifties and sixties for R&B albums to carry pictures of someone or something other than the artist in question. The cover art for James Brown's *Please, Please, Please* featured a picture of a white couple, and a photo of a baby appeared on the cover of his album *Think*. When R&B performers were actually pictured, they often were shown working up a sweat onstage or posed smiling winningly at the camera.

26   "bald was as black": Hirshey, *Nowhere to Run*, 349–50.

27   "the impact of Black Power": Craig Werner, *A Change Is Gonna Come: Music, Race and the Soul of America,* rev. ed. (Ann Arbor, MI: University of Michigan Press, 2006), 173.

27   This was the crucial: Actor Samuel L. Jackson makes this point about blaxploitation films in Isaac Julien's documentary *Baadasssss Cinema*, New Video Group Inc., 2003.

27   It's true that many: These trouble songs are far better known than Hayes's own, but he was among the first artists to record music that addressed the issues of the day, with two 1970 album tracks. While the Temptations cautioned against letting the spendthrift Joneses get you down, on *The Isaac Hayes Movement* he suggested that the bigger problem might be respectable married life itself. His "One Big Unhappy Family" chronicles the loveless marriage of a middle-class, church-going couple too proud to let anyone

know that their marriage isn't "the neighborhood example" everyone takes it for. And in "Monologue: Ike's Rap I," recorded that same year, Hayes rapped about a working-class man on the eve of leaving for Vietnam and his (likely white) co-ed girlfriend whose parents were pressuring her to ditch him.

28   "drift into accommodation": Greil Marcus, *Mystery Train: Images of America in Rock 'n' Roll Music*, rev. ed. (New York: Dutton, 1982), 101–7.

28   "deterioration": Neal, *What the Music Said*, 87.

28   "were dancing": Ward, *Just My Soul*, 354.

29   "rock steady" . . . "shakey": The references are to Aretha Franklin's 1971 hit "Rock Steady" and the Temptations' 1975 hit (on which Eddie Hazel of P-Funk played lead guitar) "Shakey Ground."

29   "black folks could go": Vincent, *Funk*, 6.

29   "harp crazy": Fred Wesley Jr., *Hit Me, Fred: Recollections of a Sideman* (Durham, NC: Duke University Press, 2005), 169.

30   "reversing the traffic": Daryl Easlea, *Everybody Dance: Chic and the Politics of Disco* (London: Helter Skelter, 2004), 70.

30   "New York funk": Nick Coleman, "Groove Is in His Heart: Chic's Nile Rodgers on the Unlikely Inspiration for 'Le Freak,'" *Independent*, July 19, 2009, http://www.independent.co.uk/arts-entertainment/music/features/groove-is-in-his-heart-chics-nile-rodgers-on-the-unlikely-inspiration-for-le-freak-1749306.html.

30   "were looking for": "Stevie Wonder: Interview with Penny Valentine," *Sounds*, February 10, 1973, 23.

30   "broken promises": Werner, *Change*, 173.

30   "smiling face trope": Shapiro, *Turn the Beat*, 120–37.

30   "Everybody knew": Even Wallace's blunt observation assumes that something has shifted in that one can now become famous. See Michele Wallace, *Dark Design and Visual Culture* (Durham, NC: Duke University Press, 2004), 209; 107.

31   "uplifted the race": Quoted in Easlea, *Everybody Dance*, 44, 97.

31   "Just come on down": Ibid., 114.

31   "People asked how": Ibid., 156.

32   "unbridled machismo": George, *The Death*, 104.

32   "hooked most black men": See Amazon.com, James Brown.

32   "We look at James Brown": Al Sharpton Jr. quoted in Hirshey, *Nowhere to Run*, 277.

33   "in a red jumpsuit": Palmer, "James Brown," 136.

33   "it makes your dick": Kempton, *Boogaloo*, 398.

33   "black stud": Ward et al., eds., *Rock of Ages,* 504.

33   "didn't take himself seriously": Richard Williams, "Black Moses Does His Thing," *Melody Maker,* January 13, 1973, 39.

33   Hayes has said: See http://blogcritics.org/archives/2002/09/05/102249.php.

33   As critic Carol Cooper: http://carolcooper.org/music/hayes-95.php.

34   "It was Hayes's": *South Park*'s co-creator Trey Parker sent up Hayes's love-man persona when he had Hayes's character, Chef, sing the X-rated "Choco-late Salty Balls," a song that Parker penned.

34   "personalized epic": Marsh, *The Heart,* 574.

34   Indeed, White so copped: Vince Aletti, "Review," *Rolling Stone,* February 14, 1974.

34   White's breakthrough single: Christgau, *Record Guide,* 418.

35   "perform any song": Jon Landau, *Rolling Stone,* July 3, 1975, 56.

35   "erased the difference": Lombardi, "Barry White," 54.

35   White presented: His first big break came with his girl group, Love Unlim-ited, whose 1972 LP was actually entitled "From a Girl's Point of View." He also created several songs to express his "masculine side," and only reluc-tantly sang them himself after he failed to find a male singer. He later said that the album was his attempt at expressing his "female side." Barry White with Marc Eliot, *Love Unlimited: Insights on Life and Love* (New York: Broad-way Books, 1999), 107.

35   "women's liberation": Heller quoted in Lombardi, "Barry White," 54.

35   Marvin Gaye's falsetto: On his 1976 LP *I Want You,* Gaye even moaned, "Baby, suck dick."

37   The Dells scored a hit: See Kelefa Sanneh, "What He Knows for Sure," *The New Yorker,* August 4, 2008, 31.

37   "intentionally made records": Chuck D quoted in Richard Iton, *In Search of the Black Fantastic* (New York: Oxford, 2008), 153, 355 n. 45.

37   "softening up": Vandross told one interviewer that he refused to go along with the injunction against a male vocalist going against masculine hard-ness. "That's society, that's rearing, that's the package," he said. Quoted in Iton, *In Search,* 153.

38   "rhymes could still sigh": http://www.pbs.org/pov/pov2004/wattstax/.

2 MORE, MORE, MORE

39   "There is a force": Siano quoted in Bill Brewster and Frank Broughton, *Last Night a DJ Saved My Life* (New York: PGW, 2000), 155.

39   "This is one massive": Larry Kramer, *Faggots* (New York: Grove Press, 1978, republished 2000), 352.

39   "Where before": Edmund White, *The Farewell Symphony* (New York: Vintage, 1998), 122.

40   "sprung up like": Ibid.

40   "sound and light": Esther Newton, *Cherry Grove, Fire Island: Sixty Years in America's First Gay and Lesbian Resort* (Boston, MA: Beacon, 1995), 244.

40   Yet disco: The author of the website nycnotkansas.com recalls "batting around the question: *When did it start?*" with friends who had opened the disco Les Mouches. He says the consensus is that it all came together in the summer of 1974 at the Sandpiper in the Fire Island Pines. Others cite other discos, of course, but the dating seems accurate.

40   "It was like": Cheren, *Keep On*, 245–6. Although gay men were most prominent in deejaying and promotion, there were gay men, such as Cheren and the legendary songwriter and producer Bob Crewe, in other areas as well. For more on Crewe, see Don Charles Hampton's very useful blog, http://popculturecantina.blogspot.com/2007/10/bob-crewe-part-two.html.

41   "solitude, shame" . . . "a depressive status" . . . "some version": My understanding of gay men's relationship to the Broadway musical has been influenced by D. A. Miller's remarkable *Place for Us* [*Essay on the Broadway Musical*] (Cambridge, MA: Harvard University Press, 1998), 27, 26, 7. Miller's essay, like much recent work in queer theory, is committed to uncovering and analyzing those parts of pre-Stonewall consciousness driven underground by gay liberation's imperative that gay is good and shame an undesirable relic of a bygone era. For example, Michael Warner writes, "Shame is Bedrock." Warner, *The Trouble with Normal* (Cambridge, MA: Harvard University Press, 1999), 35.

41   "No sad, solitary": D. A. Miller, "Cruising," *Film Quarterly* 61, no. 2 (Winter 2007/8). Miller writes that at first Friedkin was not interested in Gerald Walker's 1970 novel, which featured the usual effeminate gay men. It was only after visiting the Mine Shaft, where Friedkin wore only a jock strap and was accompanied by an armed mafia escort, that he became interested in the novel's story, transposed to this setting.

41   "going out": See David Roman, "Theatre Journals: Dance Liberation," *Theatre Journal* 55, no. 3 (October 2003).

42   "you were always": See http://www.nycnotkansas.com.

42   In 1969 alone: Figure cited in Elizabeth A. Armstrong and Susan Crage, "Movements and Memory: The Making of the Stonewall Myth," *American*

Sociological Review 71, no. 5 (October 2006). In this useful essay, Armstrong and Crage argue that the Stonewall myth—the idea that the Stonewall riot marked the beginning of the modern gay rights movement—conceals earlier activism in other cities, particularly in the Bay Area. They also advance the intriguing argument that "Stonewall made its impact on the gay movement through its commemoration" rather than through the uprising itself. They note, "The first commemoration of Stonewall was gay liberation's biggest and most successful protest event." However, in attributing Stonewall's mythic power to its successful commemoration, the authors seem to miss what was distinctive and truly memorable about Stonewall—that in contrast to other and earlier confrontations with the authorities, the rioters there could claim victory and at the site of gays' greatest oppression, the bar. By turning the tables on the police by becoming the attackers and transforming the cops into the besieged, the rioters that June could point to something other than their ongoing exploitation and discrimination.

42 "would choose": Duberman quoted in David Kirby, "Stonewall Veterans Recall the Outlaw Days," *New York Times,* June 27, 1999, 14.

42 In 1966: Charles Perry, *The Haight-Ashbury: A History* (New York: Random House, 1984), 82.

42 On the other coast: It took a protest by the Gay Liberation Front in 1969 before the *Village Voice* would allow the use of the word "gay." See Duberman, *Stonewall* (New York: Dutton, 1983), 105.

42 Even on Fire Island: Duberman, *Stonewall*, 162.

42 According to one study: See Gilbert H. Herdt and Andrew Boxer, *Children of Horizons: How Gay and Lesbian Teens Are Leading a New Way Out of the Closet* (Boston: Beacon, 1996), 36.

43 "had to take turns" . . . "All male eyes": Rodwell quoted in Duberman, *Stonewall*, 163. See Mel Cheren's corroborating account, *Keep On*, 60–1. Gay men sometimes avoided trouble by doing the Madison and other line dances, which were permissible in some bars as long as a woman was a part of the group. Perhaps this explains the early success of the Hustle in gay bars. See http://www.nycnotkansas.com. The *New York Times* obituary for the Botel's owner, John B. Whyte, says that he indeed sometimes shined the flashlight into the eyes of men whom he deemed indiscreet. See http://query.nytimes.com/gst/fullpage.html?res=9500E3DB1138F931A25757C0A9629C8B63.

43 When these groups: George Chauncey, *Gay New York* (New York: Basic Books, 1995), 170.

43 Very often dancing: Those gays, like the writer Parker Tyler, who pushed the

envelope by dancing with other men in bars, were "almost as often told to stop dancing." See Chauncey, *Gay New York*, 169.

44 It was this vulnerability: Of course, the Mafia had controlled much night-life during the Prohibition years. New York's police commissioner told the press, "gangsters had a 'piece' of nearly all the night clubs . . ." See F. Raymond Daniel, "The Big Business of the Racketeers," *New York Times,* April 27, 1930.

44 Vito Spatafore: Joseph Gannascoli, the actor who played Vito, decided to "out" his character after reading about another Vito who was gay and a hit man for the Gambino family. *The Sopranos'* actor wanted to make his Vito a "cross between Mike Tyson and Liberace." See http://www.planetout.com/entertainment/news/?sernum=1232&navpath=/entertainment/television. Mafia historian George De Stefano writes, "Gay folklore has long held that Mafiosi put their sons and other gay kin who were homosexual in charge of the gay bar they owned." See De Stefano, *An Offer We Can't Refuse: The Mafia in the Mind of America* (New York: Faber and Faber, 2007), 222. Some have connected this to the incidence of same-sex sex among men in Italy or to its incidence in prison. See http://bitterqueen.typepad.com/history_of_gay_bars_in_ne/genovese_crime_family/.

44 The unlicensed bar: See Donn Teal, *The Gay Militants* (New York: Stein and Day, 1971). Over the years the Stonewall has gone through changes in ownership; in 1997, a new owner, who had renovated and reopened it as a three-story nightclub, ran into problems with the authorities. Ironically, it was largely dancing—the owner had been unsuccessful in his bid to obtain a dancing permit—that got the bar into trouble with the city's Social Club Task Force. See David Halbfinger, "For a Bar Not Used to Dancing Around Issues, Dancing Is Now the Issue," *New York Times,* July 29, 1997, B5.

44 "you knew that": David Carter, *Stonewall: The Riots That Sparked the Gay Revolution* (New York: St. Martin's Griffin, 2004), 88. I have found evidence of other gay bars where men sometimes danced, but it seems to have still been precarious. One possible exception, although it dates back to an earlier period, is the Grapevine. According to historian Martin Duberman, "It was the liveliest gay spot in the city in the late fifties, patronized by lesbians as well as gay men, and a forerunner of the seventies' discos, which thought themselves *sui generis.* Indeed one of my diary entries from April 1958 reads like a press release from the disco-queen delirium of twenty years later: absorbed and yet released in a concatenation of emotions, bathed and abetted by the heat and excitement, the stimulation of the liquor and the

music." Although I take Duberman's point here that the ecstasies of gay disco were not unprecedented in gay male life, I would still maintain that the beat, the heat, the drugs, the freedom from raids, and the absence of women made for a different, more intensely tribal experience. See Duberman's wonderful memoir, *Cures, A Gay Man's Odyssey* (New York: Basic Books, 1999), 48.

45 "Indeed, the only time": Both David Carter and Martin Duberman note that the bar, with its thick door, blackened windows, and tough guys at the door, offered marginally better security than its competitors. See Carter, *Stonewall*, 68; Duberman, *Stonewall*, 187.

45 "I had such a thrill": Carter, *Stonewall*, 71. The Stonewall had two dance floors, one in the front room or "white room," so named because of its music and its patrons, and the other in the "black" or "Puerto Rican room," where soul was the music of choice. Carter, *Stonewall*, 73.

45 "money machine": Duberman, *Stonewall*, 183. Carter (*Stonewall*, 114) argues that by the summer of 1969 the Stonewall's business was down and that it was drawing a somewhat rougher crowd. However, on the night of the riot the bar was packed. Seymour Pine, the policeman who led the raid on the Stonewall, apologized for it in a 2004 event that was meant to help launch Carter's book. Pine said the police raided gay bars because they were concerned about the Mafia, not gays. They raided the Stonewall, he said, because of their suspicion that the Mafiosi there were involved with stolen European bonds. See Lincoln Anderson, " 'I'm Sorry,' says Inspector Who Led Stonewall Raid," *Villager*, June 16–22, 2004.

45 Despite the fact: According to David Carter and to the police officer leading the raid, the police raided the bar because they were convinced that its Mafia owners were involved in major bond theft, which they achieved through blackmailing homosexual employees of Wall Street. See Carter, *Stonewall*, 100–3.

45 And it was the first time: There is no shortage of theories about why the riot occurred. Historian John D'Emilio has argued that the death of gay icon Judy Garland, whose memorial service had been held earlier that day, put gays in no mood to cede any gay ground. He also argues that the Stonewall's patrons had grown unaccustomed to bar raids, which he says had largely ceased by then. See D'Emilio, *Making Trouble* (New York: Routledge, 1992), 240. David Carter emphatically argues against the Garland thesis, which he says fails the evidence test. If anything, he believes, as did gay activist and Garland fan Vito Russo, that the singer was symbolically allied with the old order that Stonewall upended. See Carter, *Stonewall*, 260–1. Martin Duberman pays little attention to Garland's death. He also notes that Stonewall

was regularly raided, and had been just two weeks earlier. See Duberman, *Stonewall*, 191–4. Six months *after* the Stonewall uprising, the Gay Activists Alliance was calling for an end to police harassment of gay bars. See Kay Tobin and Randy Wicker, *The Gay Crusaders* (New York: Paperback Library, 1972), 36.

45 "things were completely changed" . . . "beautiful—they've lost": Duberman, *Stonewall*, 208.

45 "kind of seismic shift": Ibid., 206.

46 Even Stryker: Susan Stryker and Jim Van Buskirk, *Gay by the Bay: A History of Queer Culture in the San Francisco Bay Area* (San Francisco: Chronicle Books, 1996), 53.

46 "None of that!": Ibid., 210.

46 Several historians: See Newton, *Cherry Grove*; Elizabeth Kennedy and Madeline Davis, *Boots of Leather, Slippers of Gold* (New York: Routledge, 1993); John D'Emilio, *The World Turned: Essays on Gay History, Politics, and Culture* (Durham, NC: Duke University Press, 2002); Allen Drexel, "Before Paris Burned," in Brett Beemyn, ed., *Creating a Place for Ourselves* (New York: Routledge, 1997).

47 "old gay": Carter, *Stonewall*, 83–4.

47 However, its leaders: See ibid., 213–4, 259. The SLA penalized bars that served homosexuals on the grounds that their gatherings were "disorderly." It wasn't unusual for bartenders to refuse drinks to those they suspected of being gay or to order them to sit facing away from other customers as a deterrent to cruising, or to throw them out in order to prevent the SLA from moving against the bar.

47 Activist Craig Rodwell: Rodwell quoted in Duberman, *Stonewall*, 205.

47 "tacky and cheap": Ibid., 207.

48 "real dive": Ibid., 181.

48 Lesbian feminists: Locating feminist and lesbian feminist antipathy to drag in this period is not difficult. See Robin Morgan's collected essays, *Going Too Far* (New York: Random House, 1978); Janice Raymond, *The Transsexual Empire* (Boston, MA: Beacon Press, 1979); Eric Marcus's interview with Jean O'Leary in *Making History: The Struggle for Gay and Lesbian Equal Rights* (New York: HarperCollins, 1992), 266. O'Leary, however, says that her views have since changed. In an interview in this same book, Stonewall veteran and transgender activist Sylvia Lee Rivera claimed that lesbians were more hostile to drag queens than gay men (194).

48 "a genuine eroticism": Dennis Altman, *The Homosexualization of America* (Boston: Beacon, 1982), 85.

49 GLF dances: Dennis Altman, *Homosexual: Oppression and Liberation* (Sydney: Angus and Robertston, 1972), 121. The fondness for circle dances apparently extended to London's gay liberationists. Richard Dyer writes that a "utopian/romantic aspect of disco is realized in the non-commercial discos" where, he says, "a moment of community can be achieved, often in circle dances." Dyer, "In Defense of Disco," in Simon Frith and Andrew Goodwin, eds., *On Record* (New York: Pantheon, 1990), 417.

49 However, GLF dances: This was the view of a group called the Radicalesbians. See Duberman, *Stonewall*, 247.

49 "These were by far": This account is from Karla Jay's wonderful memoir, *Tales of the Lavender Menace* (New York: Basic Books, 1999), 91. It is worth noting that although lesbians contrasted their own behavior to that of gay men, the "women's dances" that they subsequently sponsored were hardly prim affairs. GLF activist Martha Shelley recalls women stripping to the waist and others stripping "to the altogether. It was primeval ritual time." Shelley quoted in Marcus, *Making History*, 184.

49 Gay Activist Alliance: GAA had split off from the GLF.

49 "These were great": Cheren, *Keep On*, 101.

49 Ray Caviano: http://www.djhistory.com/interviews/vince-aletti.

50 "stroll": See http://gaytoday.com/garchive/viewpoint/083099vi.htm. Evans says the zap occurred in June 1970, but according to Martin Duberman, GAA did not lease the Firehouse until six months later. Judging from newspaper accounts, June 1971 seems the more likely date. Duberman, *Stonewall*, 233.

51 Stonewall meant little: Lawrence, *Love Saves*, 29.

51 It's been argued: Ibid., 29.

51 "aftermath of Stonewall": Cheren, *Keep On*, 144.

52 This, as much as: Vince Aletti points out that some of the discos that were big early on were private clubs that didn't have to worry about these ordinances. However, they would still have to be concerned about violating a variety of city ordinances, including those related to drug-peddling and noise. http://djhistory.com/interviews/vince-aletti.

52 Once homosexual sociability: Interview with Francis Grasso at http://djhistory.com/interviews/francis-grasso. Even Vince Aletti, who doesn't believe that Stonewall was the decisive factor in disco's development, thinks that it likely had an effect "little by little."

52 "temples to despair": White, *Farewell Symphony*, 40. Writing about the 1940s, Mel Cheren says that most of his "paramours" were straight men, especially sailors. He notes the greater willingness of heterosexual men in

that period to take part in gay sex, especially if they were on the receiving end of a blow job. See Cheren, *Keep On*, 42.

52 "The music's": http://www.nycnotkansas.com.

53 "arch and bitchy": White, *Farewell Symphony*, 340.

53 "people as people": Dyer, "In Defense of Disco," 417.

53 "so many bodies": Kramer, *Faggots*, 352, 354.

53 "boring and pacified": Fag Rag Collective, "Second Five-Year Plan," in Karla Jay and Allen Young, *Lavender Culture* (New York: Harcourt, Brace Jovanovich, 1978), 485–6.

53 Dennis Altman: Altman, *Homosexualization*, 85.

53 Scott Forbes: Lillian Faderman and Stuart Timmons, *Gay L.A.* (New York: Basic Books, 2006), 235.

54 Even when these critics: See Richard Sennett, *The Fall of Public Man* (New York: Knopf, 1977); Midge Decter, *The New Chastity and Other Arguments Against Women's Liberation* (New York: Berkley, 1972); Christopher Lasch, *Haven in a Heartless World* (New York: Basic Books, 1977) and *The Culture of Narcissism* (New York: W. W. Norton, 1979).

54 "pioneer of the new kind": Altman, *Homosexualization*, 96. Queer writers such as Michael Warner and Guy Davidson, for whom gays' avid consumption is not shameful, have built upon Altman's argument.

54 "no other minority": Ibid., 20.

54 "the anarchy of capitalism": Dyer, "In Defense of Disco," 413. Ellen Willis was among the first radicals to argue for the transformative possibilities of capitalism. See her book of essays, *Beginning to See the Light* (New York: Knopf, 1981).

55 Albert Goldman, *Disco* (New York: Hawthorn, 1978), 42.

55 Dependent on jukeboxes: Andrew Kopkind, "The Dialectic of Disco," *Village Voice*, August 12, 1979.

56 "didn't feel like": http://www.djhistory.com/interviews/vince-aletti.

56 "By the end of 1970": Lawrence, *Love Saves*, 23–5.

56 The Loft: Brewster and Broughton, *Last Night*, 149.

56 "depraved": Ibid., 133.

56 Sanctuary: Lawrence, *Love Saves*, 30.

56 Francis Grasso: See http://www.djhistory.com/interviews/francis-grasso.

57 "the cute little": Shapiro, *Turn the Beat*, 27.

57 "know how to": Brewster and Broughton, *Last Night*, 131. Mancuso used sound effects to bridge together tracks, according to Lawrence. Although most histories credit Francis Grasso with first using slip-cueing, Mel Cheren

says that mixer Tom Moulton was the first to introduce it to club deejays. See Cheren, *Keep On*, 148.

57   "throbbing lights": Kopkind, "Dialectic."

57   "Without drugs": Douglas Crimp, "Disss-co (A Fragment) From *Before Pictures, A Memoir of 1970s New York," Criticism* 50, no. 1 (Winter 2008): 11–12.

58   poppers: Kopkind, "Dialectic."

58   "I would call": Cheren, *Keep On*, 163.

58   "I would turn": Lawrence, *Love Saves*, 108.

58   "dance orgasms": Ibid., 424.

58   "Every once in a": Brewster and Broughton, *Last Night*, 153.

59   "put your balls": Lawrence, *Love Saves*, 47.

59   "pounding to the beat": Kramer, *Faggots*, 352.

59   "drugs and the music": Edmund White, *States of Desire* (New York: Dutton, 1980), 270. D. A. Miller writes of taking off his soaked shirt as "the last vestige of propriety." *Place for Us*, 49.

59   Yet the very first: Tim Lawrence has emphasized that the first discos were not exclusively gay, and sees this as part and parcel of the gay liberation movement's early promotion of bisexuality. However, the gay liberation movement was hardly united in its support for bisexuality as the more liberated sexuality. Even if it had achieved something like consensus on this issue, the gay movement wielded no influence with club owners. It is more likely that these spaces permitted women in those early years because of the uncertainty about safety and security. After all, the authorities were slow to back off in their policing of gay spaces. In an early 1970 raid on the Snake Pit, one gay man, an immigrant, nearly died when he jumped out the window to escape arrest. Most contemporaneous accounts identify as gay the clubs in which disco took root. For example, we know that women were admitted into the Loft, and yet Mel Cheren recalls panicking about testifying before a public agency on behalf of the club's owner, David Mancuso, because he was not "out" at work and the Loft was "one of the pre-eminent gay dance clubs." Cheren, *Keep On*, 156.

60   Galaxy 21: Brewster and Broughton, *Last Night*, 159. Galaxy 21 has garnered very little attention despite the fact that legendary deejay Walter Gibbons spun records there.

60   "opulent with steam": Ibid., 158.

60   "dark, sexually charged": Lawrence, *Love Saves*, 44.

60   "It was like": Brewster and Broughton, *Last Night*, 158.

60 "terribly chic": Lawrence, *Love Saves*, 73.

60 "regular-clothed": Ibid., 188.

61 "in case you": Lynne Van Matre, "Secure Sexuality . . . and the Scene Sells," *Chicago Tribune*, April 7, 1974.

61 "great little": Easlea, *Everybody Dance*, 65, 66.

61 "the public began": Andrew Holleran, *Dancer from the Dance* (1978; reprint New York: Harper Perennial, 2001), 116.

61 "a total gay": Shapiro, *Turn the Beat*, 190.

61 "churning like a": Capote quoted in Ed McCormack, "No Sober Person Dances," in Abe Peck, ed., *Dancing Madness* (Garden City, NJ: Rolling Stone Press/Anchor Books, 1976), 11. Deejay Bob Casey argues that Diana Ross's appearance at the premiere of Le Jardin marked that moment when disco "came above ground." See Brewster and Broughton, *Last Night*, 171.

62 Andrea True Connection: My account is drawn largely from http://www.70disco.com/andtruec.htm.

63 Indeed, it climbed: Chet Flippo, "For Andrea More Is Less," *Rolling Stone*, May 20, 1976, 26.

63 "arbitrariness": Charles Kronengold, "Exchange Theories in Disco, New Wave and Album-Oriented Rock," *Criticism* 50, no. 1 (Winter 2008): 51.

64 "mere verbal": Walter Hughes, "In the Empire of the Beat: Discipline and Disco," in Ross and Rose, eds., *Microphone Fiends*, 149.

65 "gave never took": Lawrence, *Love Saves*, 187. On heterosexuals "elbowing out" gays, see Charles Silverstein and Edmund White, *The Joy of Gay Sex* (New York: Crown, 1973), 82–3.

65 The same process: www.discomusic.com.

65 Even though: Peck, *Dancing Madness*, 13.

65 "industrial, hi-tech": http://djhistory.com/interviews/vince-aletti.

65 "three-hundred-pound": Lawrence, *Love Saves*, 80.

65 "wanted to open": Ibid., 75.

66 "a white male": Ibid., 79–80.

66 This had the effect: Cheren, *Keep On*, 162.

66 Although those who ran: Lawrence, *Love Saves*, 139.

66 "going after": Ibid., 193.

66 "The door of the Anvil": Brad Gooch, *The Golden Age of Promiscuity: A Novel* (New York: Hard Candy Books, 1996), 296.

67 When pricey door fees: Even a casual glance at the gay press at the time reveals that some gay discos practiced discrimination against gays of color.

67   "homosexual lives": Robert Mott, "Homosexual Lives as Varied as Those of Any Other Group," *Washington Post*, April 24, 1973. Mott reports that a group of gay men had formed the Open Gay Bars Committee to break down racial discrimination at gay establishments in D.C.; on "super discos," see http://www.rainbowhistory.org/SocialGeography.htm.

67   "Hollywood Golden Boy": See Richard Cromelin, "Disco Kids in Gay L.A.," *Rolling Stone,* August 28, 1975; Faderman and Timmons, *Gay L.A.*, 236.

67   "a completely safe": Lawrence, *Love Saves*, 193.

67   And that wasn't: Ibid., 193–6.

67   Doubtless some men: This was the case in many gay communities. Documentary filmmaker Mark Page reports that through the Stud Bar he developed friendships with black men for the first time. Interview with Mark Page, February 14, 2009.

68   "but he knew": Lawrence, *Love Saves*, 419.

68   "was NOCD": Ibid., 427.

68   "Suddenly": Ibid., 420.

68   Most revisionist: See, for example, Tim Lawrence, "I Want to See All My Friends At Once: Arthur Russell and the Queering of Gay Disco," *Journal of Popular Music Studies* 18, no. 2 (2006). See also http://www.djhistory.com/interviews/vince-aletti.

68   "[t]he boy passed": Holleran, *Dancer*, 40.

69   "thrill of exclusivity": Holleran, *Dancer*, 38. Mel Cheren suggests that Holleran's disco was based upon 12 West and the Tenth Floor. Vince Aletti claims that at least the disco's look was based on that of the Tenth Floor. http://djhistory.com/interviews/vince-aletti.

69   Too much writing: For example, it is often assumed that gay discos were characterized by more underground sounds, and yet one of New York's most experimental deejays, Walter Gibbons, played at Galaxy 21, a predominantly straight club. Tim Lawrence, "Disco Madness: Walter Gibbons and the Legacy of Turntablism and Remixology," *Journal of Popular Music Studies* 20, no. 3 (2008).

69   subcultural capital: See Sarah Thornton's important book *Club Cultures* (Hanover, NH: Wesleyan University Press, 1996).

69   "the favored domain": Cheren, *Keep On*, 105.

69   Operating as private clubs: See Seymour Kleinberg's insightful discussion of women in post-Stonewall gay bar culture in *Alienated Affections: Being Gay in America* (New York: St. Martin's Press, 1980), 148.

69   When the Sanctuary: http://www.djhistory.com/interviews/francis-grasso.

69   Indeed during the filming: Peter Braunstein, " 'Adults Only': The Construction of an Erotic City," in Bailey and Farber, eds., *America in the 70s*, 143.

70   *Thank God It's Friday*: The film has not generated much discussion in disco studies. However, for an interesting treatment see Tavia Nyongo, "I Feel Love: Disco and Its Discontents," *Criticism* 50, no. 1 (Winter 2008).

70   "the ladies": On the Saint, see http://www.nycnotkansas.com. Only by having a friend on the inside, who informed her of the latest off-limit items, could Kathleen Clemans, a disco enthusiast, gain entry to Studio One. Author interview with Clemans, November 2007. On the predominance of women vocalists (and male falsetto vocalists) in disco, see John Rockwell, "Why Are the New Stars of Disco Mostly Women?," *New York Times*, March 4, 1979, D23.

3 LADIES' NIGHT

71   "Music Inferno": "Music Inferno" weds Madonna's 2000 track "Music" with the Trammps' 1976 disco classic "Disco Inferno."

72   Disco was all beat: Carolyn Krasnow, "Fear and Loathing in the '70s: Race, Sexuality and Disco," *Stanford Humanities Review* 2, no. 3.

72   "inflate it back": Tom Smucker, "Disco," in Jim Miller, ed., *The Rolling Stone Illustrated History of Rock & Roll*, rev. ed. (New York: Random House, 1980), 430.

73   "boogie down, baby": Some scholars have argued that rock's antagonism to disco stemmed in part from its investment in controlling the body, the irrational, and the sexual Other: woman. See Susan McClary, *Feminine Endings: Music, Gender and Sexuality* (Minneapolis: University of Minnesota Press, 1991), particularly the passage on 153; Krasnow, "Fear and Loathing," 37–45.

73   "dance floor is": Nick Hornby, *Songbook* (New York: Riverhead, 2003), 128.

73   "If I am sober": Chuck Klosterman, *Fargo Rock City* (New York: Scribner, 2001), 65. Many years earlier, Ed McCormack's article, "No Sober Person Dances," appeared in Peck, ed., *Dancing Madness*, 11.

74   "outside of the rock": Herbst quoted in Robert Draper, *Rolling Stone Magazine: The Uncensored History* (New York: Doubleday, 1990), 270. The point was made as well by Dave Marsh in the pages of *Rolling Stone*. Marsh argued that young men were hostile to disco because it was too gay, black, and Latin. See Marsh, "The Flip Sides of '79," *Rolling Stone*, December 27, 1979–January 10, 1980, 27.

74   "they would discover": Lavinia Greenlaw, *The Importance of Music to Girls: A Memoir* (London: Faber and Faber, 2007), 66.

74   "reduced women": See Werner, *Change*, 210. Werner was characterizing feminists' views of disco. However, I have found little evidence of this criticism among feminists. Jeanne Cordova, a founder of the L.A. newspaper *The Lesbian Tide*, reports that disco was "very big in lesbian clubs and in lesbian–feminist movement dances." Email communication with Cordova, June 15, 2009.

74   "an inflatable sex": Stephen Holden, "Donna Summer's Hot-to-Trot 'Bad Girls,'" *Rolling Stone*, July 12, 1979, 72. African American studies scholar Mark Anthony Neal argued that the liberatory message behind Summer's early hits such as "Love to Love You Baby" soon gave way to "pervasive constructs of insatiable women, who are objectified by the pulsating and repetitive rhythms of the dance floor." See Mark Anthony Neal, *What the Music Said*, p. 123.

74   "multiorgasmic kewpie dolls": Ken Emerson, review of "The Handwriting Is on the Wall" and "Get It Out 'Cha System," *Rolling Stone*, September 21, 1978, 66.

75   "actually heralded": Ted Polhemus quoted in the very useful book by Jeremy Gilbert and Ewan Pearson, *Discographies* (New York: Routledge, 1999), 13.

75   In their view: For example, see Peter Braunstein, "Adults Only," in Bailey and Farber, eds., *America in the 70s*. Braunstein, borrowing from Walter Hughes, maintains that before the disco tsunami hit—that is, during the first half of the seventies—"disco had been an ongoing dialogue between black female vocalists and gay male dancers" (147).

75   "classic disco singer": Eric Weisbard, the incisive critic and director of the Experience Music Project, quoted in Bernard Weinraub, "Here's to Disco, It Never Could Say Goodbye," *New York Times*, December 10, 2002, Arts, 2.

75   "releases you": Dyer, "In Defense of Disco," 414. Carolyn Krasnow, following Dyer, contended that with disco there was "no particular endpoint; in its proper context in a club, a tune would never really end at all; it would simply riff back to its beginning and then dissolve into the next groove" (Krasnow, "Fear and Loathing"). Literary critic Nancy Miller made a similar argument about women's more diffuse, multiorgasmic sexuality, which she argued made for a different kind of plotting in women's fiction. See Nancy K. Miller, "Emphasis Added: Plots and Plausibilities in Women's Fiction," *PMLA* 96 (1981). By contrast, Mark Anthony Neal locates the exploitive character of "mass-commodified" disco at least in part in its repetitiveness. Neal, *What the Music Said*, 123.

75 "disturbed the very": Hughes, "In the Empire," 151, 153. Hughes contends, somewhat contradictorily, that disco embodies both the fluidity and diffuseness of feminine sexuality *and* the unnaturalness of the machine.

75 Disco did represent: Stephen Holden, review of *Once Upon a Time, Rolling Stone*, January 12, 1978, 54.

75 "wasn't exactly": David Nathan, *The Soulful Divas* (New York: Billboard Books, 1999), 56.

75 "ease off": See Vince Aletti, review of *Four Seasons of Love, Rolling Stone*, January 27, 1977, 70.

76 "pivot": Brewster and Broughton, *Last Night*, 175.

76 "the mix starts": Danae quoted in Andrew Kopkind, "Dialectic."

77 "break it down": Lawrence, *Love Saves*, 112.

77 "get off": "You were fucking me with your music!" is the way one male dancer put it. See Kopkind, "Dialectic."

77 "psychic Intifada": Richard Goldstein, "Big Science," in Larry Gross and James D. Woods, eds., *The Columbia Reader on Lesbians and Gay Men in Media, Society, and Politics* (New York: Columbia University Press, 1999), 414.

77 Women, who had: See Lawrence, *Love Saves*, 189.

77 "absolutely narrowest notion": Vince Aletti, "Metropolitan Nightlife: Fran Lebowitz Has Her Memories," *Village Voice*, March 20, 1990, 42.

77 As for female artists': Initially, disco did not favor female singers. In the first article in the States devoted to "discotheque rock," Vince Aletti focused on records by the O'Jays, the J.B.'s, Stevie Wonder, Earth Wind and Fire, the Temptations and ex-Tempt Eddie Kendricks, and several lesser-known artists—virtually all of them male. Aletti, "Discotheque Rock '72: Paaaaarty!" Deejays' actual playlists and the *Billboard* charts corroborate this.

78 In many clubs: Peter Shapiro makes an intriguing argument about Travolta's floor-emptying solo turn, that it was a feature of Brit Nik Cohn's original story upon which the movie was loosely based. He also argues that this sort of dancing characterized the British Mod scene that danced to Northern Soul, and with which Cohn would have been familiar. See Shapiro, *Turn the Beat*, 203.

79 How likely was it: Even feminist theorist and baby boomer Marianne DeKoven, who felt that disco signaled the end of her beloved sixties, nonetheless found disco irresistible. Marianne DeKoven, *Utopia Unlimited: The Sixties and the Emergence of the Postmodern* (Durham, NC: Duke University Press, 2004), xiii. The documentary *Army of Lovers* apparently does show lesbian feminists denouncing the disco singer Grace Jones.

79 all kinds of women: Certainly plenty of white singers recorded disco music, but the best known of them, such as Cher and Barbra Streisand, are not known primarily as disco singers. As for Madonna, by the time she hit the newly renamed dance charts it was late 1982, past disco's heyday.

80 "Being asked": Easlea, *Everybody Dance*, 161.

80 "Isn't sex more erotic": Stephen Holden, "Donna Summer's Sexy Cinderella," *Rolling Stone*, January 12, 1978, 56.

81 However, more typical: Important exceptions include Freda Payne's "Bring the Boys Home," a 1971 hit record that the U.S. High Command banned from its American Forces Network in Vietnam on the grounds that it would give aid and comfort to the enemy, and Aretha Franklin's cover of Nina Simone's "Young, Gifted, and Black." See http://www.superseventies .com/1970_4singles.html.

81 what feminists were calling: Second-wave feminism is often treated as a white phenomenon that trickled down to women of color. For example, in an otherwise perceptive review of albums by Ann Peebles and Millie Jackson, Ken Emerson argues that women's liberation "seeped out of the white middle class and into the black community," where it made its way into these and other R&B releases. See *Rolling Stone*, September 21, 1978, 66. Recent scholarship has argued that feminism was developing independently and somewhat differently in communities of color.

81 Perhaps this calling out: For contemporaneous accounts see Frances Beal, "Double Jeopardy: To Be Black and Female," in Robin Morgan, ed., *Sisterhood Is Powerful* (New York: Random House, 1970), and bell hooks, *Ain't I a Woman: Black Women and Feminism* (Boston: South End, 1981). For an excellent historical account of black women's relationship to Black Power see Wini Breines, *The Trouble Between Us* (New York: Oxford University Press, 2006).

83 As Vince Aletti: Vince Aletti, *Rolling Stone*, April 13, 1970, 70.

84 Their understandable discretion: On Washington, see Guthrie P. Ramsey Jr., *Race Music: Black Cultures from Bebop to Hip-Hop* (Berkeley, CA: University of California Press, 2003), 44–5. See also Etta James and Davis Ritz, *A Rage to Survive* (New York: Villard, 1995), and Tina Turner with Kurt Loder, *I, Tina* (New York: Avon, 1987).

84 "party girls": Hirshey, *Nowhere to Run*, 181.

84 By contrast, the earliest: http://www.jazztimes.com/articles/20072-the-women-jacketed-by-records. Both black and white women were used for "greaser covers." In some cases, female musicians *were* provocatively

positioned. Liberty Records posed Abbey Lincoln and Julie London in come-hither poses.

86   "they're trying": Paul Gambaccini, "Singles: Pillow Talk," *Rolling Stone*, June 21, 1973, 16.

87   "matriarch of the black": Neal, *What the Music Said*, 77.

87   "fire, war, heat": Her surname is that of her first husband, an East Indian. See David Nathan, *Soulful Divas*, 197.

87   "naturalness": See Kobena Mercer's "Black Hair/Style Politics," in Russell Ferguson, Mertha Gever, Trinh T. Minh-ha, Cornel West, eds., *Out There: Marginalization and Contemporary Cultures* (Cambridge, MA: MIT Press, 1990), 248.

87   Doubtless this was: Sol Stern, "The Campaign to Free Angela Davis and Ruchell Magee," *New York Times*, Books, June 27, 1971.

88   "Church of Khan": http://www.guardian.co.uk/music/2008/jan/19/urban.theatre.

88   "Kansas City bootlegger": Chaka Khan with Tonya Bolden, *Chaka! Through the Fire* (Emmaus, PA: Rodale, 2003), 18.

88   "half-past time": Ibid., 49.

88   *Rufusized*: She was sometimes knocked, as was Joplin, for oversinging. Jim Miller criticized her "histrionic displays." See Miller, review of *Rufusized*, *Rolling Stone*, March 27, 1975, 53.

89   "white band": Khan, *Chaka!*, 58.

89   "black hippie": Maureen Mahon, *Right to Rock* (Durham, NC: Duke University Press, 2004), 37.

89   "dropping acid": Khan, *Chaka!*, 55.

89   "went through some": Jay Grossman, "From Smoke to Rufus to Rags to Riches," *Rolling Stone*, October 24, 1974.

89   "sex symbol": Khan, *Chaka!*, 94. She also told David Nathan that she worried that her label was trying to put her across as a "sex bomb," Nathan, *Soulful Divas*, 200.

89   "what I got": Fred Schruers, "Chaka Khan: Earth Mother," *Rolling Stone*, April 5, 1979, 18.

89   No other black female: Also important, musically and for the daring way she presented herself, is Betty Davis (born Betty Mabry), the self-described "nasty gal." Davis, who was briefly married to jazz musician Miles Davis, made Chaka look tame by comparison, but she never achieved anything like mainstream success.

90   "wardrobe malfunction": See "Maybe Next Time," *Sounds*, March 29, 1975,

42. I'm borrowing the term from the imbroglio surrounding Janet Jackson's appearance at the 2004 Super Bowl.

91 "We were all Chaka": http://www.oreoluwa.com/AnitaBaker/archive/people weekly1986.html. Note that this 1996 *Billboard* interview can no longer be found through Google.

91 "I'm a Woman": See Rob Mackie, "Death-Defying, With a Punch Like the Prettiest," *Sounds*, March 15, 1975, 22.

91 "childlike": Toni Morrison, "What the Black Woman Thinks About Women's Lib," reprinted in Dawn Keetley and John Pettegrew, eds., *Public Women, Public Words: A Documentary History of American Feminism* (Lanham, MD: Rowman & Littlefield, 2005), 75. Her essay was originally published in the August 22, 1971, issue of the *New York Times Magazine*. See also the discussion in Breines, *The Trouble*.

91 "subfemininity"; Eldridge Cleaver quoted in Paula Giddings, *When and Where I Enter* (New York: Bantam, 1985), 321.

92 Yet Khan transformed: This view of black women as sturdy and uncomplaining—the Sapphire stereotype—would resurface some twenty years later when the prominent black sociologist Orlando Patterson criticized Anita Hill for behaving like a white woman by not toughing it out with Clarence Thomas's "down home courting." Patterson's position elicited a firestorm of protest from black feminists. By the time of the Hill–Thomas imbroglio black women's so-called toughness was understood as a nefarious stereotype, but in the early seventies black women's strength and resolve was understood by some black feminists as a way in which black women were way ahead of white women, who seemed dependent and weak. And it is certainly true that in many ways African American women modeled independence, fortitude, and competence. See Morrison's abovementioned 1971 essay, "What the Black Woman Thinks About Women's Lib." In it she issues a stinging rebuke to the idea of sisterhood as she excoriates white feminists' appropriation of what she called "our thing," by which she meant black cultural conventions. She included in her laundry list of hijacked cultural practices "common-law marriage (shacking)" and "children out of wedlock," which, she noted, "is even fashionable now if you are a member of the Jet Set (if you are poor and Black it is still a crime); families without men; right to work; sexual freedom, and an assumption that woman is equal to man." That these practices and stances were heralded as liberatory in white women when black women were still stigmatized for them (and had little choice but to engage in these practices) was the final insult for Morrison and some other black women.

92   "right on time": Khan, *Chaka!*, 111.

92   "more of a feminist": Schruers, "Chaka Khan," 19.

92   "woman-power": Khan, *Chaka!*, 49.

93   "blur the lines": Chic singer Alfa Anderson quoted in Easlea, *Everybody Dance*, 159.

93   "a vast, multiethnic": Carol Cooper, "Disco Knights: Hidden Heroes of the New York Dance Music Underground," *Social Text* 45 (Winter 1995), 160.

93   "disco sucks": See http://www.queermusicheritage.us/jan2005s.html.

94   But perhaps: Other scholars working in this area include Maureen Mahon, Daphne Brooks, and Sonnet Retman. See Retman's "Between Rock and A Hard Place: Narrating Nona Hendryx's Inscrutable Career," *Women & Performance: a journal of feminist theory* 16, no. 1 (March 2006); Daphne Brooks's forthcoming *Subterranean Blues: Black Feminist Musical Subcultures from Minstrelsy to the Post Hip-Hop Era* (Cambridge, MA: Harvard University Press); and Maureen Mahon's forthcoming *When the Levee Breaks: The Presence of Black Women in Rock 'n' Roll Music.*

94   importance of Simone: Ruth Feldstein, " 'I Don't Trust You Anymore': Nina Simone, Culture, and Black Activism in the 1960s," *Journal of American History* 91, no. 4 (March 2006). See, of course, Nikki Giovanni's "Poem for Aretha," reprinted in Giovanni, *The Selected Poems of Nikki Giovanni: 1968– 1995* (New York: William Morrow, 1996).

94   "Zora Neale Hurston": Alice Walker, *In Search of Our Mothers' Gardens* (New York: Harcourt, 2003), 91. See also Cheryl Walls's *Worrying the Line: Black Women Writers, Lineage, and Literary Tradition* (Durham, NC: Duke University Press, 2005), and Michele Wallace, "Blues for Mr. Spielberg," *Invisibility Blues* (London: Verso, 1990). Wallace notes that "the black female blues singer as a paradigm of commercial, cultural, and historical potency pervades twentieth-century Afro-American literature by women" (69).

94   Indeed, Khan: Celia McGee, "The Many Shades of Chaka Khan, Now in Purple," *New York Times,* December 30, 2007, Arts.

94   "Krudde": Mike Flood, "Rags to Rufus to Riches," with photos of Chaka and the band, *Sounds,* October 19, 1974, 35. Their record company actually used this word in a full back page ad for the band's new LP, *Rufus Featuring Chaka Khan.* See *Sounds,* February 15, 1975.

94   "appearing in long": Nathan, *Soulful Divas,* 203.

94   "classy": Christgau, *Record Guide,* 336.

94   "bad-girl cheekiness": Laura Fissinger, *Rolling Stone,* August 6, 1981, 49.

95   Before there was Labelle: Hershel Johnson, "From Bluebells to Labelle of

New York," *Rolling Stone*, October 24, 1974, 17. This article appeared on the same page as the magazine's first feature about Rufus.

95 If girl-group music: See Susan Douglas, *Where the Girls Are: Growing Up Female with the Mass Media* (New York: Three Rivers Press, 1995), 90. Tellingly, Janis Joplin may be the only serious sixties' rocker in America to have covered a girl-group classic—the Chantels' "Maybe"—but then her version was nothing less than an assault on the original. Until the late seventies, when Blondie and other new wave groups acknowledged the Ronettes' influence, girl groups seemed positively antique. See http://spinner.aol .com/rockhall/ronettes-2007-inductee.

96 "Nobody in England": Art Harris, "Mmmm Unnhaaah Oh God Oooh It's So Good It's Labelle," *Rolling Stone*, July 3, 1975, 46.

97 "When we were": Johnson, "From Bluebells," 17.

97 "black girls": Wickham quoted in Gillian G. Gaar, *She's a Rebel* (Seattle: Seal, 1992), 198.

97 "the other side": Hendryx quoted in Johnson, "From Bluebells," 17.

97 "You could be": Author interview with Nona Hendryx, April 24, 2009.

97 "I fought the whole": Vince Aletti, liner notes for Labelle, *Something Silver,* 1997, Warner Archives, 2–46359.

97 "I didn't want": LaBelle quoted in Robin Katz, "Wear Something Silver," *Sounds,* February 15, 1975, 14.

98 "almost like another": Author interview with Nona Hendryx, April 24, 2009.

98 "pushed into shape": Dave Marsh, review of *Smile, Rolling Stone,* May 6, 1976, 62.

98 "Hollywood": "Hollywood" is rumored to be about Elton John's ascension to stardom and subsequent snubbing of Patti LaBelle. However, Hendryx says the song is about what happens to the "star of the moment" who enters the "realm of the bodyguard." Author interview with Nona Hendryx, April 24, 2009.

98 "darlings of the pop": Aletti, liner notes for *Something Silver*. Some producers prevented them from performing Scott-Heron's "The Revolution."

98 glam rockers: In 1973 Dash and Hendryx sang backup for glam/shock-rocker Alice Cooper, and they would have already seen the glam phenomenon in Britain. See Retman, "Between Rock," 115, n. 1.

99 "decidedly right": Johnson, "From Bluebells," 18.

99 "The right song": Jon Landau, review of *Nightbirds, Rolling Stone*, May 22, 1975, 63.

100   "Voulez-vous": Harris, "Mmmm." According to one account, Patti LaBelle initially had qualms about recording it.

100   "sophisticated": Aletti, liner notes for *Something Silver*.

100   "This whole image": Robin Katz, "Magnetic Space Women Take Earth By Storm," *Sounds*, March 15, 1975, 14.

100   "Now we like to" . . . "handcuff fetish" . . . "healthy homosexual": Harris, "Mmmm."

101   "A place where": See Kevin Clarke's account at http://gaytoday.com/gar-chive/people/040901pe.htm.

101   "There's six different": Penny Valentine, "How the West was Won—Nearly," *Sounds*, April 26, 1975, 20.

101   "heavy feminist": Harris, "Mmmm."

101   "We saw ourselves": Hendryx acknowledged this change. Author interview with Hendryx, April 24, 2009.

101   "I don't know": Harris, "Mmmm." Wickham and Hendryx are in a long-term partnership. Wickham has talked about her sexuality in a 1999 *Guardian* interview, available at http://www.guardian.co.uk/Archive/Article /0,4273,3936463,00.html. See also http://www.cpinternet.com/mbayly/ article32.htm. Hendryx describes herself as bisexual. Author interview, April 24, 2009.

102   "as if to a cause": Aletti, liner notes for *Something Silver*.

103   Disco's only self-declared: David A. Moore, "Dueling Divas," *Advocate*, April 28, 1998, 22.

103   They were joined: Writing in *The New Yorker*, Ellen Willis noted Stevie Wonder's "huge interracial audience." "The Importance of Stevie Wonder," *The New Yorker*, December 30, 1974, 56. Quoted in Philip Harper, "Synesthesia, 'Crossover,' and Blacks in Popular Music," *Social Text* 23 (Autumn 1989).

103   The early seventies: Others, from Rick James to the future Chic founders Bernard Edwards and Nile Rodgers, tried to make hybrid music. Edwards and Rodgers only moved into disco after record labels passed on their rock music.

103   "progressive black": Johnson, "From Bluebells," 17.

103   As journalist Nelson George: George, *The Death*.

103   They scored: A dramatic case in point is P-Funk bassist Bootsy Collins, whose "Bootzilla" held down the number one R&B spot in the spring of 1978, but never even cracked pop's Top 100. Kempton, *Boogaloo*, 405.

104   "shuffling minds": Frank Rose, *Rolling Stone*, October 7, 1976, 70.

105   Labelle called it quits: See http://emol.org/music/artists/labelle/.

106 "in unison": Dave Marsh with John Swenson, eds., *The Rolling Stone Record Guide* (New York: Random House, 1979), 352. British music critic John Peel described "TSOP" as sounding like a backing track waiting for a singer. "Singles," *Sounds*, April 13, 1974, 28.

106 And few: Sixties' girl groups, like Ross's Supremes, sometimes found themselves at the mercy of their producers and their labels, but they were hardly compliant. Legendary Motown songwriter and producer Eddie Holland has said that he preferred writing for women because they have a greater affective range. But he emphasizes that the women of Motown were anything but tractable. Male groups took better direction, he says, whereas the women "got away with much more in the studio." See the interview with Holland in the SoulPatrol.com article on Honey Cone, http://www.soul-patrol.com/soul/honeycone.htm.

106 Especially in disco groups: I would not call the women of Chic powerless by any means. But Nile Rodgers of Chic even boasted to the head of his record label that he and his band could make anyone, even someone who had never sung professionally, a disco star. As Rodgers saw it, "our rhythm section is the star, we'll just put whoever in it." Easlea, *Everybody Dance*, 134.

106 Ross's vocals: Critics of Motown founder Berry Gordy frequently faulted him for elevating Ross as the Supremes lead singer over Florence Ballard, who was a belter and, many thought, more soulful. For another view, see Ann Powers's excellent essay, "Pop Diva, Soul Sister," at http://articles.latimes.com/2007/jan/28/entertainment/ca-dreamgirls28.

106 "having a ball": Rich Wiseman, "Singles: Love Hangover," *Rolling Stone*, July 1, 1976, 17.

107 "a clean-cut": Donna Summer with Marc Eliot, *Ordinary Girl: The Journey of Donna Summer* (New York: Villard, 2003), 63.

107 "top European music": Mikal Gilmore, "Donna Summer: Is There Life After Disco?," *Rolling Stone*, March 23, 1978, 15.

107 "something sexier": Gainsbourg originally recorded the song with his then girlfriend Brigitte Bardot, but after they broke up she begged him to not release their version, and he recorded it with his new lover Jane Birkin. Summer and Moroder covered the song in a duet for the movie *Thank God It's Friday*.

107 "a very catchy": See Vince Aletti's 1978 interview with Moroder at http://homepage.ntlworld.com/clive.hocker/moroder/mor_2002/index.htm. Bellotte's account differs somewhat, as he cites instead the four-to-the-floor bass drum that the Crusaders had recently used and the hi-hat pattern on the Hues Corporation's hit "Rock the Boat." See Tom Bishop, "In Tune with

Britain's Disco King," *BBC News Online Entertainment*, September 29, 2004. Available at http://news.bbc.co.uk/2/hi/entertainment/3697806.stm.

108   British charts: http://www.rocklistmusic.co.uk/banned.html.

108   Not a chartbuster: Bellotte's account appears in Bishop, "In Tune." Moroder told a different story to the British paper *New Musical Express* in December 1978. There he said that when the four-minute version of the song failed to ignite, he decided to stretch the track over a full side of an LP, using as his model Iron Butterfly's hit "In-A-Gada-Da-Vida." See http://www.italfree .com/giorgio_morodernme.html.

108   "Love to Love You Baby": Gilmore, "Donna Summer"; Robert Fink, *Repeating Ourselves* (Berkeley: University of California Press, 2005).

108   "Did you come": Christgau, *Record Guide*, 380.

108   "erotic Muzak": Holden, "Donna Summer's Sexy Cinderella"; Gilmore, "Donna Summer." Gilmore, however, had a change of heart.

109   "her knees bent": Richard Cromelin, "Love on the Road," *Rolling Stone*, March 25, 1976, 18.

109   suggestive ad campaign: Gilmore, "Donna Summer."

109   "garbage and pollution": Werner, *Change*, 210. Operation PUSH threatened a boycott of what it called "X-rated disco sex-rock." See Fink, *Repeating*, 42.

110   "stylish, sleek": Kopkind, "Dialectic."

111   "skinflick variety": Holden, "Donna Summer's Sexy Cinderella."

111   During the film's trial: Killen, *1973 Nervous Breakdown*, 199.

112   "great for five": Male rock critics were more likely than feminists to become incensed about disco's treatment of women. Much of this criticism focused on disco's biggest star, Donna Summer, who was attacked for both her *Cosmo*-like sexual assertiveness and for her sexual submissiveness.

112   "popcorn tracks": Gilmore, "Donna Summer."

112   "thrilling": Ken Tucker, review of *I Remember Yesterday, Rolling Stone*, August 11, 1977, 63.

112   "luxurious voice": http://tech.mit.edu/V110/N44/eno.44a.html.

112   disCOINTELPRO: Tate quoted in Reynolds, *Generation Ecstasy*, 13.

112   "worst tendencies": George, *The Death*, 154.

113   "Teutonic": Shapiro, *Turn the Beat*, 110–1.

113   "they just feel it": http://homepage.ntlworld.com/clive.hocker/moroder/ mor_1978/parto2.htm.

113   "soft songs": Gilmore, "Donna Summer."

113   After all, she tended: You hear her coquettish, little-girl voice on her 1976 release *Love Trilogy* and 1978's "The Deep (Deep Down Inside)."

113 "dazed mechanical mask . . . this monstrous": Gilmore, "Donna Summer," 11.

113 "undersexed": Elliot Mintz, "The Penthouse Interview with Donna Summer," *Penthouse*, July 1979. It is available at http://www.donnasummer.it/interview.html.

114 "When you start out": http://www.superseventies.com/1979_4singles.html.

116 "a Seventies masterpiece": Stephen Holden, "Donna Summer's Hot-To-Trot 'Bad Girls,'" 72. Two decades later, Mark Anthony Neal echoed Holden in objecting to "Bad Girls"' "hypersexualizing" of Summer and to the title track's celebration of "prostitution as a liberatory activity." See Neal, *What the Music Said*, 122.

116 "collaborative role": Dave Marsh, "A Rock 'n' Roll Map of Donna Summer's Soul: Review of *The Wanderer*," *Rolling Stone*, March 19, 1981, 61. See also the incisive chapter on Donna Summer in Barker and Taylor, *Faking It*.

117 "Having her biggest": This interview by Vince Aletti originally appeared in *Numéro* (France) 39, December 2002. See http://homepage.ntlworld.com/clive.hocker/moroder/mor_1978/part02.htm.

117 Summer's experience: Moore, "Dueling Divas," 22.

119 "felt about the sexual": Ellen Willis, "Coming Down Again," in *No More Nice Girls* (Hanover, NH: Wesleyan University Press, 1992), 262.

119 "wild-natured type": Nathan, *Soulful Divas*, 200.

120 "shock troops": Miller, *Place for Us*, 50.

4 THE HOMO SUPERIORS

121 "These bodies": Douglas Crimp, "Disss-co," 6.

122 Gay men's macho: Dennis Altman, *Homosexualization of America*, 217.

122 "was like being": Aletti, "Metropolitan Nightlife," 42.

122 "phys. ed. Fashion": Sobel quoted in Altman, *Homosexualization*, 97. It is ironic, of course, that gay men tricked out in macho drag, not reactionary Bible-thumpers, were the ones who drove a stake into the more androgynous styles of the sixties.

122 "Ever notice": Joe Parisi, "What's It All About?," *Advocate*, August 27, 1975, 27.

122 "straights don't see": Kopkind, "Dialectic."

123 Whether gay macho: However, once the new style became known to homophobic toughs it did not totally deter attacks. See Seymour Kleinberg, *Alienated Affections: Being Gay in America* (New York: St. Martin's Press, 1980), 155.

124 Men such as Alexander: See Chapter Four of Chauncey, *Gay New York*, for his fascinating discussion of the reconfiguring of male homosexuality; see also Ina Russell, ed., *Jeb and Dash: A Diary of Gay Life, 1918–45* (New York: Faber and Faber, 1993).

124 "young, effeminate": Jeffrey Solomon, "Young, Effeminate, and Strange: Early Photographic Portraits of Truman Capote," *Studies in Gender and Sexuality* 6, no. 3 (2005).

124 "natural and complete": Gore Vidal, *The City and the Pillar* (New York: Vintage, 1995), 66.

124 *The Boys in the Band*: As Ben Brantley noted in his review of the 1996 Broadway revival, the emergence of gay liberation quickly made Crowley's play seem embarrassingly anachronistic. See Brantley, "Theater Review: As the Boys Return, the Party Isn't Over," *New York Times,* June 21, 1996. The author of the meticulously detailed, richly rendered website nycnotkansas .com saw the original production of *Boys* and recalls feeling that even at the time it seemed anachronistic, offering theater-goers a portrait of the "Fifties as if it were the present." However, he also admits that the play probably accurately reflected the lives of many gay men, and that his own frustration with it may have been because it hit a little too close to home.

125 "the few worked-out": See http://www.nycnotkansas.com.

125 "perfectly muscled": Duberman, *Cures*, 49.

125 "ideas of morbid": Christopher Nealon, *Foundlings* (Durham, NC: Duke University Press, 2001), 102.

125 "physique ideal": Nealon, *Foundlings*, 123.

125 Historian Martin Meeker: We would recognize these bars today as s/m or leather bars. Personal communication with Martin Meeker, July 3, 2008.

125 And *Mattachine Review*: See *Mattachine Review,* November/December 1964.

125 "college boy": The website nycnotkansas.com offers further evidence of this trend.

126 "too swishy": Martin Meeker, *Contacts Desired* (Chicago: University of Chicago Press, 2006), 170.

126 "red-blooded, all-American": Burke quoted in Meeker, *Contacts*, 194. The article was illustrated with a photograph of two leathermen being stopped by a police officer offended at the way they had decked out their bike with a "Just Married" sign and cans. Over-the-top displays of masculinity in *Life* and *Esquire* might also communicate that homosexuals weren't really masculine, they were simply performing a kind of empty masculine drag. The *Esquire* article was sufficiently controversial that

in its May/June 1972 issue the gay Toronto newspaper *The Body Politic* referenced it in "The Myth of the New Homosexual." See Meeker's fascinating chapter on mainstream representations of gays and lesbians in *Contacts Desired.*

126   "lumberjack masculinity": This term seems to have been in fairly wide circulation. "Some call him the Lumberjack," begins an article on "Butch" in the *Advocate*, August 27, 1975, 24. Decades later, Mel Cheren used the term in his autobiography. See Cheren, *Keep On*, 89. It is worth noting Monty Python's popular "The Lumberjack Song," in which a conventionally masculine lumberjack reveals himself to be a cross-dresser. The comedy troupe first performed the song at the end of 1969, and it may have reflected some vague awareness of gay men whose self-presentation was conventionally masculine. On "The Lumberjack Song" as a gay anthem, see http://www.guardian.co.uk/music/2006/nov/12/popandrock22.

126   "audio orgasmatron": Frank Owen, "Spirituality Having Flown," review of *Larry Levan Live at the Paradise Garage*, in *Village Voice*, September 12, 2000, 137.

126   "They *had* to take": Lawrence, *Loves Saves*, 190. Although Fesco takes credit for this, Holleran's *Dancer from the Dance* features bare-chested men, and it's meant to be at least partially based upon the Tenth Floor. Mel Cheren says that the Flamingo had cross-ventilation, but that as you moved through the space it went "from cooler to hotter to very hot." Cheren, *Keep On*, 163.

126   "Within a short five years": Crimp, "Disss-co," 11–12.

127   "hunters after the same": Cheren, *Keep On*, 43.

127   "We're brothers": White, *Farewell Symphony*, 340.

127   Although gentrification: See nycnotkansas.com for a very useful discussion of the effects of gentrification on neighborhood bars.

127   Gay liberationists ... androgyny: "Our biggest failure," wrote Dennis Altman, "was an inability to foresee the extent to which ... a new gay culture/identity would emerge that would build on existing male/female differences." Altman, *Homosexualization*, 211. It is worth mentioning that gay and lesbian liberationists, who were more apt to favor androgyny and in some cases even greater sexual fluidity, comprised a sliver of the larger gay and lesbian community. See John D'Emilio, *Making Trouble: Essays on Gay History, Politics, and the University* (New York: Routledge, 1992), 87.

127   "Judy Garland style": Newton, *Cherry Grove*, 240. See also Arne Kantrowitz, "Snap, Snap!" *Advocate*, August 27, 1975, 34.

127   Gays' camp style: Yet to younger generations of gay men, disco apparently

seems camp. See Gregory W. Bredbeck, "Troping the Light Fantastic: Representing Disco Now and Then," *glq* 3, no. 1 (1996).

128 "All I could hear"; Russo quoted in Newton, *Cherry Grove*, 244.

128 By 1975 the *Advocate*: "Zap!" *Advocate,* August 27, 1975, 25. The new macho was also discussed in Jack Nichols's 1977 essay "Butcher Than Thou: Beyond Machismo," in Len Richmond, ed., *The New Gay Liberation Book* (Palo Alto, CA: The Ramparts Press, 1979).

128 "fast disappearing": Altman, *Homosexualization*, 58.

128 "They used to sit": Newton, *Cherry Grove*, 245.

128 "ridiculous and a sham": Ibid., 275.

129 "new sense of masculine": Ibid., 270.

129 "Pines People are Plastic": Ibid., 271.

130 "These people were weird!": Ibid., 269.

130 "When I knew her": Holleran, *Dancer*, 179. At another point, Malone says about an available gay neurosurgeon, "But he's a block of ice. So exact, so competent, so macho" (186).

130 "an industry": Ibid., 156.

130 "old-time queens": Ibid., 15.

130 "like a lumberjack": Ibid., 118.

130 "being looked at": Ibid., 205. Other characters in the novel also suggest that homosexuality entails being consumed by others (205, 248). See also Martin Levine, *Gay Macho* (New York: New York University Press, 1998), 98.

130 "smell of grass": Holleran, *Dancer*, 194.

131 "Is that what you really": Ibid., 146.

131 "There is no love": Ibid., 97.

131 "fucking uniform": Brent Harris, "Andrew Holleran," 1979 *Advocate* interview reprinted in Mark Thompson, ed., *Long Road to Freedom:* The Advocate *History of the Gay and Lesbian Movement* (New York: St Martin's Press, 1994).

132 Randy Jones: *Behind the Music: The Village People*, E Entertainment, June 2000.

132 "the effeminacy": See http://www.nycnotkansas.com.

132 "Radical Fairies": Stuart Timmons notes that several years earlier gays known as "the Sissies" criticized STIFS—straight-identified faggots." Timmons, *The Trouble with Henry Hay: The Founder of the Gay Movement* (Boston: Alyson Books, 1990), 250.

133 In San Francisco some: White, *States*, 46.

133 "ever more standardized": Parisi, "What's It All About?," 27.

133 "unreflecting conformist": White, *Farewell Symphony*, 339. The protagonist of *The Farewell Symphony* recalls that by the end of the seventies some younger gays who were actively hostile to the clone look had taken to stenciling "Death to Disco" and "Kill a Clone" on the sidewalks of the East Village.

133 "it's okay to be a fag": Altman, *Homosexualization*, 14.

133 Seymour Kleinberg: Kleinberg, *Alienated Affections*, 155.

133 "Our old fears of": White, *States*, 51.

133 "political act": White, *States*, 51; White, *Farewell Symphony*, 339.

133 "hiding": Kramer, *Faggots*, 32–3. Rehearsals for "The Temperamentals," a play about homosexual activists of the 1950s, revealed that the most contentious debate concerned how effeminate the man should be. Patrick Healy, "Closet Doors Were Shut Tight, but Some Gays Oiled the Hinges," *New York Times*, June 17, 2009, C1.

133 While it may have: It seems counterintuitive, but I'm suggesting here that gay men who had been deemed effeminate by virtue of their sexuality may have avoided anal sex. However, when they were muscular and decked out in leather chaps and work boots, anal sex may not have destabilized masculine identity. The author of nycnotkansas.com thinks that the new masculinism actually enabled the "de-feminizing" of anal sex, even when receptive, which seemed to acquire "its own peculiar macho." In *Faggots*, Kramer skewers gay men's exploration of the asshole, and in such a way that it can't help but bring to mind feminists' interest in the clitoris as a stigmatized erogenous zone in need of liberation.

134 "gang-banged": Kleinberg attributes this change to the fact that gay male leisure increasingly took place in female-free zones. Gay men can behave like women precisely because these spaces are emptied of women. But certainly gay men had been having sex in all-male spaces before the 1970s. See Kleinberg, *Alienated Affections*, 148.

134 "passive": Ibid., 148.

134 "Our assholes": Miller, "Cruising," 73.

134 "not your run-of-the-mill fruit": http://www.reviewjournal.com/lvrj_home/2003/Jun-01-Sun-2003/news/21430299.html.

135 "Get Dancin'": http://www.hotdiscomix.de/stars_clubs/djs/lederer_en_interview.htm.

136 Morali came up: Rose's mother was Puerto Rican and his father Native American (Lakota Sioux). See http://www.feliperose.com.

136 "You know, this is": See Abe Peck, "The Face of Disco: Macho Men With Their Tongues in Their Cheeks," *Rolling Stone*, April 19, 1979, 13.

136 "I think to myself": Ibid., 13. In his interview with the gay newspaper the *Advocate*, Morali said, "I'm gay and I wanted to make a top star gay group." *Advocate*, April 19, 1978, 31. The paper characterized the group as "openly gay" in an earlier issue: *Advocate,* December 28, 1977, 30.

136 "high-marketplace": Houston Baker, "Hybridity, the Rap Race, and Pedagogy for the 1990s," in Ross and Penley, eds., *Technoculture,* 198.

136 "very strong, positive": Peck, "Face of Disco," 13.

137 "I think that really": http://www.rotten.com/library/culture/village-people.

137 "goose-stepping": Stephen Holden, "Village People," *Rolling Stone,* June 14, 1979.

137 "They love 'em": Kopkind, "Dialectic."

138 "male-image show": Peck, "Face of Disco," 14. It turns out that Morali's first interview with *Rolling Stone* in 1978 had caused a "mild freak" within the Village People camp.

138 "He's no dummy": Ibid., 13.

138 "six very positive": Ibid., 14.

138 "audio-visual package": Ibid., 12.

138 "fast food of popular": Michael Schneider, *Rolling Stone,* September 7, 1978, 118. It's interesting that at least within gay circles some were arguing that gay men were "into sex as fast food." See Brent Harris, "Andrew Holleran."

138 Plans were under way: Peck, "Face of Disco," 13–14.

138 The militantly homophobic: "Village People," *Advocate,* December 27, 1979, 32.

139 "phallic form": Dyer, "In Defense of Disco," 415. The Village People complicated Dyer's argument that disco was more fluid, less phallic than rock music.

139 "deliberately closeting": Kopkind, "Dialectic."

139 "the Osmond Brothers": "Village People," *Advocate,* 31. The A*dvocate*'s criticism began earlier with Charles Herschberg, "Prophets or Profits? The Village People," *Advocate,* April 19, 1978, 31.

139 "strenuously denied this": Altman, *Homosexualization,* 1.

139 "sticking our tongues": Peck, "Face of Disco," 14.

140 "Look, make no mistake": "Village People," *Advocate,* 32.

140 "slaves, dancing dolls": Ken Emerson, "The Village People—America's Male Ideal?," *Rolling Stone,* October 5, 1978, 27.

140 "gay people could": Lester Bangs, *Rolling Stone,* April 19, 1979, 90. The Village People remain pariahs among almost all critics and academics. Frank Owen sums up the critical response with his pithy, "Of course, the Village

People aside, disco never really sucked." See Owen, "Spirituality." Judith Peraino contends that the group "presented urban gay macho identities as banal media products." Peraino, *Listening to the Sirens* (Berkeley, CA: University of California Press, 2005), 184. Pretty much the lone dissenter is Gregory Bredbeck, who believes that with the Village People one finds the convergence of the "marketing of disco and an idea of anti-bourgeois eroticism," which he does not condemn. Bredbeck, "Troping the Light Fantastic," 89.

140   "in the life": Michael Branton, "Sylvester Finds Heart in San Francisco," *Rolling Stone*, April 19, 1979, 34. However, he remained close to his mother and grandmother, judging from a subsequent *Rolling Stone* article.

141   "a cross between": Joshua Gamson, *The Fabulous Sylvester: The Legend, The Music, The Seventies in San Francisco* (New York: Henry Holt, 2005), 5.

141   He performed in drag: Maitland Zane, "Les Cockettes de San Francisco," *Rolling Stone*, October 14, 1971, 34. Gamson notes that he had been taking female hormones even when he was still in L.A. Gamson, *Fabulous Sylvester*, 154.

141   "among the Cockettes": Ibid., 57.

141   "like the reverse": Ibid., 65.

141   "Vegas showgirl version": Vilanch quoted in ibid., 167.

142   "big act to break out": Thompson, ed., *Long Road,* 62. This article originally appeared in a 1971 issue of the *Advocate.*

142   "*destroy* reality": Quoted in Gamson, *Fabulous Sylvester*, 92.

142   "And people complain": Christgau, *Record Guide*, 383.

142   "Magnetta Washington": Gamson, *Fabulous Sylvester*, 142.

142   "Here were all these": Sylvester quoted in Tim Lawrence, "I Want," n. 1. For more on his attitude towards disco, see also John Schauer, "Sylvester: The Disco Ticket," *Advocate*, January 25, 1979, 33.

142   Sylvester told the press: Branton, "Sylvester." Although Sylvester stressed the importance of the forum, it occurred in mid-June, just days before the release of his disco record *Step II.*

143   "positively dowdy": See Sylvester's obituary by the music critic John Rockwell, *New York Times*, December 18, 1988.

143   "Joan, honey": Gamson, *Fabulous Sylvester*, 246. When anthropologist Maureen Mahon was a youngster, she saw Sylvester perform on *Solid Gold*, and remembers finding the combination of his makeup, falsetto, and sexuality confusing. Sylvester gave a spirited performance and she found his energy infectious, but she recalls feeling relieved that she was watching the show alone, without her mother, because she realized there was something

"dangerous or too out there" about his performance. Personal communication with Maureen Mahon, June 27, 2008.

144   "fifteen bracelets": Gamson, *Fabulous Sylvester*, 158.

144   "Everybody felt like": Ibid., 132.

146   "backup singers": Ibid., 137.

146   "songs that I *really*": Branton, "Sylvester."

147   His falsetto: Critic Abe Peck compared Sylvester's "funky urban mantras" favorably to the "MOR-disco" of the Village People. See Peck, "Face of Disco," 12.

147   "a sexual utopian": Frith quoted in Gamson, *Fabulous Sylvester*, 152. Rock critic Robert Christgau called Sylvester "everyone's favorite black transvestite," suggesting that something other than musical talent explained his appeal. Christgau, *Record Guide*, 383.

147   "at the origin": Walter Hughes, "In the Empire," 154.

147   Having fixed on Sylvester: However, Tim Lawrence has argued for the classically trained, experimentally inclined cellist Arthur Russell as the embodiment of queer disco's anarchic sexual impulse. In Lawrence's typology, "queer" is more fluid, provisional, and anarchic than "gay," which here assumes an almost conservative cast. Lawrence, "I Want."

147   "I Was Born This Way": See http://www.discostyle.com/artist/bio/carl_bean.asp. Motown released a number of gay-oriented songs. The Dynamic Superiors, whose lead singer, Tony Washington, was openly gay, recorded "Nobody's Going to Change Me," and the Miracles recorded "Ain't Nobody Straight in L.A."

148   "heterosexual hegemony": John Gill, *Queer Noises* (Minneapolis: University of Minnesota Press, 1993), 137.

148   "make no mention": http://www.discostyle.com/artist/bio/carl_bean.asp.

148   Did "It" refer: According to Lawrence, Russell wanted his "It" to be read both ways. See Lawrence, "I Want." The liner notes to *The World of Arthur Russell* claim that Russell did not write the lyrics, but Lawrence says he wrote most of the lines. Email communication with Tim Lawrence, May 13, 2009. Lawrence's book, *Hold On to Your Dreams: Arthur Russell and the Downtown Music Scene*, is forthcoming from Duke University Press.

148   "made it into": Lawrence, "I Want." This minimalist track continues to be controversial. Some regard it an overrated piece of junk with out-of-tune vocals, while others praise its experimental, avant-garde ambitions. See http://www.discomusic.com/forums/disco-music-70s-80s/8367-defense-loose-joints-all-over-my.html.

148   "gay up": Miller, *Place for Us*, 35.

148   "Free Man": "Free Man" was made somewhat ambiguous by the fact it is a duet whose female vocalist sounds quite plausibly male.

148   Discologists could be: Lawrence, "I Want."

149   "disco became *disco*": See also Cheren's account of this, *Keep On*, 278–9.

149   "It was like": Levine quoted in Shapiro, *Turn the Beat*, 85.

150   "was that there": See David W. Dunlap, "As Disco Faces Razing, Gay Alumni Share Memories," *New York Times*, August 21, 1995, http://www.nytimes .com/1995/08/21/nyregion/as-disco-faces-razing-gay-alumni-share-memo ries.html?scp=1&sq=saint%20disco&st=cse.

150   The club's sound: Levine quoted in Shapiro, *Turn the Beat*, 86.

150   "To get one": Cheren, *Keep On*, 276. Note that "Doug from Brooklyn," on http://cinematreasures.org/theater/527, puts the membership fee at $250.

150   "fuck yourself up": Levine quoted in Shapiro, *Turn the Beat*, 87.

151   "The apotheosis" . . . "headiest experience" . . . "dancing on the edge": Dunlap, "Disco Faces Razing."

151   "seemed to snipe": Randy Shilts, *And the Band Played On*, rev. ed. (New York: St. Martin's Griffin, 2007), 149.

151   "Saint's disease": Dunlap, "Disco Faces Razing."

151   "gay men don't": Ibid.

152   "the pleasurable discipline": Hughes, "In the Empire," 154.

153   And, of course, AIDS: Ibid., 156.

153   "ostensibly celebrated": Werner, *Change*, 208.

153   "phenomenology": Michael Warner quoted in Caleb Crain, "Pleasure Principles," *Lingua Franca*, October 1997.

153   "'anonymous sex'": Edmund White, *Arts & Letters* (San Francisco: Cleis, 2006), 18. Gooch, however, seems to take a more judgmental stance toward the period. His novel ends with the appearance of Patient Zero.

154   "32 bed partners": Cheren, *Keep On*, 165.

154   "lousy deal": Brent Harris, "Andrew Holleran."

154   Whereas just years: Kate Flint characterized gay men's presence as hypervisible rather than merely visible. Personal communication, Kate Flint, January 6, 2007.

155   *Dancer from the Dance*: *Faggots,* which appeared in the same year as *Dancer,* conveys this ambivalence less well because Kramer is so plainly condemnatory. Holleran has said that when he and Kramer did a joint book tour in 1978, Kramer "took all the brickbats" in the gay press. Richard Canning, *Gay Fiction Speaks: Conversations with Gay Novelists* (New York: Columbia University Press, 2000), 143. Holleran is often accused of romanticizing the

fast-lane gay life of the seventies in *Dancer*, which seems a strange charge given the novel's sometimes scathing portrait of the gay circuit life. When the book was first published Holleran told the *Advocate* that the novel "was written out of a certain amount of anger" about why gay men "treat each other as shabbily as we do." See Harris, *Advocate*, 1979. In a 1997 interview Holleran said he was surprised by the accusation that he had romanticized gay life because he felt that he hadn't romanticized the Fire Island circuit scene at all. However, in the next breath he admitted, "I guess I had in a way, because part of me did love it," before emphasizing that *Dancer* "was also a very critical book." Canning, *Gay Fiction*, 143.

155 "a site not of foreplay": Lawrence, *Love Saves*, 25, 27, 50.

156 Peter Shapiro: "Mainstream disco's abandoning of its original constituency and its values, its unseemly greed, its whitewashing of race and, to a certain degree, gender," writes Shapiro, "made it the perfect bridge from the liberalism that largely dominated the '50s and the '60s to the neoconservatism that has shaped the Anglo-American axis since the 1980s." Shapiro, *Turn the Beat*, 227.

156 "lose its queer": Lawrence, "I Want."

156 "the masses": Staff Report, "The Age of Disco," *Advocate*, 1975: reprinted in Thompson, ed., *Long Road to Freedom*, 126.

156 "didn't want to remain": Lawrence, *Love Saves*, 116.

156 "underground idea": Aletti quoted in Frank Broughton and Bill Brewster, liner notes for *Larry Levan Live at the Paradise Garage*, released 2000. Vince Aletti, "Disco Stays More than Alive," *Village Voice*, February 13, 1978.

156 "quintessential mainstream": Shapiro, *Turn the Beat*, 227.

156 "patriarchal heterosexuality": Big-city discos that catered primarily to heterosexuals were often sites of dance-floor interracialism. I have come across several such mentions in contemporaneous accounts. See Peck, "Face of Disco," 27. It's generally assumed that gay discos played the most cutting-edge music, yet Walter Gibbons, one of the most innovative deejays in New York City, worked at Galaxy 21, a straight disco. See Lawrence, "Disco Madness."

5 SATURDAY NIGHT FEVER

159 "how surprised": Dave Godin, "The Dave Godin Column: Disco Boom or Gloom?," *Blues and Soul Review*, March 23, 1976, 26. Perhaps because discos in Britain were a mainstream rather than a minority taste, seventies' disco

culture in Britain attracted a largely heterosexual and white following. See Sara Thornton, *Club Cultures* (Cambridge: Polity, 1995), 44.

160 "the little disco": Oakes quoted in Sam Kashner, "Fever Pitch," *Vanity Fair,* 2007, http://www.moviesrock2007.com/article-fever-pitch-3.php#article-body.

160 a modish Oscar Wilde: Barry Gibbs describes Stigwood as looking "Oscar Wildeish" in a 2001 interview with *Mojo*, http://www.beegees-world.com/archives13.html.

160 "a real carnival": Bob Spitz, *The Beatles: The Biography* (New York: Little Brown, 2005), 163.

160 "We told Brian": McCartney quoted in the Beatles, *Beatles Anthology* (New York: Chronicle Books, 2000), 268.

160 Beatles got rid of: Spitz, *Beatles*, 222.

161 "the first British": Kevin McCormick quoted in Kashner, "Fever Pitch."

161 In contrast to: Up until the making of *Fever*, gay men had been a significant force in disco, but primarily as deejays, mixers, clubbers, and record promoters. Sylvester and the Village People had yet to score hits when *Fever* was being filmed. Although he never "came out," Stigwood's involvement with *Fever* made him the most high-profile gay man in disco.

161 "smart set": The U.S. music business can boast very few openly gay men in positions of power. Label executive David Geffen and *Rolling Stone*'s founder and editor-in-chief Jann Wenner came out many years after the disco seventies. The situation was very different on the other side of the Atlantic, where Stigwood lived and worked. In Britain, the "pink mafia" wielded considerable power. When it came to music management, gay men were the norm. Brian Epstein (the Beatles), Kit Lambert (the Who), Vic Billings (Dusty Springfield), Simon Napier-Bell (Yardbirds, T.Rex, and Marc Bolan), and Larry Parnes (Billy Fury, Georgie Fame) were all gay. Andrew Loog Oldham, who managed the Rolling Stones, was at the very least bisexual. See www.circa-club.com/gallery/gay_history_icons_simon_napier_bell.php.

161 "down the social": Hector Cook, Andrew M. Hughes, and Melinda Bilyeu, *The Bee Gees: Tales of the Brothers Gibb* (Omnibus Press: London, 2001), 406.

161 "There'd been": Cohn quoted in Cook et al., *Bee Gees*, 405.

161 "Black Nureyev": Nik Cohn, "Tribal Rites," reprinted as "Another Saturday Night" in *Ball to the Wall* (London: Picador, 1989), 326.

162 "a most extravagant": Cohn's portrait of Tu Sweet—"the Black Nureyev"— is fabulous, particularly his description of the dancer's precarious financial

circumstances. Tired of seeing the breaks always go someone else's way, Tu Sweet asked Cohn if Nureyev might not find it daunting "if his partner just walked out the door? And he couldn't get his tights back from the cleaners?" "Tu Sweet, No Sweat," in Cohn, *Ball to the Wall*, 343–46.

162 "There were automotive": Ibid., 328.

162 "looked out of place": Steven Kurutz, "The Legend of Saturday Night," posted May 26, 2005, on Nerve.com, http://www.nerve.com/dispatches/kurutz/legendofsaturdaynight.

162 Cohn spent a couple: Cohn admitted that his research consisted of nothing more than a couple of weekend nights at 2001 Odyssey, where he had only a few superficial conversations. Kurutz, "Legend."

162 "thoroughly male": Kurutz, "Legend," 4.

162 "Tribal Rites" emphasized: It is worth noting that Walter Hughes argued that disco, like bodybuilding and s/m, functioned as a disciplinary practice for gay men of the era. Hughes, "Empire."

162 "troops": Cohn, *Ball to the Wall*, 330. Cohn's portrait of disco is uncannily reminiscent of theorist Theodor Adorno's argument, first put forward in 1941, that the "standardized meter of dance music and of marching" encourages "rhythmic obedience." See Adorno, "On Popular Music," in Frith and Goodwin, eds., *On Record*, 312. There are echoes of Adorno in Geoff Mungham's essay on dance-hall youth, "Youth in Pursuit of Itself," in Geoff Mungham and G. Pearson, *Working Class Youth Cultures* (London: Routledge & Kegan Paul, 1976).

163 "the same automaton": Cohn, *Ball to the Wall*, 329.

163 "a killer": Ibid., 323.

163 "that the rest": Kurutz, "Legend," 6.

164 "they were West London": As Peter Shapiro notes, savvy British readers (and this should have included Stigwood, who, after all, managed those über Mods, the Who) should have been alerted to the falseness of Cohn's story by his use of "Face." Being a "Face" was "tantamount to becoming a saint in British Mod culture." See Shapiro, *Turn the Beat*, 203. Indeed, everything about *Fever*'s Faces—their narcissism, fastidiousness, and homosociality—pegged them as Mods for anyone in the know. See Terry Rawlings, *Mod: A Very British Phenomenon* (London: Omnibus Press, 2000).

164 "a complete invention": Kurutz, "Legend."

164 "I had no instinct": Cohn quoted in Kurutz, "Legend." Cohn apparently told the same story to the authors of the Bee Gees' biography. See Cook et al., *Bee Gees*, 405–7.

164   However, according: Anthony Haden-Guest, *The Last Party: Studio 54, Disco, and the Culture of the Night* (New York: William Morrow, 1997), xxv.

164   "I see a hundred-million-dollar": Ibid., xxv.

165   $90,000: Kashner, "Fever Pitch."

165   $150,000: Haden-Guest, *Last Party*, xxvi.

165   "hip humor": Tom Vallance, "Obituary: Norman Wexler," *Independent* (London), August 27, 1999, at http://findarticles.com/p/articles/mi_qn4158/is_19990827/ai_n14242925.

166   Wexler, who was diagnosed: Jesse McKinley, "Obituary: Norman Wexler," *New York Times*, August 25, 1999.

166   When it came time: As in Cohn's story, Wexler's script had the protagonist kissing a girl who reacts by swooning that she's just kissed Al Pacino, and cruelly rejecting another after she admits she's not on the pill and is without any form of contraception. Finally, Wexler incorporated the turf war between Bay Ridge's Italians and Puerto Ricans.

166   "The Bee Gees weren't": Kashner, "Fever Pitch."

167   "discoey": Cook et al., *Bee Gees*, 410.

167   However, just weeks: This is the account that director John Badham gives in his commentary on the *Saturday Night Fever* DVD. "Lowdown" was subsequently used instead in *Looking for Mr. Goodbar.*

167   "Travolta's too fat": Producer McCormick quoted in Kashner, "Fever Pitch."

167   Badham had no: The Bee Gees are often characterized as disco Johnny-come-latelys. Typical are Alan Jones and Juzzi Kantonen, who claim that the Bee Gees were "never a disco group." See Jones and Kantonen, *Saturday Night Forever: The Story of Disco* (Chicago: A Cappella, 2000), 142. Likewise, Mark Anthony Neal contends that the Bee Gees' disco illustrates the distance that disco had travelled from its "organic roots." See Neal, *What the Music Said*, 121.

167   "original ersatz": Dave Marsh, "The Pleasures of Their Company," *Rolling Stone,* June 30, 1977, 98.

167   "never before has": Jim Miller, "Bee Gees' 1st," *Rolling Stone,* December 21, 1968, 29.

168   "a complete rip-off": Weaver quoted in Cook et al., *Bee Gees*, 414.

169   "that this voice": Ibid., 375.

169   "I think if you": Over the years the Bee Gees have embraced and disavowed the falsetto. In this same interview, he said the falsetto was "actually something I ought to be proud of." Ibid., 376.

169   "find out about": "Burdon: Two Years on the Killing Floor," *Sounds,* June 2, 1973, 7.

169   Jeff Beck spoke: Indeed, Beck had hoped to record Wonder's song "Super-stition" for his own solo LP, but Motown insisted that Wonder record it first rather than handing it over to Beck. Pete Erskine, "Beck, Bogart and Appice," *Sounds*, September 29, 1973, 10; "Wonder: Music on His Mind: Stevie Wonder Talks to Penny Valentine," *Sounds*, January 27, 1973, 16.

170   "a *really* funky": Martin Kirkup, "Diamond Dogs: Interview with Bowie," *Sounds*, May 4, 1974, 16. Interestingly, Humble Pie's Steve Marriott was rather cynical about the attention Bowie was garnering for employing black girl backup singers. Marriott said, "he really hasn't stumbled on anything new . . . It seems to me he's a bit late with the old black and white minstrel bit. I mean it's been around a few years." See Ray Telford, "Pie: Fresh as Ever," *Sounds*, October 19, 1974, 8.

170   "emerging disco scene": Easlea, *Everybody Dance*, 65.

170   "Fame" came about: John Lennon's lover at the time, May Pang, was in the studio and relates the story in Britain's *Independent*. See http://www.independent.co.uk/arts-entertainment/music/features/the-ballad-of-john-and-yokos-secretary-495046.html.

170   "Fame," and the rest: Bowie usually sings in a rather low register, but here he forced his voice into a falsetto, especially on "Young Americans" and "Fasci-nation." Bowie continued to use the falsetto through *Station to Station*, after which point he shed both it and disco.

170   "plastic soul": John Abbey, "B.T. Express," *Blues and Soul Review*, July 27, 1976, 3.

171   "are among": Ray Telford, *Sounds*, February 16, 1974, 26.

171   "the main vein": Charlie Bermant, "Back on Course with the Bee Gees," *Sounds*, August 9, 1975, 15.

171   Whatever the reason: Billy Altman, "Bee Gees Banquet," *Rolling Stone,* September 11, 1975, 15.

171   "That's fucking": Jagger quoted in Cook et al., *Bee Gees*, 381.

171   "Atlantic didn't want": Ibid., 381.

172   "Wall of Percussion": See Richardson's interview, http://www.fortheloveofthebeegees.com/archivenews.htm.

173   "We spent as much": Maurice Gibb quoted in Cook et al., *Bee Gees*, 408.

173   "If we had known": Robin Gibb quoted in Ibid., 410.

173   "insistent": See Galuten's interview on http://www.fortheloveofthebeegees.com/archivenews.htm.

173   "Then there were the locals": See Kashner, "Fever Pitch."

173   "We thought" . . . "monster hits": Priestley and Gorney quoted in ibid.

174   "sounding pretty": Miller, "Bee Gees' 1st," 29.

174   Its guitar riff: Cook et al., *Bee Gees*, 415.

175   The middle: Critic David B. Wilson noted the similarity. See http://www
       .warr.org/odd70stemp.html#SaturdayNightFever.

175   "people crying out": Cook et al., *Bee Gees*, 416.

175   Dave Marsh misheard: Dave Marsh, *The Heart of Rock & Soul: The 1001
       Greatest Singles Ever Made* (New York: Da Capo, 1989), 457.

175   What the Bee Gees apparently meant was that the vision of nightlife offered
       by Studio 54 was proving seductive to young people, who were unable to
       see much of a future for themselves beyond the dance floor. Of course, this
       betrays a certain misapprehension about most of the characters in *Fever*, for
       whom 54 was way out of reach. Cook et al., *Bee Gees*, 410.

175   "macho": Martin quoted in ibid., 416.

175   "mechanical mice": Christgau, *Record Guide*, 43.

176   "sissy soul": Jon Landau used the term "sissy soul" in his year-end review,
       "Rock 1970," *Rolling Stone*, December 2, 1970, 43. In his "Singles" column,
       John Peel noted Bowie's falsetto cries on *Young Americans*. See *Sounds*, Feb-
       ruary 22, 1975, 36.

176   "virile": Bud Scoppa approved of the way that Average White Band's Hamish
       Stuart used his falsetto with "the daring of an aerialist," but his enthusi-
       asm seemed contingent on Onnie McIntyre's guitar work, which he claimed
       "fills out the backgrounds in a sparing, virile way." Scoppa, *Rolling Stone*,
       October 10, 1974. Tony Washington of the Dynamic Superiors might be gay,
       but "he doesn't sound wimpy," noted another reviewer. Russell Gersten, in
       Rolling Stone, September 25, 1975, 111. To Joe McEwen, Earth Wind and
       Fire's Philip Bailey has a "flaccid" falsetto. McEwen, "Review," *Rolling Stone,*
       December 16, 1976, 78.

176   *Saturday Night Fever* owed: Stephen Holden noted that the slowness of
       the Bee Gees' tracks didn't conform to the "rigid guidelines for disco that
       were devised after the film became popular." "The Beat Goes On—And On,
       And On," *Rolling Stone*, June 14, 1979, 96. However, slowish songs, includ-
       ing Diana Ross's "Upside Down" and Chic's "Good Times," from 1979 and
       1980, respectively, were massive hits.

176   Likewise the dance: Like almost everything else in *Fever*, the smoke was
       done on the cheap, made from a mix of burning tar and car tires that the
       crew had "pinched from a Bay Ridge alley." See Kashner, "Fever Pitch."

177   Skittishness about: Reporting on a Stylistics concert in London, Paul Gam-
       baccini remarked upon lead singer Russell Thompkins's "falsetto rap" to the

audience, which reacted in both "awed adulation and disgusted ridicule." Gambaccini, "Performance," *Rolling Stone,* June 20, 1974, 102.

177   Maria Torres watched: Peter Shapiro attributes Travolta's solo dancing to the fact that he was drawing on the more individualistic style of Northern Soul, but the solo dancing was something the actor himself demanded. See Shapiro, *Turn the Beat,* 203.

177   "really killed": http://www.empsfm.org/programs/index.asp?articleID=625.

177   However, in other: One of the reasons that much of the dancing seems mediocre, as Torres notes, is that about 50 percent of the people filmed during the dance sequences were Odyssey regulars.

178   "a lot of" . . . "give the illusion" . . . "amazed" . . . "dive" . . . "Quiana shirts" . . . "guys coming to meet": Kurutz, "Legend." The material on 2001 Odyssey is drawn largely from Kurutz's in-depth treatment.

182   "It looked like": Ibid., 5.

183   For well over: See http://www.beegees-world.com/bio_gplat.html.

183   "vulgar . . . the worst": See http://www.variety.com/review/VE1117794638 .html?categoryid=31&cs=1.

183   Gene Siskel: http://rogerebert.suntimes.com/apps/pbcs.dll/article?AID=/ 19990307/REVIEWS08/401010357/1023. It was Siskel's all-time favorite movie, and according to his colleague Roger Ebert, he watched it at least seventeen times. He also bought Tony's white suit at a charity auction.

183   "stylized sensuality": Marsha Kinder, Review, *Film Quarterly* 31, no. 3 (Spring 1978), 40.

183   "deft and vibrant": Janet Maslin, review of *Saturday Night Fever, New York Times,* December 16, 1977.

184   "pop music at": Christgau, *Record Guide,* 343.

184   "dreamy and aggressive": Stephen Holden, review of *Spirits Having Flown, Rolling Stone,* April 5, 1979.

184   "peculiarly piercing": Vince Aletti, "Disco Fever Stays More than Alive," *Village Voice,* February 13, 1978, 53.

184   "subcultural" . . . "made disco safe": Kopkind, "Dialectic."

185   "whitened up": See Joshua Gamson, *Fabulous Sylvester,* 163. There are many such examples. Brian Ward has called the Bee Gees' music disco "white face." See Ward, *Just My Soul,* 426. Mark Anthony Neal has also criticized the Bee Gees' music as the "ultimate appropriation" of Philadelphia International Records. See *What the Music Said,* 121. And Michael Bérubé defends "righteous disco—Gloria Gaynor, the Tavares, Trammps, and Sylvester"—against the Stigwood machine and the Bee Gees, which

"needed to die." See http://www.michaelberube.com/index.php/weblog/comments/732.

185 According to this: Braunstein, "Adults Only," in Bailey and Farber, eds., *America*, 147. Kopkind's language—that *Fever* made disco "safe" for mainstream groups—has been used time and again by other commentators suggesting that his really is the foundational essay. See also Easlea, *Everybody Dance*, 112. I, too, drew upon Kopkind's work in my essay "Ball of Confusion," *LA Weekly*, April 29–May 5, 1994, 24–32.

185 "repatriated": Tim Lawrence maintained that *Fever* was instrumental in the "reappropriation of the dance floor by patriarchal heterosexuality." Lawrence, "I Want," 144. A leading historian of the seventies treats the movie as "ludicrous . . . the Bee Gees' falsetto vocals, Travolta's white leisure suits, the melodramatic dance contest." See Schulman, *Seventies*, 144–5. And Peter Carroll argues that the movie promotes a "conservative message of conformity, expensive dress, and self-discipline." Carroll, "It Seemed Like," 266.

186 According to Freddie Gershon: Cook et al., *Bee Gees*, 406.

186 Tony dances: Although dancing was hardly at odds with conventional masculinity in African American and Puerto Rican communities, for much of America dancing was the domain of women. Indeed, Travolta admitted that he devised Tony's strut in conscious imitation of African Americans. Travolta calls his *Fever* strut "the walk of coolness." "I went to a school that was 50 percent black, and that's how the black kids walked through the hall." Kashner, "Fever Pitch."

186 "all kinds of hassle": Ibid.

187 "helpless cries": Aletti, "Disco Fever."

188 Cohn's story: Travolta was also struck by the misogyny of the Bay Ridge disco. Kashner, "Fever Pitch."

190 "like undershirts": Barbara Ehrenreich, *Hearts of Men* (Garden City, NJ: Anchor Press, 1983), 139.

191 "genius": Nile Rodgers quoted in Shapiro, *Turn the Beat*, 204–5. Although Bay Ridge disco is not presented as transformative, the larger world of music and dance is.

192 "cool things off": Production designer Charles Bailey quoted in Kashner, "Fever Pitch."

193 "Travolta and members": Unamused, the executives are thought to have ordered the film destroyed.

193 "non-bureaucratic": Stephen Holden, review of *Spirits Having Flown, Rolling Stone,* April 5, 1978, 69.

194 "politically, socially": Rodgers quoted in Shapiro, *Turn the Beat*, 205.

6 ONE NATION UNDER A THUMP?

195   "Disco's so *straight*": Erectus quoted in Frank Rose, "Discophobia: Rock & Roll Fights Back," *Village Voice*, November 12, 1979.

195   Just before: Lawrence, *Love Saves*, 285.

195   Studio 54 . . . Leviticus: Cooper, "Disco Knights," 160.

195   Mel Cheren . . . Rubell: Cheren, *Keep on Dancin'*, 185. For a splendidly full account of 54, see Haden-Guest's *The Last Party*.

196   "They wouldn't let": Stanley M. Friedman, Roy Cohn's law partner, is the speaker here. See Charles Kaiser, *The Gay Metropolis* (New York: Houghton Mifflin, 1997), 255.

196   first anniversary bash: Leslie Bennetts, "An 'In' Crowd and Outside Mob Show Up for Studio 54's Birthday," *New York Times,* April 28, 1978, B4.

196   "hell bent": Ibid.

196   "This is the nightclub": Capote quoted in ibid.

196   "peon": Rich quoted in Kaiser, *Gay Metropolis*, 258.

196   "resembled the": Miezitis quoted in Lawrence, *Love Saves*, 282.

196   "ultimate discotheque"; "playpen": Judy Klemesrud, "Discothèque Fanatics Mob Latest Addition," *New York Times,* June 9, 1978.

197   "disco hit": Lee quoted in Eric Messinger, "Questions for Spike Lee: New Kid on the Block," *New York Times Magazine*, June 27, 1999, 14.

197   A year after: Shapiro, *Turn the Beat*, 194.

197   "lining up for": Kopkind, "Dialectic."

197   "seduced Middle America": Stephen Holden, "The Evolution of a Dance Craze," *Rolling Stone*, April 19, 1979, 30.

197   Arthur Murray: http://www.dancecoquitlam.ca/pag_cms_id_22_p_hustle .html.

197   The vast majority: In some locations, Holiday Inns and Hilton hotels had started to "go disco" as early as 1976, but this process accelerated in the wake of *Fever*. *Newsweek* noted the trend in its 1976 feature on disco.

198   All across America: Jesse Kornbluth, "Merchandizing Disco For the Masses," *New York Times Magazine,* February 18, 1979.

198   "the local rock": Kopkind, "Dialectic."

198   "the disco for people": Kornbluth, "Merchandizing Disco."

198   the McDonald's: Shapiro, *Turn the Beat*, 194.

198   "geared like IBM": Kornbluth, "Merchandizing Disco."

198   "entertainment equivalent": Ibid.

198   "When I was": Boyd quoted in Lawrence, *Love Saves*, 315.

198   By 1979: Holden, "Evolution," 30.

199   Investigators of the 1978: Kornbluth, "Merchandizing Disco."

199   Television ramped: For a thorough historical account of the backlash, see Gillian Frank, "Discophobia: Antigay Prejudice and the 1979 Backlash Against Disco," *Journal of the History of Sexuality* 16, no. 2 (May 2007): 290.

199   Even *Sesame Street*: Easlea, *Everybody Dance*, 113.

199   "institutionalized disco": http://www.empsfm.org/programs/index.asp?articleID=625.

199   After *Fever*'s release: See http://www.ejumpcut.org/archive/onlinessays/JC21folder/BrazilStamJohnson.html.

200   England, France: For the internationalizing of disco, see Lawrence, *Love Saves*, 317–8.

200   "havens" . . . "growing like": News of the Soviet Union's disco market appeared in a *San Francisco Examiner* article in early September 1978, and was noted by Vince Aletti in his September 16, 1978, *Record World* disco column. According to Kate Flint, who went to a Communist hotel ballroom on New Year's Eve 1974, Russian discos often featured live bands playing hit disco songs. Personal communication, Kate Flint, May 11, 2009.

200   "cocaine dens": http://www.mio.co.za/article.php?cat=&id=532.

201   "authentically fiery": Simon Frith and Peter Langley, *Creem*. See www.creem magazine.com for their March 1977 review, which was positive.

201   Anticipating massive demand: Lawrence, *Love Saves*, 371.

201   That same month: Ibid., 364.

201   By 1979, Chic: Easlea, *Everybody Dance*, 148.

201   "disco-ize": Caviano quoted in Lawrence, *Love Saves*, 330.

201   The press was full: Bruce Dancis, Abe Peck, Tom Smucker, and Georgia Christgau, "Disco! Disco!: Four Critics Address the Musical Question," *In These Times*, June 6–12, 1979.

202   *Rolling Stone* was never: The magazine's first substantial disco feature was in 1975. Both Abe Peck and Tom Smucker, who were involved with the *In These Times* forum, wrote pieces for *Rolling Stone*'s April 19, 1979, disco issue. They were not disco haters, and Peck has said that he and the others working on the issue were committed to presenting it fairly. Telephone interview with Abe Peck, February 20, 2009.

203   "malaise speech": Edward D. Berkowitz, *Something Happened* (New York: Columbia University Press, 2006), 131. Gordon Stewart, co-author of this speech, notes that it included no mention of malaise, and that it was initially extremely popular, judging by the calls to the White House. See Stewart, "Carter's Speech Therapy," *New York Times*, July 19, 2009, A21.

204 "producing [disco] records" . . . "President Carter, homosexuality": See Frank, "Discophobia," 306, n. 116.

205 Indeed there was: Ibid., 304.

205 "play a couple of bars" . . . "electrocutions" . . . "intelligence": Quoted in Rose, "Discophobia."

205 "cultural void" . . . "antidisco army" . . . "write DISCO SUCKS": "Random Notes," *Rolling Stone*, August 23, 1979, 34.

206 Almost 5,000: Rose, "Discophobia."

206 10,000 card-carrying: Frank, "Discophobia," 297.

206 Disco Demolition: The best historical account of Disco Demolition is Gillian Frank's "Discophobia."

207 "Oh, God": Joe LaPointe, "The Night Disco Went Up in Smoke," *New York Times*, July 5, 2009, Sports, 8.

207 The day after: Cheren, *Keep On*, 258.

207 "national hook-up": "Random Notes," *Rolling Stone*, August 23, 1979, 34.

208 "disco was superficial": Rose, "Discophobia."

208 In the summer of 1979: This June 30, 1979, *Melody Maker* article is cited in David Buxton, "Rock Music, the Star System, and the Rise of Consumption," in Frith and Goodwin, eds., *On Record*, 440, n. 27.

208 pronounced disco "over": Lebowitz interview quoted in Vince Aletti, "Disco File," *Billboard*, April 8, 1978.

209 "disco was so": Cheren, *Keep On*, 259.

209 "faggots": Frank, "Discophobia," 293.

209 So straightforward: Dave Marsh, "The Flip Sides of '79," *Rolling Stone*, December 27, 1979–January 10, 1980, 28. It's worth noting that even though *Rolling Stone* did not embrace Dahl, in 1980 the paper listed him among the most influential people in the industry. See "The Heavy Hundred," *Rolling Stone,* March 6, 1980, 11.

210 "decidedly racist": Robert Draper, *Rolling Stone Magazine: The Uncensored History* (New York: Knopf, 1981), 270.

210 fan reaction to Prince: See http://prince.org/msg/7/266058. Someone with a bootleg tape of the concert has posted the following about Prince's set at one of the Stones' Southern California concerts: "But the audience is not that into it—at the start of the second song, someone—presumably the taper, says 'One more song, and that'll be ENOUGH for THIS band!' The second song is 'When You Were Mine,' another hard rocker with no falsetto. Then comes 'Jack u Off,' the taper yells, 'LOOK AT ALL THE TRASH!'—I guess the stage was being pelted. As the song ends, a loud chorus of 'boo's' can be heard from the audience. Dez graciously thanks the crowd and continues playing. Prince seems to have disappeared—there are no vocals at

213 "mass-produced . . . retained artisanal": Buxton, "Rock Music," 439, n. 1.

213 "Disco's so": See Rose, "Discophobia."

213 "Once it became": Trabulus quoted in http://www.empsfm.org/programs/index.asp?articleID=625.

214 "seemingly making": Lawrence, *Love Saves*, 378.

214 "It takes ecstasy": Morris quoted in Reynolds, *Rip It Up*, 398.

215 "You mean you" . . . "an underlying tone": Rodgers quoted in Easlea, *Everybody Dance*, 216.

215 "little disco tart": Madonna quoted in "The *Rolling Stone* Interview with Madonna," *Rolling Stone*, September 10, 1987, 88.

215 "white suit": Barry Gibb quoted in Bob Cannon, "Disco's 'Fever' Pitch," *Entertainment Weekly*, January 22, 1993. There was little let-up in the nineties for the Bee Gees. In 1996, when they appeared on the BBC show *Clive Anderson All Talk*, they put up with a number of putdowns before Barry Gibb, followed by his brothers, walked off the set. See http://www.youtube.com/watch?v=mdvfmGPDVkk.

215 Chris Rock . . . "If everyone owned": Chris Rock said at a tribute for Richard Pryor that the older comedian came on the scene "between the two great plagues, disco and AIDS." See Irvin Molotsky, "Laughs and Pathos at Pryor Tribute," *New York Times*, October 22, 1998, B13. The Camaro advertisement ran in 1996.

216 "cued up 'Stairway'": Jon Pareles, "Disco Lives! Actually It Never Died," *New York Times*, October 17, 1999, Arts & Leisure, 40.

216 "The death of disco!" . . . "We still went out": Moulton and Gomes quoted in Lawrence, *Love Saves*, 393–4.

216 Radio deejay: Electrifyin' Mojo is frequently credited with playing Kraftwerk, and thereby helping to lay the foundation for Detroit techno. I remember hearing the group's "Tour de France" on his show, but if memory serves, Mojo favored funk, especially by Detroit's P-Funk crew, but including that of Was (Not Was) and fellow Midwesterners Prince and the Time. He also played Cameo, the Gap Band, Queen, Billy Squier, Rick James, the J. Geils Band, and the Stones, among others.

217 posters for early: See Tricia Rose, *Black Noise*, for reproductions of these early hip-hop posters. For rap's connection to disco, see Chapter Five of her book, particularly 211, n. 13.

217 "percussive": Cooper quoted in Easlea, *Everybody Dance*, 166.

217 "macho nature": Jones quoted in ibid., 167.

218 Ian Dury and the Blockheads': M's "Pop Muzik" used disco, both sonically and in the figure of the deejay in their popular video, to critique the disposability of pop music.

218 "Heart of Glass": See http://www.blender.com/guide/68206/greatest-songs-ever-heart-glass.html.

218 "screw people up": However, Burke was not opposed to using a disco beat, as some narratives suggest. *Fever* was one of his favorite records, he claims, and on "Heart of Glass" he tried to capture the groove of the Bee Gees' drummer. This was not widely known at the time, however. Burke's account of "The

Disco Song" appears in "*Parallel Lines*," *Rolling Stone*, December 11, 2003, 128.

219   to many punks, disco epitomized: According to Adele Bertei, who was part of New York's punk scene and played keyboards in the Contortions, "When it came to disco, we were like these vicious little misanthropes with Tourette's syndrome. You'd get a torrent of abuse." Bertei quoted in Reynolds, *Rip It Up*, 68.

219   "It doesn't have" . . . "I've always" . . . "It's sort of": Chance quoted in Reynolds, *Rip It Up*, 68.

221   "We only wanted": Cameron Macdonald, "The Seconds Column—Public Image Limited: Fodderstompf," *Stylus*, September 3, 2006. http://www.stylus-magazine.com/articles/seconds/public-image-limited-fodderstompf.htm.

221   "as mental as"; "the studio as": Reynolds, *Rip It Up*, 13.

221   "the studio": Ibid.

221   "anti rock & roll": Patricia Romanowski, Holly George-Warren, and Jon Pareles, *The New Rolling Stone Encyclopedia of Rock & Roll*, rev. ed. (New York: Fireside, 1995), 799.

221   Reggae: From the beginning disco music carried at least a hint of the tropical, and over time artists and producers began to work the intersection between reggae and disco. Jamaican-born Grace Jones was the best-known disco artist to work with veteran reggae producers Robbie Shakespeare and Sly Dunbar.

221   "just left me": Lydon quoted in Reynolds, *Rip It Up*, 7.

221   "boot boy harassment": John Lydon, *Rotten: No Irish, No Blacks, No Dogs* (New York: Picador, 1994), 67.

221   "loved disco": For his love of disco, see John Payne, "His Way," *LA Weekly*, August 8–14, 1997, 44. See http://www.youtube.com/watch?v=mhiFGo3mt RI for his slagging off disco, particularly Donna Summer's "Bad Girls."

221   never an Abba fan: Lydon, *Rotten*, 232.

222   Some of the key: There were of course many more, including Chic's Nile Rodgers. Although he was not especially interested in exploring the interstices of rock and disco, Arthur Russell was interested in taking disco into more experimental territory. August Darnell and Andy Hernandez (a.k.a. Coati Mundi), first of the disco band Dr. Buzzard's Original Savannah Band and then of Kid Creole and the Coconuts, are another example of a one-off whose work brings together Latin, big band, funk, and rock in a wonderful collision. The South Bronx group ESG is also important.

222   In Britain: Sarah Thornton observes that in Britain the anti-disco backlash was not driven by homophobia and racism, as it was in the U.S. "British

anti-disco sentiments are more directly derived from classist convictions about mindless masses and generational conflict about the poor taste of the young." She ascribes this national difference largely to the fact that in Britain disco was not associated with gays and racial minorities, and instead enjoyed a "huge straight working-class following." See Thornton, *Club Cultures*, 44.

222   Certainly the path: Still, in 1978, British music critic Simon Frith, who was not a disco hater, wrote, "Everybody hates [disco]. Hippies hate it, progressives hate it, punks hate it, teds hate it . . ." Quoted in Easlea, *Everybody Dance*, 149.

222   "all you big heads": Reynolds, *Rip It Up*, 163.

223   "urban gay men" . . . "same forces": Cheren, *Keep On*, 260–1.

224   "thirty-five percent": Caviano quoted in Lawrence, *Love Saves*, 369.

224   "meant that they cost": Aletti quoted in ibid., 369.

224   "track date": Pareles, "Disco Lives!"

226   "less and less disco and more and more freaky": As he notes, the spaces where Eurodisco lingered were usually gay bars that featured hi-NRG disco. See interview with Vince Aletti, DJ History Archive, http://www.djhistory .com/interviews/vince-aletti.

227   more naming: In his effort to chronicle the music of rave culture, Simon Reynolds included a nearly thirty-page appendix mapping the permutations of techno. See Reynolds's excellent *Generation Ecstasy*, 397–436.

227   microgenres: A thorough treatment of eighties' dance music is beyond the scope (and the purpose) of this book. Readers looking for such a study should consult Tim Lawrence's forthcoming book, *Life and Death on the New York Dance Floor: A History, 1980–87*.

227   "gay discos": Cooper, "Disco Knights," 161.

227   "on a budget": See Jon Pareles, "Paradise Garage: A Gay Club That Forever Changed Night Life," *New York Times,* June 18, 2000. Although "house" is frequently described as music that grew out of the music that Larry Levan played at the Paradise Garage, Mel Cheren says he hears very little resemblance: "When the Chicago kids wanted to start recording, they couldn't afford [to do so with big live orchestras such as MFSB] and the computer came into being. So they did it at home and it was stripped down, with no vocals." See http://query.nytimes.com/gst/fullpage.html?res=9403E3D91F 3EF93BA25755C0A9669C8B63&fta=y.

227   "We came to this" . . . "All the stuff": Knuckles quoted in Lawrence, *Love Saves*, 409.

228   relentless splintering: There is some evidence that the relentless splinter-
       ing and mutating of dance music into ever more particularistic microgenres
       sometimes encouraged greater parochialism. Deejay Larry Levan's fans at
       the Paradise Garage reportedly resisted his initial forays into rap. "This
       is Garage music," they would say, "and that doesn't belong here." Deejay
       Danny Krivit quoted in Shapiro, *Turn the Beat*, 271.

228   "massive": See interview with Oakey at http://www.gay.com/entertain
       ment/news/splash.do?sernum=7035&navpath=/channels/entertainment/
       music/&page=2.

229   "all the nice boys"; "rock edge": Reynolds, *Rip It Up*, 500–6.

229   Michael Jackson or Prince: See Ken Tucker, "Someday My Prince Will
       Come," *Rolling Stone*, February 19, 1981, 55. Tucker writes of Prince's "pae-
       ans to bisexuality." Nelson George faulted both Prince and Michael Jackson
       for the way they "ran fast and far from blackness and conventional images of
       male sexuality." See George, *The Death*, 174.

229   "feminine and masculine" . . . "unladylike": Vince Aletti, "Madonna," in
       Peter Guralnick and Douglas Wolk, eds., *Da Capo Best Music Writing* (New
       York: Da Capo, 2000), 157. Aletti's interview with Madonna was originally
       published in a 1999 issue of *Aperture*.

229   Barry Walters, "New World Disco," *Village Voice*, February 15, 1994, 67.

230   "prefab disco": On Madonna, see her entry in Romanowski et al., eds., *New
       Rolling Stone Encyclopedia of Rock & Roll*, 613.

230   "English haircut": On English bands, see Reynolds, *Rip It Up*, 534. Christo-
       pher Connelly wrote of the "seemingly endless influx of English synthesizer
       bands" in "1982 In Review," *Rolling Stone*, February 17, 1983, 46. Most of
       these bands were comprised of men, although several included women.

230   Frequently criticism: One *Rolling Stone* writer criticized Soft Cell's music
       as "sleazily sexual" and faulted its lead singer for his "affected tenor" in
       Romanowski et al., eds., *New Rolling Stone Encyclopedia of Rock & Roll*,
       922.

230   "New authenticity movement": Simon Frith, *Taking Popular Music Seriously*
       (London: Ashgate, 2007), 62.

230   "scruffy guitars": Reynolds, *Rip It Up*, 519.

230   "was built": Touré, "In the End, Black Men Must Lead," *New York Times*,
       August 22, 1999, Section 2, 1.

231   "new world": Walters, "New World Disco," 67.

231   On techno: Techno and other genres of dance music were affected by the
       arrival in the eighties of MIDI, or Musical Instrument Digital Interface,

which allowed "any sonority to be thrown into the mix." It also permitted the exploration of even lower ranges of the bass. For a terrific discussion of this see John Payne, "Music of the Heart and Other Organs," *LA Weekly*, November 2–8, 2001. For an example of the hype surrounding techno, see Robert Hilburn, "Can Techno Save Rock & Roll?," *Los Angeles Times,* March 30, 1997, Arts.

231   "mostly witless": D. James Romero, "London's Calling Again," *Los Angeles Times,* March 30, 1997.

231   "shunned dance": Mike Rubin, *Rolling Stone*, November 28, 2002, 88. This was not true of Moby, however.

231   "people would buy": Ed Ward, "Creating Dance Music Worth Sitting Through," *New York Times*, June 11, 2000, Arts, 28.

231   On P.M. Dawn: KRS–1 once busted up a performance by P.M. Dawn. The best essay about this is Ernest Hardy's "Home of the Brave," *LA Weekly*, December 25–31, 1998, 35.

231   "emasculate": Rose, *Black Noise,* 152.

232   the genre's studio manipulations: For example, the electronically simulated handclap that Chic began to use with such effectiveness on tracks like "Good Times" was produced by an early drum machine—Roland's Analogue TR–808 model. But even after this drum machine was upgraded to a digital model, the electronic handclap produced by the TR–808 had come to sound so natural that producers and musicians sampled their own electronic simulation from the analog machine rather than from "real handclaps." See Andrew Goodwin's excellent essay "Sample and Hold: Pop Music in the Digital Age," in Frith and Goodwin, eds., *On Record,* 266.

232   "Disco . . . once mocked": Pareles et al., "Disco Lives!"

232   "Disco Inferno": Barney Hoskins, "Disco Inferno," *Rolling Stone,* March 20, 1997, 82.

232   Two years later: Ann Powers, Rob Sheffield, and David Fricke, "Dance + Pop," *Rolling Stone,* May 13, 1999, 79–83.

232   *The Last Days of Disco* and *54 . . . Fever* made its Broadway: None of these productions was strong; nonetheless, their anemic box office performance suggested that America was not quite ready for a disco revival.

232   the Village People: Shapiro, *Turn the Beat,* 281.

232   Fans looking: Writing in *Rolling Stone*, critic Ernest Hardy lamented the fact that American lovers of disco had spent the last several years buying French disco. Hardy, review of *Funky Green Dogs, Rolling Stone*, March 4, 1999, 82.

EPILOGUE: DO IT AGAIN

234   "Sea change": Sasha Frere-Jones, "Ladies Wild," *The New Yorker*, April 27, 2009.

235   Digitally downloaded music: According to Professor Jonathan Berger of Stanford University, young people accustomed to listening to digitally compressed MP3 files actually prefer the tinny sound offered by iPods to the dynamically richer range offered by vinyl. See http://www.independent.ie/entertainment/music/manic-compression-its-killing-rocknroll--but-the-kids-like-it-1672755.html.

236   *American Idol* near-winner, Adam Lambert: http://www.rollingstone.com/rockdaily/index.php/2009/00006/09/the-new-issue-of-rolling-stone-the-liberation-of-adam-lambert/#.

237   Chris Martin of Coldplay: http://www.theinsider.com/news/1039318_Chris_Martin_Urges_All_Men_To_Change_Diapers.

237   "young people just can't": http://theconversation.blogs.nytimes.com/2009/06/03/guns-gays-and-abortion/?scp=7&sq=gay%20rights%20polling&st=cse.

237   Mark Christopher's 54: http://www.ew.com/ew/article/0,,284645,00.html.

238   "to try and change"; "uneasy hybrid": Tennant quoted in http://www.glbtq.com/arts/pet_shop_boys.html.

238   "Poker Face": Gaga said this in an interview with MTV. See http://www.mtv.com/news/articles/1610702/20090505/lady_gaga.jhtml. It's worth noting that "Poker Face" not only features the thump; it is also about the very obliqueness that characterized seventies' disco.

PLAYLIST

What follows is not the greatest hits of disco. Although Abba and the Village People are conspicuously absent, more than a few of the usual disco classics turn up
here. This playlist reflects my dance-floor favorites over a ten-year period, beginning in 1974. These were the records I was hearing, first in Albuquerque and then
in Detroit—on the city's airwaves and in its discos—and reading about, mostly in
the pages of the *Village Voice.* I have included the year that these records entered
the *Billboard* charts.

The playlist is meant to run about four and a half hours, but my estimated running time is predicated upon the user relying upon the extended 12-inch versions
of these songs, most of which are available on iTunes. (The LP version of Donna
Summer's *Bad Girls*, however, provides a ready-made mix from "Hot Stuff" into
"Bad Girls," and I would advise it here.) Seventies' disco mavens will recognize
my strategy of the slow buildup to climax, repeated here twice. When the music's
tempo plummets, as it does after "Disco Inferno," it is intentional, a gesture to
dancers' need for fortification of various sorts. Songs with an abrupt end, which
are marked here with an asterisk, allow one to segue into a track with a radically
different tempo like "Love Hangover," or to mix into a song that is already so musically busy that it presents difficulty when one is trying for a smooth mix. Listeners
with deejay experience who trick their stereos out with the standard disco setup
of two variable-speed turntables and a mixer (and two copies of the record so as to
segue into the segue-friendly middle of the song) or who use the sort of computer

program that today's deejays use, should find that these tracks mix fairly well. However, I am assuming that people will play this without actually trying to achieve the seamless beat-on-beat mix that most seventies' deejays labored to achieve.

PART I

"Rock Your Baby"	George McRae	(1974)
"More, More, More"	The Andrea True Connection	(1976)
"Runaway Love"	Linda Clifford	(1978)
"My Forbidden Lover"	Chic	(1979)
"Back Together Again"	Roberta Flack with Donny Hathaway	(1980)
"Can't Get Enough of Your Love"	Barry White	(1974)
"Ain't No Stopping Us Now"	McFadden and Whitehead	(1979)
"Lady Marmalade"	Labelle	(1975)
"Behind the Groove"	Teena Marie	(1980)
"Put Your Body In It"	Stephanie Mills	(1978)
"Stomp"	Brothers Johnson	(1980)
* "I Zimbra"	Talking Heads	(1980)
"Love Hangover"	Diana Ross	(1976)
"Shake Your Body"	The Jacksons	(1979)
"Let's Start the Dance"	Bohannon	(1978)
"Don't Stop 'Til You Get Enough"	Michael Jackson	(1979)
"Got to Give It Up"	Marvin Gaye	(1977)
"Controversy"	Prince	(1981)
* "Tell Me That I'm Dreaming"	Was (Not Was)	(1982)
"Found a Cure"	Ashford and Simpson	(1979)
* "Dancer"	Gino Soccio	(1979)
"Never Can Say Goodbye"	Gloria Gaynor	(1974)
"Disco Inferno"	The Trammps	(1977)

PART II

"More Bounce to the Ounce"	Zapp	(1980)
"Heartbeat"	Taana Gardner	(1981)
"Don't Stop the Music"	Yarborough and Peoples	(1981)
"Brick House"	The Commodores	(1977)

* "Flashlight"	Parliament	(1978)
"Upside Down"	Diana Ross	(1980)
"Pull Up to the Bumper"	Grace Jones	(1981)
"Which Way Is Up?"	Stargard	(1977)
"Ain't Nobody"	Rufus with Chaka Khan	(1983)
"Rapture"	Blondie	(1980)
* "Me No Pop I/Que Pasa"	Coati Mundi	(1981)
"Funkin' for Jamaica"	Tom Browne	(1980)
"The Breaks"	Kurtis Blow	(1980)
"Good Times"	Chic	(1979)
* "We Are Family"	Sister Sledge	(1979)
"Love Town"	The Originals	(1976)
"Bad Luck"	Harold Melvin and the Blue Notes	(1975)
"Don't Leave Me This Way"	Thelma Houston	(1976)
"Running Away"	Roy Ayers Ubiquity	(1977)
"Hit and Run"	Loleatta Holloway	(1977)
* "Is It All Over My Face?"	Loose Joints	(1980)
"Take Your Time (Do It Right)"	S.O.S. Band	(1980)
"Hot Stuff"	Donna Summer	(1979)
"Bad Girls"	Donna Summer	(1979)
"This Time Baby"	Jackie Moore	(1979)
"Vertigo/Relight My Fire"	Dan Hartman	(1979)
"Cuba"	The Gibson Brothers	(1979)
"You Should Be Dancing"	The Bee Gees	(1976)
"I've Got the Next Dance"	Deniece Williams	(1979)
"You Make Me Feel (Mighty Real)"	Sylvester	(1978)
"Shame"	Evelyn "Champagne" King	(1977)

PHOTOGRAPH CREDITS

INDEX

Page numbers in *italics* refer to illustrations.